Mental Health: From Infancy Through Adolescence

REPORTS OF TASK FORCES I, II, AND III AND

THE COMMITTEES ON EDUCATION AND RELIGION

BY THE JOINT COMMISSION ON MENTAL HEALTH

OF CHILDREN

HARPER & ROW, PUBLISHERS

NEW YORK, EVANSTON, SAN FRANCISCO, LONDON

1817

Official distribution of this book has been made possible through a grant from the Foundation for Child Welfare, Inc.

FIRST EDITION

STANDARD BOOK NUMBER: 06-012228-5

LIBRARY OF CONGRESS CATALOG CARD NUMBER: 78-123939

Designed by Sidney Feinberg

Contents

Figure and Tables

MENTAL HEALTH: FROM INFANCY THROUGH ADOLESCENCE

I

STUDIES OF INFANCY THROUGH AGE FIVE

(REPORT OF TASK FORCE I)

Edited by Halbert B. Robinson, Ph.D.,
and Nancy Robinson, Ph.D.

This volume focuses on the mental health aspects of human growth and development from conception to young adulthood and on ways in which we, as members of society, might enhance the developmental potential of our nation's children and youth. Although present knowledge does not permit an authoritative and final statement, there is little doubt that the course of human development is determined by a complex of interrelated factors—biological, psychological, social, and cultural—which we, as a nation, have not dealt with effectively. Thus, the reports of the Commission's Task Forces and Committees included in this volume are not simply a portrayal of the needs and potentialities of children and youth but also an analysis of the roles and failures of their adult mentors and of the institutions designed to serve them. The analysis begins with the Report of Task Force I on Studies of Infancy Through Age Five.

—EDITOR

MEMBERS OF TASK FORCE I

Chairman: PETER B. NEUBAUER, M.D.
Director, Child Development Center
New York, New York

RUTH ABBOTT, R.N.
Visiting Nurses Association of Hartford
Hartford, Connecticut

MILLIE ALMY, PH.D.
Professor of Psychology and Education
Teachers College
New York, New York

HERBERT G. BIRCH, M.D., PH.D.
Research Professor
Albert Einstein College of Medicine
Bronx, New York

PARK S. GERALD, M.D.
Associate Professor of Pediatrics
Harvard Medical School
Boston, Massachusetts

LOUIS M. HELLMAN, M.D.
Chairman, Department of Obstetrics
and Gynecology
State University of New York
Downstate Medical Center
Brooklyn, New York

HYLAN LEWIS, PH.D.
Fellow, Metropolitan Applied
Research Center, Inc.
New York, New York

RICHMOND S. PAINE, M.D.
Professor of Pediatric Neurology
George Washington University
School of Medicine
Washington, D.C.

NORMAN A. POLANSKY, PH.D.
Professor of Sociology and Social Work
Child Research Field Station
Asheville, North Carolina

SALLY PROVENCE, M.D.
Assistant Professor
Yale University
Child Study Center
New Haven, Connecticut

HALBERT B. ROBINSON, PH.D.
Professor of Psychology and
Director, University of North
Carolina Child Development
Research Institute
University of North Carolina
Chapel Hill, North Carolina

Preface

The report of Task Force I of the Joint Commission on Mental Health of Children is the product of many months of analysis and evaluation of the contemporary needs of infants and young children. We plan for a nation dedicated, with compassion and hope, to its generations to come, and for a people increasingly aware that it is only through the young that its own cherished goals may be realized. This report presents both a dream and an imperative. The dream is reflected in setting the goal to provide the very best we can devise for the growth and development of our children— *all* of our children. The imperative results from the recognition that, as a nation, we have failed to meet the needs of most of the youngest and most vulnerable among us. We alone are guilty if we do not immediately take action to meet these needs.

As a nation we now possess neither the facilities nor the trained manpower to realize the dream in its entirety. A set of priorities, of first steps, is therefore necessary. Task Force I recommends the following guidelines for immediate action.

1. Emphasis should be assigned to programs of prevention and early intervention rather than later remediation. The adage that "an ounce of prevention is worth a pound of cure" is nowhere more valid than in the realm of early childhood. Wounds inflicted during this period of life are likely to be so deep, so serious, and so pervasive that many can never be overcome. It follows, thus, that in turning our resources to children, ultimate priority of effort must be assigned to the early years. The most efficient time in which to extend help to family and child is the period which begins even before conception and extends to age three. This does not mean, of course, that we should not strive to create high-quality remedial and preventive services beyond the early years.

5

2. Planning and intervention should have, as their basic context, the family as the primary child-rearing institution. However, we must recognize that the family of today is subject to increasing pressures of a complex, demanding, and fragmented society. Therefore, our ultimate goal should be a compact of the society with all parents, for the cooperative planning for and care of all children. Under modern conditions of living, most parents need community assistance in child care. It is the responsibility of the community to provide supplementary or complementary services, in a variety of degrees and forms appropriate to each concrete situation.

3. Emphasis should be placed on comprehensive, continuous, and coordinated programs with the developmental needs of children in the forefront. Piecemeal programs, even if of excellent quality, can seldom fulfill reasonable goals in our complex society. They often discourage and alienate the families most in need, and because they provide only parts of the total package of requisites for healthy development, the whole is seldom realized. The beneficial effects of limited programs are too often reversed by continuing unmet needs. In the beginning, the numbers of children directly served with this approach will necessarily be relatively small, but such programs can serve as models and can provide training for professional workers who will then assist in the development of further services.

4. In order to break the intergenerational spiral of disorder and defeat, the emphasis in programming at first will have to be with children in that neglected population which has lived in poverty over the years. While this group will receive emphasis, it is important to avoid the notion that problems of the poor are theirs alone. We should seek to decrease rather than increase the separation of social groups.

5. There are a few programs which can be mounted immediately on a large scale and operated with relatively little expenditure of funds or of highly skilled professional personnel. These should be vigorously pursued.

a. The child who grows up in a home in which he is unwanted lacks the security and trust which are absolutely basic to mental health; furthermore, he constitutes a burden both on his often already overwhelmed family and upon programs which seek to serve children. At present, it is the poor of our nation who most strongly desire fewer children, and who have more than they wish, but population growth in all segments of society threatens us. Family planning techniques are highly developed and amazingly inexpensive. In fact, the prevention of unwanted births costs considerably less than mere delivery of those same children. We have the means available to accomplish now the goal of family planning for all who desire it.

b. A nation so rich in food that it limits production must face squarely that it fails to provide the basic nutritional requirements of pregnant mothers and young children in a large segment of the population.

Errors of generosity would be greatly preferred to errors of penury. Damage wrought by dietary inadequacies, especially during gestation and infancy, are probably irreversible and are enormously expensive in the long run.

6. Planning for programs which are comprehensive, continuous, and coordinated should be concentrated, at this point, in research and development. For too long, research has been largely confined to laboratories removed from the scenes of action and programs of action have operated with the merest token of innovative development and evaluative research. We must develop services to children and families which are carried out in research and demonstration settings, in which a variety of the best professional talent is dedicated to inquiry into ways in which best to serve, to discovering what *can* be done effectively and what *should* be done, and to testing which comprehensive models are appropriate for communities which differ both in resources and in the unmet needs of children.

7. Together with the unanswered questions about effective action, the unavailability of manpower severely restricts the immediate mounting of wide-scale programs for families and children. Therefore, we recommend increased emphasis in training in early childhood development (particularly the first three years of life) for all professionals across disciplinary lines; we also recommend the development of new occupations, many of them subprofessional, which will enable us to carry out programs of service. Even the minimal programs attempted so far have foundered too often on lack of knowledge and training, and on the necessity for employing persons whose abundant good will could not compensate for their poor skills. How much more acute will be our needs of tomorrow!

Mental health in children derives from a very wide variety of sources: in physical integrity and vigor, in the economic, social, and emotional climate of families, in opportunities for education and learning, in the early recognition of problems, in the promptness and effectiveness of remediation experiences, in the physical environment, in the skill and affection of those who care for children, in the role models available, and so on. A significant handicap of any sort—physical, psychological, or environmental—constitutes a strong deterrent to optimal mental health. Every day which passes sees unwanted children born, damaged children doomed to frustration and discouragement, families wracked by heartbreak. To the extent to which these tragedies can be avoided, we cannot in good conscience delay.

Introduction

A nation's most important and precious resource is its children. They constitute its hope for continued achievement and productivity, for world leadership, and for eventual peace and harmony among nations. Any waste of this resource, especially in a land as powerful and wealthy as the United States, is intolerable. This report indicates that we can recognize and remedy the circumstances that allow too many of our children to be irreparably damaged even before birth, to be born into homes ill prepared to meet their needs, and to grow up with such impairments of mental and physical health that they must disappoint our hopes for them and remain dependent upon, rather than be contributors to, the society of tomorrow.

A distressingly large number of facts provide testimony to this nation's failure to answer the needs of young children:

• Almost one-quarter of all pregnancies enduring twenty weeks or more are accompanied by often-preventable complications which are potentially damaging.

• An estimated 85,500 children die each year before they are one year old; the majority of these deaths could, with minimum health care, be prevented (U.S. Dept. of HEW, 1968a).

• An estimated 50,000 children under the age of seven die each year as the result of clear neglect such as failure to take reasonable precautions for safety, failure to provide a minimal diet, and failure to pursue minimal medical treatment for illness.

• The mothers of more than 4 million children younger than six years of age work outside the home; more than 1.5 million of their children are below the age of three. A shocking percentage of these children are inadequately cared for, and as many as 21,000, six years and younger, receive no care at all while their mothers work (Greenblatt, 1968).

• Fully one-third of our children younger than six are living in homes at or near the poverty level, and yet in 1965 fewer than 700,000 children of all ages received welfare services such as adoption, foster care, casework, or protection (U.S. Dept. of HEW, 1966a).

• The incidence of emotional disturbance in schoolchildren, severe enough to warrant special therapeutic and/or educational attention, is approximately 8 to 10 percent. Based on 1960 figures, it is estimated that there are 2.7 million children of elementary school age who need professional help because of emotional disturbance (Glidewell, 1968).

• At least 110,000 children are born every year who are destined to be mentally retarded to at least a mild degree—approximately 3 percent of all live births (President's Committee on Mental Retardation, 1967).

• In 1967, 3,907,000 children under eighteen, in 1,273,000 families, were being served by the program of Aid to Families with Dependent Children, an index of the size of programs needed by a compassionate nation to cope, in even a minimal fashion, with the needs of children in homes of destitute poverty (U.S. Dept. of HEW, 1968c).

During the extensive discussions of the problem areas bearing on the mental health of children, the members of Task Force I have been led to strong and unanimous convictions about several basic issues.

1. *The Need for Preventive Services*

In a society in which manpower, clinical and research facilities, and financial support are inadequate to meet all needs of children, priority should be given to prevention and early detection. Few remedial programs of any sort achieve full restoration of normal development to children with moderate to severe handicaps. Far more expense, effort, and heartbreak must be expended to meet the minimal needs of emotionally handicapped children than would have been necessary for the prevention of the same disorders. Moreover, we have already within our technical grasp more effective methods for prevention than for the treatment of most handicapping conditions.

2. *Emphasis on the Period from Conception to Age Three*

There is no more crucial period of life than the short span between conception and age three. It is during this period that the child is most vulnerable and malleable, and it is then that many barriers to normal development and continuing mental health are erected.

Damage sustained before or at birth is the prime etiological factor among a very large percentage of mentally retarded children who will ultimately be institutionalized (Yannet, 1957). For a great many more children not so severely handicapped, damage prior to birth produces mild brain injury which interferes with learning, productivity, and mental health.

The accumulated evidence concerning the first years after birth clearly indicates the importance of these formative years. Learning is very rapid and basic, and the effects of this learning are extremely persistent. Longitudinal studies have indicated that emotional and experiential deprivation during this period can be seen in much later periods. Moreover, young children who live with severely disturbed parents may exhibit even more severe handicaps as time passes than they do in the early years.

Maternal attitudes and practices in the first 18 months of life have been related to the children's achievement motivation much later in life; clear differences in intelligence level appear in the second, and especially the third, year among groups from different socioeconomic levels; differences in vocalization patterns can be detected between middle-class and lower-class children as early as the third month of life.

A concentration of efforts to provide for the optimal development of children from conception to three years of age can provide a firm and absolutely necessary base from which to formulate services to older children. That this period of development is the most neglected by our society is both self-defeating and unconscionable. Early protection and nurturance are essential to ensure that all of our children are granted their basic rights to the conditions necessary for their maximum development.

3. *Primacy of the Family*

The development of children occurs for the most part within the context of family life. The early parent-child, particularly mother-child, relationships constitute the matrix within which are to be found not only those life-damaging factors which may endanger the child's mental health, but also those life-enhancing factors which safeguard and advance it. The parent figures, as principal caretakers, subsume a host of functions of critical significance for the physical, intellectual, and emotional development of their children. The most important place to begin to improve our population is by helping parents do a better job of caring for our children. This is also the most efficient place on which to concentrate.

The ability of the family to support the growth of the child can be enhanced by appropriate, flexible, community-based combinations of family and community resources, from short-term and intermittent child-care assistance to complete residential care. Such comprehensive and accessible services should be directed toward strengthening the role of the parents, rather than substituting for or absorbing it. Under modern conditions of living, most parents need community assistance in child care. More communities need to assume increased responsibility for such assistance.

4. *Need for Comprehensive Services*

In our complex, demanding, and fragmented society, it has become more and more difficult to be an effective parent, whatever the family's socioeconomic status. Many parents experience difficulty in effectively fulfilling their roles as providers, protectors, nurturers, tutors, disciplinarians, and interpreters of the cultural heritage. It is impossible for many to contract individually for the wide variety of specialized services which are necessary for their children's optimum development. Supporting services are needed by every family but most frequently and most acutely by those families least able to deal effectively with the demands of parenthood. They are unable to recognize what is needed before emergency strikes, to seek out appropriate services, and to cope with specialized facilities which are too infrequently provided at minimal cost and too frequently with maximal inconvenience and impersonality.

While many programs exist that are designed to provide for the health, education, and general welfare of young children, they are too limited in number and scope, and especially in coordination. Their services are offered in piecemeal and independent, sometimes competing fashion, and access to them is often difficult. This disorganization has particularly serious consequences for the children whose parents are least capable of providing for their needs.

Comprehensive services oriented toward the needs of families and children must be provided if we would seek to avoid imposing on our children the disorganization of our society. Convenient neighborhood comprehensive centers for children and families, providing integrated services such as general medical and dental supervision, day care, education, recreation, social services, family planning, mental health services, and close ties to the public schools, should become the pattern of the future, playing an integral role in the lives of most children.

The problem of providing accessible and comprehensive services in sparsely populated rural areas is difficult to solve, especially in mountainous regions and others where transportation is difficult. Traveling teams of workers can partially alleviate the problem, but further imaginative solutions will be needed to effectively reach isolated families and small communities.

5. *Deviance Occurs Within a Social Context*

No specific deviance of behavior, and no specific clinical condition, can be considered apart from the social context in which it is bred and developed. The social context thus becomes the focus of concern, and solutions need to be sought in the matrix of social conditions which produce and maintain pathology in children. Many aspects of today's society have relevance to the young child, in their direct impact or their indirect effect as mediated through the child's interactions with his parents. Solutions to the specific pathological conditions of children cannot consist exclusively in attempts at remediation.

Because society as a whole is changing rapidly—for example, not only in its technology but in its underlying values and its primary organization —parents often feel isolated from their children and unsure of themselves. This is perhaps most apparent in the insecurity of parents about methods and goals of disciplinary interaction with their children. Inconsistency and insecurity on the part of parents is clearly damaging to many young children.

The role of violence, and its encouragement in young children, must be faced squarely. Some children meet abuse and angry outbursts at the hands of their parents; nearly all children are exposed routinely to graphic violence over the television screen. Through possible imitation of and identification with these models, patterns of violent behavior may be acquired. Of at least equal importance are the patterns by which the young child is taught to handle his own frustrations, his own angry feelings, and the constructive and destructive acts for which he comes to feel responsible. Possibly no other area represents as profound a source of pathology in our culture as the handling of anger and aggression.

Other aspects of the total society which impinge upon the child are problems of sex education and the provocative use of sexual material in the culture, in advertising, and so on. Again, the feelings of the young child toward his parents, toward his body and his impulses, are likely to be distorted because of the profound societal conflicts in this area.

The increasing isolation of the various segments of our society has an impact which is difficult to assess. Television may bring the large world closer to the child, but it offers him little assistance in interpretation or clarification. The child of the slums, or of the suburbs, sees people and places in his everyday life which almost invariably match his own background. He seldom sees his parents or other adults at work; he has little idea of what it means to "grow up"; his own isolation may result in a dependence upon his segment of the world as he knows it, and a distrust of the "different."

6. *The Developmental Approach*

The child's needs, potentialities, and vulnerabilities, along with the avenues open to him for development, are in continuous change from one period of life to another. The attributes of development that are most important, the most relevant conditions of environment, the adjustment pattern of the individual, and accordingly the opportunities for intervention, differ from period to period. The continuity of approach permitted by attention to the changing characteristics of the growing child is essential if truly comprehensive and integrated programs for children are to be achieved. In this report, such a developmental approach makes possible the appropriate organization of the relevant data. More importantly, it permits the formulation of potentially effective and flexible strategies for the organization of resources on behalf of children. The recommendations contained in the Task Force's report are, therefore, presented in terms of the particular opportunities for intervention at each age level.

7. *Mental Health and Mental Retardation*

Mental retardation, a handicap of intellect which produces deficits in the child's ability to attain maturational mastery, to learn in school and/or to cope with the demands of everyday living, has been considered by the Task Force to be a problem falling under the general rubric of childhood mental health. This inclusion of mental retardation among the problems of mental health rests on several bases.

First, a high percentage of the individuals diagnosed as mentally retarded in middle childhood and adolescence have no demonstrable biological defect. Many, if not most, of them are retarded because of depriving or damaging life experiences.

Second, a great many mentally retarded children exhibit symptoms of emotional maladjustment, which may be causally related to the retardation, may be a result of the difficulties of living as a retarded child, may stem from the same source as the retardation, or may be coincidental. A great deal of professional energy has been wasted upon attempts at differential diagnosis to distinguish emotional disturbance from intrinsic mental retardation, an extremely difficult and often mistaken task in any child who exhibits both. It is especially fruitless with very young children, who tend to react totally when there is disturbance in any sphere of normal growth.

Third, measures which generally are conducive to the mental health of children are also, in most instances, positive forces in the development of intelligence.

Fourth, the continued fragmentation of programs for the retarded as distinct from the emotionally disturbed perpetuates the disorganization of services to children, and frequently requires that a child who exhibits both retardation and emotional disturbance must receive services which are one-sided and fail to take cognizance of the totality of his needs.

The Task Force recommends, therefore, that services to children with a wide variety of handicapping conditions be coordinated and integrated at national and state levels, in clinical facilities offering help to families, and in support for research and training. While the availability of specialized services and specialized personnel is required for optimal care to children, the continued independence of these programs at higher administrative levels and the competition for funding are detrimental to the development both of research and training endeavors and of optimal services to families.

8. *Priorities for, But Not Segregation of, the Poor*

Members of Task Force I recognize that one of the most dangerous aspects of life in our society is the increasing gulf between the affluent and the poor in all areas of participation. To eliminate these discrepancies, every resource will be needed; the highest priority should be given these efforts.

Current efforts to combat poverty and the degenerative conditions which result have typically led to a continued and, in some instances, increased separation between the "haves" and the "have-nots." Future programs should be broadly based and should include children and families from all segments of the community.

9. *The Need for Research and Demonstration Programs*

The most pervasive and strongly expressed opinion at every facet of Task Force deliberation was that research and demonstration programs are desperately needed in almost every area bearing on the developmental problems of young children. Research in child development, initiated in the first quarter of this century, has only begun to reveal the vastly complex processes of physical growth and psychological development. While it is clear that much can be done to improve the quality of life for children and the opportunities for healthy development open to them, it is equally clear that effective long-range solutions will be forthcoming only from imaginative, large-scale, long-term, and therefore expensive research and demonstration efforts.

The considered and strongest recommendation, wholeheartedly endorsed by all members of the Task Force, is that every type of program for children and families be undertaken with careful provision for research, development, and evaluation. Far too many of the existing programs have been inadequately planned and executed, and consequently their benefit to the children involved has been too little. In some instances, there has been no measurable benefit at all.

A realistic budget guideline, for almost every large-scale program touching on the problems of young children, would be the provision of a minimum 10 percent of total expenditures for research, demonstration, and evaluation of programs. Very few programs are so "tooled up" and ready to go that they could be immediately applied to large segments of the population. One possible exception is programs in birth control, except that even here the manpower needs demand research into more effective use of trained second-level personnel and into methods of assuring prolonged cooperation of women.

It should perhaps be pointed out that no industry which contemplated expansion of its facilities would do so without comprehensive research into the efficacy of its projected plans, without research into methods of accomplishing its goals more successfully, without constant evaluation of its productivity and product quality, and without building models to "get out the bugs" before replicating similar facilities all over the country. Concerted, all-out efforts in the physical sciences have made possible explorations in space once undreamed of. Programs which have such potential import for the lives of children can hardly afford to do less.

The Prenatal Period

GENETIC FACTORS IN HUMAN DEVELOPMENT

Genetic transmission of disorders, or the susceptibility to them, follows complex patterns. Some disorders are caused by abnormalities in the number of chromosomes or by their being distributed in unusual ways; other genetic disorders are caused by abnormalities in single pairs of genes, the much smaller units of heredity which make up the chromosomes; still other disorders that have a hereditary component depend upon combinations of genes, working additively or in interaction. Some of these modes of transmission are as yet little understood, and many are not yet predictable. Tools already exist, however, for the detection of many chromosome disorders and some disorders in specific gene pairs; further tools are rapidly being developed for the detection of other such genetic abnormalities. Thus, the possibilities have been opened for anticipating, if not yet eliminating, the passage of these abnormalities to the succeeding generation. There are many disorders of which prospective parents who can be identified as carriers (but who are not themselves damaged) could be warned.

In some instances, there are environmental manipulations which, if instituted very soon after birth, can prevent the tragic damage which otherwise would be caused by defective genetic material. Parents of genetically damaged children need especially careful counseling about the probabilities of their having other damaged children. Moreover, the effect on the mother's own image of the birth of an abnormal child, and the impact that it may have on siblings, may be very profound from a mental health point of view. Unable to produce a normally developing child, the parents may feel too guilty or may reject him. Counseling, therefore, must include attention to the mental health components, which are always present with these forms of deviations.

16

More than a quarter of a million children are born each year in the United States who may then or later demonstrate abnormalities known to result from faulty prenatal development (National Foundation, March of Dimes, 1968), and according to some authors, as many as one-half million stillbirths and miscarriages have the same causal origin. While some obvious physical deformities are immediately apparent at birth, others—such as congenital deafness or blindness, mental retardation, or some heart defects —may not be detected until months or years later. Cystic fibrosis, an inborn error of metabolism, for example, strikes as many as 4,000 infants annually (Cystic Fibrosis Foundation, 1968); a small percentage are diagnosed at birth and the rest are detected only later in infancy or childhood, although a test now under study may permit regular detection at birth.

Too little is yet known about the hereditary basis for human development to permit categorical statements concerning the role of genetic determination in the mental health of children. Nevertheless, in at least some children, conditions of "genetic deprivation" or "genetic susceptibility" may exist, even when the child does not exhibit clear-cut symptoms of genetic abnormality. Even in these children, of course, environmental factors will significantly affect the level of functioning and of development. Improvement of environmental factors, however, may not prove sufficient to effect complete alteration in the child's ability to use environmental opportunities or to cope with environmental stresses and deficiencies. Thus, it is probably unwise to assume that even the best environmental engineering will of itself ensure the mental health of all children.

RECOMMENDATIONS

Prevention: 1. Encouragement and financial support should be given for the establishment of genetic laboratories, and for the provision of mechanisms for referral and transportation to such laboratories of materials from physicians in contact with patients, especially including prospective parents and newborn infants.

2. Application of screening tools for the detection of carriers of genetic and chromosomal abnormalities should be evaluated for possible incorporation in premarital examinations.

3. Genetic counseling services should be made a part of, or available to, every medical center. Such services should be conducted by individuals with competence in both genetics and mental health skills. It should be clearly understood that counseling concerned with childbearing is an area of great sensitivity.

4. Examination of aborted fetuses should be undertaken for the identification of chromosomal anomalies and other conditions which may be familial, or at least likely to be repeated in subsequent children.

5. As appropriate means for treatment become available, screening of

newborn infants for remediable genetic abnormalities should be expanded. Since, however, this is an area requiring study and development, mandatory legislation regarding the application of screening tests should for the present be avoided.

Treatment programs: 1. The means for early identification and treatment of genetic abnormalities (e.g., phenylketonuria, cretinism) should be made readily available.

2. The medical examinations of disordered children and adults should incorporate routinely an examination for suspected genetic abnormalities (e.g., sex-chromosome disorders).

Research: Increased support should be given for research into the identification of both carriers and affected individuals, and for means of treatment. Basic research into the mechanisms of genetic transmission, including polygenic interaction, should be expanded. Research into those modifications of the environment which may be appropriate to the function of the individual child with genetic disorders must be undertaken. The evolvement of compensatory mechanisms for almost any deficiency or disorder is theoretically possible; the outcome of specific genetic disturbances need not be "inevitable."

Manpower: 1. Support should be given to the training of researchers, technicians, and medical counselors.

2. Dissemination of information relevant to this area should be energetically undertaken and continued, a primary target being the physician in patient contact.

UNWANTED CHILDREN

Every child has the right to be wanted, and the right not to be born if unwanted. His conception should be the outcome of a positive act of choice by his parents. Yet, it is well known that many people in the United States today have children that they did not plan and do not want. There is often a high psychological cost to parents of unplanned births, particularly if the addition of a child causes excessive strains upon their limited resources (economic, social, and psychological) for raising a family. The unwanted child in a family too often adds, by his very existence, to the complex of deficiencies and distresses which have already given rise to latent or overt disturbances in his family and which will characterize the primary setting for his early years of life. The approach of an additional child can have a significantly adverse impact on all family members.

The phenomenon of "willful" exposure to unwanted pregnancy, in spite of the availability of contraceptive methods, is frequently attributable to unconscious or ambivalent desires for pregnancy on the part of parents who are immature, psychoneurotic, or subject to emotional stress. The child who is the product of this "willful unwantedness" may be victimized, during the earliest years, by the same psychological inadequacies of his parents which led to his conception.

Of far greater significance is the fact that in parts of the United States contraceptive information and devices available to private patients, and particularly to those with greater means, are not readily available to the poor. For example, more than half the women in need of subsidized family planning services live in our 110 largest metropolitan areas. Only 17 percent of these women received guidance in family planning in 1967. These cities provide the most highly developed family planning facilities, yet approximately 2,211,000 low-income women in these areas were left unserved. The 764 large non-Catholic hospitals in these areas which offered no family planning services in 1965 delivered more than one-quarter of all infants in the entire nation (Jaffe and Bernsohn, 1967). Most of the poor do not have adequate access to those services that will enable them to choose to limit their families, any more than they have adequate access to many other kinds of health services. Furthermore, many of these families are limited in foresight, poorly informed about the nature of the help they might seek, and accustomed to seeking medical aid only on an emergency basis.

Not least among the factors that have rendered contraceptive information in effect unavailable has been the tendency for it to be presented to low-income families in the negative terms of avoidance of family, with all the corresponding overtones of disparagement. In contrast, contraception permits childbearing to be a positive event, the child thus being assured of a welcome into a family which sees itself as adequate to provide not only physical but affectional sustenance.

It is highly significant that there are an estimated one million illegal abortions annually in the United States—one for every four or five births. By the time of an attempted abortion, an increasingly intense but helpless sense of the need for some form of fertility control has foundered on sheer ignorance.

Among families with children, those below the poverty line have an average number of children approximately 40 percent greater than the number in nonpoor families (Sheppard, 1967). Indeed, of all youngsters growing up in poverty, approximately 43 percent are in homes having at least five children (Orshansky, 1965b). Such families often breed defeat. For example, in 1964 it was revealed that about 70 percent of young men who were rejected by selective service because they performed intellectually at the fifth-grade level or below came from families of four or more children, and nearly 50 percent came from families in which there were six or more children. Four-fifths were school dropouts (President's Task Force on Manpower Conservation, 1964). In 1963, 49 percent of families with six children had incomes below the poverty level compared with 12 percent of those with no more than two, and 17 percent of those with three children (Orshansky, 1965b).

These differences in size of family are not because poor families wish to have more children, but can be attributed to the reduced availability of birth control methods to the low-income group. Several studies have demonstrated that low-income mothers actually wish to have fewer children than do upper-income women; nonwhites desire fewer children than whites (Jaffe, 1964); and 90 percent of unwed mothers wish they had not had the child (Greenleigh Associates, 1964).

Where birth control services are presently offered by governmental and private sources, their utilization has been high, and the proportion of women continuing to participate in the program has remained high, usually at or above 70 percent. In one study in Mecklenburg County, North Carolina, for example, 74 percent of the patients continued to take the oral contraceptive regularly for one year, and 66 percent for two years. There were no pregnancies in this group although previously these patients had been quite prolific (Corkey, 1964; Jaffe, 1964). A Chicago study found effective continuation by 72 percent after two years (U.S. Dept. of HEW, 1966e). Other studies indicate that there are approximately 5,300,000 medically indigent women who desire family planning assistance. Only about one in ten of these women is currently receiving such aid from public or private agencies (U.S. Dept. of HEW, 1966e).

The cost-benefit ratio for family planning services is extremely positive. Costs of providing family planning services are only about $20 annually per woman when provided through an independent clinic; when such services are provided in conjunction with prenatal, obstetric, and postnatal care, costs drop to $10 to $15 per woman per year (U.S. Dept. of HEW, 1966e).

It is estimated, moreover, that for every $10 million expended, up to at least the level of $90 million per year, family planning services would prevent approximately 49,000 unwanted births, 2,000 infant deaths, and 48 maternal deaths (U.S. Dept. of HEW, 1966e). Each birth prevented would cost only approximately $200, less than the cost of prenatal care and delivery for that child. Furthermore, because the incidence not only of infant mortality but all varieties of morbidity is so high in the medically indigent group, the incidence of mental retardation, neurological handicap, learning disability, sensory deficit, and emotional disturbance could substantially be reduced by adequate birth control services.

Not every infant who is at first unwanted is headed for disaster. However, he is a child "at risk." If his parents find it impossible to provide him with loving care, the chances are very great indeed that he will develop significant personality or character problems. This is true whether he is born to the affluent or to the poor.

As a public mental health problem, the sheer number of unwanted and therefore often poorly cared-for children is staggering. Moreover, the seriousness of the disturbance in the individual child who has lived his early childhood with one or a series of adults who cannot meet his major emotional and experiential needs makes his situation one of the most urgent.

RECOMMENDATIONS

Prevention: 1. Although elements of avoidance of unwanted births play a necessary role, the philosophy of family planning should evolve into a view of childbearing as a positive choice among alternatives, and a recognition that every child has the right to be wanted and the right not to be born if unwanted. There are plentiful means now available to achieve this goal.

2. Family planning and birth control constitute perhaps the single most important means for the prevention of disorders in children and the enhancement of the effectiveness of families to provide for the children they have. Vigorous methods of education and delivery of services are recommended at the highest priority level. Birth control methods should be furnished without cost, as needed, and carried to target groups through accessible clinics in which the individual is made to feel comfortable. Special efforts should be made to reach the very young woman, the group aged thirty-five to forty-five, the mother who has as many children as she wants, the woman who for any reason would probably not be able effectively to nurture a child, and the unmarried as well. Medical priority ratings of high-risk groups have been developed and should be more widely used in actively giving contraceptive counseling.

The exploration of the conditions that determine whether the child is wanted must deal with many emotional factors, in addition to the economic and educational ones. Birth control programs which are made available to the unmarried or married woman, to the adolescent girl as well as to the more adult woman, must take into account the responsibility for the mental health aspects connected with such programs.

Treatment: 1. States should be encouraged to liberalize abortion laws so that (1) pregnant women seeking abortion will not be endangered by treatment at the hands of unqualified practitioners, (2) unborn children whose existence endangers the health or adjustment of the mother or the family can be legally aborted, and (3) unborn children bearing a high risk of significant damage can be legally aborted.

2. Sterilization should be made more readily available as a means of preventing pregnancy.[1]

1. In its final resolution, the Joint Commission endorsed the recommendation of the Planned Parenthood–World Population organization that abortion and sterilization be removed from criminal law. The Commission's final report also concurs with the

3. Birth control assistance to mothers who are physically or emotionally ill should be actively advanced, not left to personal initiative.

Research: Ample support should be given to the search for more effective, more acceptable, and easier means of birth control. Research is also needed into the means of influencing attitudes toward birth control. Studies into the relationship between sexual behavior and the maternal role need to clarify an issue that has plagued mankind for centuries.

Manpower: For expansion of facilities to take place, need exists for the concomitant expansion of the pool of trained medical personnel, and for more effective use of specialists in tandem with paramedical personnel.

CHILDREN OUT OF WEDLOCK

The number of children born out of wedlock has risen from fewer than 90,000 in 1940 to an estimated 291,000 in 1965, nearly one-twelfth of all live births in that year. Of the 142,000 children placed in adoption in 1965 88,000 (nearly five-eighths) were born out of wedlock; yet, these constitute fewer than one-third of the estimated number of illegitimate children (U.S. Dept. of HEW, 1966a). Further, unmarried mothers have constituted an increasingly large proportion of the almost 5 million heads of families with children but no fathers (U.S. Dept. of Commerce, 1967a), nearly two-thirds of which have been estimated to be living below the poverty line (Orshansky, 1965b).

Despite widespread misconceptions, a number of studies have ruled out any accurate stereotype of unmarried mothers—whether along clinical, psychodynamic, or sociocultural lines. Bearing a baby out of marriage is not limited to any single age period, educational or income level, social class or ethnic group, nor is it limited to any one kind of family background, intelligence, or personality make-up. Although there has been a marked increase in births out of wedlock in recent years, this rise is not due primarily to an increase of births among teen-agers. The number of such births to girls between fifteen and twenty is larger than in any other five-year age group, but the majority of unmarried mothers are not teen-agers. In fact, teen-agers now form a smaller proportion of the total than they did earlier (U.S. Dept. of HEW, 1966b).

Age, education, ethnic group, and especially economic status are correlated, however, with the incidence of births out of wedlock (Herzog, 1967). These factors, unfortunately, are even more closely related to the availability and utilization of prenatal, perinatal, and postnatal services.

Unmarried mothers who are most in need of prenatal services are least

resolution of the American Public Health Association's stand that it is the right of every woman to decide whether or not she will bear a child. See *Crisis in Child Mental Health: Challenge for the 1970's* (New York: Harper & Row, 1970).

likely to receive them. Such services have been given primarily to those who are white, above the poverty level, and likely to place the infant for adoption (Herzog, 1967). It is estimated that fewer than one-third of the white unmarried mothers are served by public or private child welfare agencies; the proportion of nonwhite unmarried mothers so served is less than one-tenth (Herzog, 1966). For mothers from the low socioeconomic groups, services tend to focus on the later stages of the prenatal and immediately postnatal period, so that little is known about the subsequent development of these children.

RECOMMENDATIONS

Prevention: The relatively high incidence of infants born out of wedlock is a reflection of the state of our society, and to a large extent reflects sexual practices embedded in complex cultural conditions. Therefore, the methods and philosophy of birth control should be extended to the unmarried woman as well as the married woman who engages in extramarital sexual relationships.

Programs and services: 1. Services should be extended to a larger proportion of unmarried mothers, with less selectivity based on those intertwined factors of class, color, and income. Services must include social supports to encourage natural mothers to care adequately for their children if they want to; therefore, services not only should cover the period of pregnancy and childbirth but also should be continued for several years when it seems necessary to protect and promote the mental health of the child. In public health agencies, the provision of such broadened services will necessitate a reexamination of priorities and a reassessment of the use of all manpower.

2. Services should include early identification of children to be placed; help in using placement services, when indicated; and an increased number of placement services.

3. Community services should be offered in such a way as to minimize the disruption in the life of the unwed mother, so that this additional burden does not make even more difficult her adjustment, which is frequently already tenuous. This is most important for the young, unmarried mother, whose schooling needs to be continued, whose identification with a stable social group needs to be strengthened, and who most needs the support of familiar figures if she is to retain her potential to become a successful wife and mother. The experience of an illegitimate pregnancy during adolescence, with all the accompanying conflict of decisions which must be made, often exacts a great emotional toll. A heavy burden is placed on the psychic reaction of the adolescent, regarding not only her pregnancy but also her response to her social environment, which is most often critical of her deeds.

Repetition of pregnancies out of wedlock is frequently symptomatic of poor adjustment. Thus, these community services must strongly emphasize the emotional aspects of this experience.

4. Adoption and foster care should be extended through a number of changes recommended on pages 47–49.

5. The often neglected factor of *time* is extremely important in the life of the illegitimate infant. In order to provide him with the kind of care that will support development and prevent mental disorders, a stable place is needed for him from the moment of birth. If he is to remain with his mother, the supports that will enable her to provide adequate care must be immediately available. If he is to be adopted or to be in foster care, the time lags and changes of setting must be reduced to a minimum through good and sufficient services to biological and other parents.

Manpower: Training is needed for social workers and others involved in counseling, placement, and supervision. Child-care training to adoptive parents and foster parents would also serve both educational and screening functions.

PRENATAL DAMAGE

The complexity of the developing organism and its complete dependence on the prenatal environment create vulnerability to insult from the moment of conception onward. At least 250,000 infants are born annually with major birth defects so obvious that they can be identified immediately (National Foundation, March of Dimes, 1968). It is impossible to determine how many other children are born with damage which is less easily detected, or which makes its presence known only later in speech defects, mental retardation, epilepsy, perceptual-motor problems, reading handicaps, and a variety of behavior problems. It is widely accepted that a great number of mildly handicapped children, including many of those whose disorders seem to result from socialization and enculturation problems during childhood, actually suffered minor degrees of injury to the central nervous system before they were born.

Major damage may be caused by the injury or death of only a few of the small cluster of cells which constitute the unborn children during the earliest days of pregnancy. The most critical period of brain development, for example, lasts from as early as the second week of pregnancy to about the eleventh week, roughly the first trimester. The entire period of gestation is, however, a period of vulnerability to insult.

A great many agents of damage in the prenatal period have been indicated, among them a wide variety of maternal nutritional deficiencies, viral infections such as rubella, cytomegalic inclusion disease, and possibly with lesser frequency, influenza and other viruses (some of which cause minimal illness in the mother but are highly dangerous to the unborn child), bacterial infection by congenital syphilis and toxoplasmosis, maternal sensitization to Rh-positive blood type, maternal hypertension, maternal diabetes, hypoxia, a wide variety of drugs including some present in tobacco, pelvic radiation, and a complex of as yet incompletely understood factors which are related to social class and background of the parents. Additional risks are attendant on pregnancies in very young mothers, in older women, in women with chronic poor health, and in women who bear too many children too rapidly. Even maternal emotions may play a significant role in the development of the unborn child. Complications of pregnancy, such as bleeding and toxemia, also apparently play a causal role in brain injury.

From such selected facts, it is clear that the prenatal period is crucial in the mental health of children. The factors that bear upon the ability of the child to survive and upon so many aspects of his functioning are varied and far-reaching. More importantly, many of these factors are preventable.

Far too few women receive adequate obstetric care. Furthermore, our society makes little effort to enhance the environment of the pregnant mother in order to support her chances for producing a healthy child. Nutritional supplements, for example, known to be beneficial to the mother with a poor diet, are not made readily available. Prenatal or postnatal maternity leave with pay is seldom granted to the mother of low occupational status. Perhaps most striking is the correlation between social class and the amount and quality of obstetric care. Not only do mothers in the lowest social classes tend to seek health care later in pregnancy, but when they do so, they tend to use a general practitioner or clinic services rather than the obstetric specialists heavily used by women in higher classes. In many major cities, one-fifth of the mothers receive no prenatal care at all (Lesser, 1963). In New York City, the figures for married mothers show that only 13 percent of white mothers receive no prenatal care during the first six months of their pregnancy while this holds true for 38 percent of Negro mothers and 39 percent of Puerto Rican mothers (Birch, 1967). In these mothers, poor general health and inadequate health care compound in their effects.

The possibilities of risk to the unborn infant by environmental factors during the gestation period are so clear as to make systematic, continuous, and widespread prenatal care and support an essential condition for improving not only the physical but the mental health of children. The improvement in public mental health will come through decreasing the number of infants born with preventable defects which render them more vulnerable to both normal and unusual stress. Similarly, the infant who is intact has a much better chance for normal development.

Preventive efforts, moreover, must in many instances begin long before pregnancy. Women from lower social classes, for example, presumably because of poor nutrition and poor health during childhood, frequently fail to attain optimal height and pelvic growth, and the outcome of their pregnancies is affected (Baird and Scott, 1953). Efforts to increase the immunities of the mother should be undertaken prior to pregnancy because of the high risks concomitant with infection during the early period of pregnancy. Nutritional deficiencies and the use of potentially damaging drugs should be reduced during the entire childbearing period, for the same reasons. Birth control measures clearly play a role, as has been emphasized elsewhere in this report.

RECOMMENDATIONS

Prevention: 1. Efforts to improve the nutrition, general health, and medical care of girls throughout life, beginning in infancy, will have ultimate payoff in the mental and physical health of their offspring.

2. Adequate, early, systematic medical care should be made available to all pregnant women. Reorganization of medical functions and support of paramedical personnel will be needed to achieve this goal. Offering impersonal, inconvenient, or marginal-quality clinics is neither medically defensible nor likely to reach the group of women most in need.

3. Efforts should be made to support the general health and functioning of the pregnant woman, as appropriate to her needs. Reduced working hours, paid maternity leave, homemaking services, as well as nutritional supplements and other supportive practices would be beneficial to many high-risk mothers.

4. In view of the wide variety of factors potentially responsible for damage to the unborn child, special efforts are necessary to protect women of childbearing age. These efforts include prepregnancy immunization and other measures for the prevention of many illnesses, and extensive testing and strict control of the drugs made available to them.

5. Educational efforts aimed at teen-agers and young adults should emphasize the importance of good health and suitable timing of pregnancies, and the kinds of efforts necessary to protect the unborn child.

Treatment: Further efforts should be made to detect damaged or chromosomally abnormal fetuses and to undertake abortions when advisable.

Research: Support should be given to research aimed at the identification and control of the many factors potentially responsible for damage to the unborn child.

Manpower: 1. The capacity of the specialist to provide care may be increased through experimentation with programs involving the reorganization of medical services and the use of paramedical personnel.

2. Support is needed for training programs for all personnel involved

in rendering obstetrical care. Only about 850 obstetricians are currently being admitted to the board of qualified specialists each year; this number exceeds only slightly the number of obstetricians who retire. In 1966, there were only 415 nurses enrolled as students in graduate programs in maternal and child health (National League for Nursing, 1966), and only 29 graduate programs that prepared nurses in this area or in obstetric or pediatric nursing (National League for Nursing, 1967).

3. Although there is some controversy surrounding the advisability of heavy reliance on nurse-midwives, it is clear that some such solution will be required in order to provide the necessary services. Since there are presently only 10 schools which offer such training, and fewer than 1,000 trained midwives practice now in the United States (American College of Nurse Midwifery, 1968), research should examine the efficacy of the use of well-trained individuals in various kinds of settings.

The Perinatal Period

Neonatal and infant deaths have many consequences for the mental health of the parents and surviving children. The ramification of the death of an infant on the emotional life of the mother and the rest of the family can be great indeed under many circumstances. Feelings of guilt in the parents, fantasies in the siblings as to the precariousness of life, or the problem of rivalry may all be accentuated in the family when death occurs at such an early age.

Mortality rates also serve as rough indices of the much greater number of children who survive the infant period handicapped by physical and psychological damage resulting from the same sets of causes which produce death in more vulnerable organisms, or which occurred in lesser strength, or at less crucial periods.

The mortality rate for nonwhite infants is twice as high as that for whites (U.S. Dept. of HEW, 1966d), and the correlation of infant mortality with prenatal care is substantial, though also related to the health and socioeconomic status of mothers who do or do not successfully seek to obtain such care. The rate of fetal deaths among mothers who have had one or more visits to a prenatal clinic is approximately 0.7 percent, while the rate of fetal deaths among mothers who have received no prenatal care is about 4 percent, or more than 5½ times as high (Birch, 1967).

Data are not available to establish the relationship between the death rate of mothers in childbirth and the extent of prenatal care, yet the relationship between maternal death in childbirth and ethnic origin is all too plain. In 1940, twice as many nonwhite as white mothers died in childbirth; by 1960, that ratio had become three to one, and by 1965, four to

28

one (U.S. Dept. of Commerce, 1967b). Although the overall death rate for mothers in childbirth has now reached an all-time low for the United States, the reduction has occurred at a more rapid rate among white mothers than among nonwhite mothers (U.S. Dept. of HEW, 1968b).

The relationship between social class and the amount and quality of obstetric care is striking. The President's Panel on Mental Retardation (1962) has found that 35 percent of the babies born in cities with a population of more than 100,000 are born to mothers who must receive free service if they are to receive any at all. Yet, one study in New York (Shapiro *et al.*, 1960) found the perinatal mortality rate (fetal and newborn) to be considerably higher among infants delivered in general service (ward) facilities than among those delivered by qualified specialists in private services, although this may be as much a result of the high-risk population as of the quality of the clinic service. Only 17 percent of white mothers were delivered in general service, whereas approximately 88 percent of nonwhite mothers were delivered there. Approximately 6 percent of nonwhite mothers were delivered by midwives, 21 times the rate for white mothers (U.S. Dept. of HEW, 1966c).

By 1966, the steadily declining position of the United States among developed nations with regard to infant mortality rates brought it to thirteenth place, with a rate of 23.4 per thousand live births (U.S. Dept. of HEW, 1966d). Within the United States there is striking variation among counties in infant mortality. It is fair to assume that a great many cases of infant mortality are avoidable. The shortage of trained personnel can probably be blamed for much of this distressing state of affairs, together with other problems inherent in disadvantaged families. It is for this reason that the Children's Bureau has indicated that only 56 key counties, containing most of the highly urbanized population, hold "the key to any successful effort to reduce sharply the nation's infant mortality rates" (U.S. Dept. of HEW, 1966d). In fact, nine of the largest counties have infant mortality rates exceeding 30 (U.S. Dept. of HEW, 1966e).

Mortality rates during the last eleven months of the first year of life constitute an inverse index of nutrition, protection, and general health care, including medical services and their utilization. During this period, the rate of mortality of Negro infants is nearly three times that of white infants (U.S. Dept. of HEW, 1966d). The majority of these infants can be presumed to have been viable at birth.

RECOMMENDATIONS

Prevention: The medical and other measures recommended for the prenatal period would also be strongly preventative of perinatal mortality and morbidity. In addition, the rate of death during the first year indicates that intensive educational efforts aimed at the socially disadvantaged groups would help ensure the minimal care of children during this period, with consequent reduction in the wastage of human life.

Manpower: In addition to obstetric and pediatric physicians and allied personnel, there is need for specialist neonatologists, practicing in large centers but serving primarily to train other pediatricians and to continually bring to their attention current findings in the field.

PREMATURITY AND OTHER FACTORS RELATED TO INCREASED RISK

A serious problem related to the mental health of children is prematurity at birth, which occurs in about 7 out of every 100 live births (U.S. Dept. of HEW, 1966e).

It has been demonstrated clearly that premature infants of very low birth weight suffer high rates of mortality and of serious handicaps such as brain damage, mental retardation, blindness, and other disabilities. Many are born with congenital anomalies.

It is difficult to tell whether prematurity itself, except in infants of extremely low birth weight, carries a high risk to the infant. In damaged infants, it is often impossible to ascertain whether the prematurity caused the damage, or whether the prematurity and the damage both stemmed from some other source. There appears to be evidence that, even with social class held constant (an essential feature of any follow-up study of premature infants compared with normals) and even when neonatal care has been excellent, there is some risk of handicap to children of low birth weight. Premature children, on the average, are slightly less bright than their siblings who were born at term. In pairs of twins of whom one later becomes schizophrenic, that twin was usually lighter in weight at birth. Studies suggest that, in later life, prematurely born infants exhibit more school and behavior problems and more learning disabilities than do full-term infants (Wiener *et al.,* 1965).

Prematurity is clearly more frequent among mothers of lower social class, of poorer health, who are unmarried, or who have suffered previous complications of pregnancy. The rate of prematurity is much higher among Negro than among white infants (Pasamanick, 1959).

Premature infants need immediate and special assistance following delivery. Less developed than mature babies, they are usually incapable of adapting to extrauterine life without a great deal of help. Their lungs, for example, are not ready for normal air breathing. The capacity to feed is often impaired. They are more vulnerable to infection. Their mothers also need special attention and education if they are to provide adequately for the needs of these children in the post-hospital period.

Other babies who need special care and intensive monitoring are those who suffer hypoglycemia (a blood-sugar shortage), hypoxia (oxygen starvation), and accumulations of bilirubin, a by-product of the breakdown of red blood cells. The first of these is seen particularly in underweight or low-birth-weight infants, while the second is generally transient and due to conditions of delivery. Blood-type incompatibility with the mother accounts for some cases of hyperbilirubinemia, although this condition, seen as jaundice, has other etiologies as well.

The early neonatal period also constitutes a critical period for laboratory studies to detect inborn errors of metabolism. Some of these metabolic processes are crucial to normal brain function, and increasing numbers of them can be alleviated if detected and treated early enough.

RECOMMENDATIONS

Prevention: The same sets of operations designed to enhance the health of the mother during pregnancy and to minimize the prenatal risk to the child operate with respect to complications surrounding delivery. Care between pregnancies should receive more emphasis for every mother of a premature infant who wishes to have another child at a future time.

In addition, support should be given to increased services during the newborn period, including specialized premature nurseries, surveillance for hypoglycemia, anoxia, and jaundice, and screening for inborn metabolic errors.

An infant known to be unusually vulnerable is a great emotional burden on the family. Special attention is given to this newcomer. The mother may sense a feeling of inadequacy to provide for this infant, and her maternal impulses may become inhibited. The preferential attention may unduly affect the siblings. Depending on the degree of immaturity, the family balance may be changed for quite some time. Those preventive aspects of dealing with this and other questions must be part of the services offered to these families.

Programs: 1. See recommendations concerned with prenatal period.

2. Increased services are needed by the premature group after hospital release, particularly among the poor, since it is known that the premature infant is at greater risk in one environment than another.

Research: 1. Increased attention to the problems of the newborn should be encouraged.

2. Research into the causes and prevention of prematurity is essential.

3. Research exploring better ways in which to care for the newborn with special needs should be continued. As one example, increased stimulation of the premature child still in the hospital nursery appears promising.

4. Further longitudinal research following different subgroups of prematures through their school years is needed in order to compare their

eventual adjustment with that of other children who have the same pattern of postnatal experience.

Manpower: Reorganization of the use of medical manpower, and training support for new professional and paramedical personnel, will be necessary in order to provide medical services to every mother, prenatally, perinatally, and postnatally.

The Child in His Family

As has been indicated, some of the factors associated with complications of pregnancy and delivery are present long before the mother becomes pregnant. These factors have been related to the mother's nutritional history, her height and weight, and the social class of both her husband and her father. Women who were born in the lowest socioeconomic classes and remained there following their marriage have been found to be not only an excessive risk with regard to prematurity and Caesarean section and perinatal death, but also to be in poorer general health, more stunted in growth, and to possess less adequate nutritional and health habits.

The incidence of cases of severe malnutrition is low in this nation today, although far from nonexistent. Among the poor there are subtle, subclinical forms of malnutrition that may be responsible, at least in part, for the generally higher rates of mortality and physical and mental ill health among children of these groups. Malnutrition with regard to the intake of iron, for example, has been shown to be widely prevalent among lower-class infants. Subclinical forms of malnutrition are present also among middle-class groups. Despite a rising standard of living, there is some indication that poorly balanced diets may be becoming more prevalent among these more affluent groups. This may result, in part, from the upward mobility of parents whose own childhoods were characterized by poor nutritional habits.

The nutritional differential among white and nonwhite infants is striking, however. In nine out of ten cases of malnourishment, the cause lies in the character of the family diet. One study of white and Negro children found that 35 percent of the former as opposed to 71 percent of the latter

33

subsisted on grossly inadequate diets. In the southeastern part of the United States, approximately 50 percent of the nonwhite and 30 percent of the white children suffer from iron deficiency anemia during the first two years of life (Birch, 1967). The highest percentage of malnourishment in this country has been found among Negro migrant agricultural workers, but Negro slums in the big cities are known to contain the greatest concentration of anemias, growth failures, and other signs of malnutrition.

Conditions of ill health, including undernourishment, may have severe consequences for the physical and emotional well-being of the child. The development of the nervous system may be directly affected with the resulting impairment of the potentialities of the child as a learner. Deficient nutrition may also have a direct impact on the relationship of the child to his body image and the sense of pleasure and comfort he derives from the environment. Energy variations with irritability, restlessness, or lethargy can often be observed with nutritional problems. Children who are ill nourished are reduced in their responsiveness to the environment, distracted by their visceral state, and impaired in their ability to progress and endure in learning situations. Interference with the learning process during certain critical periods may have long-term results and lead to significant backwardness at later periods—with all the social and psychological threats to mental health that such backwardness entails.

RECOMMENDATIONS

Prevention: 1. There is no defensible reason why, in a country in which the production of food has had to be limited rather than encouraged, any mother or child should suffer basic malnutrition. Programs aimed at furnishing foodstuffs to pregnant or nursing mothers and young children in need of assistance should be generous.

2. Education of families whose habit of food purchase and preparation are inadequate should be strongly undertaken. Schoolchildren, who will be parents, are a primary target. Home economists and public health nurses can be utilized to bring group and individualized services to families aimed at improving nutrition habits.

Programs and services: Strenuous efforts at prescription, maternal education, and supervision should be aimed at children who are discovered to be suffering even mild malnutrition.

HEALTH SERVICES AND SCREENING

During the period from birth to entry in school, many children essentially disappear from professional (private or agency) surveillance. Even though there are a great many facilities for well-baby care, these are not sufficient to the need. Further, many families fail to take advantage of available services. Consequently, developmental problems go unnoticed until the child enters school. This period, however, covers essential years when development is extremely rapid and malleable.

During this time, the child is especially vulnerable to trauma of all kinds: infections such as meningitis, encephalitis, ear infections, and other illnesses with long-range consequences; accidents including poisoning and anoxia; preventable diseases such as whooping cough, measles, rheumatic fever, diphtheria, and tetanus; uncontrolled dehydration and high temperatures associated with illness; uncontrolled epileptic seizures, and so on. Early in this period, some metabolic errors undetected in the newborn are still amenable to treatment. Corrective measures for children with hearing, motor, speech, and visual handicaps can often prevent the interference with learning which produces retardation in mental development or which may be complicated by emotional problems. It has been estimated that approximately 20 to 30 percent of chronic handicapping conditions of childhood and later life could be prevented or corrected by comprehensive health care to age five, and approximately 60 percent if health care were extended to age fifteen. Current handicapping conditions could be severely reduced by a comprehensive program of child care throughout the childhood years; uncorrected visual problems could be reduced by 80 percent; hearing problems by more than 50 percent; and unmet dental needs by 100 percent (U.S. Dept. of HEW, 1966e).

Early detection and intervention are among the most promising possibilities for the improvement of current and future mental health of the child. The same facilities and programs that make somatic problems more visible can be utilized to screen for the danger signs—in both the child and his environment—that are known to jeopardize mental health. We have no way of estimating the benefits, because this kind of screening has never been done in a systematic way. There is no doubt, however, that such screening methods can be taught, and that we need to apply them on a broad scale.

RECOMMENDATIONS

Prevention: Regular contact with facilities which are designed to look at the whole child is essential throughout childhood. Through regular surveillance and screening, many handicaps can be prevented, or if present, minimized in their handicapping influence on the child. These facts should be publicized and brought home to mothers. One possible mechanism for reaching children might be tied to health insurance plans, with periodic examinations required for continued coverage. Such requirements might also be part of AFDC programs and others.

Treatment: 1. Emphasis and support should be given to programs which deal with potentially handicapping conditions in the very young.

Child guidance clinics and individuals, groups, and agencies dealing with emotional disturbance should afford priority to younger children. Persistent follow-through with many families will be needed to ensure contact and continuation with treatment plans.

2. Diagnosis in the infant and young child should emphasize functions and deficits rather than diagnostic labels, and should provide the rationale for treatment.

Manpower: Each facility offering medical surveillance and screening might involve individuals whose primary responsibility is follow-up of referral and treatment prescriptions with families who are likely to need special assistance with carry-through. Competent individuals with only short-term training might be supervised by public health nurses; these individuals might well be selected from social-ethnic groups similar to the target families.

CHILD ABUSE AND NEGLECT

Child abuse occurs when a nonaccidental physical attack or physical injury is inflicted upon a child by a person charged with the responsibility of caring for him. Neglect, on the other hand, while closely related in cause and effect, appears in its most severe form as a "failure to thrive," a syndrome of infancy and early childhood that may include signs of severe malnutrition, growth failure, and developmental retardation. While precise data are lacking, it is believed that cases of severe child abuse are to be counted in the thousands or tens of thousands, and that cases of severe child neglect run into the hundreds of thousands (Polansky and Polansky, 1968).

Until recently there has been slight attention paid to these clinical syndromes. Since they have been systematically recorded and reported for only about five years, the recent marked increase in the number of known cases may primarily reflect increased awareness and reporting. The spectrum of cases routinely brought to light ranges from deprivation and neglect to gross physical and emotional abuse. Some experts have suggested that if this problem could be adequately assessed, the result would reveal that maltreatment is the most common cause of death in children.

Child Abuse

The abused victim is usually only one among several children in the family. Frequently, it is the child who was conceived or born extramaritally or premaritally, or who symbolically represents something which under some circumstances can trigger extreme anger in the parent. There is a tendency for the abuse to be repetitive. The fact that the marital partner often does not intervene may be a function of sadistic vicarious satisfaction, recognition that the child is diverting the anger which could be directed elsewhere, or fear of similar abuse.

Parents who abuse their children come from a wide variety of educational, socioeconomic, racial, and ethnic backgrounds. Ninety percent have serious social problems, marital discord, financial difficulties, etc. Many appear to be in a state of continual anger which needs only the stimulation of some normal difficulty of child-rearing for its direct and violent expression. Others have marked attitudes of rejection toward the child and feel that he is a real and constant threat to them. Some parents evince impulsiveness in areas other than child care, as well as an unusual degree of instability and a history of emotional deprivation in their own infancy. Defects of the child are often greatly resented, particularly those defects which lead to lack of responsiveness or other frustration-creating reactions.

Serious child abuse is not one act, or even many, but rather a basic condition about which the offending parents are rarely given to seeking help. Such parents typically withhold information and remain evasive or contradictory about the circumstances surrounding any one incident. They may show neither remorse nor concern about the child's condition but instead seem to be angry with him for having been injured.

Active casework and intensive psychiatric treatment has yielded little improvement for a large proportion of the parents reached by these services. This is, perhaps, of little practical importance. Treatment attempts are offered in an infinitesimal proportion of the cases; adequate facilities are unavailable in most areas of the country; and few parents can be persuaded to participate in programs aimed at changing their behavior. Thus, prospects are discouraging for rehabilitation, and intervention must in most instances take other forms. We assume, however, that some reduction in prevalence might occur if more child-care services of the kind already described were available.

How being a victim of abuse will be psychologically reflected in the child depends upon the child's own make-up and resources, and his age at the time of abuse. Because acts of abuse so frequently occur in the context of a disordered family, their effects cannot be separated from the total pattern. Since, however, there is a strong likelihood that children so treated will develop sufficient hostility toward the world in general to become the next generation's perpetrators of violent crimes, early treatment of the syndrome may not only prevent the possible permanent injury of the child but also break the cycle of disorder bred by violence.

Childhood Neglect

While the concept of childhood neglect could be extended to cover any withholding, or failure to secure, optimal sustenance for the child—nutritional, affectional, disciplinary, educational, medical, and so on—it has, for practical purposes, been limited to those severe instances in which there is gross inattention, abandonment, starvation, and/or unusual isolation. Studies of neglectful parents and neglected children are practically nonexistent except for a few dealing with the medical picture of the resulting "failure to thrive." However, it is clear to social workers, physicians, and others concerned with child welfare that this is a syndrome of widespread and national importance.

Parents who are prone to neglect children may come from many walks of life. However, neglect is not always so apparent in the middle class because of the "child-centered" mores. The possibility of compensating for a mother's neglect through the substitution of surrogate caretakers, and the ability of the more adequate parent to make up for the deficiencies of the partner, are practices which tend to mask the more subtle forms of neglect in some middle-class families. The results of disturbed parent-child relationships of this kind can be seen in a variety of developmental delays and behavior problems in children and occasionally in the syndrome of severe failure to thrive.

Parents who severely neglect their children exhibit a variety of personality problems—psychosis, low intelligence, impulse-ridden character, and others. In some ways, many of them resemble abusive parents, except that ordinarily their problems are not manifested through the acting out of aggressive impulses. Frequently, the neglected child is one in a family of several children and holds some special symbolic meaning for the parents.

A large percentage of neglectful mothers exhibit a characteristic pattern of apathy and futility. This pattern may stem, in part, from discouraging and frustrating social conditions or from chronic physical health problems, or it may be a defense against conflicts within the mother's personality. Among these mothers, the following patterns are reported: a pervasive aura that "nothing is worth doing," an emotional numbness and withdrawal, the absence of intense relationships beyond a kind of forlorn clinging, a passive mode of expressing aggression, low competence in most areas and an unwillingness to become sufficiently invested to acquire new skills, low self-confidence, relative difficulty in verbalizing important feelings, and, not surprisingly, an almost uncanny ability to infect with the same feeling of futility those who try to help them. However, it is incorrect to consider this diagnosis only when there is an overtly disturbed or inadequate mother. Many mothers living in relative isolation, whether in the ghetto or in suburbia, need far more support for child care than they receive. With the assistance of others they can often nurture their children with reasonable adequacy; alone they become depressed, disorganized, and inadequate as caretakers.

Children suffering from the most severe forms of neglect exhibit a clinical failure to thrive, without sufficient organic disease to account for it. The syndrome is characterized by failure to grow and gain weight, by developmental slowness, by occasional vomiting and/or diarrhea and other bodily symptoms, by feeding difficulties, and by weakness, tiredness, and irritability. Typically, with the warm attention and sustenance of a pediatric hospital setting or a foster home, they show marked improvement, only to lose ground again upon being returned to their homes, if no changes have been made in the home conditions. Clearly, this represents a syndrome which calls for intervention.

RECOMMENDATIONS

Prevention: Many abused and neglected children are the products of unwanted pregnancies, and many constitute a distinct threat to the parent who might have been discouraged from parenthood on the grounds of mental illness, alcoholism, etc. Aggressive provision of birth control techniques, including in some instances sterilization or abortion, should reduce the incidence of child abuse and neglect. Certainly parents who abuse or neglect their children should be actively discouraged from having more children.

Treatment programs: 1. Because of the nature of the psychological problems involved, often including severe character disorder in the parents, mass programs cannot be employed in the treatment of child abuse and neglect. For effective marshaling of services, it is clearly best that treatment of these problems be regarded as a local responsibility, supported by the federal government only in terms of propaganda, education, finances, and in some instances permission to make innovative use of funds (e.g., use of AFDC funds temporarily in nonfamilial situations).

2. Wherever there is clear, or even persuasive, evidence of abuse of a child under the age of three, he should be removed from the parental home, with return to that home the exception rather than the hoped-for norm. The parents should be forbidden to remove any other children from the possibility of continuous and intensive surveillance by the court of jurisdiction.

3. Children neglected to the point of starvation or actual abandonment by their parents should also be promptly removed from the home, with the expectation that they will not be returned for a considerable period of time, if at all. Reconstitution of the family, if it is attempted, should be undertaken cautiously, with the assumption that change in the parents is a process which will require a number of years.

4. The failure to thrive syndrome has been reasonably well established, and the findings regarding those cases in which its source lies within the mother's psychological make-up should be made general knowledge among the relevant medical and social agency personnel. Specifically, pediatricians,

obstetricians, and general practitioners should be alerted to the nature of the psychological pattern, as should nursing personnel in the hospital setting. The law should require that when this is the diagnosis, the child must be returned for regular check-ups at a suitable and reputable clinic.

THE DISADVANTAGED FAMILY

Problems related to mental illness in children seem to be greater and more severe among disadvantaged segments of the population. Although we have touched upon this point previously, some further discussion is needed. This section of the report will be held to minimum essentials not elsewhere covered, and will deal primarily with customs and necessities of living which affect the child-rearing practices of such families.

While it should be clear that economic indices alone are not synonymous with what is often termed "cultural deprivation," financial hardship is highly correlated with inadequate child care and unhealthy attitudes toward children. However, there are many impoverished families who, given the bare essentials needed for survival and physical health, can by dint of healthy interaction with their children raise mentally healthy youngsters who are happy, productive, alert, and socially adjusted.

The economic variable, which is most salient and easiest to measure, provides a startling index of the number of children living in high-risk families. In 1966, some 19 million children, about one of every four, were growing up in families which had too little money to meet their basic needs (Orshansky, 1967). The 16 percent of the families that were living below the poverty line tended to have more children than the national average.

In 1966, about 1.7 million nonwhite families and 4.4 million white families were poor—about one-third of the nonwhite and one-tenth of the white (U.S. Dept. of Commerce, 1967b). The proportion of families headed by a female was significantly higher among the nonwhite subgroup than among the poor white group, although in actual numbers there were more white families in this group. Among nonwhite families, then, there are the cumulative effects of extensive poverty, a high proportion of single female parents, and the added hazards of being nonwhite in a white culture.

The child-rearing attitudes and practices of the typical family living in poverty are largely dependent upon the physical and economic limitations of the environment, overwork on the part of the mothers, and family composition. Other aspects of child-rearing, however, stem from the cultural attitudes and personal characteristics of the parents which may be part of the cycle of poverty but are less directly dependent upon current economic circumstances. The pervasive influences of the "culture of poverty" which are destructive to the mental health of children will be outlined below; however, it should be emphasized that the culture of poverty is merely a convenient concept which describes life styles among various low-income subgroups in a very generalized way. The poor are by no means a homogeneous group, and the following points are not applicable to many.

1. Physical circumstances: Homes which are chaotic, crowded, dangerous to health, and lacking in either the physical necessities for learning (e.g., toys, crayons, books) or the privacy, focus, and consistency necessary for constructive learning activities.

2. Family structure: Frequently characterized by lack of two parents, and the power residing in the mother even when the father is present; large numbers of children, mixtures of nuclear families, with a wide spread of generations; disorganization; and fluctuating appearance and disappearance of family members.

3. Child-rearing practices: Frequently characterized by

a. encouragement of passivity: strict, unreasoned demands for unquestioning obedience, and conformity in children;

b. fatalistic attitudes: luck, not hard work or foresight, determines outcomes;

c. conviction that one works out of necessity, not pleasure, and that one has little choice of vocation or other activity;

d. discontinuity in training for mastery: children are prohibited from engaging in small steps toward goals of independence, but are suddenly thrust into positions of responsibility when they are thought to be old enough;

e. reliance on punishment, often physical punishment, as a means of discipline, with omission of rewards and explanation;

f. emphasis on external rather than internal controls, with little encouragement for learning to work for future goals;

g. prohibitions against expression of negative feelings, particularly anger, toward the parents; channeling of aggression toward the peer group and external authority;

h. low ratio of adults to children; fatigue and preoccupation with household tasks by working mothers, reducing the amount of attention to children and their steps toward new achievement, and producing constant frustration for the child who needs adult help in mastering a given task;

i. stereotyped, authoritarian, poorly articulated, and poorly focused verbal interactions with children;

j. lack of concern with the protection, self-esteem, educational achievements, or desires of the children;

k. monotony, with affective and cognitive deprivation.

4. Provision of adult (parental) models who are immature, depressed, impulse-ridden, fatalistic, apathetic, constricted and distrustful, magical in

thinking, lacking in goal commitment, low in self-esteem, and lacking skills to effectively participate in the mainstream of society.

The effects on children of these complex patterns are deep-seated, and make themselves known early in the child's life. Among the obvious consequences are inadequate fine motor skills, depressed ability to learn, lack of investment in tasks involving mastery, reduced verbal abilities, impulsiveness, overactivity, low self-esteem, lack of trust in the environment, low achievement motivation, fatalistic attitudes, depression, little foresight and ability to work for future goals, inability to focus on potential learning experiences, heavy loads of unresolved aggression under poor control, hostility toward authority figures and the larger society, underlying expectations of failure, pseudo-independence, and a lack of responsiveness to the potentially positive opportunities in school, recreation, and so on. Such children often do become adept at manipulation of others, in a shallow, affectionless manner, and they learn early to share their possessions with others because they have little sense of belonging or of possessing belongings. This propensity to share, while highly valued by the middle-class culture, conflicts with the attitudes toward saving and accruing resources.

Although the matrix of problems is easy to describe, prescriptions for intervention are harder to determine. Various models will be later described under the heading "Family and Community Child Care." It is possible that the syndrome of deprivation cannot be handled simply by increasing the economic capacities of poverty families, although some of the pressures (e.g., the overworked mother, the lack of resources) lifted in this manner would greatly improve the child-rearing potential of poor families. Models of intervention which provide varied and enriched life experiences which contrast with the home will probably be necessary. To be effective, such intervention efforts must begin very early in the lives of children (see p. 9). They must be worked out in coordination with the families, both to circumvent rejection and to improve the capacities of the parents to be effective in providing healthy experiences for their children.

RECOMMENDATIONS

Prevention: The only reasonable way to prevent the recurring, intergenerational cycle of poverty is to prevent the development of handicapping conditions in impoverished children. Emphasis should be given to comprehensive programs of intervention in early childhood which seek to provide for the optimal development of the children enrolled.

Treatment programs: Programs aimed at the eradication of poverty, per se, are obviously of value, but should be aimed primarily at increasing the effectiveness of parents, enhancing their self-esteem, increasing the alternatives open to them, and making possible improvement of their life circumstances through meaningful work and planning. Decent living conditions (e.g., housing, neighborhood recreation) for children and parents are also essential.

Research: There is plentiful evidence concerning the general composite picture of the effects of social deprivation on children. Further research should concentrate on particular deficits and motivational patterns, specific parent-child interactions and their consequences, the development and long-term evaluation of programs aimed at prevention and remediation at an early age, and ways of involving parents in parent-education experiences.

Manpower: The overwhelming number of families to be dealt with makes it obvious that large numbers of professional and subprofessional personnel will be required for the many programs which will be developed in this area. Involvement of the poor in such programs is to be encouraged; however, in order to break the cycle of intergenerational transmission, a careful evaluation should be made of the roles they can play, the positions in which they can be most effective, and the training they should receive.

WORKING WOMEN AND CHILD CARE NEEDS[2]

The growing trend for mothers with young children to enter the working force is part of the great social revolution of our time. Working mothers now account for 24.7 percent of all mothers with youngsters below the age of six, and their children represent 15.6 percent of all youngsters in that age group. The provision of high-quality care to children of working mothers is a problem of considerable magnitude, encompassing, by 1968, almost 4.5 million children under the age of six (U.S. Dept. of Labor, 1969).

Eighty-six percent of working mothers with young children give "economic need" as the primary reason for working outside the home; their more specific reasons range from the provision of the subsistence-level income to the purchase of a new car, a home, or a college education. From Table 1 it is possible to infer that there is a very sizable group whose incomes are quite low. They cannot be expected to purchase high-quality care inside or outside the home, unless subsidized.

There are a number of possible solutions to the provision of care for young children of working mothers. Data show that nearly half (47 percent) of such children are presently cared for in their own homes—by father, relative, nonrelative baby-sitter, or nonrelative who also does household chores.

Three children in ten are cared for in a surrogate's home, that of either a relative or a nonrelative. Some children (15 percent) accompany their mother to her place of work; a few (1 percent) have mothers who work only during the child's school hours.

A very small percentage (0.08) of children under six receive no super-

2. Data in this section largely from Greenblatt (1968).

Table 1.—CHILDREN UNDER SIX YEARS OLD OF WORKING MOTHERS, BY OCCUPATION
OF MOTHER, 1965

OCCUPATION	NUMBER	PERCENT
Total	3,813,000	100.0
Professional and managerial	574,000	15.0
Clerical and sales	1,255,000	33.0
Craftsmen, operators, and laborers	743,000	19.4
Household or service workers	904,000	23.7
Farmers or farm laborers	337,000	8.8

SOURCE: Children's Bureau. Preliminary data from report on child care arrangements of
the nation's working mothers, Dec. 1967.

vision whatsoever for at least part of the day; this percentage, while small,
amounts to 21,000 children who can be assumed to be seriously endangered.
Not all of these children come from impoverished families. Ten percent
come from homes with incomes between $6,000 and $10,000. At least a
third have mothers who have completed high school, and an additional 10
percent have mothers who completed at least one year of college.

Only about 6 percent of the children are in group care. There exist,
in fact, very few licensed day-care centers or family day-care homes. In
1968, public, voluntary, and commercial licensed day-care centers and
family homes cared for a total of 531,000 children of all ages (U.S. Dept.
of Labor, 1969). The overwhelming majority of day-care homes are
unlicensed, are not required to meet any standard, and are completely
unsupervised. Adequate facilities to meet the day-care needs of the rapidly
increased force of working mothers fall far short of the demand.

In view of the present need, it is evident that families, communities, and
state and federal governments must assume a responsibility to ensure that
all children are afforded care designed to enhance, not to hinder, their
health and learning. Far too many programs are substandard, and even
those which meet standards for physical care and protection fail to offer
more than custodial care to young children. This report will later outline
basic requirements to meet the needs of young children. However, there is
probably no single model which will best meet the needs of all children and
their working mothers. In each family, considerations of cost and convenience, as well as availability and quality of facilities and personnel, will
determine the method of child care the parents choose.

There is a current trend toward expanding facilities for group care and
early education for children of working mothers, and in some instances for
children whose mothers are not working. Such programs are even beginning
to reach below the age of three, although most are concentrated in the

three-to-five age range. This trend toward group care reflects the growing conviction that the crucial and vulnerable years of early childhood are precious and must be filled with experiences that reflect our best knowledge of child development. The number of group-care centers is still pitifully small, however, and is not adequate to meet the needs of both children and parents. In a low-income area in one large city, there were 7,000 children in need of day care; the area had four licensed day-care homes and one commercial day-care center, with a combined capacity for 87 children. A study in one state revealed that nearly three-fourths of its day-care centers provide only part-time care; that most full-time centers are proprietary and charge higher fees than most low-income families can afford; and that subsidized centers have far more applicants than they can accommodate.

During the past few years, support for early childhood programs has burgeoned (see Table 2). Programs such as day-care services under welfare auspices, Head Start classes under the antipoverty banner, and preschool classes within the sphere of education have been established. They represent an explicit assumption of national responsibility for assistance in the care and rearing of children under school age which, except for

Table 2.—FEDERAL FUNDS FOR PRESCHOOL PROGRAMS, BY FEDERAL ORGANIZATION AND TYPE OF AGENCY PROGRAM, U.S., 1967 FISCAL YEAR

ORGANIZATION AND AGENCY PROGRAM	PRESCHOOL PROGRAM	
	NURSERY SCHOOL AND KINDERGARTEN	DAY CARE
All Agency Programs	$320,485,000	$86,915,000
Office of Economic Opportunity		
Head Start (part year and summer)	$244,500,000	
Head Start (full year)		$70,000,000
Community Action Program		$ 1,245,000
Migrant Families (Title III, EOA)		$ 4,000,000
Work Experience (Title V, EOA)		$ 4,270,000
Office of Education		
Preschool (Title I, ESEA)	$ 65,485,000	
Preschool (Title III, ESEA)	$ 10,500,000[1]	
Children's Bureau		
Child Welfare		$ 6,700,000[2]
Small Business Administration		
Small Business Loans		$ 700,000

1. Combined expenditures for both 1966 and 1967.
2. Expenditure for 1966.
SOURCE: U.S. Department of Labor, Federal Funds for Day Care Projects, 1967.

emergency measures during the Great Depression and World War II, breaks sharply with former policies. The quality of these services, that is, the extent to which they meet the developmental needs of the very young, is a matter of utmost importance.

RECOMMENDATIONS

Because standards and models for child care will be described later, few specific recommendations will be made in this section. Some guiding principles can, however, be formulated:

1. The entry of mothers of young children into the working force is increasing. Therefore, priority should be given to the provision of suitable methods of surrogate care. This implies the setting of adequate standards based on current knowledge of the specific needs of the infant and young child, the provision of training for surrogates in child care, and subsidization of adequate facilities so that economic necessity alone will not force the decision of the mother to leave her child in less than optimal surroundings.

2. We need to reevaluate the current prevailing attitude that the child's own mother is inevitably the best person to care for all his needs. It is undoubtedly true that a stable, warm, and healthy relationship between mother and child is an important part of the context in which healthy growth occurs. It is also clear that the infant's development can be supported by effective surrogates and that the effectiveness of many mothers is enhanced when they share responsibility for their children. This has been a common and seemingly successful pattern among more affluent families who have long shared the responsibility for the nurturance of their children with nurses, maids, nursery schools, and so on.

3. There is a growing body of research data, supported by clinical impressions, which indicates that the mere fact that a mother works exerts no negative influence upon her children. In fact, income considerations aside, the mother who works through choice and/or who takes pleasure in her work may rear children who are happier, healthier, and more responsible citizens than the nonworking mother who in subtle ways feels imprisoned at home and somehow allows these feelings to adversely affect her relationships with her children. On the other hand, the mother who works unwillingly and/or who receives little compensation for her efforts may be a happier and more adequate mother if she remains at home while her children are very young.

4. Provision of day-care facilities, or surrogates in the home setting, must include some provision for care of the young child when he is ill. Comprehensive facilities, including medical care, present one solution to this problem; others may be worked out in home settings.

ADOPTION AND FOSTER CARE

For children whose own families are unable and/or unwilling to meet their minimal needs, even with financial, psychological, and social support, placement outside the family is essential. Because of the often stressful nature of the child's experience prior to placement, and because of the poor prenatal obstetric care of many of the unwed mothers who subsequently place their children, these children constitute an especially high-risk group. Babies born out of wedlock constitute a large proportion of those for whom long-term placement is sought. Adoption services are insufficient to meet this need, however, especially for nonwhite babies. In 1965, about 142,000 children were adopted. Eighty-eight thousand of these adoptees were born out of wedlock, but they constituted only one-third of the estimated 275,700 illegitimate babies (almost 7 percent of all live births) born in this country in 1964. Of the children adopted by non-relatives, only 9 percent were nonwhite (U.S. Dept. of HEW, 1966a).

Long-term, permanent placements, preferably beginning during the first six months of life, are often a fully acceptable solution to the problems of the child who needs a foster home or adoptive home. Support to the child's own family would reduce by perhaps 25 percent the number of children needing placement. However, in most instances children who need placement should be removed from the home or institution more promptly than is generally the case (Jenkins and Sauber, 1966).

In various ways, the typical short-term placement procedures fail to meet the needs of young children:

1. Early care, especially for children of unwed mothers, too often takes place in conditions of deprivation in large, institutional, understaffed nurseries. The retardation which is likely to result from such deprivation may make the child unadoptable. If the deprivation is continued, the long-term handicapping effects are likely to be as severe upon personality development as upon intellectual development.

2. Children placed in foster care after infancy, or in circumstances where it is thought that the parents might seek to reclaim them, are rarely adopted. Such children frequently journey through a succession of foster homes, unable to build meaningful and long-term relationships with anyone, and are likely to develop poorly in intelligence, in character strength, or in investment in the world of people.

3. Various barriers (e.g., religious, ethnic) block the free adoption of children by families who could very adequately provide for their needs.

4. Subsidization payments to foster parents are inadequate in most states to make possible and encourage greater numbers of competent persons to welcome children into their homes. Moreover, the foster parent

who develops the desire to adopt a child must face the cessation of these payments.

5. Early placement is frequently held up by legalities and red tape which work to the detriment of the child. Psychological testing has been relied upon unduly in the past. This practice fortunately is no longer so prevalent, since these tests have been shown to be unreliable in the first year as a precise predictor of intelligence, except in instances of marked handicap. Although early assessment of the child's progress sometimes yields valuable information, delay of placement until reliable results can be obtained often is self-defeating.

RECOMMENDATIONS

Prevention: 1. Proposals already advanced with respect to the unwed mother are equally applicable here. Prompt counseling and adequate pre-natal health care and delivery services would reduce the scope of the problem. Those studies which suggest the possibility of an increased rate of brain damage among adopted children may be largely attributable to these lacks.

2. Since by far the majority of children needing placement were un-planned, birth control methods vigorously extended would also reduce the scope of the problem.

3. Family services to support natural parents would reduce the number of children needing placement.

Programs: 1. Prompt work with unwed mothers and parents from whom children are removed would expedite the early placement of children in permanent arrangements. Time is a crucial dimension in the life of the very young.

2. Greatly increased support for the expansion of adoptive services is necessary.

3. Decisions to remove children from homes in which they are abused or deprived should be prompt and firm; in most instances, such children should be placed in permanent, not temporary, homes. However, there should be safeguards against injustice to parents.

4. Elimination of legal barriers to adoption by qualified families, re-gardless of religion or ethnic group, would increase the pool of adoptive homes.

5. Improvement of nursery facilities (such as boarding nurseries in hospitals) and early placement of children in adequate homes would re-duce the effects of early deprivation.

6. Financial subsidies should be offered to families who are adequate to meet all but the economic needs of their children. Subsidies in some instances might continue to foster parents who adopt the child.

7. Payments to foster parents should be more realistic.

8. The full range of services, including day care, should be available to foster and adoptive families. There is no evidence to suggest that working mothers cannot be adequate foster or adoptive parents.

9. The need for involvement of the mental health professionals in working with unwed mothers, with parents who are neglecting or abusing their children, and in assisting foster and adoptive parents can be readily seen. For some, the contact will be direct; for others it will be in a supervisory or consultative role to health and welfare agencies and to the courts. There is a great need for children's mental health services and for individual clinicians to devote time to the large number of children that fall in this group.

CHILDREN NEEDING TEMPORARY CARE

A great many families that ordinarily meet the needs of their children quite adequately undergo periods of crisis and disruption which can be damaging to the young child. Typically, this crisis revolves around the illness or temporary incapacity of the mother or father, the hospitalization of another child whose needs for the mother are great, the prolonged absence of the mother from the home because she is needed elsewhere (e.g., death or illness of a relative), or the temporary chaos which can result from myriad factors (e.g., mental breakdown). Such crises are particularly acute in one-parent homes. If there are no relatives or friends who can help to maintain the family, the child is subjected not only to the temporary loss of support from his parent, but also frequently to living conditions which are damaging of themselves.

At times of crisis, the child who is unaccustomed to removal from his home should not be suddenly thrust into an unfamiliar environment, among strangers. Very young children who have been removed to residential care under such conditions often show signs of deep disturbance. The mental health impact of crisis periods could be ameliorated by the availability of a temporary homemaker, trained in child care, who would assume 24-hour responsibility, would care for the children during the working hours of other adults in the home, or would aid the mother for a part of the day.

RECOMMENDATIONS

Facilities and programs: 1. The live-in or part-time homemaker should be a resource to be called on in times of family crisis, when the parent responsible for child care is incapacitated, absent, or undergoing unusual stress. Preservation of the family setting for the very young child, particularly the child under the age of four, should take precedence over the possible economy of the residential or group-care setting. If it develops that the crisis period will be an extended one, appropriate longer-term arrangements can be made eventually, with careful preparation of the child for their occurrence.

2. Premature discharge of mentally ill parents from hospitalization without adequate provision being made for the children is to be avoided. When parents of preschool children are discharged, careful follow-up is necessary to make sure that the parent is capable of meeting the needs of the children, and that the burdens of child care are not so stressful that further pathological episodes are likely to occur. A homemaker should often be made available in such situations.

Manpower: A corps of homemakers will be required to carry out such services. These women should be carefully trained not only in homemaking skills but in the recognition and satisfaction of the needs of children. Women who are capable of caring well for children and acquiring new skills to further their mental health can be recruited from many socio-economic and ethnic groups.

MANAGEMENT OF HOSPITALIZATION TO REDUCE SEPARATION OF
MOTHER AND CHILD

Hospitalization, especially for the very young child, creates a crisis for him at a time when he is least prepared to cope with it. A number of research studies have revealed that the child's separation from his family during hospitalization not only adversely affects his physical recovery but produces in many children profound psychological disturbances which are often persistent. Infants under six months of age frequently show "global" reactions in their adjustment patterns (e.g., disturbances in feeding, sleeping, elimination); infants six months to one year frequently exhibit anxiety, depression, and/or adverse psychophysiological responses; one-to-three-year-olds tend to manifest a sequence of "protest, despair, and detachment," and/or regressive behavior, quite aside from the illness; four-to-six-year-olds tend to show lessened anxiety about the actual separation, but have more severe fears about the aspects of their treatment which involve pain and imagined mutilation.

In this entire age group, it is particularly important to provide as normal an environment as possible, within the requirements of the hospital situation, and to provide for continuity of experience with the parent(s). This can be accomplished in a number of ways, preferably utilizing several avenues of approach.

1. Some, but not all, hospitals with pediatric facilities provide "live-in" arrangements for the mothers; these, however, tend to be used by only a

minority of families because of the expense and the fact that mothers often have other young children to care for. An additional barrier is the general but usually erroneous feeling on the part of the staff that mothers tend to interfere with the care of the child.

2. In some hospitals, mothers are encouraged to assume much of the care of the child during the day, with staff cooperation.

3. In conjunction with the above, increased contacts between mothers and nurses have been found to hasten the child's recovery.

4. Patient-care representatives—nonprofessionals familiar with hospital procedures who support families and help to personalize care—are used in only a fraction of hospitals, although with encouraging results.

5. Motel-like arrangements in or near hospitals to accommodate mothers whose children are undergoing essentially outpatient diagnosis or limited treatment can minimize the traumatic aspects of hospitalization as well as separation, and represent considerable financial savings.

6. Playrooms, educational experiences, and/or freely supplied toys appropriate to the age and mobility of the child, and the staff to utilize these resources, are found in about half the general hospitals serving children and in only about three-quarters of hospitals specifically devoted to children. Volunteer workers can also be utilized in enriching the young child's experience and the personal attention he receives.

Hospitalization of the mother produces some of the same problems in the interruption of the mother-child relationship as does hospitalization of the child. In response to this situation there is, for example, increasing use of the "rooming-in" arrangement of mothers and newborn infants, although because of contagion little has been done to permit visiting of such mothers by their older children. In a very few programs, mothers hospitalized with post-partum psychosis are also accompanied by their young infants. These programs report a significant improvement in the response of both mother and child.

RECOMMENDATIONS

Prevention: There is an encouraging trend, which should be fostered, to postpone elective procedures requiring hospitalization until a time when the child can better understand what is happening to him, why, and for how long.

Facilities and programs: Programs supplementing hospital care, such as those described above and other innovative arrangements, are highly recommended. Many of these require a minimum investment of staff time, and some, by utilizing the services of mothers and volunteers, may actually represent a net saving. They provide, in addition, important benefits to the mother-child relationship and the child's mental health.

Manpower: Nursery teachers for the hospitalized young child, and patient-care representatives, are examples of the kinds of nonmedical personnel which can be employed in programs. Individuals who work with families and children under stress generally need training, but short-term training courses for sensitive and warm individuals without specialized backgrounds should suffice.

THE BRAIN-DAMAGED CHILD IN THE HOME

Some young brain-injured children present such problems of physical care and management that supplementary aid to the families is highly desirable. Particularly difficult to live with is the young child with problems of hyperactivity, distractibility, and general problems of impulse control. Many communities are experimenting with day-care programs and recreational facilities, and a great many school systems have special classes for retarded brain-damaged children. Additionally, many families would benefit from available resources of trained baby-sitters, foster homes, or residential institutions in which a child might be boarded while a family vacations, etc. With increasing resources within communities for retarded and brain-damaged children, many families are finding it possible to keep these children at home and at the same time to preserve the integrity and the effectiveness of the family.

It should also be recognized, however, that because of intense and special needs, not every brain-injured or severely retarded child should be kept in the home. If a home is adequate to meet the needs of the child, he can generally benefit from family living; however, at the same time, the parents and siblings in some instances suffer consequences which must be taken into account. The decision concerning institutionalization is a highly individual matter, one which must be considered in the context of the rest of the family and the community. Professional guidance can be extremely helpful in aiding a family to make a decision rationally and confidently, but the decision, of course, must remain in the hands of the family.

RECOMMENDATIONS

Facilities and Services: 1. For families who keep the brain-injured or retarded child in the home, the present trend toward a wider and more plentiful supply of services of all kinds should be continued, including facilities for short-term care. Relief of the family is at times as important a consideration as are the needs of the child, especially when the child's behavior patterns are particularly taxing.

2. Realistic professional guidance, based on the family and community

situation, should be readily available to families who need to face the decision concerning institutionalization. At the same time, such decisions need not be seen as permanent or irrevocable; the child's behavior patterns and the family situation undergo significant changes over the years, and parents need not be made to live with decisions which become inappropriate.

Family and Community Child Care

The several components of this section will outline the basic needs of children during the first five years, and will suggest programs which might be designed to meet these needs. Basic to the mental health of all young children at this age is a stable, supporting family situation capable of nurturing, protecting, and teaching.

It is, however, unrealistic to assume that most families can alone, as exclusive units, meet all the needs of their children. What is required is a compact between the larger society and families, a cooperative arrangement designed to strengthen family life and to offer a reasonable and productive mode of interaction between outside services and parental roles.

A number of forces interfere with the smooth development of such a compact. Among the most outstanding of these forces are the fragmentation of services to families and children and the idealized notion of the "good family" as the exclusive agent responsible for the child. There is a tendency to view the family as being capable of providing alone the complex matrix of conditions which constitute the optimal environment for the young child.

There are several major faults with the arguments of those who tend to romanticize the role of the family in child-rearing. First, the idealized American family has never been as prevalent as many believe. There have always been homes broken by death, divorce, and desertion; there have always been ignorance, poverty, ill health, and despair in large segments of the population. Second, the families most successful in raising children have tended to be those who did not attempt to accomplish the job alone; they have made the best use of the facilities and services available, employed surrogate caretakers, and supported many experiences for their children outside the home. Third, families until recently have existed in economic and social contexts very different in a number of important respects from the urban and specialized society of today. Fourth, the goals of child-rearing have been very different from generation to generation. In the past, our goals for the growth and health of children were much less ambitious than they are today. Many more infants died; more children had serious health problems of all kinds; fewer children were educated, and those who went to school began later, left earlier, and endured much poorer school conditions than are common today.

We want and expect much more for our children today. We are no longer contented to do a fair job for some children; our standards are now much higher. The advances of our society, however, have created new and very difficult problems of coping for parents, at the same time that they have presented new opportunities.

The proposed compact between parents and society was designed to take into consideration the very difficult requirements being posed for parents today. Not only must they establish their own homes for the nuclear family, earn the money to provide a decent standard of living, feed, clothe, and supply the material props for growth, health, and learning, cope with the social and political systems in which they are citizens, and be available and nurturing to their children day and night; they must, in addition, be wise counselors and tutors, first-aiders, disciplinarians, protectors, and even interpreters of the values of a society in which they themselves do not necessarily share but in which they want their children to participate. Moreover, it is necessary that they be contractors for specialized and uncoordinated services of all kinds: family planning, prenatal medical attention and delivery, pediatric supervision, dental services, special-interest experiences, day care (if the mother works), nursery school, kindergarten, contact with welfare agencies, specialized diagnosis and therapy, and so on. These extrafamilial services, of course, are needed most acutely by families which are least able to afford them, to cope with the demands of parenthood, to anticipate needs, and to seek out services which may not be easily available.

A number of the models to be proposed in the succeeding sections involve the use of group facilities in the care and early education of young children. These programs are based on clear evidence that simple maturation in the circumscribed home environment does not automatically produce maximal growth. Children need not only affection and security but challenge, not only shelter but stimulation, not only a waiting to be adults but an active zestful involvement in the play and work of childhood. Many people still doubt the value of providing extrafamilial experiences to the infant and very young child. Specifically, a great many professional persons and parents question the value of group experiences, such as day-care centers, particularly for the very young. They question whether such programs can support the family and do as good as, or better than, the typical family does. There is no doubt that the answer is *yes*, that well-run daytime group-care programs can be beneficial to children of the tenderest ages and also add to the stability and general well-being of families. The damaging effects which have been found in the understaffed and sterile residential institutions studied by Rene Spitz, Wayne Dennis, and others are not the consequences of group care per se. Just as some families provide good, and others somewhat worse, settings for the care of children, so too, group-care experiences can be good or bad, depending upon many variables such as personnel, equipment, opportunities for learning, grouping of children, and so on. The designation "well run" means that such settings must meet the developmental needs of children.

It is not suggested that all parents be encouraged to enter their children in group-care programs at an early age. However, society needs to offer not only this kind of experience but a comprehensive and coordinated package of services to both children and their families. It is expected that the 30 to 50 percent of families who are least able to manage would choose most often to utilize these programs of family planning, day care, early education, health care, guidance in personal and economic matters, and the like. Many middle and upper socioeconomic group families would probably also choose to avail themselves of these services, since they already contract for them. It is imperative that the programs offered be of such high quality that all families will recognize them as providing a reasonable alternative to the prevailing child-rearing system.

While our knowledge about the needs of infants and very young children has increased, much remains to be investigated regarding many practical problems concerned with various programs of care for this age group. Only a very few studies of comprehensive care techniques in these early years are presently funded by public or private agencies in this country. Even nations with extensive programs for the care of young children outside the home (e.g., Israel and the Soviet Union) have conducted little research bearing on the crucial questions involved. Many states are presently formulating standards of child care in foster day-care homes, day-care centers, and institutions, but there is no body of empirical research to determine optimal caretaker-child ratios, space requirements, suitable scheduling of the child's day, and so on. Little is known concerning the relative long-term efficacy of programs of direct parent education, programs of educational intervention in the infant's home, programs of day care (full day or part-time), and so on. The development of sequential, possibly structured, learning experiences for the infant and young child, various methods for the provision of health care integrated with caretaking facilities, methods for developing important personal relationships within the multiple-mothering situation, methods for providing for solitude in the group setting, and a great many other areas are likewise untouched.

The virtual explosion of programs to serve the infant and very young child is beginning, but there exists practically a complete vacuum in the needed pool of individuals trained to meet the needs of this age group and to deal in a helpful way with their families.

THE FIRST THREE YEARS

There can be no doubt that a healthy, mature newborn has a better chance of developing normally than does the child who starts life with any kind of handicap. A healthy, intact body makes it possible for the infant to respond to the various influences in his environment in a way that promotes total development. Moreover, the fact that he is healthy and responsive makes it less difficult for the mother to provide the kind of care that is supportive of optimal development.

Important though they are, organic deficits, whether congenital or acquired, constitute only a part of those seen in the many infants and very young children with problems of development. There are a large number of children who require urgent attention because they do not receive from adults the kind of nurturing care upon which good development depends. The nurturing of the child's mind and the nurturing of his body are at first inseparable. His emotional needs and his need for experiences that facilitate learning are met, in early infancy, mainly in conjunction with his bodily needs; being fed, kept warm, changed, lifted, held, and bathed are all daily events around which a multitude of sensorimotor and affective experiences occur. These child-caring activities are normally carried out by a person who interacts with the infant in a feeling way, smiling at him, talking in soothing or stimulating tones, handling him in different ways to induce sleep or wakefulness.

In this report, knowledge about the infant and young child is organized around the types of care, experiences, and comprehensive services which should be provided in order to safeguard him and support his mental and physical development. Planning can then be anchored firmly in the developmental characteristics and needs of the child. Further, the major emphasis should be determined by a commitment to support and strengthen the family as the way of life in which most children are likely to develop well in relation to our society's preferences.

Experiential Needs in the First Three Years

1. The infant needs a person with whom he can interact and who responds to his distress signals and to his needs for comfort, for relief of tension, and for a social partner. Such a person constitutes the most important need-satisfying adult with whom emotional communication can be established. This is the person who loves and cares for him and whom he comes to love and trust. In family life, the mother usually has this role;

she may share the caretaking responsibilities with others, but she retains her central importance to the child. Even in situations of group living, the importance of a primary attachment to a specific person cannot be overemphasized. If, because of the realities of group living or surrogate care, several caretakers are necessary for each infant, every effort must be made to enable the infant to develop a close attachment to one of them. The infant's attachment to his own mother may provide this base for children in day care, and should be supported strongly. It appears that there may be essential differences in personality development and probably in styles of learning and adaptation between children who develop a strong primary attachment in infancy and those whose attachment is about equally diffused among several "mothers"; it seems likely that the differences are detrimental ones for the latter group.

2. The provision of adequate shelter and food is, of course, of prime importance. Poorly housed, malnourished parents and children are vulnerable to a host of influences that interfere with their physical and mental health and their capacities to cope with the demands of everyday existence.

3. The prevention and treatment of physical illness is of crucial importance (see p. 34). It must be stressed that our capability for preventing and treating illness far outstrips our effectiveness in reaching many of those who need it.

4. Holding, cuddling, bathing, lifting, changing of clothing, and other everyday events that are a part of infant care are of great importance to the development of young children. These experiences are rich in social communications. They are important in the development of gross motor skills, the child's concept of his body self, and his capacity to act. Intentional action in relation to the external environment is an essential component in the development of the child, and influences his learning through active observation, manipulation, play, exploration, experimentation, and the testing of his own abilities and limitations.

5. A speaking social partner is essential to the development of the child. It is unlikely that language can develop optimally except in an environment rich in language. The speech of the adult is one of the principal channels through which information comes to the infant about himself and his world. His first meaningless babblings can be interpreted and reinforced in such a way that his repertoire of sounds with specific meaning steadily increases. Adults influence children not only through their words but through the feelings that color the words and help to determine their significance. Talking in a manner which organizes and extends understanding also influences development and differentiation of thinking. This becomes especially apparent in the second year, when the early phases of the development of inner mental representations, symbolic thought, and logical thought become increasingly visible in the child's speech and behavior.

6. An atmosphere in which consistency and repetition are prominent is important to the young child. The consistency of the person who cares for him in a certain way day after day is a natural part of a good family environment, supportive of feelings of security, learning, and adaptai on. In disorganized family situations such care is difficult to achieve and its provision requires the services of others. In group care, continuity is hard to achieve because the child relates to several different caretakers. It is important to realize that consistency resides mainly in people and not in the clock, and that excessive routinization and rigid scheduling must be guarded against.

7. Novelty, variety, and contrast within an atmosphere of consistency and repetition are of importance. These attributes of environment sharpen the infant's perceptions and create those mild tension states that call for adaptive responses. As long as the tension state is not so massive as to overwhelm and disorganize, it stimulates development. Group settings, both day care and residential, have tended to provide monotonous and bland environments which fail to stimulate the children to look, to act, to listen, or in other ways to use or develop their capacities.

8. Toys and other playthings are a necessary part of a child's environment. They bring to him a variety of stimuli, challenges, and satisfactions. They are also important as objects with which to discharge feelings of aggression, pleasure, and excitement without getting back a response. As the infant grows older, he uses them independently to support his imagination and to work out some of the normal and the unusual difficulties in the long process of developing controls and becoming responsible for his own behavior.

9. Of crucial value to the developing child are opportunities to move about, to play, to use emerging skills, and to pursue emerging interests in a supportive and safe atmosphere. A combination of freedom and protection becomes increasingly important as the infant becomes a toddler. In addition to enlarging his experience and stimulating mental and physical development, moving about and playing contribute to the development of the awareness of his own body and person. As the child moves from toddlerhood into the third year, children of his own age become increasingly important to his development.

10. Children need to encounter limits, prohibitions, and frustrations appropriate to their age level. Every child needs to learn how to wait, how to behave toward others, how to recognize danger, and how to distinguish between what is permitted and what is prohibited. Reasonable requirements help him to learn to live with others in a society that has particular customs, ideals, and standards. Such requirements inevitably give rise to anxiety, frustration, displeasure, and conflict within the child. It is important for adults to realize that aggressive angry feelings are a normal and necessary

part of development. Adults can help children learn ways of expressing these feelings that will neither harm others nor get them into trouble or danger. Children should be allowed to protest and complain, though not abuse others physically; there should be a few things that they can treat roughly to express their negative feelings. Then they can be calmed or comforted, if need be, and reassured that they have not alienated anyone. Education and guidance, of course, should take place in an atmosphere in which attention, affection, comfort, and satisfaction predominate.

11. Children should have plentiful opportunities for moments of peace during which they are not asked to interact with people or other outside stimuli. Quiet moments help to replenish the child's energies and allow him to begin to be aware that he has an inner world of thought, fantasy, and feeling. A constantly stimulating, highly charged environment, an overcrowded home, or well-intentioned parents who keep the child almost continuously in the center of things may retard movement toward autonomy and may increase demandingness or dependence. Moreover, the child who is constantly stimulated may learn to "tune out" his environment in self-defense, so that he has difficulty in achieving focus and attention when they are appropriate.

12. Many children have little opportunity to know men. The world of young children tends to be a world of women. As the infant becomes a toddler, it becomes increasingly important that he have frequent constructive contacts with men. In the close-knit family, the father and other male relatives provide these contacts. There are in our society, however, thousands of intact families in which the father is regularly away for long periods, and even socioeconomically privileged parents often live in relative isolation. Lonely mothers and lonely children are by no means rare. Appropriate concern has been voiced about the children in fatherless families. Some of these children do find meaningful relationships with men in the relatives, friends, and consorts of their mothers. Special attention should be paid to the various ways in which men with meaningful roles can be introduced into group-care settings for young children.

13. Children need appropriate opportunities to be a part of the adult world. In a family setting, the mother has to respond to many demands not related directly to infant care. These events become a part of the child's experience with his mother. He learns that he must wait for some things, that others have needs and make claims on his mother's time, and that she will react with feelings which may be unrelated to him. This participation in the world of adults enriches his experience in countless ways and includes the important communication that he and his family are part of a larger society. In day-care and residential programs, it requires ingenuity to provide experiences that make the child aware of a world beyond his immediate one.

RECOMMENDATIONS

Prevention and early intervention: In infancy and early childhood there are several settings in which services appear to offer the best possibilities for exerting a significant influence upon the child's chances for good health and development.

1. Own home. This includes financial support to families when needed, and a more vigorous and systematic effort to bring the knowledge of the physician, nurse, social worker, psychologist, and early childhood educator into the home. Direct contact by the professionals will often be necessary, but the services of nonprofessionals under supervision should be utilized as much as possible. In addition, the provision of household help and baby-sitting services, at times, is of great importance in supporting the parents as individuals and in their nurturing role. Assistance to the mother in planning and carrying out homemaking and child-care tasks is among the areas of great need. The presence of interested people with knowledge of child development permits early recognition of problems, for which appropriate help can then be mobilized.

2. Comprehensive centers. One possible vehicle for the provision of the kinds of facilities envisaged is the comprehensive center, providing not only a program of basic nutrition and health supervision but also a full program of stimulation, affection, and education appropriately suited to the needs of the baby and child. Public schools for older children could be closely integrated with such facilities. Medical, educational, casework, and other compensatory and preventive programs for adults and children in such a setting could be instituted very early. The neighborhood comprehensive center, with referral lines to highly specialized services, might effectively reach out to the segment of the population most underserved today.[3]

3. Day-care centers and nursery schools. The term "day-care center," unfortunately, sometimes has the connotation of a custodial arrangement. What is emphasized here are facilities which provide an environment that

3. The proposal for a comprehensive center is one which appears, in various forms, in several Commission documents. In formulating its final recommendations, the Commission recognized the merit of such centers and endorsed their support. After careful study, however, the Commission abandoned the idea of adopting the centers as a *major* recommendation. Among the deciding considerations was the recognition that these centers would not ensure that every child receives the services he needs. Further, the practical difficulties involved in replacing our present system of fragmented services with comprehensive centers placed their reality in the distant future. For these reasons, the Commission proposed, as its major recommendation, a child mental health advocacy system, operating at all governmental levels, but designed, at the neighborhood level, to ensure that each child and his family receive the services they need. See *Crisis in Child Mental Health: Challenge for the 1970's* (New York: Harper & Row, 1970).

not only protects physical health but also provides learning experiences and contacts with others that are geared to the child's developmental needs. For the two-and-a-half- or three-year-old much of the program may resemble that of a nursery school, with the exception that the long day and the child's needs will require modification of some of the existing programs of nursery school education. For the infant and toddler a greater proportion of the experiences will occur in contact with adults in eating, sleeping, toileting, bathing, dressing, and other such activities. The young child with symptoms of disturbance, deprivation, or abuse should be admitted, along with those for whom the facility may be seen as primarily preventive. Staff people can plan how the center can best serve each child. Supports to the parents can be supplied by the center and its allied agencies which should, when feasible, be part of a larger neighborhood center which provides a variety of services to families.

4. Foster day care. The extension of foster day care deserves special attention for the infant and very young child. Some working mothers privately arrange for quality care for their children, and licensed day foster homes under supervision are quite successful in many places. Many arrangements are questionable or overtly damaging, however, not only because some of the caretakers involved are inadequate to care for young children but because of the frequency with which they are changed. There is a need to increase the availability of effective day foster mothers. They should have available to them, when needed, the kind of health and social services referred to earlier, and most important, they should be well compensated. In addition, an educational program should be available for part of the child's learning opportunities.

5. Foster family care. Twenty-four-hour care in a family setting may be for emergency care, for short-term placement, or for permanent placement. Unfortunately, many children now live in a series of foster homes, and with each change there is an increasing risk that their chances for healthy development will be permanently jeopardized. In addition to the need to increase the number and quality of available foster families through more adequate compensation and more vigorous recruitment, the provision of such additional aids as household help, baby-sitters, educational programs, and more direct help from child-care specialists could preserve many of the foster homes that are now lost.

6. Group residential care. Some authorities deeply concerned with the welfare of infants and very young children believe that there is a legitimate place for good institutions in the broad spectrum of services required to take care of these and other children at risk in our society. The emphasis is on the word "good," which means that more and better-trained personnel, more careful attention to the needs of the children, and a more creative and flexible use of the facilities are required. There are several obvious ways in

which such a residential setup could function effectively. First, it could serve as a home for infants without families. Hopefully, this would usually be a temporary state of affairs, while a family was being sought. It appears inevitable, however, that some children will be reared in congregate-care settings. Second, it could provide emergency or short-term placement for young children of disordered families while active efforts are being made to help the family and to preserve the family for the child; thus, it could be used to maintain the contact between the child and his parents rather than to separate them. Finally, it could be used as a setting for diagnostic evaluation of young children. There are times when the distinction between disturbed functioning owing to a biological defect and disturbed functioning from noxious or impoverished experiences can be made only as one observes the young child's response to a therapeutic residential environment over a period of time, as assessment of and work with the family continue. Such a resource would free the pediatric wards of young children who become "boarders" in an inappropriate hospital setting. It would also avoid some of the hazards implicit in both the premature placement of children outside their families and the dangers of returning them to parents who endanger their development or survival.

There are many other settings in which some of the recommended objectives for young children can be accomplished. The existing child guidance clinics, casework agencies, health departments, child placement agencies, community mental health centers, preschool educational programs, inpatient and outpatient medical facilities, and others can and should be a part of a network of essential services. Multiple-function agencies that deal not only with health, education, and social services but also with problems of housing, recreation, legal assistance, employment, and other human needs are being recognized increasingly as essential approaches to the problem.

Research: 1. Because of the paucity of firm knowledge concerning the care of the young child, generous support should be given to a wide variety of studies. Many different models for support of the family in caring for the child of this age should be tried and evaluated. Wherever possible, evaluation of a long-term nature is desirable.

2. Because of the very recent awareness of the necessity for beginning intervention, screening, and family support in the very early years, and more pressingly because of the increasing number of mothers entering the working force, we are faced with the possibility of proliferating programs of caretaking and education for the very young child. It is imperative that research efforts be mounted immediately so that serious mistakes will not be made with infants and children who are so vulnerable, so that inadequate facilities will not be allowed to function, and so that ineffective programs will not become solidified and difficult to change. Perhaps in no other

area is there such a pressing need for basic and applied research, drawing for its direction upon the many disciplines involved in the comprehensive care of infants and children.

Manpower: There is need for a vast increase in personnel from the helping professions specifically trained to deal with this group: nurses, social workers, pediatricians, child psychiatrists, psychologists, nursery school teachers, and so on. In addition, there will have to be created a large pool of individuals for roles practically nonexistent at present. Among these are:

1. Child care workers, or caretakers. These individuals, who will often be working without the close supervision of professional individuals, need training in recognizing and meeting the needs of infants and young children, in utilizing daily experiences as opportunities for learning, and in the management of groups of children. Women *and men* who are basically accepting of young children need not be highly educated, but they should be carefully selected and trained. Curriculums for their training are as yet practically nonexistent. The community college or technical school, in conjunction with a model facility able to provide practical experience in caring for infants and young children, might well be the most appropriate setting for such training. The first task may be the education of teachers capable of training other adults in this work; widespread training programs cannot exist until they can be staffed.

2. The specialist in the development and learning of the infant and very young child. Few educational specialists have ever engaged themselves with these tender years, and few other professionals concerned with the very young are skilled in methods of helping them to learn. The development and supervision of "curricular experiences" for this age group requires not only major research efforts, but also the training of specialists who can apply the findings to the actual setting in which the child is found. There is no profession at present whose training produces experts in this important area. Knowledge and practical experience in caring for very young children must be combined with an awareness of how the child's experiences with activity, persons, and materials enhance his development. Such specialists expedite and enhance the capacities of the on-the-job caretaker and teacher.

3. Teachers of the very young. In addition to child care workers primarily responsible for meeting the basic needs of the infant and young child, there is a need, in many settings (home, day care, foster day care home), for the intervention of the individual trained to provide specialized educational experience, both preventative and remedial, to this age group. For infants and perhaps toddlers, the teacher might best operate in bringing integrated programs to the child and in teaching the parent or caretaker how to create and utilize learning experiences. Beginning with children two and three years old, teachers might work in more specialized areas (e.g.,

language development; precursors of mathematical concepts and reading), especially in settings in which groups of children are involved. These teachers, relying upon the supervision of more highly trained specialists and with the backing of prepared programs and materials, need not themselves be highly trained, although short-term training programs would obviously be required.

THREE-TO-FIVE-YEAR-OLD CHILDREN

After the third birthday, young children need safeguards for the support of physical and mental development that are similar to and continuous with those required in infancy and toddlerhood. To the extent care in the earlier period has been adequate, children are less vulnerable to a large variety of risks. Changing status, however, brings with it new potentialities for hazards, as well as new opportunities for mental and physical growth.

The three-to-five-year-old, moreover, has new and expanding needs. His healthy development profits from association with other children in expanding numbers. His horizons are broader, and within carefully defined limits, he can begin independently to explore the world outside his home. Along with his developing cognitive, motor, and expressive abilities there develops increased need for educational experiences. The children of privileged families, at this age, have for many years been afforded nursery school and kindergarten experience. As at younger ages, children are eager to learn and happiest when they are learning and expanding their competence.

The three-to-five-year-old's increasing body competence and his ability to use language combine to make him better able to take care of himself. He can better comprehend what is expected from him and can communicate his wants more directly. In the push to investigate, to explore, and to test growing powers, he may endanger his physical safety. Moreover, without support by adults who understand the varied facets of his thinking and feeling in this period, his expansiveness may largely be replaced by apathy or confusion.

Comprehensive planning for the three-to-five-year-old should reflect the same concern for the provision of good care for the child in his family and in other settings as that which goes into planning for the infant and toddler. Additionally, the early identification of emotional and learning disorders and the initiation of educational experiences demand special consideration. These two aspects of comprehensive planning are closely interwoven.

Early Identification of Disorders

Clinicians and educators are routinely confronted with developmental deviations, learning difficulties, and behavioral problems which should have been detected earlier. The number of children referred for help before they are five is quite low. Three major factors are involved. First, young children are rarely exposed to responsible extrafamilial adult observation. Second, observations are often brief and sporadic in those situations to which most children are brought for routine professional care and therefore do not uncover many signs of emotional or developmental maladjustment. Finally, even in those instances in which parents have become concerned about symptoms that later prove to have been harbingers of serious emotional disorders or developmental deviation, there exists a combination of limited knowledge and unrealistic optimism among medical practitioners which results in the often inappropriate reassurance that the child will grow out of the problem.

Particular attention needs to be given the possibilities for the early identification of learning disorders (see p. 89). Estimates indicate that from 5 to 15 percent of the school population have serious difficulty in reading, 2 to 10 percent have speech problems, and 20 to 30 percent have less than adequate motor development (Bateman, 1966). Such estimates do not include children characterized as slow learners, aphasoid, emotionally disturbed, visually handicapped, and so on. Many of these disorders could have been prevented or remediated if discovered earlier.

Although knowledge of the etiology of learning disorders is necessarily sketchy, it may still be possible to develop some predictive indices. The results of at least one study (based on a small number of children) indicate that a combination of tests administered at kindergarten can be used to identify nearly all children who will fail in second grade, although a few children who will be successful may be erroneously identified (De Hirsch, Jansky, and Langford, 1966). Screening of gifted children who are likely to be eligible for early school admission and for whom ordinary school experiences may be inappropriate can also be initiated in these early years.

It seems reasonable that information derived from successive observations of the child in the years before he is five might contribute greatly to the screening process. The astute nursery school teacher can be taught to assess the level of the child's perceptual-motor and language functioning, the kinds of problems that are too difficult, the extent to which he can control impulsive behavior and stay with a problem, and so on. If such assessments can be explicit and reliable, they can be added to more formal testing devices to assist in the process of early identification.

The Initiation of Early Educational Experiences

The increasing involvement of women in out-of-the-home activities, concerns for intellectual and academic performance engendered by technological advances, revision of public school curriculums, the war on poverty, and many other factors have focused attention on the relevance of preschool educational experiences to later learning and adjustment. A variety of programs have evolved, most of them focused on the children from the disadvantaged segments of our society.

Few of the present programs, however, involve comprehensive programming for the three-to-five-year-old. Generally, these do not represent new patterns but modifications of established nursery school, kindergarten, or day-care programs. Some are concerned with cognitive development almost to the exclusion of other aspects of the child's development; others ignore cognitive development in favor of social development. Where there has been experimentation, it has been along the lines of involving parents in the program, introducing more direct and focused instruction into the curriculum, developing planned sequential experiences, varying the length and frequency of the sessions, and widening the use of paraprofessionals.

On the whole, the experimental programs of intervention for three-to-five-year-olds have shown significant initial advantages for the very young child. However, follow-up studies after school entry have tended to be discouraging. Control-group youngsters have tended to exhibit a spurt in development upon entry to school, and the advances made during the preschool period by the experimental group children have tended to be lost by the time the child has been in school for a few years. A few studies, however, have demonstrated continuing gains in social and intellectual behavior other than those measured by standardized tests (Robinson and Robinson, 1968).

There exist several possible explanations of these data. First, the programs themselves may not have been designed astutely enough to prepare the child for a continued high rate of social and cognitive growth. Second, the school programs into which they have later gone may not meet their needs well, especially the needs of children who have become accustomed to a very rich and stimulating preschool environment. Third, the interaction patterns within families may take a form during the elementary school years which counteracts the earlier gains. Fourth, gains may be made in areas not easily tapped by standardized psychological tests. Finally, and perhaps most important, the intervention of the preschool programs may not have begun early enough or been sufficiently intensive; therefore, the time actually had to be spent in efforts at rehabilitating children who had already suffered damage to their learning capacities by the time they entered the preschool at age three, four, or five.

Because of present limitations both in the availability of professionally trained staff and in curriculums for programs of early intervention, stress must be laid initially on research and experimentation with new models for service. Emphasis should be on devising models better adapted to the children's conditions of living, to their learning abilities and their deficits, and to the school systems into which they will go.

Meanwhile, within the facilities which are available, changes can be made which appear to offer promise of improved effectiveness. Among these modifications, the following points should be considered:

1. The present numbers of nursery school and day-care center "drop-outs" who cannot be contained in the group setting of existing facilities reflect problems in the children, the parents, and/or the programs. The services which may be required by a particular child (more specialized programs, part- or full-time hospitalization, counseling for the parents) are often unknown to the isolated staff of the school or center, even when they exist in the community. It is hoped that eventually every group setting for children will be integrated in some fashion with a comprehensive package of services to children, including continuing and close health and dental supervision, casework, and access to treatment facilities. Meanwhile, staff members, whose professional training is often limited, need consultative services in order to make existing services available and to improve their own functioning.

2. The traditional nursery school provides for a considerable degree of autonomy in the child's choice of activities. With improved assessment, the experiences provided can be tailored more precisely to the capabilities of the individual child. The child with deficits will often avoid, rather than spontaneously seek, elements in his environment which are potentially corrective. Planned remediation programs are required.

3. What has become a traditional pattern of grouping according to age needs reexamination to see how opportunities can be created for more constructive contacts among older and younger children. Such groupings would also simplify and strengthen the contacts of parents and staff, if siblings had a common caretaker.

4. The hours of operation of preschool centers need to be more realistic. In an effort to increase their effectiveness some centers have turned to two days a week for some children and three days a week for others and to morning and afternoon sessions. Closer scrutiny of how well programs away from home coordinate with family needs and patterns might lead to more appropriate and varied modifications, and perhaps also to a better "spread" of available services, especially to those children with available caretakers at home or in foster day-care homes.

5. The introduction of nonprofessional staff would make possible the extension of services to a larger number of children and free the teacher for more specialized and more individualized interactions with the children.

6. For the past few years, controversy has revolved around the importance, or even the advisability, of including structural conceptual and skill learning in curriculums for use with very young children. The traditional nursery schools, designed in the main for middle-class children, have been formulated around the notions that the years of early childhood are

almost exclusively years of social learning, and that given a rich environment, children will learn by themselves. It was felt this period should be unfettered by cognitive training, and that there should be only a minimal imposition of controlled patterns of responding.

Recent research already alluded to demonstrates clearly that the early years are crucial to subsequent intellectual development. Early programs can indeed teach children much more than they had ever been thought capable of learning. It is not clear at this point whether any specific skills or abilities are crucial to this early learning period. It is clear, however, that the child's motivational pattern which results from joyful and rewarding learning is of basic importance. Early attitudes toward exploration, self-instigated investigation, and pleasure in learning and mastering are probably critical.

The matter no longer appears to be an either-or decision; many types of learning probably have their place. There is growing awareness that the young child is happiest when he is expanding his capabilities, not only in the social and motor spheres, but also in the cognitive sphere. New methods of teaching have to be developed for this age group. Longitudinal data are badly needed to guide decisions about which concepts and skills are best taught early and which delayed, and about the best ways to foster positive self-concepts, urges toward achievement, and productive engagement with the world.

RECOMMENDATIONS

Prevention: By the age of three, socially disadvantaged children are clearly behind middle-class children in language ability, in fine motor coordination, in their concepts, skills, and mastery of the world, and in confidence and self-control. It is probably also true that many middle-class children fail to develop to their fullest potential in cognitive, motor, social, and emotional spheres. In order to avoid the necessity for massive programs of remediation after the age of three, it is essential that programs for the birth-to-three age group be included in the integrated services and facilities available to families.

Facilities and services: A variety of services need to be developed for this age group, particularly those which provide out-of-home experiences and those which provide treatment and screening for the many handicaps which can be detected at this age. It is essential that emphasis be given to developing programs which will offer a comprehensive package of services to children and their families as well as a wide range of experience and assistance both to the young child and to those responsible for him.

It is clear that there will need to be marked expansion in the number and perhaps the size of facilities available, though this should be accomplished carefully so as not to sacrifice the quality of care provided. Indeed, most existing services need to be upgraded if they are to be of benefit to children, other than mere custody and protection.

Meanwhile, within the facilities which are available, modifications can be made which appear to offer promise of improved effectiveness:

1. means of providing easier access to psychiatric, pediatric, psychological, casework, and other services; a great deal might be accomplished through more experienced nursery school staffs;

2. more individualization within programs;

3. greater flexibility in age grouping;

4. more realistic hours of operation of preschool centers;

5. expanded use of paraprofessionals and volunteers;

6. recognition of the importance of cognitive as well as social learning (although the cognitive should not be overstressed).

Research: Before rushing into massive programs of providing services to young children, stress should be laid upon research and training. Slow growth of programs, especially in the beginning, is certainly to be preferred to premature, ill-staffed, and ill-equipped programs which probably will be of little advantage to children and may lead inevitably to public reaction against further support for such services.

1. Particular support should be given to research centers which, in sum, approach the development of comprehensive patterns both from laboratory studies and from applied settings. Existing programs and those being developed in diverse patterns should be carefully and continuously evaluated.

2. A significant segment of research in this area should be longitudinal in design, continuing to follow during the school years children who have come from different backgrounds, who have experienced various kinds of programs, and who have entered varied public school experiences and programs supplementary to school. Such research is expensive and demands long-term funding commitments.

3. Among the research questions to be considered in the development of new educational programs are the following:

 a. long-range effects of early-childhood learning in a variety of areas; new methods and materials to support such learning; effects of early learning on children's motivational patterns and self-concepts;

 b. assessment of the resources and activities available to children within their homes, revealing areas which need supplementation in service programs;

 c. assessment of the ways in which needed experiences can best be provided (in a group setting, directly by professionals or paraprofessionals, or indirectly through work with the parents);

d. areas in need of direct instruction, methods of diagnosing assets and deficits, and individualizing instruction accordingly;

e. differences, if any, in the provisions to be made for boys and girls;

f. methods of enhancing the children's participation in the world of adults;

g. methods of providing opportunities for children to incorporate and practice learnings provided in structured situations balancing spontaneous play and privacy with structure and group participation;

h. provision of a suitable balance between direct, immediate experience and vicarious experience through books, television, and mechanical aids;

i. optimal types of locations for educational programs and means of integrating the programs with other services to children;

j. methods of providing children with a wide range of interpersonal experiences, including contacts with individuals of different ages, styles, and backgrounds which will enable the children to identify these people as individuals who care about them, and with whom continuous friendships can be established;

k. methods of working with parents and other caretakers so that their abilities to provide for the child are both strengthened and supported.

Manpower: 1. Just as outlined in the previous section, programs should be immediately developed for the training of professional and paraprofessional personnel to staff the services to be provided for young children. Emphasis in the early years of such programs should be given to the training of persons who will be able to offer training to other adults who will staff the services. It is impossible at this time to begin massive programs of educational, medical, or social care to young children because sufficient pools of personnel simply do not exist.

2. Special efforts should be made to recruit men for both professional and paraprofessional positions.

HEAD START PROGRAM

Head Start, a nationwide program for the children of the poor, was initiated in 1965 by the Office of Economic Opportunity. According to the official document setting out the aims and nature of the program, the overriding goal "should be to create an environment in which every child has the maximum opportunity and support in developing his full potential." Seven more specific goals were then indicated as follows:

1. Improving the child's physical health and physical abilities.
2. Helping the emotional and social development of the child by

encouraging self-confidence, spontaneity, curiosity, and self-discipline.

3. Improving the child's mental processes and skills with particular attention to conceptual and verbal skills.

4. Establishing patterns and expectations of success for the child which will create a climate of confidence for his future learning efforts.

5. Increasing the child's capacity to relate positively to family members and others while at the same time strengthening the family's ability to relate positively to the child and his problems.

6. Developing in the child and his family a responsible attitude toward society and fostering constructive opportunities for society to work together with the poor in solving their problems.

7. Increasing the sense of dignity and self-worth within the child and his family (Planning Committee of Project Head Start, 1965).

The report also emphasizes that "research and evaluation should be a key part of both local and national efforts."

If Head Start is to be judged by its own criteria, a mixed picture emerges. On the one hand, at the most general level, there is no question that the program has served to make visible the very large number of children who need assistance and has aroused community responsibility throughout the nation. Up to one-half million children have in some summers been enrolled in Head Start programs; approximately 260,000 were enrolled during the summer of 1969, with greater emphasis on the more extensive year-round programs for approximately 62,500 children. On the other hand, if one seeks signs of accomplishment with respect to these seven specific program areas outlined in the Statement of Policy, progress is uneven, and indeed one-sided. The one-sidedness is strikingly reflected in the character of research that has been done in Head Start programs at both a national and a local level. An overwhelming proportion of the studies reported focus on objective 3, the development of conceptual and verbal skills, with the remaining six areas receiving minimum attention. Moreover, the selective emphasis in research reflects a similar bias in program as well. Throughout the country, Head Start centers defined as their major task (and were so perceived by the public as well) improving the child's intellectual capacities so that he might do better in school. As a result of this selective distortion of the original comprehensive aims of the program, the success of Head Start is frequently judged on how well the child performs on entry into a conventional kindergarten or first grade. Yet application of this criterion does violence to both the fundamental assumptions and the operating principles of the Head Start program which emphasized that changes in the child could be expected only with appropriate and enduring changes in the child's everyday environment.

Program Recommendations. Under these circumstances, we can make no more pointed recommendation than to urge that Head Start programs be modified and expanded in accordance with their original mandate to provide more balanced emphasis across the seven objectives set for the program. In this connection, it is important to recognize that these objectives call initially for changes in the child's environment rather than in the child himself. In this perspective, the child's family, neighbors, and friends assume a far greater importance than has been usually accorded in operating programs. Far too many of these are content to define parent involvement as participation in advisory committees and classes in adult education, with little attention or opportunity being afforded for the interaction of parents, older children, and neighborhood adults with the children themselves, and the development of special opportunities and activities appropriate for such interaction. Further specific recommendations include the following:

1. Given the philosophy and aims of Head Start, a year-round program is clearly far more appropriate than one limited to a few weeks during the summer. Accordingly, continuation of the shift in emphasis from summer to year-round programs is strongly indicated.

2. Given, too, the importance of prevention rather than remediation in programs dealing with children, the age of entry into Head Start programs should be extended downward to at least age three, possibly to age two, with continuous experience in the program until the child reaches the age of school entry. Even by the age of two, intellectual, emotional, and social handicaps are already detectable in the group of children for whom the program is intended; a program begun at age four or five offers too little, too late, and has too much ground to make up.

3. Much greater attention needs to be paid to the mental health of the child. Some programs have been totally disrupted by the presence of a large number of children who are so seriously disturbed that education cannot proceed. Some of their problems of adjustment may reflect difficulties within the program itself; there have been a number of hastily put-together programs, staffed by poorly trained workers, which offered very little to the children enrolled and were not sensitive to their immediate needs. In view of the prevalence of deep-rooted problems within this high-risk group, however, mental health consultation should be available, preferably through a mental health group or center, in order for collaboration between resources to take the form of working alliances. Assessment outlines need to be developed in order to give the consultant, teacher, and others the opportunity to inventory strengths and problem areas of the children so they can plan suitably for them, as individuals and subgroups. Consultation may take many forms, including clinical evaluation of the child, direct observation in the program, participation with the teacher, and in-service training of the staff. In some instances, special classes or

therapeutic aides for severely disturbed children may be deemed advisable.

4. The staffs of Head Start programs, both professional and nonprofessional, are overwhelmingly female. There should be far more males involved in the program at all levels.

5. Perhaps the most neglected aspect of the Head Start program has been the utilization of "preadolescent and adolescent models" which was strongly urged in the original mandate for the program. This, incidentally, offers a major source for participation by males.

6. Present regulations limit to 10 percent the proportion of children in Head Start programs above the poverty criterion. In view of the demonstrated advantage to lower-class children of being placed in groups including substantial numbers of middle-class children, the 10 percent limit should be raised.

7. Special attention should be given to the child's transition from Head Start to kindergarten or first grade, particularly in those situations where Follow-Through programs are not already available. In this connection, the opportunity for the child's Head Start teacher to continue on with him as he moves into the early grades is especially valuable and can be accomplished by making joint appointments of teachers in Head Start and in primary grade classes.

ENVIRONMENTAL SETTINGS FOR FAMILY LIVING

In the current emphasis on providing specific services to children and families, communities have tended to ignore the importance of the environmental settings in which family living occurs. In all walks of life, families with young children find themselves forced to accept living conditions which were constructed without reference to their activities and needs. Some provisions can be made with little additional expense when community and architectural planning take these needs into account; others, such as the provision of decent housing, will involve considerable expenditures. A few examples of desirable qualities of the environmental setting for families with young children are the following:

1. Housing which meets at least minimal requirements for health, cleanliness, and space. Millions of infants and young children whose families are of marginal or poverty economic status are growing up in homes which are hazardous to healthy development. Many substandard homes lack functional plumbing and adequate heat control and may be infested with rats and other disease-bearing organisms. Overcrowding not only breeds contagious disease but stifles the child's play. Fire and other safety hazards take their toll in death and accidents. Such homes and those which are otherwise substandard are directly injurious to the development of the infant and young child. While there are many valid bases on which

to argue for the provision of decent housing to all citizens, perhaps the most powerful of these is the protection of children.

2. The need for privacy. To foster the sense of belonging to a family unit, to provide the opportunity for expansive behavior in young children, and to permit freedom of response between parents and children, privacy of living is highly desirable. The young child needs space for quiet moments, for play and other activities; he and the older child alike need a place which they feel to be theirs alone. The mother who must be concerned about what the neighbors will hear will behave differently with her child than the mother who is assured of privacy. The young child's noisy play, the baby who must cry before he goes to sleep, the child's protests at unwanted restrictions, and the occasional outbursts of parent or child cannot be allowed to occur naturally if they will be disturbing to others. Moreover, the child who knows that his protest will bring immediate action very early learns this powerful means of manipulation. Restrictions of privacy beset families of many socioeconomic levels; they are not confined to the poor.

3. The need for aesthetically satisfying surroundings. Beauty and organization are thought to encourage a joyful alertness and satisfaction with one's environment which is mentally healthy for both parents and children. Those whose homes are chaotic and ugly typically seek to escape them either by leaving home or by "tuning out" the environment. The young child responds to attractive belongings, an attractive home, and pleasant outdoor areas as positively as do adults. We suspect that children who are surrounded with beauty learn to search for the beautiful and to produce it in their own surroundings as they grow older.

4. The need for safety. Accidents in early childhood constitute an important, and largely preventable, cause of fatalities and serious incapacities. Aside from the many hazards in homes which are poorly constructed or organized from a safety standpoint, it is also necessary to provide outdoor space which is safe for children. The young child whose mother must stay too close to him learns little independence or self-confidence. Playground areas for toddlers and very young children probably need to be separate from those of other children; playground equipment needs to be carefully selected so that it requires a minimum of supervision; fencing is imperative to protect the child who might wander into the street. Pedestrian travel with the parents also needs to be made safe.

5. Facilities for family recreation. The lack of convenient parks, playgrounds, and other family recreational facilities in many cities reveals the low-order value which is placed upon care for the young. Small neighborhood parks and playgrounds are useful to most families with young children both because of their ready accessibility and because small groups of people are more inviting to very young children than are crowds in which they

may feel insecure. The young child also profits from being able to participate with his family in an outing, a picnic, a walk, and other activities which require larger and different spaces than the small playground.

RECOMMENDATIONS

Prevention: All planning of community resources, housing developments, schools, and other aspects of community living should include the services of individuals who are knowledgeable about the needs of young children and their families. Membership of local planning boards should include at least one such individual. Preservation of space for neighborhood playgrounds and for recreational facilities should take high priority in urban planning.

Facilities and programs: Community improvement funds should be channeled into the provision of decent housing, the development of aesthetically satisfying surroundings, the renovation of unused small spaces for playgrounds, the purchase of undeveloped lands for recreational facilities, the provision of safety in existing facilities, and the provision of privacy for families with young children.

Clinical Conditions

It has long been evident that diagnostic assessment of children is most meaningful when carried out according to developmental rather than symptomatic considerations. The hallmark of psychological health in the child is not absence of symptoms, but unhindered progression in personality and intellectual development. Transitory symptoms occur normally in the course of early development and do not necessarily reflect pathological trends. Every new phase of growth creates new conflict situations, but, also, new ways to deal with these conflicts. In addition, each new phase of maturation carries with it the possibility of modifying the impact of earlier conflicts.

It is evident, then, that meaningful diagnostic assessment in the child requires an accurate evaluation of the course of overall psychic progression. Certain characteristics of developmental progression in very young children, however, cause theoretical and methodological problems which render developmental assessment in the child under five an arduous task, fraught with uncertainty. First, progression does not occur smoothly, but takes place in discontinuous fashion, with considerable ebb and flow and significant overlapping, or even simultaneity, of behaviors belonging to different developmental phases. Second, patterns of development vary considerably from one individual to another. Finally, the personality is in flux during the early period and so responsive to environmental conditions that, except in cases of massive developmental disturbance, it is sometimes difficult to distinguish between transitory phenomena and permanent changes. Diagnostic assessments leading to crucial decisions as to whether to intervene in children's lives thus require rather hazardous predictions.

Yet, diagnoses must be made, and decisions regarding intervention cannot often be postponed. The very decision to postpone may have important

77

impact on the course of the condition. It is incumbent upon the clinical investigator, therefore, to utilize the methodological tools and theoretical construction available to him in such a manner that the task is accomplished as accurately as possible within the limitations imposed by existing conditions.

The broad conceptual framework supplied by the modern unitary theory of disease is especially useful in conceptualizing the problems of the earliest years. Health and disease are seen as phases of life, and in this framework the concept of stress plays a central role. Stress is defined as any external or internal influence that interferes with satisfaction of basic needs or disturbs the adaptive equilibrium. It is always related to the maturational level and capacity of the person at any given point in time. Health is the state of successful adaptation and, in the child, of growth and maturation. The healthy young child is able to deal effectively with the demands of everyday existence, provided that the environment is responsive to his developmental needs.

Physical growth and maturation and the progress and differentiation of a variety of functions are signs of health, as are freedom from disability and effectiveness in physical and social interactions. Restriction of adaptive functions, growth or development, and adaptive breakdown can be said to represent disease states which derive from multiple etiological factors. Some symptoms manifested by the sick are the result of attempts to maintain adaptation, to obtain satisfaction of basic needs, or to effect restitution; others directly reveal stressful interferences in specific functions of organ systems. In the context of concern for mental health it is important to note that even when major stress is of a predominantly physical nature, the resulting changes in physiological systems may significantly influence psychological and social levels of organization. When stress is predominantly psychological or social the emotions involved may result in concomitant physiological change in a variety of organ systems.

In very young children, crystallized and circumscribed symptom pictures are unusual. Rather, disturbances tend to be more global reactions. Some of the more common problems probably deriving primarily from psychosocial influences are outlined below:

1. Disturbances in eating, elimination, and sleeping: too much or too little food intake and sleep, disturbances in cycles of tension and relaxation; appetitive disturbances (food avoidances, ingestion of nonedibles); conflicts with parents around these areas.

2. Delayed or disordered growth: poor weight gain, retarded skeletal growth, and failure to thrive may occur even when food intake is adequate.

3. Specific organ-system symptoms: vomiting, rumination, poor absorption of food, diarrhea, constipation, skin rashes, wheezing and rhinarrhea, etc.

4. Delayed acquisition or deviant nature of specific developmental steps: motor skill and activity, control over sphincters, communication (verbal and nonverbal), and intellectual growth.

5. Delayed or disturbed relationships with others.

6. Loss of previously acquired skills or regression in levels of psychosocial organization.

7. Disturbances in the capacity to play.

8. Accident proneness.

9. Fears of familiar and new situations, doubts about one's own capacities for mastery.

10. Mood disturbances: overreaction to minor stress, sadness, prolonged anger, lack of tolerance for frustration, etc.

RECOMMENDATIONS

Prevention: Since most disorders stem from predisposing or precipitating factors in the first five years of life, early intervention offers considerable potential for ameliorating the actual condition, providing for continued normal development, and preventing subsequent occurrence or exacerbation of the pathological variation. The potential for effective and economical therapeutic intervention is unequaled in any other life period and is highly recommended.

Facilities and services: Facilities for developmental diagnosis and intervention must be made easily accessible to all segments of the population.

Research: Among the questions to be given research priority are:

1. Elucidation of earliest signs of variation from normality (developmental delay, pathological symptoms, high-risk patterns of behavior).

2. Investigation of correlations between early variation and subsequent pathology; long-range implications of various indices of difficulty which can be obtained through professional and paraprofessional observation, testing, and parental report.

3. Effectiveness and efficiency of personnel other than mental health specialists in screening clinically disturbed children; development of instruments to facilitate screening.

4. Means of making sure that meaningful surveillance of every child takes place during the preschool years, in order to initiate remediation.

Manpower: Aside from the numerous steps toward prevention outlined elsewhere, all professional personnel who will be involved with young children should receive training in the basic aspects of child development: motor, emotional, social, intellectual, moral, and motivational facets; age-appropriate expectations, both of growth and of natural "problem behaviors"; and cognizance of the needs of children. Such training should enable a large number of persons who have contact with child and family to enhance their sensitivity to possible disordered patterns of development and thus to serve an initial screening function, which would be followed by referral for more specialized evaluation. Their common training should also facilitate communication and cooperation among them.

Insofar as possible, subprofessional personnel should likewise receive training to permit them also to become sensitive to distortions in development and symptoms of emotional disorder during early childhood, so that children with questionable problems can be more closely observed and appropriate referrals made.

INCIDENCE OF EMOTIONAL DISORDERS

The incidence of emotional disorders in early childhood is largely unknown, but it is unquestionably a mental health problem of considerable proportions. The number of children actually under psychiatric care is indeed very small, and is in no way a reflection of those who need such services. When careful studies are undertaken of high-risk target groups, such as populations of children in nursery schools or day-care centers, approximately a third of these children at any one time are seen by teachers and clinicians as suffering from at least mild emotional conditions which interfere with their development, and approximately 30 percent more show transient difficulties (Population Study of a Day Care Center, 1967). The careful longitudinal study of one group of middle-class children of intact families revealed that, at some time before age six, 23 percent were identified by mothers' reports and psychiatric evaluation as having exhibited emotional problems more significant than the normal gamut of transient problems inherent in growing up (Thomas, Chess, and Birch, 1968).

The difficulties in obtaining clear data about the incidence of emotional disorders of varying degree stem from a number of sources. Some of these have already been mentioned. Young children are rarely exposed to responsible adult observation outside of the family, and it is left to the skill, sensitivity, and initiative of the family to seek diagnosis and therapeutic intervention. When children are seen for routine medical care, these brief observations often fail to uncover signs of maladjustment. Even when the parents are sufficiently concerned to seek help, there is an unrealistic tendency, on the part of those who advise them, to wait for the child to "grow out of it." There are, indeed, complex problems involved in the evaluation of troublesome symptoms, which may be harbingers of handicapping disorder or may be merely the temporary and normal product of the child's dealing with important developmental tasks. Too few professionals in any discipline concerned with mental health are trained in the assessment and treatment of children who suffer from emotional disorder in the first years of life. Too few facilities exist which would encourage families to seek help.

With few exceptions, there is no clear confrontation of community responsibility for the child until he reaches school age. At school entrance, rigorous demands for achievement, conformity, and maturity are imposed upon the child, and it is often at this point that cognizance is first taken of the child's emotional problems. Clearly, by this time, the maladjustment patterns of many children are deeply entrenched and difficult to treat; primary symptoms, of a physical or psychological nature, have been overlaid with secondary symptoms and disturbance in the organization and behavior of the entire family.

RECOMMENDATIONS

Manpower: In spite of the insufficient attention paid to this age group thus far, persons with sufficient skill are able to make early diagnosis of such disorders as infantile autism, childhood schizophrenia, depressive states, psychosomatic conditions, and developmental deviations, and identify the children who belong in the atypical group. The number of persons with such skills must be greatly increased by training if the extent and severity of emotional disorders during early childhood are to be discovered.

Research: Screening procedures at present are rough and inexact. Procedures for detection and evaluation of early childhood disorder must be developed if accurate estimates of the magnitude of this mental health problem are to be made.

PSYCHOSIS AND DEPRIVATIONAL SYNDROMES IN YOUNG CHILDREN

Included in this section are summary statements concerning the current status of the problems of children five and under with psychosis and with failure to thrive and other deprivational syndromes (Gair and Bullard, 1968). These clinical areas are presented jointly because they subsume the most severe psychiatric reactions in early childhood from the point of view of current risk to the child's well-being and/or his subsequent development.

Recommendations follow each summary, but the emphases in the two major areas are different. Basic research in clinical definition and methods of assessment of degrees of disorders are stressed for psychosis, while prevention and practical management aspects are emphasized for the deprivation syndromes. These emphases in the recommendations reflect directly the difference in the clinical strategy that is appropriate at this time for expanded work in each of the two areas. Psychosis is not yet reliably defined by etiology but rather by a manifested picture which in itself needs more precise delineation before more accurate reconstructions of causation and definitive follow-up studies can be conducted. The deprivational syndromes on the other hand are defined by their cause; children exposed to this pathogenic situation can be identified as soon as the deprivation is discovered. This allows for immediate application of preventive and other treatment and management methods and points to the need to expand the facilities for early recognition.

Psychosis in Young Children

Basic facts about which there is little dispute: 1. There are children who demonstrate striking and persistent withdrawal from their parents, some as very young infants and others in their first years following periods of normal relatedness. Such children recoil from or ignore other adults and children, and demonstrate other signs of major psychological deviations: in speech, emotional expression, responsiveness to stimuli, and handling of the physical environment. These children are called "psychotic," "atypical," "autistic," "schizophrenic," and other less common labels, provided that they show signs of neither organic brain disorder nor primary mental retardation.

2. Children who do show signs of organic brain disorder, or cerebral dysfunction, and children who are afflicted with primary mental retardation may also present behavioral pictures identical or very similar to those outlined above.

3. The majority of children with onset of psychotic symptoms before five do not find their way to psychiatric evaluation until after age five.

4. The parents of such children tend, under stress, to become perplexed and often handle their anxiety in maladaptive ways; whether or not they have entered into the original etiology of the disorder, they as well as the child need assistance.

Facts that are less certain but little disputed: 1. The prognosis of children diagnosed as psychotic under the age of five, as a group, is poor; only 20 to 30 percent achieve a fair to good recovery.

2. Of those who have no communicative speech by age five, only 5 percent are subsequently able to manage without institutionalization or total supervision outside an institution.

3. Of those who have communicative speech at age five, no higher than 50 percent subsequently manage at better than an institutional adjustment, while some 5 to 10 percent return to normal, or nearly so.

Sharply disputed areas: 1. Whether or not there is one psychotic disease state in childhood, whatever name may be assigned it, is not agreed upon. Some assert and purport to demonstrate that there is one disease process. Others, citing the unproven etiology in many instances and the variable manifestations and courses, as well as the similarity in manifestations in which probable causations are different, insist that the behavioral manifestations describe a syndrome with multiple possible separate or interlocking causes. Those who insist on the unity of the disease state are not all of the same mind as to the essential problem. Some point to central psychological factors, others to a specific maturational disharmony, others to extrinsic cerebral damage as the exclusive and defining core of the disease.

2. The disputes about etiology are not always along lines of homogeneity and divergence of psychotic states. Genetic causation (metabolic or neurophysiological), genetic predisposition, brain damage (or cerebral dysfunction), and parental psychopathology are not only cited as exclusive or contributory causative factors in all or some instances of psychosis, but are also the target of extensive disproofs.

3. There is some agreement in the reported studies of large series of cases that no conclusive evidence can be cited to demonstrate that prognosis with treatment of various sorts is much different from prognosis with little or no treatment ("no treatment" in such children often implies simple custodial supervision). Despite this, convictions of efficacy of treatment and parallel disproofs are as fervently recorded as are elaborations of etiologic theory. The lack of common diagnostic criteria, not to mention criteria for assessing severity of disorder, makes reliable comparison of treatment results impossible.

There is a voluminous literature on treatment, including psychotherapy, special educational practices, parent education, parental counseling, parental psychotherapy, operant conditioning, drugs, residential treatment, and electric shock treatment. Here, as with etiology, many detailed longitudinal reports of treatment efforts are persuasive and suggest, in the aggregate, that no one treatment is specific for all children with psychosis, but that some treatments do make a difference to individual children's courses. In practice, choice of treatment stems from the prevailing orientation of the treatment center to which a child is taken.

Areas of little agreement but little dispute: 1. There is wide divergence in criteria for the diagnosis of psychosis cited in the literature, and in many articles no criteria are specifically enunciated. Rather than enter into dispute, there often exists the tacit assumption that others are referring to "the same" kinds of children and the conclusions of the articles are either supported or attacked without questioning the basis for diagnosis.

2. It is not surprising, in view of the ambiguity of diagnostic criteria, that incidence as well as other epidemiologic data are vague and sparse.

3. There are interesting theories implicating specific brain dysfunction in the severe withdrawal of some psychotic children. The theories are speculative and divergent, although there is little active debate about this subject. Direct studies in this area are difficult, few, and fragmentary. Attributions of central nervous system implication in psychosis are derived from gross findings of dysfunctions *not necessarily relevant* or from histories suggestive of damage.

RECOMMENDATIONS

Facilities and services: Achievement of earlier identification of children with psychotic reactions requires the development of facilities for broader and more effective professional examination of all children in a community. For diagnostic and treatment purposes, screening facilities should be physically and administratively related to special educational facilities, regular school settings, preschool centers, pediatric hospitals, mental health centers, and residential units. The residential units suitable for children under five should be small and their use should be flexible, allowing day care, single overnight care, or more nights as tolerable to the child and productive of diagnostic and therapeutic gain.

It is premature to underwrite one specific form of treatment or attempt at prevention for psychosis. The great pressure for treatment can be answered concurrently with evaluative programs recommended here.

Research: It is highly desirable that research programs of different orientations currently studying psychotic children be coordinated. The existing fact of research proliferating along divergent lines, each confident of its own validity, perpetuates fruitless schisms and concomitant ambiguities of basic criteria for diagnosis, severity, and change. Even where research is carried out in separate centers with similar orientations, lack of common criteria and of agreement on methods of study minimizes the applicability of findings.

Regional programs on the model of the Maternal and Infant Health study are probably necessary. Long-range studies are needed of a large number of children under five representing all (or a known percentage of all) cases in a given region evaluated by the same methods and against the same criteria for psychosis. Such groups of children should be followed into adolescence through further study and systematic treatment by the different systems in practice.

Collaboration among studies, including those of deprivation and cerebral dysfunction, should be encouraged. Some workers dealing with problems of deprivation are unaware of the clinical questions about psychotic children that their work might help answer. The overlap between deprivation and psychosis studies is in the area of etiology. Although it is generally accepted that deprivation does not alone cause psychosis, deprivation is thought to be a potential contributing factor. Studies of deprived children reveal an incidence of psychosis in about 2 percent, a rate known to be much higher than the rate in the general population. The possible relation between the two areas needs more understanding. It may be that a psychotic state in a child, manifested as withdrawal or as hyperreactivity to stimuli, antedates deprivation and, by stimulating adverse maternal reactions, precipitates a deprivation syndrome such as failure to thrive. On the other hand, deprivation may be predisposing or precipitating to psychosis. Because of the concomitance of the two, a common or related etiologic factor is likely to be operating.

It is premature to ignore children exhibiting psychosis with demonstrable cerebral dysfunction or with mental retardation, and to study only those without them, when the psychotic aspect of their clinical picture is similar. Inclusion of these groups for research attention, while identifying them as carefully as possible, will enhance the clarity of understanding of the roles played in the psychotic picture by the other conditions. Such inclusion does not imply the absence of differences; it allows for clarification of what such differences may be.

Many if not all of the attitudes implicit in these recommendations have been embodied in work already begun at different research centers. Research, however, has not been conducted on what appears to be the necessary multicentered collaborative level which could be greatly facilitated by federal support and encouragement.[4]

The Deprivational Syndromes

The deprivational syndromes are usually taken to include the battered-child syndrome, severe neglect, and marked failure to thrive. They do not include, but are often related to, less severe forms of disturbance stemming from more general aspects of what is often termed social or cultural deprivation.

A substantial incidence of the deprivational syndromes occurs in clinical practice in hospitals, outpatient facilities, agencies, and private medical practice. This incidence does not represent, however, the true extent of these disorders in our society. The deprivational syndromes occupy increasing proportions of available hospitals, institutions for delinquents, facilities for retarded and disturbed children, and casework agencies, further stressing these already maximally used institutions. The large time demands of such children make great inroads on the schedules of medical and paramedical personnel. The resulting expense of the diagnosis and immediate treatment of children who suffer from the deprivational syndromes represents a significant economic drain, involving as it does a multitude of studies and the need for close follow-up supervision.

The long-range untoward effects of deprivation have been shown to be significant, and a wide variety of disorders follow the various deprivational syndromes. These include the impairment of physical growth, intellectual function, emotional and personality development, and social adaptation in later childhood and adult life. These long-term effects are not completely

4. The final report of the Commission, cited in the previous footnote, added specificity to this recommendation by urging the creation of research centers, under the auspices of NIMH or NICHD. Research on early childhood disorders would be one area of concern in these research centers.

reversible by today's methods and hence represent a lifelong drain on community resources, the full cost of which has not been determined.

In addition to the primary effects, the secondary effects on family function of a chronically ill child have long been recognized but until recently poorly documented. While it is doubtful that other studies of chronic disease are all applicable to these syndromes, the evidence is overwhelming that any life-threatening illness poses a severe stress on family function and often results in immediate and long-term family difficulties secondary to the illness.

The detectable forms of the deprivational syndromes are completely preventable and in their early stages reversible. Sufficient knowledge has accumulated to successfully treat many of these children in the acute phase of their disorder. In the past 50 years, prevention has reduced the incidence of some of these disorders. In the more subtle and currently more common forms of these syndromes, prevention awaits the more careful study of the causal factors. Only then can education lead the public and the professional community to recognize and to detect the early signs of these disorders.

At the present time our knowledge is sufficient to provide a basis for programs of early recognition and treatment of at least the more obvious forms of the deprivational syndromes. These forms of deprivation, which include battering and gross neglect, are still insufficiently reported by hospitals, physicians, and public health agencies. The recent spate of state laws has not substantially increased the numbers of reported cases, nor have the states provided adequate facilities for the care of these children.

The more subtle forms of these disorders remain complex and obscure conditions in which neither the conceptual framework nor the clinical data have sufficiently defined the disorder. For example, such factors as the critical periods of development, environmental versus innate and biological influences, the character of the mother-child relationship, and the importance of accidental factors have not yet been fully elucidated. Careful investigation will be required to establish more clearly the nature of these disorders before early diagnosis and prevention can be accomplished.

RECOMMENDATIONS

Prevention: Further education of the public to the emotional needs of children and sound child-rearing practices is needed. Prevention of these disorders can easily be seen to intertwine itself in the problems of marital stability, economic necessities, and cultural values. As has been stressed, day-care centers for young children should be extended to include infants and young babies. Such centers should extend their operations to provide classes for mothers of young babies with both group and individual instruction in the care of their child and more specifically the opportunity for these mothers to watch a successful caretaker in action.

Facilities and services: Practices in well-baby clinics should be extended to include more careful behavioral assessment of young babies so that various deviations from the norm which are the prodromal signs of the deprivational syndromes can be established and remedial steps taken early in the course of the disorder. This will require use of more comprehensive behavioral criteria in the assessment of development.

Once recognition is accomplished, an expansion of outpatient and follow-up care facilities will be necessary to increase the continuity of treatment and to decrease the episodic medical care which has in the past encouraged partial and, therefore, unsuccessful treatment regimens. A considerable expansion of the facilities for handling foster home care of children is indicated. This should include increasing the pool of applicants to raise the quality and variety of parents available and able to take care of foster children of varying ages and increasing the number of personnel in placement agencies for the proper study of foster homes and supervision and follow-up of the children who have been placed.

The expansion of these facilities must be accompanied by an increased public awareness of the extent and importance of the needs of children who suffer from deprivational syndromes. Therefore, an increase in expenditures for the education of the public is indicated and is a prerequisite for their participation in the care of these children. Finally, more sophisticated legislation must be enacted to promote a wider recognition of these disorders and more comprehensive legislation to provide the facilities for the proper care of these children.

Research: Further study is indicated in several areas. Epidemiological research to document the extent and demographic characteristics of these disorders is necessary for appropriate planning for case finding, diagnosis, treatment, and rehabilitation. Specific study of each syndrome of deprivation will be required before appropriate diagnostic and preventative measures can be undertaken. These studies should include further investigations of the subtleties of the distortions of the mother-child relationships which result in deprivational syndromes. The relationships of the specific traumas and disruptions of family life to the child's development in different time periods should be investigated. Research is required for the appropriate and most sensible method of diagnostic study of these children and also to evaluate the efficacy of the initial treatment methods. Further study of the outcome has already been mentioned and needs emphasis if the extent of these disorders is to be recognized.

PREDELINQUENT STATE: PREVENTION AND EARLY SCREENING
OF DELINQUENCY

Juvenile delinquency, primarily a later-childhood and adolescent phenomenon, has some of its important roots in the early childhood period. While little is known with certainty concerning the relationship of early-childhood experience to later delinquency, a number of variables have been indicated whose roots stretch back to the early years. Among these are the following:

a. lower socioeconomic status (slum areas, population density, mobility, substandard housing, high crime rates, median education);

b. "status deprivation" (i.e., lower-class environment where middle-class goals are emphasized but unattainable);

c. socialization practices which are unsuccessful in developing internal controls and the ability to delay gratification; lack of affection toward child;

d. intermediate sibling status and membership in a large family;

e. broken homes (especially in boys who become delinquent as pre-adolescents);

f. parental marital maladjustment, uncooperativeness, disagreement between parents;

g. parental discipline which is characterized by lack of "fairness," by inconsistency, and by overuse of physical means of discipline; role uncertainty by parents.

Obviously, juvenile delinquency is not a unitary phenomenon. There are at least three definable subgroups: the gang delinquent, the occasional delinquent, and the maladjusted delinquent. The last, in particular, reflects emotional disturbance or character disorder, and these youngsters tend to be characterized by high-tension homes, school retardation, "lone" delinquencies, poor peer relations, parental rejection, and nervousness.

Because so few programs for combating delinquency in older children have been successful, it is important to try to identify early those individuals with a high risk of becoming delinquent, and to institute preventative measures. Thus far, measures of early identification have centered on the early school years, by which time many patterns have become solidified and a good many boys are already known to be transgressors. Even with boys at this age, there has been little success at identifying *individuals* who are likely to become delinquent; predictions have been made only for sub-groups which appear to present a high risk.

RECOMMENDATIONS

Prevention: Emphasis should be given to preventive rather than to treatment methods because of the discouraging results in handling delinquency in children who have already been identified. General methods which attack the socioeconomic isolation, deprivation, unsuccessful child-rearing practices, family size above that desired by the parents, and so on should eventually yield a lower rate of juvenile delinquency.

Research: Efforts should be made to devise methods for the very early identification of youngsters who are likely to manifest repetitive delinquency, particularly the maladjusted group. Measures designed to carefully describe both the child and his family setting should be incorporated into the large-scale longitudinal studies of childhood development and intervention so that antecedent-consequent relationships may be studied in this area. Early childhood longitudinal studies should be continued through the adolescent period so that the emergence of delinquency can be observed; frequently, the child who is legally identified during adolescence as a delinquent has been well known to teachers, school authorities, and even the police during his earlier years.

LEARNING DISORDERS

The terminology used to designate the burgeoning field of "learning disorders" today strongly suggests that the area is ill defined, heterogeneous, and characterized by dispute over matters covering the entire range of definition, etiology, treatment, and prevention.

Definitions in current usage by various investigators and other interested parties vary widely. Some definitions, for example, specifically exclude children with "emotional handicap"; others specifically include and, indeed, emphasize this group. Some definitions exclude children with neurological impairment; others concentrate on this aspect.

In order to define learning disorders broadly enough to include all the problems currently labeled as such, it is necessary to describe them simply as those deviations in the learning processes which are associated with an educationally significant discrepancy between apparent capacity for language or cognitive behavior and actual level of language or cognitive performance. Language is understood as including vocal and motor expressive behaviors as well as the reception and manipulation of symbols. Clearly, when such a definition is used, it encompasses a very large percentage of children. It seems very likely that the term includes a number of different syndromes which are, as yet, undifferentiated.

In the consideration of etiology, the same degree of disagreement is to be found. Underlying causes of learning problems have been postulated, for example, in hereditary disorders, in biochemical variations, in mixed or nonestablished cerebral dominance, in damage to the reticular system of the brain, in the slow tempo of neuromuscular maturation, in developmental lags in specific portions of the brain, in mother-child (usually mother-son) interactions in the early years, in early frustrations and failure experiences, in disturbances in the language relationships of child and parents, and so on. Probably the largest group of workers postulate some sort of organic substrate of neurological impairment, but even they do not agree about the nature of this source of difficulty.

Whatever the definition, and whatever the cause, the child with problems in learning faces a situation which is almost sure to be detrimental to his mental health. He is met with constant failure; he achieves poorly in school and usually develops immature patterns of relationships with other children; he may passively withdraw or become the "class clown"; he is often depressed and despairing about his own future; he is concerned about himself, his body image, and his own integrity.

A wide variety of treatment approaches has been tried with school-age children who exhibit learning disabilities, but very seldom has the preschool child been included in such efforts. It is impossible at this time to assess the relative efficacy of the various approaches, or their suitability for the younger child.

Although children with learning disorders are not commonly identified until they reach school, when they must measure up to standardized requirements at specific age levels, nearly all workers agree that the condition is manifest in some form long before school entry. It is, therefore, imperative that identification leading to attempts at treatment and remediation be instituted as early in the preschool years as possible.

RECOMMENDATIONS

Prevention: Because of the lack of agreement about etiology of this disorder, or group of disorders, it is impossible at this time to specify precise measures of prevention. However, because of the emphasis by many on organic pathology, much of which can be presumed to be congenital, early efforts at prenatal and perinatal care are one method of approach, which has been strongly recommended elsewhere. Services supportive to families and parent education programs may also yield improvement in the incidence of learning disorders.

Facilities and services: Early identification and treatment programs are highly desirable, although these cannot proceed without supporting and exploratory research.

Research: At this state of development, research must be given special emphasis, to the point of taking precedence, if necessary, over the provision of facilities and services. Among the research areas to be explored are:

1. Etiology—emphasis on organic and experiential primary factors, but also on the role of secondary emotional disturbance resulting from the disability and its effects on the child's self-concept and his interaction with others.

2. Identification of early signs that the child will be unable to profit in the ordinary way from regular school experiences. Attention must be given to disorders of perception, language, fine and gross motor control, "soft" neurological signs, personality immaturity, and emotional disturbance.

3. The possible identification of subgroups of children, differing in etiology or in nature of disability, or both.

4. The development of more effective remedial programs to be instituted both with preschool children and with school-age children. Model programs of remediation should receive thorough evaluation before they are proliferated; this evaluation will need to be not only careful but longitudinal.

Manpower: Eventually, a program of prevention and remediation of these common disorders will require involvement of a considerable number of workers. It is, however, too early to specify the level, training, or approach of the personnel who will be needed.

THERAPEUTIC PROGRAMS

The wide variety of emotional disorders of early childhood and the variation in treatment programs necessary to alleviate or to cure each condition as it arises in individual children preclude the specific discussion of each configuration. A few general principles of early treatment, however, deserve special attention.

1. *The younger the child, the more his treatment is linked to child care.* It is clear that the treatment of any disturbed child will be most effective when his total experience is oriented to his specific condition of pathology as well as to his nonpathological needs. For the young child, however, this integration of experience is even more essential than for the older child. Since the organism at this stage has not yet developed specificity of function, and still shows the intimate interrelationship among somatic, emotional, and intellectual spheres, the treatment cannot separate one from another. Thus, the professional direction of treatment must be closely allied to the total life experience of the child, and professional knowledge must be translated to terms of daily child care. Continuous and close contact of professional staff with family and others who care for the child is required.

In the earlier and milder disorders, it is frequently possible after diagnosis to bring about considerable improvement by appropriately modifying the child's environment, without bringing him into a special psychotherapeutic treatment setting. The lack of personnel experienced in working with parents of very young children has tended to minimize the frequency of therapeutic intervention into the daily environment; yet in many instances emotional disorders can be effectively managed in this way.

2. *Family and community share the responsibility of care for the disturbed young child.* Earlier in this report we outlined an approach to early child care in which the family is supported in a flexible way by a combination of many possible community resources. For children with specific emotional disorders in early life, the need is intensified for such a general, flexible interrelationship of caretaking by family and community. By our present tendency to polarize, assigning *either* to the family *or* to the com-

munity the total care of the disturbed young child (as, for example, in residential treatment or foster care), inappropriate programs of care are too frequently developed. The translation of professional knowledge into child care procedures by guidance to the parents, by demonstration, and by direct caretaking will be an essential feature in dealing with the emotional disorders found in early childhood.

The nursery school is being increasingly utilized in the mental health field, and expansion of such programs recommended in this report provides the opportunity for further use of this setting as a tool for detection and early treatment. Mental health consultants attached to nursery schools; specialized nursery and day-care facilities for disturbed and handicapped children; nursery programs within clinical facilities such as pediatric or psychiatric hospital settings and community clinics; and preventive recreational and educational services coordinated with high-stress experiences (such as hospitalization for medical treatment) have been increasingly utilized for the past few years. This sort of approach has special value because it coordinates a treatment-oriented educational experience and individual therapy, and provides an environment for at least a part of the day which is more suitable to the needs of the child than those conditions in the home which have been pathogenic. As these possibilities are extended to the age group below nursery school, early child care programs can be developed to fulfill the same functions.

One of the new questions raised by this approach deals with the relationship of individual care to group care. Individualization of recommendation and treatment is unquestionably necessary to deal with the unique problems of young children. The crucial questions to be answered deal not with whether the group *or* individual approach is preferable, but with the amount and quality of individual attention possible in various kinds of group care, the numbers of children who can be brought together without sacrificing the individualized approach, the particular constellations of disorders during the early years which are amenable to group experience, and the ways in which workers of the mental health professions can be trained and utilized in planning, supervising, and carrying out group experiences for young children.

3. *Individual therapy has an important place in the treatment program for many young children with emotional disorders.* Emphasis has been given in most of the report of this Task Force to the design of preventive approaches and group experiences for young children. Enhanced awareness of the number of children who are in need of professional attention increases the pressure to design helpful programs which will provide minimal treatment to most children who exhibit emotional disorders, with resulting emphasis on modifying the child's daily environment and the expansion of group programs. It is clear that a major mental health approach is required to change the conditions in which children grow up, in order to support

normal development as well as to modify those factors in the surroundings and the family which lead to the specific pathology of the child. There is need at the same time to stress the significant aspects of individual treatment and care of children which must be a part of therapeutic and preventive measures. Individual care must not be overlooked or too severely restricted under the pressure of mass programming.

Individual variations among children are too great, even when the children come from similar circumstances or share a similar disorder, to devise an appropriate uniform program. The younger the child, the more important it is to recognize his unique potentiality, his particular capacity for growth, and his special pathology. Moreover, the younger the child, the more he is dependent upon a consistent and continuous relationship with *one* person. Whereas the child whose development is proceeding normally may rely strongly on his relationships with his parents, even when he spends a large part of his day away from them, the child with disturbed relationships has greater needs for a special relationship with one other person. The working through of pathological conflicts or developmental deviation often demands the availability of a person whom one can trust and by whom one feels understood. These are tools of treatment which need to be maximized in the therapeutic programs appropriate for many children.

Events which appear the same to the adult observer may have very different effects on different children, depending upon their individual make-ups, their stages of development, their potentialities, and their specific past experiences. Only exploration of the inner life of the child will permit final assessment of the environment, through understanding how this child has experienced it and the consequences he has sustained. There is no shortcut to this approach, and thus the assessment of the environment, of its nurturing and life-sustaining influences as well as those which lead to deprivation and conflict, must be coordinated with any decisions about the timing and form of therapeutic intervention.

Moreover, there are emotional conditions which have become an integral part of the internal psychic structure of the child, or which overlie a structural pathology, and thus are less responsive to changes in the daily environment. Internal alterations in such children frequently require individual treatment. It will continue to depend upon the individual child and his disorder as to which combination of the environmental and internal approaches is most appropriate for him.

RECOMMENDATIONS:

Facilities and treatment: 1. Expansion of a number of programs recommended elsewhere in this report will provide the opportunity for shared responsibility between parents and community for the detection and treatment of emotionally disturbed children. With the age group not yet in school, it is particularly essential that treatment be linked to and incorporated with child care.

2. Group settings which provide essential parts of a treatment program need to be expanded; early nursery school and child-care programs which are specifically therapeutic in orientation are needed to provide comprehensive programs of care.

3. Careful diagnosis and prescription based on individual study of a child, his family, and his special experiences cannot be replaced by group diagnosis. Individualized work with parents and individual psychotherapy with the child will continue to be essential in the treatment of many children.

Manpower: Workers in many disciplines concerned with mental health have insufficient experience with the preschool child, especially during the first three years of life. While there are many nonprofessional people who can participate in programs of early child care, we will need specialized, trained persons at both professional and paraprofessional levels for work with emotionally disturbed young children. At the present time there is an increasing gap between the need in this field and the very small number of trained personnel.

References

Abbott, R. "Review of Research Concerning Child and Maternal Health with Implications for Nursing." 1968 (unpublished).

American College of Nurse-Midwifery, 1968.

Baird, D., and Scott, E. M. "Intelligence and Childbearing," *Eugenics Review*, 45 (1953), 139–154.

Bateman, B. "Learning Disorders," *Review of Educational Research*, 36 (1966), 93–119.

Birch, H. "Health and Education of Socially Disadvantaged Children." Paper presented at Conference on Bio-social Factors in Development and Learning of Disadvantaged Children. Syracuse, New York, Apr. 19–21, 1967.

Corkey, E. C. "A Family Planning Program for the Low-Income Family," *Journal of Marriage and the Family* (Nov. 1964), p. 480.

Cystic Fibrosis Foundation, 1968.

De Hirsch, K., Jansky, J. J., and Langford, W. S. *Predicting Reading Failures*. New York: Harper & Row, 1966.

Gair, D. S., and Bullard, D. "Psychosis and Deprivational Syndromes in Young Children." Background paper for the Joint Commission on Mental Health of Children, Inc., 1968 (unpublished).

Glidewell, J. C., and Swallow, C. "The Prevalence of Maladjustment in Elementary Schools." Special report prepared for the Joint Commission on Mental Health of Children, Inc., 1968.

Greenblatt, B. "Planning Models for Daytime Care of Preschool Children." Background paper prepared for the Joint Commission on Mental Health of Children, Inc., 1968 (unpublished).

Greenleigh Associates. "Facts, Fallacies, and Future." 1960, p. 19 (as cited in Jaffe, S. "Family Planning and Poverty," *Journal of Marriage and the Family* [Nov. 1964]).

Herzog, E. "The Chronic Revolution: Births out of Wedlock," *Clinical Pediatrics*, 5, 2 (1966).

―――. "Unmarried Mothers—Service Gap Revisited," *Children*, 14, 3 (1967), 106.

Herzog, E., and Bernstein, R. "Health Services for Unmarried Mothers." Children's Bureau Pub. 425 (1964), p. 7.

Jaffe, F. S. "Family Planning and Poverty," *Journal of Marriage and the Family* (Nov. 1964).

Jaffe, F. S., and Bernsohn, C. J. "Closing the Gap in Subsidized Planning Services in 110 Metropolitan Areas with More Than 250,000 Population." Department of Program Planning and Development, Planned Parenthood-World Population (Oct. 1967).

Jenkins, S., and Sauber, M. "Pathways to Child Placement." New York: The Community Council of Greater New York, Research Dept., 1966.

Lesser, A. Current problems in maternity care. U. S. Dept. of Health, Education, and Welfare, Welfare Administration, Children's Bureau, 1963.

National Foundation, March of Dimes. "Birth Defects Incidence, 1968."

National League for Nursing. "Some Statistics on Baccalaureate and Higher Degree Programs in Nursing, 1966." New York: National League for Nursing, 1966.

―――. "Masters Education, 1967." New York: National League for Nursing, 1967.

Orshansky, M. "Counting the Poor: Another Look at the Poverty Profile," *Social Security Bulletin*, Jan. 1965(a).

―――. "Who's Who Among the Poor: A Demographic View of Poverty," *Social Security Bulletin*, July 1965(b).

―――. Background material prepared for Citizens Committee for Children, Conference on Children's Allowances. Oct. 1967.

Pasamanick, B. "Influence of Sociocultural Variables upon Organic Factors in Mental Retardation," *American Journal of Mental Deficiency*, 64 (1959), 316–320.

Planning Committee of Project Head Start. Report prepared for the Office of Economic Opportunity. Feb. 1965.

Polansky, N. A., and Polansky, N. F. "The Current Status of Child Abuse and Child Neglect in This Country." Background paper prepared for the Joint Commission on Mental Health of Children, Inc., 1968 (unpublished).

Population Study of a Day Care Center, Child Development Center, Pre-School Liaison Project, New York City. Jan. 1967.

President's Committee on Mental Retardation. MR:67. *A First Report to the President on the Nation's Progress and Remaining Needs in the Campaign to Combat Mental Retardation.* Washington: U.S. Government Printing Office, 1967.

President's Panel on Mental Retardation. Report. 1962, p. 52.

President's Task Force on Manpower Conservation. *One-third of a Nation: A Report on Young Men Found Unqualified for Military Service.* Washington: U.S. Government Printing Office, Jan. 1964.

Robinson, H. B., and Robinson, N. M. "The Problem of Timing in Preschool Education," in R. Hess and R. Bear (eds.), *Early Education.* Chicago: Aldine Press, 1968.

Shapiro, S., *et al.* "Further Observations on Prematurity and Perinatal Mortality in a General Population and in the Population of a Pre-paid Group Medical Practice Medical Care Plan," *American Journal of Public Health*, 50 (1960), 9.

Sheppard, H. L. *Effects of Family Planning on Poverty in the United States.* Kalamazoo, Mich.: W. E. Upjohn Institute for Employment Research, Oct. 1967.

Thomas, A., Chess, S., and Birch, H. G. *Temperament and Behavior Disorders in Children.* New York: New York University Press, 1968.

U.S. Department of Commerce, Bureau of Census. "Household and Family Characteristics, March, 1966," *Current Population Reports*, Series P-20, No. 164. Apr. 12, 1967(a).

————. "Social and Economic Conditions of Negroes in the U.S." BLS Report 332. *Current Population Reports*, Series P-23, No. 24. Oct. 1967(b), p. 64.

U.S. Department of Health, Education, and Welfare. Welfare Administration, Children's Bureau. "Adoptions in 1965." Child Welfare Statistics—1965. *Children's Bureau Statistical Series*, No. 84. Washington, D.C., 1966(a).

————. Public Health Service. "Supplement to Monthly Vital Statistics Report." National Center for Health Statistics. Vol. 15, No. 3. Washington, D.C. June, 1966(b).

————. Public Health Service. *Vital Statistics of the U.S., 1966.* Vol. I: *Natality.* Washington, D.C.: U.S. Government Printing Office, 1966(c).

————. Welfare Administration, Children's Bureau. *Infant Mortality: A Challenge to the Nation.* Washington, D.C.: U.S. Government Printing Office, 1966(d).

————. *Program Analysis: Maternal and Child Health Care Programs.* Oct. 1966(e).

————. Public Health Service. "Monthly Vital Statistics Report—Advance Report." Vol. 16, No. 12. Supplement. Mar. 12, 1968. Washington, D.C.: U.S. Government Printing Office, 1968(a).

————. Public Health Service, National Center for Health Statistics. *Vital Statistics for the U.S.* Washington, D.C.: U.S. Government Printing Office, 1968(b).

————. Welfare Administration, Children's Bureau, 1968(c) (unpublished).

U.S. Department of Labor. Women's Bureau. "Day Care Fact Sheet." Apr. 1969.

Wiener, G., Rider, R. V., Oppel, W. C., Fischer, L. K., and Harper, P. "Correlates of Low Birth Weight: Psychological Status at Six to Seven Years of Age," *Pediatrics,* 35 (1965), 434–444.

Yannet, H. "Classification and Etiological Factors in Mental Retardation," *Journal of Pediatrics*, 50 (1957), 226–230.

II

STUDIES OF CHILDREN FROM KINDERGARTEN AGE THROUGH EIGHTH GRADE

REPORT OF TASK FORCE II

Edited by Mary Engel, Ph.D.

The report of Task Force I has pointed to the crucial importance of providing high-quality, comprehensive care in the early years of life. It is during this period that the foundation is laid for the later developmental stages. For this reason, the promotion of healthy growth in the very young child emerged as a major priority in the Commission's final deliberations on the prevention of mental and emotional disorders.

Proper nurturance, good physical and mental health care, a wholesome environment, and the opportunities for learning so essential to early development retain their importance throughout childhood. Each determines how well the child of kindergarten and school age can meet the challenges posed by his expanding world. It is at this point that Task Force II picks up the thread of the developmental analysis to consider the mental health needs of children from the age of their entry into school until they reach the age of twelve or so.

—EDITOR

MEMBERS OF TASK FORCE II

Chairman: MARY ENGEL, PH.D.
Associate Professor
Department of Psychology
City College of the City University
of New York
New York, New York

HERMAN S. BELMONT, M.D.
Professor and Head
Child Psychiatry Section
Hahnemann Medical College
Philadelphia, Pennsylvania

BARBARA BIBER, PH.D.
Distinguished Research Scholar
Research Division
Bank Street College of Education
New York, New York

GEORGE B. BRAIN, ED.D.
Dean, College of Education
Cleveland Hall
Washington State University
Pullman, Washington

ROBERT E. COOKE, M.D.
Given Foundation Professor of
Pediatrics
The Johns Hopkins University School
of Medicine; and
Pediatrician in Chief, the Johns
Hopkins Hospital, CMSC 2-116
Baltimore, Maryland

CLAIRE M. FAGIN, PH.D.
Director of the Graduate Programs in
Psychiatric Mental Health Nursing
New York University
New York, New York

* Chairman until September 1967.

RICHARD L. FOSTER, PH.D.
District Superintendent of San Ramon
Valley Unified School District
Danville, California

LAWRENCE KOHLBERG, PH.D.
Visiting Associate Professor of
Education
School of Education
Larsen Hall
Harvard University
Cambridge, Massachusetts

SALVADOR MINUCHIN, M.D.
Professor of Child Psychiatry
University of Pennsylvania
School of Medicine; and
Director, Philadelphia Child
Guidance Clinic
Philadelphia, Pennsylvania

* SAMUEL M. WISHIK, M.D.
Director, Division of Program
Development and Evaluation
International Institute for Study of
Human Reproduction
Columbia University
New York, New York

MARTIN WOLINS, PH.D.
Professor of Social Welfare
University of California
Berkeley, California

Introduction

The members of Task Force II devoted their energies to the "school-age child"—that is, the youngster between the first and the sixth or seventh grade. These are somewhat arbitrary markers in time, and we frequently found it necessary to look before and after these points in the life-span in order to fully grasp the mental health implications of this developmental stage.

In pursuing this study, Task Force members met jointly on several occasions and also engaged in consultation with representatives of professional groups who were thought to have distinct views, strong positions, or special competence in a particular area. Thus, we added to our Task Force discussions and evaluations the questions, suggestions, and recommendations of groups of experts in special education and in welfare services, as well as those of interested members of the American Academy of Child Psychiatry and several persons from the field of child clinical psychology. Other important considerations led us to acquaint ourselves with current legislation in mental deficiency and public welfare and to gather information on the present status of public decision making in a number of other areas. In addition, various members elected to study and survey an area of concern in which they felt some individual competence. As a result, a number of position papers were generated, many of which contain recommendations.

There were many areas which we were unable to study. It became apparent early in our deliberations, while we were still under the chairmanship of Dr. Samuel Wishik, that our limited time demanded an eclectic approach, that we could not possibly give thorough coverage to all aspects related to the mental health of the school-age child. For example, we left unexplored the mental health potentialities of peer group relationships and the deployment of time in after-school hours. We also elected to bypass the area of mental deficiency, since at least two Task Forces have been set up by government agencies to work on criteria for mental deficiency. We felt, too, that we could not focus on particular forms of psychopathology because in doing so we would so divide our time by apportioning certain amounts of it to neuroses, psychoses, organic conditions, and so on, that we would have little time left to consider the societal aspects of mental illness in children.

Our report is a synthesis of many points of view. It reflects the minutes of Task Force deliberations, the contributions of numerous outside consultants, and the several position papers listed in Appendix A. Large sections of these position papers are included without direct quote, for the sake of continuity and sense of progression. For example, much of the education section is written by Dr. Barbara Biber, that on health services by Dr. Claire Fagin, and the foster care portion by Dr. Martin Wolins. These and other papers are sometimes paraphrased and sometimes directly quoted, and may appear under several headings, as do the studies of Dr. Salvador Minuchin. No attempt has been made to reconcile any opposing views among Task Force members; it is assumed that the public as well as the scientific community is better served by clarity than consensus. The reader is assured, however, that all recommendations for public action reflect the agreement of Task Force members, even where there is some apparent disagreement concerning the rationale or the *details* of the realities upon which the recommendations rest.

It should be made clear that we conceive of recommendations to be on at least three different levels. First, a professional group may point out to the general public as well as to the rest of the professional community *the need for altered perceptions* about a particular problem. For example, our suggestion that mental health problems be viewed in terms of the total ecological context of the child's life rather than solely on the basis of intrapsychic functioning is a recommendation for altering usual ways of perceiving mental illness. Such recommendations are not necessarily on the level of public action but deal with values, convictions, and points of view which we must assume reside either implicitly or explicitly in any public action. Second, some recommendations call for the innovative uses of existing institutions or personnel. When we suggest that the teacher's role be reformulated so as to include community-connected and child-centered decision making by the teacher, we are not suggesting the creation of a new profession or the abolishment of an old one; rather we are recommending *alternative ways of using present resources*. Recommendations on this second level naturally involve the altered perceptions suggested earlier, but carry our thinking one step beyond first-level recommendations. Third, there are recommendations which come, as it were, with dollar signs attached to them in that they call for *new forms of intervention and the creation of new social structures*. In such cases, we did not attempt to estimate costs, since we assumed that other of the Commission Task Forces with more knowledge about financing would eventually contribute the kind of specificity required for public legislation. It is our considered opinion that recommendations on levels one and two are equally as necessary as those calling for overt public action.

Rational procedure demands that recommendations for social action be based on evidence that a suggested new course will have better results than doing nothing or following old paths. However, when we turned to the professional literature for relevant evidence on particular points, the yield was often like sand running through our fingers. Hard, relevant evidence is extremely rare. The data have to be made relevant to problems of social action by a series of mental compromises which, in turn, become the bridge between what we know and what we believe in. Needless to say, such bridges are built with various degrees of certitude. Consequently, recommendations vary with regard to both explicitness and certainty.

The framework of this report will take us from considering the child alone, as a separate psychological entity, to considering him part of his family. From then we will continue our outward journey and view him as a member of the most powerful social system affecting latency-aged children, the school. Last, we will consider the child as part of the larger realities of the community and of the government agencies responsible for the welfare of children. Naturally, as we proceed, alternating vantage points as we travel along larger and larger concentric circles, the same problem will acquire different meanings. Each is an essential part of childhood mental health.

—MARY ENGEL
Chairman, Task Force II

Psychotherapy and the Child—
Alternatives for Intervention

To the extent that professional opinions about the value of psycho-therapy were adequately represented in Task Force II, we can conclude that there are currently two dominant positions which we will refer to as the interaction view and the ecological model. As will be noted, the two positions differ considerably in their approaches to therapy. While neither rules out the importance of the other, there appears to be a point beyond which reconciliation of the two is no longer possible.

AN INTERACTION VIEW

The interaction view considered by the Task Force is succinctly ex-pressed by Dr. Herman S. Belmont in "The Psychotherapies of the School-Age Child." In this paper, Belmont urges that psychiatric treatment approaches be considered as among the most important "sociomedical meas-ures" to help children who suffer from poor mental health. The various types of psychiatric treatment, however, must relate to an adequate concept of men-tal health which, in turn, is based on a workable system of diagnostic classifi-cation, such as is contained in the recently completed report of the Group for the Advancement of Psychiatry (1967). In addition, psychiatric treat-ment must always relate to a theoretical rationale arising out of a theory of development as well as a theory of psychopathology. Without such con-ceptual underpinnings, the various therapeutic approaches are likely to be used indiscriminately and professionals are apt to work without explicit therapeutic goals. Without a concept of mental health, a system of diagnostic classifications, and a theory of development and pathology, we may easily adopt "a form of treatment that attends to large numbers of children at one time, or one that focuses on purely environmental handling of all cases rather

106

than a more painstaking approach . . . ," even when a more painstaking approach, like individual therapy, might be indicated.

Professionals who are attempting to find an adequate concept of mental health must be flexible and consider symptoms as meaningful relative to the child's age and developmental stage. The definition of mental health should not be colored by individual value judgments or particular investments in certain treatment approaches to the exclusion of others.

The not uncommon conviction that what is good mental health in one situation is not good mental health in another needs to be carefully reconsidered. The relativization of the concept of mental health to varying social and cultural situations results in a "double standard." For example, because the poor mental health of a deprived child is *understandable*, this should not lead to the conclusion that such a child is in good mental health. Because it is possible to comprehend the manner in which environmental circumstances were responsible for the development of psychopathology in some children, this does not *necessarily* mean that the illness of these children requires a different therapeutic approach from that required by other children.

By this view, intrapsychic and environmental factors have to be recognized as interacting forces in development. As Belmont notes:

. . . sociological factors will play a crucial role developmentally in determining the degree of mental health a child can achieve at any particular age. That is, sociological factors certainly play an etiologic contributory role. Furthermore, at any particular point in development and given a particular degree of mental health, sociological factors are highly significant in the degree of opportunity allowed for the most effective utilization of inner personality adjustment in relation to the child's environment.

Also, we have to keep in mind that:

The ability to solve the problem of an immediate adjustment to a particular situation is not necessarily evidence of good mental health any more than the use of specific and apparently deviant measures of adjustment in a realistically stressful environment is necessarily evidence of poor mental health.

From this point of view, mental health and illness are not entirely conceptualized according to environmental factors. The environment is considered important, and recognition is given to the *contributory significance* of sociocultural matters.

Belmont conceptualizes the healthy ego as:

one which carries out its functions in a manner appropriate to the level of development of the ever-changing child, consistent with norms for these functions laid down in a now extensive and ever-growing body of child developmental studies from many different vantage points (e.g., A. Freud, B. Bornstein, Piaget,

Gesell, Escalona, Sontag, Erikson, and many others). Such functions are: age appropriate self-preservation, sense of identity, object relations, reality testing concept formation, memory and acquisition of knowledge, action and trial action (thinking), perceptual-motor function, avoidance of excessive stimuli, control and regulation of drive discharge, postponement of immediate satisfaction for future gain, experiencing of anxiety and adaptive use of mechanisms of defense, integration and synthesis of stimuli from all sources, including the various personality structures and the external environment, and finally the effective utilization of all these resources for adaptation to and making changes in the external world.

Belmont states:

What needs to be clearly understood is that no one type of therapeutic approach to all child psychopathology can be reasonably opposed to all others. Each clinical entity has a preferred form of treatment which is most appropriately indicated. For certain problems where a child's capacity to function adaptively is crucially disrupted at least in considerable degree by serious environmental handicaps, acute reactive disorders for example, environmental modification is not only helpful but required, whereas intensive individual psychotherapy would here be limited in its usefulness, inasmuch as the problem is not one of intrapsychic pathology or poor mental health, but environmental. Where the life-long experience of adverse environment has contributed to a disorder in development of basic personality structures, while environmental manipulation could have had preventive value earlier, it now can no longer lead to a complete reversal of deficits accumulated through the years. Here, if the problem is one of deficient development, a specifically prescribed educational experience might be helpful in compensating for the deficiency. If the personality development has led to intrapsychic conflictual problems, as for example conflicts about sexual role or a need for punishment, intensive individual therapies may be suggested, or a combination of approaches. On the other hand, there are disturbances of mental health in which the etiology resides predominantly intrapsychically, as for example, in certain neurotic conditions like anxiety hysteria or an obsessional neurosis, and where the *current* environment has little to do with the nature of the psychopathology. . . .

There is no objection to a massive program aimed at an improvement of environmental contributions to the child's development and life situation. Moreover, it is even desirable, since better neighborhoods, work and play opportunities, better schooling and social progress, etc., can contribute to the opportunity for healthier psychological development of many children and ameliorate some of the emotional problems of many others. However, while this is undoubtedly true, it would be a mistake to believe that this is what is needed for all types of childhood psychological disorders. Assume that such a massive shotgun approach has been undertaken and has alleviated a major portion of those general environmental contributions to emotional problems. Then, more than ever, is it necessary that adequate diagnostic resources as well as an entire spectrum of therapeutic measures be available for the range of psychological problems other than those which will respond purely to environmental intervention.

The position discussed here views with some alarm the increasing tendency to think of mental health exclusively in situational terms because the situational approach can so easily lead to overlooking basic defects in personality structure. A child may find himself in a noxious environment, may have been subjected to severe deprivations of many sorts, and he may share his troublesome symptoms with many other children—all this does not necessarily mean that he can be helped by environmental interventions aimed at factors which are *associated* with his distress. He may in fact be suffering from personality defects, character problems which are not responsive to environmental intervention. A relativistic, environmental-istic position about mental health may easily lead to misdiagnosis.

This view, of course, gives rise to the question: What should be the role of the environment in an adequate concept of mental health? According to Belmont, "The child's environment has to be considered in relation to his psychological state, both developmentally and in terms of current inter-play with personality structure."

It is important to clarify that none of the above rules out environmental intervention, "ecologic approaches," family therapy, or any of the newer forms of treatment. Rather it calls for continued interest in the development of a broad spectrum of approaches to mental illness in the hope that the dovetailing of various diagnoses and various therapies will become more and more accurate.

All of the above points are consistent with the position stated in the 1966 report of the Group for the Advancement of Psychiatry (1967):

> The committee agreed with the definition of the mature and healthy person as one who actively, flexibly, and rationally masters his environment most of the time; shows a unity and integrity of personality; is able to perceive the world and himself, including his own feelings, in essentially correct proportions; can postpone immediate gratification in favor of more long term goals; exhibits the capacity for love, work and play; enjoys a certain sense of mental well being; and possesses a set of values which permit him to organize his life and work while also tolerating the values of others. The truly mature individual may at times forsake adjustment and conformity for the less certain and more pain-ful, but ultimately more rewarding, constructive experiences of attempting to alter or influence his world in a creative fashion. He also possesses the capacity for further personality development throughout adult life (pp. 186–187).

According to this point of view, psychopathological disorders in the latency-age child can be understood in terms of the degree to which one or another criterion of this definition of mental health is satisfied. The latency-age child is seen as one who suffers more than younger children from in-ternalized conflicts. Children before the age of six are said to experience largely objective anxiety. By the time they have reached first grade the situation will be quite different, since the free and direct interchange and responsiveness to the immediately present environment will be complicated by post-Oedipal conflict resolution resulting in superego formation. Responsiveness to external danger gives way then to superego anxiety; the child is reacting to external prohibitions as he internalized them and as he saw them at some point in the past. The internal conflict situation has become more impervious to revision by alterations in external circumstance.

It is recognized, of course, that post-Oedipal children also react to environmental stresses and that the removal of these, in some cases, reestablishes equilibrium. But a central position is given to internalized conflicts and psychic structures with relative degrees of permanence along with the obvious implication of differential psychotherapeutic measures prescribed on the basis of a variety of interpretations as to the origins of psychic stress. There is a firm belief among those who adhere to this viewpoint that certain past developmental interferences do not respond to present-day environments. Consequently, there is expressed disenchantment with the growing tendency to think of mental health exclusively in situational terms, especially when it seems to emphasize the environmental approach for all. However, it is recognized that this emphasis is in the service of society's problems, that it takes into consideration the manpower shortage and the understandable wish to help many more children than can now be helped.

In the interaction view, individual therapy is not always considered the necessary treatment of choice. However, individual psychodiagnosis is seen as the necessary condition for prescribing one of many forms of psychotherapeutic interventions. Supportive therapies, treatment for parents, environmental manipulations, educational therapy, intensive psychotherapy, and child analysis are among the many forms of therapy which should be considered and matched as closely as possible with etiological considerations of psychopathology. The variegated approaches to psychotherapy are seen as amenable to administration by one person or by a team of therapists, sometimes with different disciplines working together. Therapists emerging from the ranks of medicine, social work, psychology, or education may see children alone or in groups or together with their families for different lengths of time and under various structural provisions. Because each treatment approach is in the service of different goals, the effectiveness of various therapies ought not to be compared unless their varying goals are taken into account. For example, conditioning therapies can remove symptoms; however, symptom removal would not be regarded as a primary criterion of the effectiveness of more dynamic forms of therapy.

AN ECOLOGICAL MODEL

In addition to focusing on interventive approaches which call for a variety of individual diagnoses, Task Force II considered another point of view which holds an "ecological" theory as its center. The ecological model is the conceptualization of the child as an individual involved in complex interrelationships with his surrounding world, particularly his family. Each unit of the child's "ecosystem" is so connected with the whole that intervention with any part of the ecosystem, including individual intervention with the child, will affect the entire system.

Proponents of the ecological point of view note that their views have always been part of psychiatry, to some extent, as indicated by the following statement from the above-quoted GAP report:

The child's psychosocial milieu is at first the family; his earliest and most influential experiences take place in the context of parent-child relationship, operating within the transactional field of the networks of family interpersonal contacts. . . . The child's behavioral and developmental characteristics, beginning with his first feeding response, may affect the parent as feedback operations, often setting up a "circus" movement . . . (pp. 196–197).

One cannot intervene in ecosystems successfully without a full understanding of all the parts of these systems as well as the processes which serve to maintain balance. Viewing the child in this context, Salvador Minuchin and Jay Haley state in "Broadening the Unit of Intervention: The Delivery of Services According to an Ecological Model":

Almost every ecosystem can be seen as a subunit of a larger system. The family as a social unit is a subsystem of its society. But it has its own structures, history, organization, and boundaries. Transactions among subsystems and their inter-reactions with larger systems take place, as it were, at the boundaries of each subunit. The modality of transactions, the degree of interlocking among subunits, the freedom of alternatives available: all these are dynamic equations which have to be studied by anyone attempting to understand any unit or subsystem of an ecosystem.

In the case of a child, his development is so dependent on the family system that it is extremely difficult, if not impossible, to make an evaluation of a child without simultaneously evaluating his family system.

In general, the study of normal child development has paid close attention to the family as the background within which the child becomes socialized, but has placed less emphasis on the feedback processes between parents and children in this development. It is almost as if no tradition has developed for highlighting the qualities of the child as an organizing force in the family system.

It may be that the richness of the observations of the developmental processes of the child decreased the perception of the interpersonal forces constantly interacting with him. In any case, this orientation has greatly affected the study of child psychopathology. This study has focused on intrapsychic processes, conceptualized as being internalized and crystallized phenomena only barely available to the forces of the ecosystem.

But with the ecological point of view, we see that the level of "crystallization" within the child depends upon the level of crystallization of the interactional processes of his ecosystem. A rigid crystallization "within" the child betrays a rigid crystallization of the family system; child and system "diagnoses" are interlocked.

But the "intrapsychic" concept of pathology has dictated most or all of the diagnostic definitions of child psychiatric disorders, and consequently, pathology has been defined as autonomous of *environmental influences*.

Thus, adherents of the ecological view are critical of interventions which have as their main target the "inside" of the child. Although they recognize ecological statements in the GAP report, they feel the diagnostic classifications and definitions of this group betray an essentially intrapsychic approach as illustrated by the following example from the psychiatric definitions:

Oppositional Personality: These children express their aggressiveness by oppositional patterns of generally passive character, although these patterns may have some actively aggressive implications. They may appear to be conforming, but they continually provoke adults or other children. By the use of negativism, stubbornness, dawdling, procrastination, and other measures, they covertly show their underlying aggressivity.

It is further pointed out that those who adhere to the intrapsychic framework fail to understand the importance of the environment even when talking of "reactive" disorders, since even then they emphasize the child's inner responses to the environment more than the environment itself. This point is also apparent in the GAP report:

In making the diagnosis of reactive disorder, *the dynamic state and reaction of the child should be emphasized rather than the degree of stress*. Some situations might be judged to be potentially traumatic for all or most children. Yet relatively mild stimuli may produce a reactive disorder in a particular child, depending upon its meaning to the child and to his parents, the nature of his past experiences, his original endowment, his level of development, and the adaptive resources he has available (p. 223, emphasis added).

Those who recommend interventions based upon the ecological model are highly critical of present methods of delivery of services and contend that it reflects a system of diagnosis which largely ignores the environment. The target of intervention is the "inside" of the child, and the treatment of choice is to work with the child alone, in one-to-one therapy, with the treatment of his parents relegated to an ancillary position.

The drawbacks of the traditional delivery of services are numerous. An intervener ought to recognize the close interrelationships between the individual and his surroundings, and deal with the factors that impinge upon the individual from the outside as well as from within the individual himself. When the surroundings are not taken into account, there is, for example, insufficient understanding of the social consequences of diagnosis; that is, that psychiatric labels tend to stigmatize. Also, the act of labeling puts the child into a niche. If he is diagnosed as disturbed, he is sent to a child guidance clinic. If his symptoms manifest themselves in school, he is placed in a special class for emotionally disturbed children. If he is judged delinquent, he is sent to a correctional institution. All of these children are plucked from their natural environments and introduced to a different setting for a cure. If the child is treated successfully in this new environment, it is assumed that he can be sent back to his old environment to make a clean start. Unfortunately, however, one cannot remove psychopathology like an appendix.

This traditional approach disregards the unfortunate fact that children often tend to conform to the niche in which they have been placed. A child labeled delinquent may begin to consider himself a delinquent, and act accordingly. Furthermore, if the environment to which the "cured" child is returned has remained the same or, perhaps, even organized itself more firmly around old lines of interaction, with the absent child seen as the only "family problem," it seems highly unrealistic to expect the child to maintain his "cure" in the face of reexposure to the elements which caused his disturbance.

This is not to say that the internal processes of the child are to be ignored. Individual therapy can be the treatment of choice within the framework of the ecological model. But the therapist does not proceed from a theory of dichotomy between the reactive and what has already become an internally crystallized mechanism. Rather, he assumes that a change in one unit of the family system will affect the entire system, and that a change in the system will affect each unit.

From this point of view, a crystallized intrapsychic pathology in the child that doesn't affect and is not affected by the family system is inconceivable. Therefore, those of the ecological approach do not trust either diagnosis or judgment of improvement which does not take into account the total "ecosystem" of the child. The structures, history, organization boundaries, and relationships of the family, as well as the family's place in the larger social unit of the community, are regarded as critical aspects and determinants of psychopathology in children. Thus, there can be no complete diagnosis unless there is a family diagnosis, and there can be no lasting cure unless the cure takes place within the youngster's natural environment.

Thus, it can be argued that the organization of services, based on the assumption that there is individual pathology and an individual cure, leads to a diagnosis that tends to label, to categorize, and ultimately to isolate the child, as in institutions or special classrooms for disturbed children. This means that psychopathology developed and diagnosed in one environment is treated in another environment. However, psychopathology may well not be the same in the new environment as it was in the old. Furthermore, a cure effected in the new environment may be impossible to maintain upon return to the old.

Another serious consideration is the contention that individual psycho-therapeutic approaches can never hope to have a broad enough impact. The American Psychiatric Association estimates that 12 percent of school children in this country, about 4.5 million, are in need of mental health services. There is an estimated increase of 14 percent yearly in the number of psychiatric patients who need treatment (American Psychiatric Association, 1964). Our services are not meeting the need. For example, in 1965 only about 300,000 patients under the age of eighteen were being treated in all the outpatient services in the country (National Institute of Mental Health, 1965a).

Also, methods of therapy based on the intrapsychic conceptualization are not effective with many of the children who most need help—children from the lower socioeconomic groups. Many children in the lower-class strata are socialized in a diffusely organized environment, and respond to environmental deprivations of various sorts which an individual therapist could never conceivably correct. Those who proceed from the ecological model feel that their method overcomes the limitations of intrapsychic, individual therapy-oriented approaches.

Because the family is the child's primary ecosystem, family therapy is one of the most important methods of intervention derived from the eco-logical theory. There are many methods of intervening in a family, however; family therapy is not any single procedure of family treatment, but is rather an orientation which allows many different procedures. Most of the family therapy methods are built around ways of dealing with family dynamics and resistance to change by taking them into account as part of the treatment procedures.

Various principles of family therapy are enumerated in the writings of Ackerman (1958), Vogel and Bell (1960), Bateson, Jackson, and Haley (1963), and Minuchin, Montalvo et al. (1967). For example, the child is seen as part of a feedback process, a recipient of other family members' responses as well as an activator of their responses in turn. It is impossible to affect one family member without also affecting others eventually. Families brought together and observed in interaction with one another provide data for clinical understanding that cannot be obtained by interviewing individually. Family interaction data tend to change the clinician's perception of these problems. It is contended that those who do not work with families have no opportunity to observe the kinds of interaction which form *the reality* behind the thinking of the proponents of the ecological model.

Of course, the family is not the entire focus of the ecological view, since the family is influenced by the neighborhood and the wider society in which it is imbedded. An intervention by experts from the wider society can disrupt a family, whether this is therapeutic or governmental intervention.

The factional balances in the family can be tipped in unpredictable ways by outside intervention which is naïve about the total system. For example, a father who loses his job can shift his position in the family. Or a mother given welfare may find herself in a different relationship with her husband. If the therapeutic expert intervenes and hospitalizes a child, there are effects upon the total family group, just as the imprisonment of a delinquent without consideration of his family can have unexpected effects in the total family group. From this wider view, a "child problem" is a shared responsibility of the child, his family, and the wider society.

Often the child manifests problems that merely reflect something going on within his family. These problems may disappear over time, as the family changes. The freedom of the child and his family to change may be limited by early treatment intervention; therefore, it is not necessarily wise to seek out and identify children with problems early in their school career, if this identification labels the child and pigeonholes him.

The intrapsychic and ecological points of view both have their influence on legislation. If one works from the inner-space theory, legislation will consist largely of increasing funds for training child therapists and providing more institutions for the severely disturbed. There may also be funds for improved testing facilities in the schools to select the disturbed children for individual treatment. If one proceeds from the more ecological view, legislation in relation to the mental health of children will take into account the child, the family, the neighborhood, and the wider society whose institutions are part of the child's ecological system.

One thing must be kept firmly in mind—family structure appears to be changing. We can make only partial predictions about what the government must anticipate in years to come. Legislation which seems appropriate now could have unfortunate consequences in the future, yet have become so firmly entrenched that change would be difficult.

Workers from the ecological orientation feel that a total redefinition of the nature of psychopathology is required—one which has as its core the conceptualization of the child as a member of a family network. Family therapy, of course, is not a "new method." Over the last 15 years about a dozen different family treatment approaches have been devised and "schools" of family therapy have arisen. In addition, there has been the growth of a substantial body of literature which indicates that, as individuals, members of families with problem children do not look too different from individuals of a family without problem children. However, there is some evidence that the role structure of families with problem children differs from that of others in that they have more conflict, different coalition patterns, and more inflexibility in regard to modifying their behavior.

Family therapy is the expression of a different orientation to psychiatric problems and assumes an ecological definition of mental illness. Inherent

in the family therapy approach are some basic convictions about the nature
and the purpose of the family. It is seen as primarily a child-rearing institution. In the ideal family, married couples have passed through several
major developmental crises as a couple by the time their children are five
or twelve years old. Not the least of the crises for the couple is the time
when the child goes out into the community to represent the family there.

Several key concepts in family therapy need to be briefly defined. The
concept of the generation line is essential, because it is assumed in the
family field that disturbance in the child may be related to a confusion of
generation lines in the family, as, for example, when parents behave toward
children more as peers than as young people. Blame and the choice of
scapegoat is another essential concept. Typically, children are chosen by
families as the people to blame when the family in its entirety cannot focus
on its problem. The child usually cooperates unwittingly by providing sufficient difficulty to serve as a scapegoat. The details of other central concepts,
such as patterns of nonresolution of conflict and several problems of
"parenting," are important in family therapy but beyond the scope of our
report. What is essential in this conceptual scheme is the fact that children
are seen more as indicators of a family problem than as mentally ill themselves.

The underprivileged family presents a special challenge because some
of the worst problems must be understood in the light of the influence of a
very large ecosystem. Disadvantaged families are, for instance, more vulnerable to government decrees than are middle-class families because the
government influences their life very directly through income subsidy. By
giving subsidies directly to a mother and her children, the government under-
cuts the man's economic function in his family and weakens the family's
hierarchical structure. This, in turn, affects the mental health of the children
in such families.

Family therapists who work with the poor alert us to some often ignored
facts. We are reminded that the poor are not a homogeneous group. Ethnic
differences (such as the powerful differences between the Negro and Puerto
Rican poor), geographic factors (urban or rural poor), and differences
owing to family structure are often ignored when planning programs for
the poor. Various family styles have been described in the literature, showing
that "enmeshed" families function very differently from "disengaged" family
units. In the former, attempts to change one member bring forth powerful
resistance from the other members of the family; in the latter, the parents
have abdicated their role, and the consequent disengagement of family
members from each other requires different therapeutic interventions from
those required by families functioning according to some other style.

The absence of the father, a widely publicized element in poverty
families, turns out to have been somewhat overplayed. The studies of
Alexander Leighton (National Institute of Mental Health, 1965b) and

Hylan Lewis (1967) indicate that a stable one-parent family may be better for children than a chaotic family with a father.

RECOMMENDATIONS

It is obvious that the ecological and the individual therapy models can, from various practical points of view, coexist. Several members of Task Force II have undertaken to reconcile these views on a conceptual level. Certain difficulties are obvious. The existence of pathology which is encapsulated, and which exists autonomously from the environment, is a weak reality for family therapists; the ecological point of view in fact does not allow for major investment in individual therapeutic efforts. Conversely, the individual approach does not focus upon the wide range of environmental influences which may have possible effects on mental health. However, while complete resolution cannot be reached on the conceptual level, it is difficult to see what practicalities would impede support of both types of therapeutic approaches, on the research and training level. The Task Force, therefore, makes several recommendations specific to each approach. Other of our proposals are relevant to both positions.

The Interaction View

Because there are so many different types of therapies and such a great variation in the individual approaches of therapists from different disciplines, the possibility of inappropriate or noneffectual treatment is great. However, these various forms of therapy should not be considered valueless unless formal research has more or less conclusively justified discarding them. There is a need to tighten up the rationale of the diagnostic and treatment processes currently practiced, and to conduct well-planned clinical action research to provide bases for evaluation of previous efforts. We, therefore, make the following recommendations:

1. Funds should be made available for the study of forms of psychotherapy and of therapeutic technique.

2. Psychoanalytic theory, which has up to now provided the broadest basis for a comprehensive understanding of psychological development and psychopathology, should be mined for its continued explanatory potential.

3. The appropriateness of treatment techniques based on an understanding of intrapsychic factors should not be tested under inappropriate circumstances. Task Force II recommends that greater investment be made in the training of clinicians who would be qualified to put psychodynamic theories under appropriate test.[1]

1. Three of the Task Force papers represent a summary of the position favoring continued support, professional and financial, of individual psychotherapy: see H. S. Belmont (Appendix A).

The Ecological Model[2]

Those working from an ecological approach recommend that an ecological model for delivering psychotherapeutic services for children be brought to the attention of the professional public as well as the lay public. Such a model will have to take into account the child living in his family, spending some time in school, and time in a particular neighborhood. This model would imply a differentiated view of the child in his various environments, and it would also require of the therapists the kind of clinical skills that are necessary in family therapy. For example, the initial diagnosis of the child would have to be carried out against the background of his family and community and would entail home and school visits. These visits become appropriate aspects of the diagnostic procedure. Interviewing should be done with the family as a total unit. There is a need for a differentiated view of the way in which family members assign roles to children in difficulty, in the service of maladaptive family equilibrium. In short, the diagnostic procedure involves the participation of all the significant members of the child's family, including often grandparents and aunts. The model then calls for the evolution of strategy for the treatment of the total family and each individual member within the family.

In support of the development of the enterprise of family therapy,[3] we make the following recommendations:

1. Government support should be extended to clinics and community mental health centers which organize services in terms of larger units of interventions than one-to-one therapy and which deal with the child in his natural social unit. It is regrettable that community mental health programs often reproduce the segregated method of delivery of services that existed before the creation of such centers. The Task Force argues for the continued attempts to establish and maintain neighborhood health centers of various sorts. It is recommended that neighborhood health centers blur the boundaries between service to adults and children so that adult services will deal with children of adults and child services will take into account the family, as explained above.[4] It is recommended that federal fundings be used to

2. Editor's Note: The ecological model recommended by Task Force II is not mentioned specifically in the final report of the Commission. The broad view of the ecological approach, however, is supported by the Commission's recommendations for an advocacy system and for a comprehensive network of services. See *Crisis in Child Mental Health: Challenge for the 1970's* (New York: Harper & Row, 1970).

3. Related recommendations concerning the betterment of the lives of families most typically under family therapy as well as recommendations related to the school experiences of impoverished children under such care appear in later sections of this report.

4. Editor's Note: In its final deliberations, the Commission endorsed the treatment of the child *and* his family. Certain qualifications were expressed, however, on

support the creation of comprehensive intervention units, rather than the proliferations of special services.

2. Funds should be provided for the training of family specialists. With an estimated 4.5 million disturbed children in the United States (American Psychiatric Association, 1964) and only 1,500 registered child psychiatrists,[5] the extent of the need can hardly be overstated. The "family specialist" should be developed. The mental health of different members of a family has, up to now, been divided among a number of specialists treating fragmented problems. We suggest the development of specialists concerned with the total family. But even if all the training facilities in the mental health field provided training for family specialists, this could not cover the needs of all the families who want help. The patterns of training today's mental health helpers cover a number of requirements that make training extremely long and expensive. At the same time, the population is begging for people to provide help. One could conceive of selecting people who are naturally oriented or potentially able helpers without training and giving them a training specifically oriented toward helping families, making them paraprofessional aides to facilities working with families. This area should be explored.

3. Funding for family research should be made available. Longitudinal studies of families should lead to improved understanding of what families were like before they developed their problems, or a problem child; we need to better understand the *process by* which families develop a problem child. There is a lack of base-line data from which we can judge deviant processes as they evolve in families because we do not know enough about the normal family processes in different social groups. The various developmental stages of families under different circumstances have to be highlighted and understood.

It is essential that studies be made of the strengths of lower socioeconomic groups. It is fashionable to speak of the alienation of the poor from American society. But the poor are not apart from the *values* of the society; rather, they are separated from the opportunities to live by the values of the majority. Some have unusual strengths. Some live productively and decently and raise happy, well-adjusted children. Studies must be made of what factors enable them to rise above circumstance. Research, exploring this

---

blurring the boundaries in adult and child services, as recommended above, because adult services presently receive priority in funding, manpower, and facilities. While the Commission is not opposed to the integration of child and adult services in cases in which such arrangements would better meet the needs of the child and his family, it is opposed to any effort toward integration which will perpetuate the present inequities in children's services. See *Crisis in Child Mental Health: Challenge for the 1970's* (New York: Harper & Row, 1970).

5. Personal communication, Dr. Frank Whiting.

question, must be longitudinal in nature and should focus on the supportive aspects of the environment as well as on the individual.

4. Funds should be made available to study the consequences of family therapy interventions.

Research on All Therapeutic Approaches

In addition to the above, consideration should be given to research on all forms of therapeutic interventions. At the beginning of this report we made clear that the major handicap under which we operate in drafting recommendations is the lack of information on some of the most vital problems of child mental health. This point has to be underlined now. It seems that any recommendation calling for research on the effectiveness of psychotherapeutic intervention, either in individual psychoanalysis or in the family orientation, is sure to be on the side of the angels. One can never go wrong when insisting on the need for more knowledge on any topic, and when it comes to psychotherapeutic interventions, it is especially obvious that more research must be conducted; however, there are several other truths which further emphasize the need for research in child therapy. Practices, theories, and styles of intervention in the lives of children are partly determined by personal bents and preferences of therapists. Such interventions are also extremely costly. Psychotherapeutic interventions of whatever kind are often subject to ridicule or criticism or misinterpretation on the part of the general public. For all these reasons, the absence of solid information about the long-range effectiveness of therapeutic interventions is particularly deleterious. A professional technique, albeit of many varieties, purportedly so powerful, obviously so costly, and more often than not controversial, should receive maximum financial support in the attempt to really test its effectiveness and to truly come to understand its variegated limitations with various populations and its manifold potentialities with different kinds of children.

Research findings on the effects of therapy, counseling, or casework with children are inconclusive. The findings do not indicate the presence of any across-the-board effective technique for dealing with mental health problems of children. However, these findings are often based on inadequately conducted studies. The poor control, lack of clinical sophistication in the investigator, and procedural problems render the results incomparable. The very problems of interpreting such research findings indicate the need for more careful definition of types of children, types of environment, types of therapy, and the relation of individual therapy to a variety of alternative services. In view of these shortcomings in research studies, we recommend:

1. The use of nontreated control groups in evaluation research.

2. Long-term follow-ups of both treated and control cases. This seems

essential, since sketchy findings indicate that children showing the most immediate post-therapy gains are not necessarily the children with the greatest long-range gain. Again, the need for a common diagnostic framework emerges, as it did earlier in this report.

3. It seems that planned longitudinal studies are required before effective prognostic procedures can be developed. It would be desirable if the variables of these studies would not be restricted to clinical tests, interviews, and casework information. Studies should include systematic measures of ego development and ego strength based on observational measures of classroom and peer group functioning and systematic assessment of the family environment. This suggestion is based on available longitudinal studies which indicate that such variables are among the more effective long-range childhood predictors of adult mental health.

Treatment Approaches

In the absence of more definite information about psychotherapy and awaiting the results of such investigations as are recommended here, we suggest:

1. Treatment programs should avoid rigidity in permanently categorizing children as needing different kinds of specific treatments. Flexibility should be the rule in assigning children to interventions of varying depth. It would appear sensible to determine the degree of help needed by a child by first attempting to try less intensive interventions.

2. It would also seem desirable if treatment programs would not conceive of "cure" as occurring within a fixed period of time, but as a process which once activated may show benefits 10 or 15 years later.

3. When various kinds of services in a broad spectrum of available services are tested against one another, psychoeducational and environmental interventions should not be conceived of as auxiliary services to psychotherapy but should receive as careful and intensive attention as more traditional therapies; otherwise, there cannot be any solid testing of various methods of interventions.

COMMENTS ON THE CONTINUITY HYPOTHESIS

These various recommendations regarding psychotherapy and research in psychotherapy are made in light of the review of the literature examining the assumption that emotional disturbance in children is indicative of continuing psychological difficulties which may lead to adult mental illness. This is essentially the continuity hypothesis which fares poorly when one attempts to trace particular symptoms from childhood to adulthood. Dr. Lawrence Kohlberg has studied this problem extensively for this Task

Force. The following is a glimpse of the material presented in his paper "Predictability of Adult Mental Health from Childhood Behavior."

The available data indicate that antisocial symptoms show the most continuity from childhood to adulthood, but even these symptoms do not show strong continuity with *specific* antisocial symptoms in adulthood. It appears that if continuity exists at the level of symptoms this continuity has yet to be demonstrated. However, there is considerable evidence that childhood symptoms are predictive of later pathology as *nonspecific predictors* for a variety of adult adjustment difficulties. Children showing antisocial behavior have a better than even risk of being maladjusted during adulthood, although the adult maladjustment may not manifest itself as antisocial behavior. The number of antisocial symptoms and the frequency and seriousness of antisocial episodes do permit considerable refinement of predictions for individuals. A wide range of pathological and nonpathological outcomes is possible given a particular childhood antisocial symptom. But there are indicators that general antisocial behavior creates a less than even chance of later positive adjustment.

Studies of peer relationships show that various kinds of poor peer relationships in childhood are predictive of various kinds of psychopathology in adult life. In light of this finding it is particularly regrettable that the Task Force did not have the time to fully explore ways in which the peer group structure could be utilized to promote better mental health. There is also some promising evidence that certain psychophysiological symptoms, for example, a relatively rapid GSR half-recovery score, may provide some ways of identifying individuals who are high risks for the future.

Interestingly, academic underachievement seems to be by no means as certain a predictor of future maladjustment as it is assumed. The predictive power of academic work upon maladjustment is as good as that of intelligence.

Research in psychotherapy with children of whatever type will have to take into account findings from research on child development and normal behavior in order to choose variables for investigation which are not only clinically meaningful but which also show some promise of stability or predictability over time. There appears to be a two-culture problem: clinical questions grow in a different soil from that which produced methodological skill in research.

The Child and His Family

To better understand child mental health, Task Force II thought it important to move away from the child as a central focus of our discussion and examine general problems of family life. In so doing, we limited ourselves largely to the disadvantaged family because their problems are presently so severe.

THE DISADVANTAGED FAMILY

In 1967, there were 5.5 million children under six, and 9 million more under seventeen, who were living in families too poor to feed and house them adequately. Lyndon B. Johnson (1967) noted in a Presidential Address that after three years of the war on poverty only 3.2 million of these received AFDC payments; 12 million impoverished children went without any benefits at all. Those who were granted aid were not receiving very much. There is great variability in payments among states. Some offer a mother with three children $120 a month or less; 30 states do not meet their own minimum subsistence standards.

Population statistics and dollar figures obscure the fact that the poor are not a unified group. There are many differences among lower-income groups which must be considered in planning programs. One of the most important of these lies in family structure. Stable poor families often do an excellent job of child-rearing. Unstable poor families often do not.

Minuchin, in "The Slum Family and the Slum School," provides a number of insights into the particular characteristics of unstable families. Typically, the male remains transitory or peripheral. The relationships between parents and children give rise to the phenomenon of "parental" child, one who has child-raising responsibilities while still a child himself.

The parental child's position is an extremely stressful one because his siblings displace onto him their anger against their mother. Also, the parental child is in an obvious power alliance with the mother. This parental role often pushes girls into premature marriage or unwed motherhood as a means of escaping the stressful home situation. Ironically, what they escape to is often a tragic repetition of the same experience they wished to avoid.

Another phenomenon in unstable families is the nonevolved grand-mother. Here the daughter relinquishes her own motherly role to the grandmother, who takes over the maternal functions toward the children, thus confusing generation lines.

Child-rearing practices often reflect the instability of these families. Parental responses to the behavior of children are random and often deficient in explicitness about rules, making it very difficult for the child to internalize them. Also, the emphasis of the parents seems to be on the control and inhibition of behavior, rather than on its revision and guidance into proper channels. Consequently, the experience of the child is one of either lack of responses or, at the other extreme, violent responses. The child has little feeling that his behavior can modify his world.

ENVIRONMENTAL PREDICTORS OF MALADJUSTMENT

The child development research which deals with environmental variables as predictors of later outcome yields a number of facts relative to families, some of which will be discussed below.

Drawing again on Kohlberg's analyses, it seems that social class is moderately correlated with childhood adjustment and later adjustment status. While high social class is a good predictor of later positive adjustment, the prediction of maladjustment, either in aggressive or in withdrawn forms, requires the interaction between social class and low IQ. Evidence indicates that when social class, intelligence, or childhood adjustment ratings are used by themselves to predict later adjustment, these three variables obtain about the same level of accuracy.

Studies of the relationship of family atmosphere to later maladjustment show the negative relationship between high family cohesion and antisocial behavior, at least in the legal sense. Homes which are rated as quarrelsome and neglecting are very clearly predictive of a high rate of antisocial behavior later in life. Recidivism and reformation seem to be determined more by factors of the neighborhood and by disciplinary techniques than by factors pertaining to the structure of the family. Broken homes which are both quarrelsome and affectionate also have implications for later antisocial outcome. The criminal from a broken home seems to be more person-oriented in his choice of crime than people from other types of homes. Research on parent personality as a predictor of later maladjustment indicates that parental role models and the quality of the affectionate relationships to children have serious bearing on legally defined antisocial behavior; however, there is also the suggestion that more refined variables such as reinforcement patterns and modes of communication will become fruitful variables for further research.

Antisocial behavior seems to be a frequent focus of developmental research, perhaps because antisocial acts are easier to count reliably than other forms of maladjusted behavior. The family, the neighborhood, the internal personality structure and a number of other variables may be predictive of antisocial behavior. It appears that, as far as delinquency is concerned, several predictor variables function in interaction with one another. For example, a deviant neighborhood is in itself not a contributing variable to delinquency, but in combination with a deviant family atmosphere it functions as a predictor of crime. And so it is with a number of other predictors of antisocial behavior.

RECOMMENDATIONS FOR PROGRAMS AND RESEARCH

Family Services to Juvenile Delinquents

It is recommended that government funds be extended for providing family services to juvenile delinquents. It is argued that a large percentage of disturbed children, especially those from lower socioeconomic groups, are now treated in custodial institutions at a cost which may on occasions range as high as $20,000 per year per child. Not only is this an uneconomical system of care but also it removes the child from his natural environment, which is often not the best way to treat him. While many courts have some facilities for helping families to contain their children, the case loads of probation officers are extraordinarily heavy, and services tend to be minimal. Housing services, homemaking help, job counseling, job training, and remedial and tutoring services are among the few that could be extended to the families of delinquents, in the spirit of ecological intervention.

Marriage Laws and Counseling Services

Since the state intervenes at the formation and dissolution of families, it seems important to consider the laws which could help stabilize the family unit. It is recommended:

a. that the waiting period between the decision to marry and the actual marriage should be lengthened to help avoid impulsive, ill-advised marriages;

b. that some type of premarital counseling should be built into this waiting period;

c. that consultation and counseling should be built into divorce actions as well as into post-divorce periods, particularly where there are children involved. Various forms of counseling in marriage and in divorce, however, should not be required.

Welfare Laws

Welfare laws as they are presently organized discourage the formation of the nuclear family, rewarding the female-headed household economically. The cycle of female-headed, extended, large families continues, suggesting a much-needed search for ways of modifying the social situations which create the problems of female-headed households. These problems are numerous and are difficult to separate from the problems of father absence which, *considered in isolation*, have been overstated. It is suggested that patterns of funding could be powerful change agents in breaking the cycle of one-parent families who raise children, who in turn will tend to create one-parent families. We suggest the following considerations:

1. If the negative income tax were to be adopted, the bureaucratic welfare machine and the negative label "on welfare" would disappear. The preservation of the nuclear family would no longer be financially disadvantageous.

2. It is also possible to envision patterns of funding which would encourage the nuclear family unit by arranging that the income of wife, husband, and children living together be at least as much as if they were living separately. In this way, the lower socioeconomic population would be financially rewarded for preserving the family in the same way that the stability of middle-class families is rewarded by the advantages of the joint tax return.[6]

Family Planning Services

The government must support the dissemination of birth control information and of such birth control devices as seem appropriate. Such services would allow low-socioeconomic families to cope with more manageable family size and would provide them a means to protect their children from pregnancy.

As Minuchin and Haley note, in New York City alone, it is estimated

6. Editor's Note: The Commission's final report recommends the revision of all present income maintenance programs to ensure a *guaranteed minimum income* for all Americans. It recommends, in addition, experimentation in different areas of the country with various forms of income support, such as the negative income tax, and a determination of the most feasible arrangement for different populations. Other proposals include guaranteed employment and children's allowances. See *Crisis in Child Mental Health: Challenge for the 1970's* (New York: Harper & Row, 1970).

that in the coming year 86,000 babies will be born to families now receiving AFDC. But birth control services are inadequate, and legislation in some states prohibits welfare workers from giving out birth control information to the recipients of public welfare. Therefore, the following recommendations are made:

1. The government should make birth control information available to those clients of welfare services who request it, and the availability of such information should be a requirement for the dissemination of federal welfare funds to the state.

2. However, the availability of services is not necessarily followed by adequate use of these services, and it is important to continue to study the ways of reaching and motivating those members of the lower-class population who tend to be indifferent or hostile to the use of birth control.

3. It is also recommended that such information be made available to adolescents who have the consent of their parents for the use of birth control devices.[7] We recommend the development of units of pediatric obstetrics to provide services to adolescent expectant mothers particularly in the inner-city slums.

7. Editor's Note: This qualification of "consent of parents" does not appear in the Commission's final report.

Mental Health and the School Environment

Task Force II contends that the school has an important role in the psychological development of children. We can spell this out only in a general way and then proceed to examine various aspects of the school world and attempt to suggest recommendations for the improvement of education, if it is to foster rather than impede the evolution of healthy personality. Most of the following discussion is derived from the Task Force papers of Dr. Barbara Biber (see Appendix A).

AN EXPANDED ROLE FOR THE SCHOOL

One outcome of the advances made in our knowledge of human behavior has been our awareness of the inextricable interaction between cognitive and affective realms of human functioning. In school terms, this means it is no longer feasible to separate the growth of cognitive functions—the use of the symbol systems, reasoning, judging and problem solving, acquiring and ordering information—from the growth of other developmental processes, such as self-feeling and identity, potential for relating to people, and autonomy and creativity, commonly regarded as personality development. These are interdependent developmental processes, all relevant to the broad concept of mental health. The classroom is just as much a psychological climate, which may be described in terms of expectations, sanctions, and codes for personal-social interchange, as it is a medium for the specific tasks of learning, describable as to teaching method, equipment, and assessment. In terms of the investment of time and energy alone, school is a significant life environment for the child that will have a differential impact on his evolving self-esteem. In the middle years, it has special relevance with respect to trust in the world outside the family and on the psychological positioning of the self in the larger community.

The question is not whether the school has responsibility for aspects of personality development. It is, rather, how we can move toward greater acceptance that inner processes of personality development inevitably respond to the intrinsic learning experience.[8] How can it become a matter of professional conscience that schools should hold themselves responsible for all the ramifications of the total development of the child that flow from the nature of his learning experience in school? Jules Henry (1963) cries out against modal American teaching as though it were a partly unconscious conspiracy to create a docile population. If docility and other such life-schema are not what we want, then we are obligated to describe images, models of school that have a rationale, and goals and methods for developing other kinds of people.

It should be clear that recognition of the school's responsibility for personality development does not imply that it has exclusive or even major dominion over this aspect of development. The family, the neighborhood, and the community continue to be salient influences. Perhaps the simple point is that there cannot, should not, be an exclusive dominion by any of these life influences. The family rears and teaches; the school teaches and rears.

By this view the school has both an expanded opportunity and a responsibility. If these are to be realized or even approximately fulfilled, the first step is to work with the concepts of development that are syntonic with the behavioral sciences as we proceed to specify the school's responsibility in contemporary society. The special mandate from society to the school is clear—namely, to develop ego strength. The school's first obligation is to bring competence to the highest possible levels. Thinking of the elementary years, this highlights the mastery of symbolic systems, that is, becoming literate in the discourse of words and numbers; advancing the child's differentiated perception of the natural phenomena, work processes, and social functioning of both past and present societies; developing the child's abilities to solve problems and acquire and order information by increasing his cognitive powers, such as hierarchical conceptualized reasoning and judging and inferring; and increasing doing and making skills, that is, manipulative-constructive operations as well as athletic performance.

But competence, even at grand levels of excellence, can only *serve* ego strength; it is not coextensive with it. It is only when these intellectual and performance skills (at a high level of competence) are expressed in the effective interaction of the individual with the work, the people, and the problems of his environment that we are seeing ego strength. If this is our goal, we must deal with the forces within school life which influence self-esteem, feelings of competence, motivation, and modes and models of human interchange. Furthermore, we need to be willing, through education,

8. For further elaboration of the extended responsibility of the school see Biber (1961).

to work toward projected images of optimal human functioning with the same confidence with which we work toward projected images of intellectual competence. These images of optimal human functioning, which we call basic principles of mental health, are derived from our knowledge of the behavioral sciences and a humanist view of a democratic society; they are neither more nor less ephemeral than the images of excellence in intellectual functioning which have guided curriculum and teaching method at any point in history.

So it is that while the school works at educating competent individuals who have the knowledge to make things work, get things done, and think things through, it is also responsible for nurturing individuality, for the experience that contributes to feelings of worth and self-realization, to the capacity for emotional investment, and to the building of a separate identity. In the development of the elementary school child it is within the school's orbit to support and stimulate autonomous processes, especially at this stage when the child is making major shifts in his lines of allegiance and dependence. This is a period when the child can gain differentiated knowledge of himself as a worker, a learner, a member of a group; when it is important for him to build a sense of self as someone who has a voice to question and choose, to accept help without sacrificing independence; as someone whose sense of worth derives from the competence to perform and the courage to initiate, as well as from the reflections of his image in the people around him. It is a time when he can develop a relation to learning and work that connects him deeply with the essence of his activities, generating intrinsic motivation and only subsidiary dependence on competitive superiority or external symbols of approval as the source of drive. These are processes which free him, and we can add to them the freedom intrinsic to being known by important adults and coming to know one's self as a distinct, thinking, feeling, striving being who, while heir to the universal human impulses for good and evil, is composing a way of life that is his own, that cannot be the duplicate of anyone else's. There are known ways in which the elementary school can support these autonomous processes.

The autonomous individual is presumably not the prey of psychological externals or codified social forms. At the same time, by our concepts of mental health, neither is he indifferent to the challenge of participating fully in social processes while sustaining his individual autonomy. In this connection, one thinks not only of the distinctness of self but of all the experiences in school by which the child between the ages of six and twelve can extend and embellish the self through important involvement with others— in play, in work, in talk, in argument, in sympathy or defiance—so that the self, so exquisitely unique, does not end up as an isolate. There is a further obligation of the school to equip the child with the power to communicate his expression and invention, that make him, for example, not the slave but the master of form. There is a bridge to be built, a synthesis to be accomplished, between the personal and the impersonal, so that eventually what is deeply meaningful to the individual can be universalized as an ideal, can take socialized forms, and, conversely, the nonpersonal reality in more remote social spheres can become part of a personal commitment—in other words, the formulation of a value system.

Similarly, education which, for the sake of stimulating creativity and originality, operates on the premise that open-ended, undirected exploration or play with things or ideas is an optimal first stage in learning has an obligation to provide subsequent organization and discipline of thought and activity leading toward products that bespeak control and consolidation. Basic to all these processes is the goal of sustaining the vital interchange between thought and feeling, between affective-expressive and logical-analytical modes of experience. There are known ways in which school can be presumed to support these synthesizing processes even while research in methodology is in the making on the difficult problems of securing hard-core evidence in this domain.

Proceeding from this basic orientation, we have formulated a series of recommendations which deal, first, with a model for the functioning of an elementary school geared toward comprehensive positive development during the middle years of childhood and, second, with the strategies of change and redirection of teacher preparation that might affect movement from the predominant modes of existing elementary education toward this model.

RECOMMENDATIONS: GUIDELINES FOR AN ELEMENTARY SCHOOL MODEL

Our first consideration is the altered perception of the goals of the elementary school in the direction of extended responsibility. We make the following recommendations:

1. We recommend that those who formulate educational policy and innovation or teach the philosophy of education recognize the psychological significance of the school as an institution as having differential effect on personality and that it be recognized that this effect and influence is far greater than has been recognized as a mere by-product of the process of teaching skills.[9]

2. It is also recommended that the school assume responsibility not only for educating for competence and achievement but for nurturing of individuality and the development of ego strength, and that such functions

9. The comparative group study *The Psychological Impact of School Experience,* by P. Minuchin, B. Biber, E. Shapiro, and H. Zimiles (New York: Basic Books, 1969), reports that qualitatively different school experience up to the fourth-grade level, interacting with home background, has a different effect on attitudes toward the self, perspective on life stages, images of adult roles, and evolutions of value systems.

be recognized as pivotal throughout the span of the preschool and elementary years. Schools, in general, have failed to fulfill, or have even violated, these developmental goals. Serious as this is for all children, it is most traumatic for the less privileged children in our society, for whom the negative aspects of their life situations are often reinforced by their experience in school.

In the broadest sense, we argue for an acceptance of the enhancement of developmental psychological processes as proper educational goals. This means that processes which advance self-understanding are seen to be *as* integral to schooling as learning to do arithmetic, that the facilitation of interchange with adults and peers become *as* central a concern of the school as the learning of basic skills.

3. We recommend, therefore, that all aspects of the school milieu comprising curriculum, teaching methods, administrative practices, and architectural design be focused on stimulating and guiding developmental processes. This orientation would change the position of measures of achievement in the educational scheme of things. These would no longer be regarded as the prime, if not the sole, indicators of successful learning; their importance would be contingent upon the extent to which they represented genuine progressing mastery of the tools for learning.

4. In recommending that developmental processes rather than achievement products be adopted as the goals for education, we are aware that it would not be possible to offer a universally acceptable schema of the developmental processes to serve as guideposts for education in the middle years of childhood. One problem rests in how generally, in terms of basic process, in contrast to how concretely, in terms of experiential components, one chooses to specify developmental processes. The essence of our recommendation is that for any school or school system a schema *in terms of development* be clearly conceptualized as the basic rationale for the whole edifice of a school's functioning and, further, that such a schema shall meet two criteria: first, be justifiable in terms of theory in the behavioral sciences and, second, be translatable into an educational program.

As illustration we offer, in brief, two schemata of developmental processes which meet these criteria but are conceptualized at different levels. Schema 1 is organized according to generalized modes of the individual's interaction with his environment; Schema 2 is more functionally delineated. Both are consonant with goals of development in the terms of N. Sanford (1967): ". . . Development involves ego-expansion and differentiation processes in all the major areas of the personality, integration within each of these areas, and integration among the areas." Both require imaginative translation into the most relevant learning experiences by educators ready to engage in continuous experimentation.

Even a quick perusal of the dimensions which are highlighted in these two schemata should suggest an additional advantage in the adoption of developmental processes as goals for the school. Goals such as these could provide a common conceptual framework for educative and therapeutic functions and thus build up a sadly needed common language of communication between educators and mental health specialists.

Developmental Processes as Educational Goals
Schema 1 (Bower)

Differentiation vs. diffusion
>Concerns quality, quantity, and content of a child's transactions with persons and things so that images and symbols can be focused and delineated one from another. Increasing capabilities for differentiation.

Fidelity vs. distortion
>Use of symbols accurately, tied to conceptual or action correlates—events, objects, relationships; with sufficient degree of freedom to permit change in the meaning of the symbol.

Pacing vs. overloading
>Constructive and controlled release of emotional energy.

Expansion-constriction
>New energies and inputs in order to develop new adaptive skills, to permit higher levels of symbol development and encourage conceptual breadth and depth; concepts about knowledge interpenetrate ego concepts, etc.

Integration-fragmentation
>Integration of separate parts of person and personality—emotions, skill, knowledge, thoughts, imagination; processes of integration vary; individuals have unique ways of synthesizing.

Schema 2 (Biber)

Range and depth of sensitivity to world around
>Differentiated, discriminating perception as basis for action and interaction.
>
>Attitude that there is an open, varied world all around which invites penetration; experience to be probed and unraveled; human interchange across wide range of emotion.
>
>Openness to receive and react, etc.

Cognitive power and intellectual mastery of the symbolic systems of word and number
>Search for relationships among discrete elements of experience.
>
>Reorganization of perceptual meanings to larger order concepts and generic meanings.
>
>Conceptual mastery of experiential elements.
>
>Competence in the logos of our society, etc.

Synthesis—integrating across cognitive and affective domains

Outcome of learning experience which takes symbolic expressive form. Transformation of some part of child's encounter with the outer world that reflects and utilizes the forces—the cumulated meanings, feelings, wishes, conflicts—of his inner life of impulse and affect.

Integration of diverse stimuli, general intimacy with nonrational processes as basic to creativity.

Differentiated interaction with people

Availability of variety of modes of communication, verbal and nonverbal.

Use of interchange with people as source for understanding commonness of human feelings and conflicts as well as mode of emotional refreshment.

Experience with peers for joint productivity and building codes of interpersonal relationship.

Relating to adults, selecting, as part identification figures.

Adaptation to requirements of social situations

Acceptance of denial for sake of alternate fulfillment.

Adherence to rules and regulations as protection of learning.

Internalization of regulating codes.

Recovery from frustration or failure.

Mergence of individual drive with group purposes.

Self-understanding

Depth and range of acquaintance with self.

Reality of expectations and aspirations.

Identity as an individual.

Moral judgment (see Biber, 1967).

5. The goals of a school are activated, in considerable measure, through the choice of instructional methods. When learning functions are not dichotomized from the processes of personality formation, every instructional method needs to be assessed in terms of its total complex impact. It is not hard to see learning by rote as representing an influence on personality as well as a teaching technique. It is recommended, therefore, that the suitability of every instructional method for a given child population be judged along two dimensions: first, its efficacy in relation to mastery and, second, its associated effects on broader modes of dealing with experience such as docility, autonomy, tolerance for ambiguity.

There have been several efforts to establish criteria for choosing and evaluating instructional methods. Biber (1967) has made the point that knowledge of changing conflicts, drives, and energies at different stages of development is needed as a foundation for changes in educational materials and teaching methods, and that this body of knowledge should not be regarded as having relevance only to the specialized psychological and/or guidance services of the school. She states: ". . . The educator, at all levels in this context, is being asked to exercise a kind of *binocular perception of the learning child,* so that awareness of associated emotional processes is as naturally and knowledgeably considered as is intellectual gain. This, and no less, is the standard of excellence to be held as an ideal for education in our times." Hollister (1967), with secondary education in mind, speaks of the *double-purpose curriculum,* stating:

> For a long time curriculum specialists have been working toward the formulation of a new and more potent blend, namely, a curriculum that not only imparts substance but also, at the same time, engenders greater cognitive and affective capacities. . . . These curricula are providing opportunities in prediction, inference making, formulating hypotheses, making operational definitions, and learning how to change or control variables in a process. These are being taught as part of an effort to escalate content teaching into greater development of creativity. In recognition of the interaction of cognitive factors with affective factors, these curricula deliberately reward novel ideas, observations, definitions and solutions.

Furthermore, continuous, systematic analysis of educational techniques and methods in terms of their associated effects on personality development would require the cooperative efforts of school people and mental health specialists and would tend to diminish the deleterious polarization of therapy and education which still characterizes the contemporary educational scene.

The two schemata of developmental processes presented above have sufficient generality to be relevant to successive stages of maturity from the earliest years on. To construct a rationale for a concrete curriculum for a given developmental stage, i.e., the middle years, it becomes necessary to close in on the distinctive characteristics of that stage—the qualitative changes in nature of cognitive functioning, the changing drives and allegiances associated with psychosexual maturing, the construction of self-image in terms of skills, interests, and introjected reflection of peers' images, the emergence of a value system within the microcosm of child society, and the conflicts and problems which appear to be basic in the maturing process as distinct from those which could be ameliorated by a change in life circumstance.

It is this latter distinction that presents us with both a theoretical and a practical challenge at present. The basic characteristics which constitute our image of the middle years have been derived from studies of childhood and children for whom this maturing period took place in the context of middle-class life which, despite the variations in value systems, nevertheless had a common core of being able to protect the child's needs and to send him forth with images and expectations of one or another kind of individual glory. Now we have become intensely aware that concepts of dynamic processes and sequential ordering of the course of development need to be modified in terms of life patterns which differ from the populations on which they were based. For example, the dependence-independence sequence, and the conflicts associated with it in the middle years of childhood, are circumstantially different for a poverty population than they are for the middle class. The young child in poverty necessarily assumes more independence at an earlier age in a more restricted range of experience; this may cut back his total developmental potential at the same time that it gives him a degree of competence satisfaction. This concept has been fully discussed by Marans and Lourie (1967).

When the dependence experience is shortened and more shallow in the early years, we can expect the dependence-independence conflict of the middle years to have different behavioral manifestations relevant to the set of child-learning-from-adult which, in turn, may call for radical changes in the concept of the teacher-child relationship.

6. We recommend, therefore, that while basic developmental processes be accepted as educational goals, the concrete curriculums for the elementary school should represent a high degree of differentiation in order to be adapted to the impact of life circumstance in the early years of childhood on subsequent developmental sequence. Other factors argue with equal potency for differentiation in curriculums, within schools and within classrooms as well as between schools in contrasting regions and for children of contrasting life histories. Some attention has been given (and more is needed) to individual differences in rates of mastery, modes of expression, and styles of cognition. More emphatically, we recommend that the research evidence on the rate of development and qualitative differences in development between boys and girls be taken into serious consideration and be reflected in a differentiated curriculum.

In this connection, an active contemporary trend calls for comment. Progress has been made, through new teacher education programs and curriculum revision projects, to establish greater continuity between the nature of school life and the mores of family subculture of the child population. This trend we support so long as it does not take distorted forms which might perpetuate deleterious aspects of minority-group status. There is, however, another potential danger in programs with good intentions which aim to be relevant to the mores of a subculture, namely, the assumption of homogeneity in the way individual families or individuals in families live within the mores of their subculture society. There is a complex interaction between variance within social class and variance within ethnic groups. A child comes from a particular family with its own intrafamily dynamics—not from a generalized, often stereotyped image of family life in a given subculture. This needs to be understood if the goal of know-the-child-as-an-individual-within-the-context-of-his-life-pattern is to be attained. Ultimately, education must be relevant to each child as an individual in order to sustain his motivation to learn, and some of this relevance can be found in the common characteristics of childhood—pleasure in activity, excitement, challenge, mastery.

7. Up to this point our recommendations have pointed to a series of goals for education, to a rationale for selection of method, and to bases for a differentiated curriculum which comprise a model we judge to be consonant with mental health principles. On the level of action, we recommend that federal grants be made preferentially to programs dealing with the concept of the relation of education to mental health, as spelled out above. In the selection of a school or a school system for involvement in grants, or designation as models under the Education Professions Development Act, or in future legislation, the above criteria should be adopted as essential elements in evaluation projects.

8. In the next pages we present, in brief, a series of principles for an optimal learning environment to serve as guidelines for the actual teaching-learning activities in elementary school classrooms. We endorse these principles and recommend their adoption because they represent the concrete educational mechanisms and relationships through which the school can serve the goal of contributing simultaneously to intellectual mastery and to personality development. Here again, we recommend that these principles be adopted as dimensions for analysis and assessment of experimental programs in connection with allocation of govenment funds for the improvement of education.

a. *Learning can be considered optimal when it takes shape as independent pursuit by an actively involved child; a positive learning environment presents the child with varied possibilities to observe, discover, invent, and choose; it avoids complete dependence on verbal-vicarious transmissions of information and emphasizes processes of search in which the child identifies his power and competence in being the author of inquiry and the initiator of action.* The following quote from Parsons and Shaftel (1967) places this principle in the context of psychological and educational theory and reminds us of the potential for learning through interaction with peers.

As far as education is concerned, the chief outcome of this theory [Piaget's] of intellectual development is a plea that children be allowed to do their own learning. Piaget is not saying that intellectual development proceeds at its own pace no matter what you try to do. He is saying that what schools usually try to do is ineffectual. You cannot further understanding in a child simply by talking to him. Good pedagogy must involve presenting the child with situations in which he himself experiments, in the broadest sense of that term—trying things out to see what happens, manipulating things, manipulating symbols, posing questions and seeking his own answers, reconciling what he finds one time with what he finds at another, comparing his findings with those of other children.

b. *Learning is incomplete from the developmental view unless it encompasses both cognitive and affective domains and utilizes the forces—the cumulated meanings, feelings, wishes, conflicts—of the inner life of impulse and affect; it is essential that children have opportunity to express feelings directly in their relations to people in school; it is essential that they have opportunity to reexpress indirectly, in symbolic form, the affective elements of their encounter with the outer world.* These are the appropriate ways in which school can support positive self-feeling and encourage a continuous viable interchange between thought and feeling. Crabtree (1967) develops this principle as follows:

. . . to conceive of thinking in terms of rational, ego-directed processes alone is to abstract a partial picture of what is a complex interplay of events. . . . In part, the inter-relationships considered here are interactions between the rational processes of ego-directed, logical thought and the preconscious processes by which intuitive, or creative, thinking is generated. Mediating both operations are important affective and motivational states of the learner. . . . Young children entering school face critical tasks in learning to endure loss and separation, in learning to move into new roles in a new school situation, in learning to control primitive ways of expressing normal feelings of hostility and anger, rivalry and resentment. School learning goes forward in attendance with these feelings, and with the anxieties which these feelings may, in turn, incur. Teachers can help children through transitions in ways which do not require a rejection of the self for having had those feelings in the first place. In an open and supportive class-room environment, where *feelings are accepted as part of the total configuration of responses made to problems*, children can learn more acceptable patterns of behavior without, at the same time, suffering excessive guilt or castigation of the self. . . .

What is envisaged here is the opposite of a flat, emotionally reduced human atmosphere. There is house room for positive affect—excitement, enthusiasm, laughter—as well as for the acceptance of the negative impulses as human and lending themselves to moderate, nondestructive forms of control. It is, of course, in the latter instance that slum children, already bearing an overburden of inner strife, are most neglected when they find themselves in an emotionally antiseptic school climate. For them, it is especially important that the teacher be aware of turbulent feelings—fear, anxiety, threat—and be able to help children feel comfortable in having their troubles and doubts known to her. She can become a source of emotional support even when she can do no more than listen. In her other teacher capacities she becomes a source of emotional support by providing self-enhancing experiences of mastery and avoiding the pressures that lead to self-defeating failure.

c. *The organization of the tasks of learning should make maximum use of one of the major developmental trends of the elementary years, namely, the tendency to turn to the peer group both as refuge and as authority.* At this stage the peer group is a mechanism by which children establish a desirable distance from adults and their authority and, in so doing, engage in the creation of a society—a code, a pecking order, another authority acting collectively on the individual, another set of mandates for loyalty. Unfortunately, this dynamic developmental process has all too often been neglected by the school. Instead of being enlisted in the interest of learning, it has been relegated to the playground and actually violated by excessive emphasis on interchild competition and one-to-go, question-answer modes of communication restricted to a teacher-to-child paradigm.

If the peer group is perceived as a proving ground for evolving codes of social interaction, it is part of the school's responsibility to give guidance to this process by integrating it into the curriculum design. There are many ways in which this can be done, depending on how open are the perceptions of what a peer group of children can be. The peer group can be perceived as a labile social form through which spontaneous, shifting, exploratory interpersonal reactions among the children can be expressed and worked through. This would involve freedom to talk to one another, to make and unmake friendships; it might call on the teacher to mediate instances of scapegoating, bullying, or imposition of coventry. The peer group can be perceived as a forum for opening up issues, expressing differences, pooling information, or joint planning of strategies for problem solving and further pursuit of knowledge. Here it is required that the teacher be highly skilled in the discussion method of teaching and sensitive to the nuances of group process. The peer group can be perceived as a working society, of the whole or in subgroups, in which the individual contributes skills and ideas to common goals and helps maintain the group as a viable decision-making and communicative medium. Here the teacher's role is in helping the children maximize the possibilities of production through the economy of their resources within their group. Finally, the peer group can be perceived as an instrument for the real participation of children in evolving a social order (helping to make the rules) which can coexist with the social order of the adults in authority and with the morality of the larger institution of which they are a part.

In many ways, the custom of grouping children by chronological age boundaries or according to homogeneous intellectual or achievement levels can be deterrent to the developmental potential of peer group experience in school. There is need for continued experimentation, such as is under way in certain schools, in optimal modes of composing the peer group in the elementary school.

d. *The maintenance of a rational authority structure in a school is a cornerstone in establishing an open climate for learning; its effectiveness depends on the extent to which the relations of those in superior positions to teachers are consistent with what is expected of teachers in their relating to the children.* At all levels there is established a milieu of interpersonal relationship in which there is no room for arbitrary, status-invested control that is exercised through threat, humiliation, or retaliatory punishment.

If we concentrate on the children in relation to the adults in the school, there are a few hallmarks of a rational authority structure. The adults see the importance of investing effort in having children participate in formulating and maintaining regulations and restrictions while inviting them into considerations of what is functionally reasonable in order to protect the basic purposes of school. This sometimes takes persuasion on both sides: "functionally reasonable" is a span, not a point, in social behavior, and it is not written in the stars that teachers and children can easily agree how much noise is too much noise. The rules and regulations are flexibly adapted to the requirements of different learning situations and the realities of different school activities. Rules about how to behave in the hallways en route to the water fountain or the science room are not identical with regulations on hallway conduct during a fire drill.

No matter how rational and flexible the authority structure, there will be infractions of more and less serious nature. In fact, this is to be expected in the middle years of childhood, as part of the children's testing of individual and collective strength. These need to be dealt with, but there is a crucial psychological difference between punitive measures stamping the child as "bad" and corrective measures emphasizing what it is the child must learn in order to hold his position as an individual-within-a-society.

In rejecting threat, fear, and punishment as psychologically corrosive methods of control, the teacher must build potent motivating forces in their stead—first, meaningful levels of communication and feelings of mutuality as a person with the children and, second, an image of strength and adequacy as the means through which the children can build their own strength and gain satisfaction in competence. For the slum child, entrance into this kind of an authority system is often like entering a strange world, anxiety-producing in what appears to him as indefiniteness, or a world not to be trusted because it does not fit previously learned stereotypes about school and teachers. It behooves the teachers and the school to move slowly and understandingly in response to the defensive behavior which this dislocating experience may arouse.

e. *The opportunities provided in school to achieve mastery and feelings of competence during the middle years of childhood should include genuine work responsibilities in school and in the community perceived by the children as realistically essential and as betokening the readiness of teachers to admit them into the world of adult concerns.* When planned as an integral part of the total curriculum, such work experiences extend the scope of effectance satisfaction, create new natural avenues for interchild communication, and connect the child with adult models of work through the performance of stable, repetitive, functionally meaningful tasks to which he feels responsible and committed.

There are many illustrations of jobs for children in school—chores within the classroom or story-reading projects in which older children read to younger or better readers help the weaker ones. There is also the concept of a "job-centered" curriculum design in which each grade level is committed to carrying through a needed function for the school and in which the content of the social studies program is related to the job.[10] We strongly recommend not only an extension of such functional work opportunities within the school and their integration with curriculum content, but would like to see programs of work outside school boundaries developed and supervised as part of elementary school education.

f. *The elementary school child's moral education pertains to the basic motives and principles by which he judges and acts in interpersonal situations and in the execution of life tasks; in part, his moral development will reflect the moral climate of the school as a whole and the values of the school adults with whom he identifies.* It will also be influenced by specific aspects of the learning-teaching design previously discussed, such as: degree of stimulation of ego strength, extent of peer group participation, exposure to diversity of moral views and complexity of moral issues, and capacity of teachers to establish feelings of mutual respect and trust and principles of "fair play" rather than expediency, punishment avoidance, or pressure to conform as the basis for judgment and behavior.

One of the most significant deterrents to moral education is the contradiction between the overt and covert systems of morality which exist in many schools; for the child in the slums this reinforces distrust of adult authority and deepens feelings of disillusion. This aspect of classroom life has been investigated by Leacock (1969).

The approach to sex education, an aspect of moral education, should be made as part of extending opportunities to further personality development in general, to deepen sensitivity to the emotional aspects of human interaction. Sex education should be integrated with moral education as part of the total curriculum and the basic goal of stimulating ego development rather than formalized as an isolated topic. Factual information on sex should be integrated with the health education aspects of the curriculum with consultation with parents.

g. *The teacher (or the teachers as a staff of colleagues) is the pivotal figure in the educative process; she must continuously maintain the balance of her dual position as an advocate in the interest of the children and as a surrogate of adult authority; her success is to be measured partly in the degree to which the children begin to see that these are not necessarily antipodal to each other.* The multiple functions of the teacher in the elementary school can only be indicated here, stated generally. They fall into four rubrics:

10. At the City and Country School in Manhattan, for example, the grade that serves the school's needs by operating a printing press is likely to be studying Europe at the time of Gutenberg and the impact of the invention of printing on Western civilization.

1. To stimulate and guide the acquisition of competence in a variety of skills; to promote conceptual mastery of experiential elements with full awareness of the parameters of cognitive capacity and the salience of motivation in ability to learn.

2. To establish a relation with the individual child that receives him as a person and mediates between the specific reality of his strengths and deficits and the next steps judged desirable for his learning.

3. To respect and support the processes of peer group affiliation, and to guide the peer group toward functioning as an open forum for expression of opinion, differences, problems, and as a collective means of partaking in establishing the regulations of school life.

4. To continuously monitor the balances within the curriculum between, for example, stimulation of originality and teaching of skills for communicating meanings, between open-ended exploration as the initial stage in problem solving and the disciplined consolidation necessary to productivity, between structured presentation of subject matter and techniques of learning by discovery, between the use of prepackaged instructional materials and independent selection of content and choice of technique.

In recognition of the increasing complexity of the teacher's role and functions, there is a growing tendency to diversify the learning activities in the elementary school, and thus to depart from the accustomed form and operation of the self-contained classroom. There is, at the same time, a warning to be sounded in this connection. What appears diversified to those who are doing the planning may be experienced as fragmented to the children who are learning. More importantly, too much diversification may make it less possible to provide for continuing relationships with adult figures. This loss may injure identification processes which reinforce motivation for learning and provide models for ego and sex role identity. Here again, the needs of the slum child require special consideration, especially in instances in which the transient quality of interpersonal relations in unstable families detracts from identification processes which have primary roots in the home orbit.

Kvaraceus (1967), in reporting on studies on education of disadvantaged children, states that they "offer evidence that the competency of the teacher and the quality of relationship—the rapport between teacher and child—are crucial to the improvement of service to the disadvantaged."

PREPARATION OF TEACHERS

Much time was spent by the Task Force examining ways in which the effectiveness of the elementary school teacher could be improved. All of these discussions about teachers and teaching, even where not made explicit in this document, sooner or later return to the topic of the preparation of teachers. This is because no method, model, curriculum, or point of view, written, professed, or verbalized, was felt to be realistic in isolation of the consideration of the delicate but strong fabric of the relationship between children and teachers.

In our discussions we recognize that society does not understand or value those technicians who work with people except when the people they work with are sick. Society values technicians who work with things—at least it understands them. Things are made to make money, and sick people are worked with in order to enable them to return to work in order to make money. Society tends to understand services which are specific to the world of work and economic survival. By contrast, the work of people who deal with healthy, normal processes in other people are often misunderstood. Their function is hard to explain. Their purposes and their means are misunderstood, and their reputation is lost. Some of us felt that until there is greater clarification of the objectives of the work of teachers, they will be regarded by society as technicians whose work has value only secondarily to the larger purposes of an industrial society.

But more importantly, teachers themselves suffer from a separation of function and cause. That is, they have internalized their function as technicians and do not see themselves as being the agents of revision of purposes of the society. To recommend increase in salary for teachers is not enough if then they will continue to make meaningless decisions. High pay alone might compound their already alienated relationship with the systems in which they work. Organizing strikes is not the only sign of the ability to organize for a cause. It would be good if teachers aimed at the highest level of professionalization by acting for certain causes on behalf of the children whose education is their work. Teacher groups must learn to understand the use of *responsible power* which at present they do not understand. Working for a cause is for the pursuit of an ideal, while performing can be a matter of technology. The separation between cause and function is an ailment of the teaching profession which high salaries alone are not likely to remedy.

But how do we put the sense of cause back into teaching? How do we inculcate a sense of mission in our teachers?

Some programs are experimenting with different methods of putting the teacher in direct touch with the individual child through tutoring and remedial efforts, then moving him into a seminar in which he deals with the problems presented by that child, then into a small group, and finally into the classroom. Such programs need to be closely monitored, supervised, and tended by the educators of teachers who in some cases are not very good teachers themselves. Indeed we feel that teacher education programs have to be redesigned so as to provide systematically varied experiences and relationships not only to enable teachers to become competent to teach but also for experiencing their own training as an interpenetration of intellectual and emotional functions.

Only a few guidelines can be suggested here.

RECOMMENDATIONS: GUIDELINES FOR TEACHER PREPARATION

1. Preparation should include the study of child development from a psychodynamic view, organized in terms of drives, conflicts, and capacities characteristic of successive stages of learning. The questions to be probed have no instant answers. How is social development related to the thinking process, to self-fulfillment? What is and what is not latent in the latency period? When are fantasy solutions part of a stage of growth, when a sign of anxious retreat? Is behavior a "language" to be interpreted so as to understand motivation, defense mechanisms, and individual style of thinking?

2. The student teacher needs to master a new repertory of the kind of teaching techniques which heighten motivated and active approaches to learning—how to integrate the learning of symbolic skills with the acquisition of meaning, how to turn a classroom into a workshop, how to lead natural curiosity to structured pursuit of understanding and effective problem solving, how to provide for creative reexpression of experience through play and playmaking, how to make the peer group a viable vehicle for the educative process.

3. A major challenge in teacher education is to use the teacher's direct experience with children in classrooms in ways that give theory some functional reality, on the one hand, and, on the other, generate the kind of questions that demand further theoretical search and study. This happens only under certain conditions—those which place the direct teaching experience with children at the core of the training program. Sufficient time, energy, and actual teaching responsibility have to be allotted to allow the student to become genuinely and continuously involved with a given teacher and a class of children. Seminars on principles and techniques need to be placed synchronously with actual participation in teaching functions. There should be continuous cross-referencing in seminars, discussion sessions, etc., between the teaching experience and the body of knowledge and theory being mastered concurrently. Most important of all, the experience of teaching should be worked over, thought over, and critically reviewed. To this end the training institution should establish regular mechanisms for students to engage with faculty in a critique of the student's experience as a novice teacher.

How this kind of participation in real teaching becomes a professionally maturing experience is described by Biber, Gilkeson, and Winsor (1959):

In the course of training, each student's classroom placements . . . include situations differing in age of children, in social-cultural levels of family backgrounds, and in school practice and philosophy. Experience with contrasting school situations stimulates questioning and provides the raw material out of which to shape an independent point of view. Informally, among themselves, students talk, argue, accept, reject. In guided discussions, they more systematically compare and cross-reference their differing observations. Another level of learning takes place at the same time in that the student sees her own patterns of constancy or shift in the way she responds, for example to differences of class privilege among children, of integrity among teachers, or of degrees of flexibility in curriculum. . . .

Student teaching does not long remain a depersonalized checking of theoretical ideas. . . . In the presence of children, emotions associated with one's own childhood and past experience are activated. Long established patterns of interpersonal relations, modes of response to strangeness, aggression and deviation, degree of anxiety associated with uncertainty—all of these in the constellation of total personality are active determinants of the particular blend each individual makes of the exposure to theory and practice provided for all.

4. Multiple factors influence the kind of teacher identity which the student establishes—among them the extent to which the milieu of the training situation provides models of committed educators with clearly stated educational goals and values. But exposure to models, real experience with teaching and probing analysis of the problems aroused, proficiency in techniques and methods, new and old, and understanding of developmental processes interacting with the life environment are not yet the full complement of teacher preparation. Added to this there must be provision, built in as an integral part of the program, for guiding students toward self-knowledge in the teaching role.[11] By whatever chosen method of faculty-student relationship or form of psychological or psychoeducational counseling, the student should be helped toward integrating mastery of skills and knowledge of childhood with personal values and with the personal experiences of frustration and problem solving encountered in the actual teaching role. Wilhelms (1967) has stated this point with emphasis:

In one way or another we must provide optimum opportunity for the development of self-insight and a valid self-concept. . . . If the climate in individual counseling, in courses, or in counseling-oriented seminars is such that students can bring their evocative, challenging experiences—with all the questions and doubts and exhilarations they arouse—into the open with fellow students and/or faculty, the stage is set for something highly therapeutic. One of the nicest problems of teacher education is how to secure a constant intertwining of reality experience and foundation studies, so that each progressively reinforces the other. . . .

11. For an analysis of a psychoeducational method of counseling in teacher education see Biber and Winsor (1967).

It is time to mount an aggressive campaign and fight back. As education has grown more complex and demanding, the needs of teachers for professional preparation has grown. As the behavioral sciences have reached new insights and educational research has accumulated new findings, faculties in education have developed an increasingly valuable *corpus* of helps for teachers. It is time to expand professional education, not to shrivel it.

This would be true even if we sought only to teach professional students the body of theory and practice they need to know. It is doubly true when we conceive our mission with them as also involving a time of personal/professional becoming.

There is an inevitable parallel between the experience of being a learner and the subsequent experiences of being a teacher of others. Therefore, much of what is said about the role of the teacher in the classroom applies as well to the role of his teachers in teacher education. We are for a highly individualized approach to education on all levels which addresses itself to the individual as a distinct person and paves the way between the way he is and what he is to become.

The recently formulated recommendations regarding teacher education for work with the disadvantaged by the National NDEA Institute for Advanced Study in Teaching Disadvantaged Youth point this out. We endorse those recommendations and urge support of efforts which encourage the teacher to monitor the balances within the curriculum so that there will be adequate time for learning through discovery as well as the acquiring of skills. Repeatedly, we find that what we consider necessary innovation for slum children are innovations needed in all schools.

5. During their training years, teachers should be exposed to various degrees of disturbed behavior within the classroom setting, with an emphasis on new techniques of remediation. Later during their career years, teachers should have available realistic mental health consultation. Realism in this sense means mental health consultants who themselves understand the world of education and the problems of the school system. This recommendation assumes concurrent changes and increased collaboration between educational and mental health systems under national, state, and local levels. Collaborative consultation would also reduce the unnecessary polarization of therapy and education which now exists in the schools.

6. Preparing teachers to deal with a variety of individuality in children as well as with different degrees of disturbance would render less necessary the placement of children in special classes for the emotionally disturbed. The Task Force wishes to register unequivocal disapproval of the present custodial nature of many special classes for emotionally disturbed children, while it recognizes the necessity for special classes for children with particular handicaps. Where special classes for emotionally disturbed children are actually classes for psychotic children, the true purpose of these classes

should be kept in mind; euphemisms such as "educationally handicapped" obscure the nature of these classes and make it more difficult to think clearly about their value.

7. The essential failure of special classes for emotionally disturbed children to reduce "the size of the problem," added to the increased tendency to commit children to state mental hospitals for lack of any other alternative, and the disadvantages of commitment to detention centers cause us to recommend the establishment of day-care and residential centers for the severely emotionally disturbed. We conceive of day-care and residential centers as intermediary structures in the community, standing between hospitals and schools. Such centers would be based on flexible admission and discharge arrangements so that children could stay for brief or long periods of time for day or total care and would not find their return to the community hampered by elaborate administrative procedures. The Re-ED project serves as a good model for such intermediary residential and day-care centers. It would be desirable if such centers were more closely identified with educational and public health agencies than with courts or hospitals. This recommendation reflects our concern with the deleterious effects of excluding children from the mainstream of the life of the school.

DIFFERENTIAL PATTERNS OF DEVELOPMENT
AND NEEDS IN BOYS AND GIRLS

There is reason to believe that severing or at least loosening the childish ties from home is a different task for boys and for girls. In a paper prepared for this Task Force, Dr. Mary Engel notes that writers in the field of the dynamics of childhood certainly think the task is different, although the belief that the process is more difficult for boys than for girls is not explained the same way by various theories. Some believe that girls have a more difficult development task to accomplish because in resolving the Oedipal conflict they have to make successful identification with the mother, who is also a powerful rival. Others, taking the realities of the school into account, suggest that the task of a boy in identifying with the father in the resolution of the rivalry for the mother is made more difficult because of the need for further identifications with female teachers. Boys are presented with the dilemma of moving "out of the frying pan into the fire," in which one feminine reality is no relief from the other from which the boy needs to differentiate himself. Also, the association with masculine role models is made more difficult when both home and school tend to be deficient in masculine company for the boy.

For optimum psychological development, then, the boy would be aided in leaving the female world of his mother by the availability of masculine associations and role models. Ideally, the world of the school would be facilitating if his teachers were men. Not only could men function as identity models, but also the process of learning would be facilitated by its separation from the struggle to gain independence from feminine ties. To learn, one has to identify with the teacher. Identifying with women teachers can hamper the process of learning.

Numerous studies show that the intellectual and personality functioning of boys and girls are more different than alike, at least as far as those attributes are concerned that are most relevant to school. Also, there is ample evidence that the elementary grades are more troublesome for boys than for girls. Girls are superior to boys in most kinds of verbal performance. While girls learn to read sooner than boys in general, there are also more boys who require remedial instruction. Grammar, spelling, and word fluency are subjects at which girls maintain their lead throughout the school years. These differences can hardly be attributed to the effects of schooling because they show up in the first few years of life (Maccoby, 1966). While males are somewhat better than females in mathematics and science, in the language areas girls are markedly superior to boys (Clark, 1959).

By the early school years, boys do better than girls in tasks requiring perceptual and analytic functioning, particularly when tasks require them to restructure a problem in order to solve it. The lead they have over girls in these abilities, however, does not seem to make up for the greater proficiency of girls in language tasks, and there is reason to believe that the matter of school achievement is subject to the working of rather complicated factors, affecting boys and girls differentially.

It is a fact that girls get better grades than boys throughout the school years *"even in subjects on which boys score higher on standard achievement tests"* (Maccoby, 1966). In one study (Carter, 1952), both male and female teachers were asked to assign grades and it was found that boys received lower grades from both men and women, even when their achievement was comparable to that of girls, indicating that the sex of the teacher cannot be considered the sole causal factor for the poorer performance of boys.

The relationship of personality variables such as high motility level to intellectual functioning is different in the sexes. Girls with high motility are brighter than others, boys with high motility are less bright than others, suggesting that aggression may be an inhibitor of school performance in boys but a facilitator in girls (Kagan and Moss, 1962).

Some of these results indicate differences; others point to disadvantages. Sharper arguments for the problematic nature of school for boys come from statistics such as presented by Rosen, Bahn, and Kramer (1964) in their analysis of termination rate (an index of referral rate) from psychiatric clinics (see Figure 1).

Figure 1 shows that many more boys per 100,000 population are brought

Figure 1—Clinic Termination Rates by Single Years of Age, Sex, and Color, Patients Under 18 Years of Age, 1961[1]

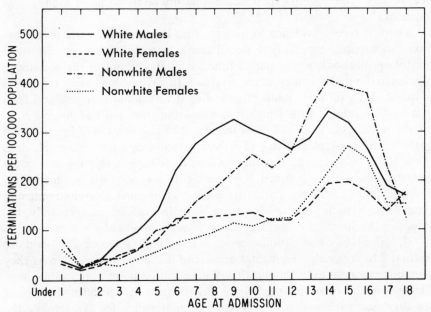

[1] Data for 525 of 616 clinics in 24 states.

Source: B. M. Rosen, A. K. Bahn, and M. Kramer, *American Journal of Orthopsychiatry* 34 (Apr. 1964), 455–468. By permission of the authors and the journal.

to mental health clinics and that the rate during the elementary years reaches its peak around the fourth grade. The greater need of boys for remedial reading also indicates greater incidence of mental health problems for them. Other decisions about children also show the greater vulnerability of boys. For example, in one school system in northwest Florida, more than 600 students were studied with interest about the likelihood of their remaining in school. Boys showed a greater probability than girls to be retained (failed) over all grades. Sixty-five percent of the retained students were boys and 62 percent of the dropouts also were boys. The first four grades combined accounted for more than 50 percent of the retentions in grade, these having been especially numerous in the first grade (Mannio, 1966).

The mental health disadvantages of elementary-school-age boys cannot be assigned either to organismic or to environmental factors. The greater vulnerability to disease of the human male is a well-documented medical fact. But psychological reactions vary greatly with environmental conditions (Hamburg and Lunde, 1966). Since boys and girls differ in qualities of intellectual functioning and personality factors such as motility level, aggression, and conformity (Maccoby, 1966), and since little if any differentiation is made in their schooling to honor these sex-linked differences on the level of experience, the school experience can hardly be the same or even similar for them.

There is recent evidence to indicate that the accepted patterns of sex-linked differences, especially those related to personality factors and social sex-role projections, are in part a function of the nature of the socializing process in the traditional elementary school. In a study comparing the effects of qualitatively different kinds of schooling it was found that girls and boys in a modern school, with a high individualizing emphasis and more autonomous value system, did not show the extent of polarization of interests and goals or the sex-typical styles of behavior that characterized the children of the traditional schools. Findings such as these suggest that the commonly described differences between boys and girls are not only a function of developmental forces but are partly a product of particular environmental conditions, including the trends of the times in a social era, generally, the values of the subculture, and the psychological climate of the school.

If, indeed, boy and girl differences in the middle years of childhood are restricted to fewer developmental areas and are not as immutable as they were once thought to be, implications for education point in new directions. Changes in the nature of the school environment may change the typical sex alignment with respect to aggression or conformity, for example. At the same time, schools may need to change in their attitudes and skills for recognizing and utilizing differences in interest, learning style, and life-role perceptions as potentially contributing to a richer, albeit more complex, learning environment.

In "Boys and Teachers," Dr. Engel draws attention to the problem of the great imbalance in the sex ratio of the faculty. Figures from 1961 show the predominance of women in the public elementary schools: 750,130 women to 127,177 men. This imbalance was about the same in 1959–60, and in 1963–64, and seems to be a characteristic of education in the United States (Simon and Grant, 1966). A search for the origins of the shortage of men in the teaching profession will serve to illuminate some of the causes.

For a long time, American education was dominated by a spirit perhaps best expressed in St. Paul's advice to Timothy: "Let a woman learn in all quietness, with all subjection, but I permit not a woman to teach, nor to have dominion over man, but to be in quietness" (Knight and Hall, 1951).

Around 1850, American women were still under civil, economic, and educational restrictions. The climate of opinion was definitely against the entire education of women, an attitude which seems to have given way under the impact of the development of the first normal schools in the United States, roughly around the years 1839–40.

Woody, in his *History of Women's Education in the United States*

(1929), concludes that in the middle of the nineteenth century, when the number of women in school positions began to increase, this increase was due largely "to the difficulty of getting men for the low salaries offered them." The rapid increase of women over men is apparent from employment statistics from the state of Massachusetts between the years 1837 and 1850. Whereas in 1837 there were 2,370 men employed in schools to 3,591 women, by 1850 the number of women became 5,238 while the number of men increased only to 2,437. Though the rapid increase of women was not as great in some other states, the general trend was the same. Woody states that by 1888 women occupied 63 percent of the school positions while the men filled only 37 percent in the entire United States. Since 1880, the percentage of men in education steadily decreased. The proportion dropped from 43 percent to 34 percent in 1890, to 30 percent by 1900, to 21 percent in 1910, and by 1918 only 16 percent of the total number of teachers were men. Comparative figures with other countries such as England, France, Prussia, Austria, Switzerland, and Italy show that around the turn of the century the proportion of men teachers in public education was less in the United States than in any of these countries.

The entrance of women into teaching professions as well as their rapidly increasing number called forth numerous pronouncements from school men and school committees, as well as from the Office of the Commissioner, regarding the desirability of these events. However, there were as many if not more opinions expressed in the educational literature as well as in the reports of committees about the disadvantages of the imbalance. A leading educator from the state of Colorado put it this way:

One of the most desirable reforms in the administration of the American common school at the present day is that whereby more men may be employed as teachers. Not that a man is a better teacher than a woman. This is not true. But, there are elements in the teaching profession which belong to sex, and the elements proper to both sexes are needed in training and character-making, the main work of the school. A complete course of twelve years can be established only by an equal allotment from teachers from each sex. I would, year by year, alternately place the pupil under the companionship of, first, the man; second, a woman, and so on, from the first to the twelfth grade. In the present condition of society and of the *financial world* this is impossible, but the change will come . . . (Woody, 1929, p. 507, emphasis added).

At the turn of the century the city of Philadelphia became profoundly concerned over the fact that there were 2,745 female teachers to only 126 men. In 1890 the Chicago Board of Education took a strong stand "for the restoration of the elements of masculinity." The New York Board of Education also became concerned about the prevalence of female teachers, but sought to remedy the psychological effects by barring married women from teaching, a decision for which it was loudly ridiculed.

But perhaps the most interesting report on this topic is one (noted by Woody, 1929) by the Male Teachers Association of New York in 1904 which was entitled "Are There Too Many Female Teachers?" It stated that women are bad for boys above ten years of age because (1) men are necessary as ideals for boys; (2) a boy needs forceful, manly control, and he should learn it from a man; (3) men are less mechanical in instruction than women; (4) women feminize the course of study; and (5) they feminize the method of teaching. While it was recognized that the educational efforts of women yield good immediate intellectual results, it was said that "the true test of educational efficiency is what the boy is and does as a man."

The summary of all these opinions by Woody (1929) gives prominence to a report by Chadwick, who in 1914 reviewed the issues surrounding "The Women Peril." He concluded that women teachers have an evil effect upon the manhood of the country and that consideration of the sex of the teacher is one of the most vital questions facing the nation. Female teachers have "feminized manhood" and produced emotional, illogical, and noncombative personalities. The feminizing of boys was seen by Chadwick to result in "supineness" in municipal affairs with reluctance on the part of men to think in terms of large forces, overall effects, powers of war and finance. Chadwick warned: "That such a state of things should continue is unbelievable. It cannot be that we shall be willing to continue this downhill process of character; that we shall continue to warp the psychics of our boys and young men into femininity." He implored that efforts of economizing were made at the expense of the national character.

Old-fashioned concepts and crusty language notwithstanding, the concerns of educators about the lack of male influence upon boys is now about 100 years old. The statistics speak for the greater problems of boys in school and for some inherent sex-linked differences which are not honored in our educational provisions.

We recommend that every effort should be made to increase the number of males in the teaching profession. Increases in salary are not enough to attract and hold men in teaching. With greater part in responsible decision making, with the organization of responsible power in teacher groups for goal-directed behavior, teacher morale could be sufficiently enhanced to offset the imbalance in the sex ratio of the faculty of our public schools

THE IMPACT OF THE SCHOOL AS A SYSTEM

The above discussion still leaves implicit the inevitable fact that no matter how teachers are trained, the way school systems are run has a heavy impact not only on the children but also on the teachers. The impact of the system on the teacher is often deleterious, discouraging, and demoralizing. Therefore, it is necessary to talk of desirable systems within which teachers can function as responsible individuals. *We advocate that schools turn from closed to open systems in which teachers are given an unusual amount of direction in order to arrive at novelty.* In such a system teachers should feel a great deal of responsibility to serve as self-correcting agents in case new procedures do not bring about the desired outcome. Curriculum choices by teachers should be encouraged, and building plans for schools should provide the physical setting in which children can be grouped, re-grouped, mixed with regard to age, and otherwise housed in a manner responsive to changing educational goals. This Task Force's position on open schools was given careful consideration by Dr. Richard Foster in his paper "The Search for Change." Our discussion on this point is taken largely from his work.

School systems which are open to change from teachers as change-making agents have certain identifiable characteristics. Some of the ongoing activities of such systems would include the following:

a. meetings before the beginning of the school year for staff on a voluntary basis in which group process techniques are used;

b. summer workshop programs on staff-developed needs in which teachers are paid a regular salary for participating in workshops;

c. demonstrations by teachers to other teachers of ongoing experiences in the classroom; for such activities teachers are to be released from classroom activities with contract substitutes available to work with their classes;

d. ongoing sensitivity training groups such as T groups and confrontation groups would be a regular part of staff development programs;

e. grade-level meetings, area-level meetings, child study groups, and groups studying learning and child growth and development would be available on a voluntary basis;

f. summer schools would be operated as experimental schools to try out ideas that have been developed throughout the year in workshop and study groups;

g. available consultants would not rate or evaluate but work with teachers as resource people to plan experiences with the children.

Foster notes that several examples exist in the United States of open systems which reflect involved functioning of the collective intelligence of a group, rather than decisions handed down by a few people. In such places, the process approach is synchronized with the systems approach. These are bridgeheads of change. However, it is necessary to say that once a model has been planned and developed in a bridgehead, a strategy needs also to be developed with the bridgehead for the movement of this model into the mainstream of education. Therefore, the development of a model should coordinate the best efforts of a department of education, a university or college, the liberal arts department, the science departments, and the public school system. With this vehicle and with the use of the model as part of the work of think centers (to be described later) a major thrust could be made toward improving the education of all children.

It is necessary that each school system or each school has within it some kind of plan for the continued evaluation of teaching innovations such as programmed learning techniques and teaching machines, which are now being sold to school systems before there has been time to test their advantages or disadvantages. Teachers and principals have to be allotted staff time to engage in a dialogue about new methods of teaching before they are adopted into the school. Particularly, the side effects of new teaching technologies have to be assessed as to their implications for the role of the teacher and the teacher-child relationship.

In addition to embodying this evaluation procedure in the local school, there should be a centralized mechanism established to monitor this activity. One possibility is to make grants-in-aid to state departments of education for a unit with responsibility to register and evaluate educational innovations adopted into public schools; such a unit could be university-affiliated and also undertake training in how to develop and apply criteria for such evaluation.

RECOMMENDATION: A CENTER FOR ADVANCED STUDY IN EDUCATION

Changes in teacher education and in the systems of schools must proceed together with increased rate of training of administrators and middle-level administrator-supervisory and specialist personnel. However, administrators must be trained in the same key of valuing open systems and responsible individual decision making on the part of the teachers as discussed above. The fact is that the educational elite in the United States is extraordinarily small in relation to the size of the educational enterprise. For this reason we recommend the development of a *Center for Advanced Study in Education,* for the training of educational statesmen for the public schools and for teacher education. This would mean a concentrated attack on all facets of the national educational enterprise, bringing together the most knowledgeable theoreticians, the most creative practitioners, and the most promising administrators. Every year one hundred Fellows should be brought to the Center for advanced training in the behavioral sciences, administrative leadership, and the dynamics of change. Each Fellow should come from a position of potential leadership from either the public schools or teacher education and must agree to return to his position following training. Full salaries as well as actually necessary expenses would be paid the Fellow. It is hoped that one hundred Fellows a year would return to their systems and become the creators of bridgeheads of change. Bridge-heading in education, moving closed systems to open systems in the manner described in this report, should be federally supported. Programs which bring universities and school personnel into close working relationships should receive particular support.

SCHOOLS AS BROAD-GAUGE COMMUNITY CENTERS

On the whole, it seems advisable that we structure our thinking about mental health and education in terms of an expectable and appreciable increase in federal support of education. Such increase is seen as the only realistic solution to problems of quantity and of quality control. We also encourage very high and noncategorical investments in education for the early grades.

The boundary line separating the schools from other communities ought to become a semipermeable boundary. Schools should be reconceptualized as broad-gauge community centers, offering many kinds of services in addition to education. In the inner-city school, this would mean that the teacher acting as a responsible decision maker would have encouragement as well as power to concern himself not only with the learning of basic skills but also with the delivery of welfare services to the families of the children under his care. In suburban areas, a school which is a broad-gauge community center might confront itself with other problems of the community such as the lack of cultural stimulation in some upper-middle-class suburban centers as well as other problems of suburbia. It is impossible to anticipate community problems in advance. And yet, it seems essential that schools be forever responsive to changing community problems. At the moment, in the inner city, this means that schools have to become sensitive to the plights of welfare recipients. However, elsewhere in the nation and in a few decades schools may have to become responsive to other community problems. If the school is an open system and does not restrict itself to narrowly conceived educational services, then we would have at least the necessary if not the sufficient conditions for building in change rather than reinforcing rigidity.

From our present perspective it is possible to suggest guidelines for these complex change processes. Parents should be involved in the formulation of the schools' long-range plans and informed of the rationale for the school's major choices and decisions in carrying out its programs. The extent of community participation shall be as great as is compatible with the conduct of school as an optimal learning environment. At the same time, the school's concept of its relevant community should extend beyond neighborhood and parent population to encompass understanding of the social-political-legislative factors which impinge upon the local community and affect the specific realities of school and family interaction.

With regard to specialized personnel in the schools, it is recognized that there is a great need for psychiatrists trained to cope with the emotional problems of physically handicapped and retarded children. Psychiatrists with a special interest in the blind and the deaf are only too few. Many more are needed. Our recommendation to support the financial subsidy of the training of psychiatrists with specialization in these areas should be taken in the full context of the general intent of our deliberations. We see more virtue in a general and massive support of the development of teachers' competence and of the teachers' decision-making role than we see in our provision of an infinite army of specialists to whom teachers could "refer."

TEACHERS FROM SLUM SCHOOLS

We have noted the extent to which slum schools call on capacities of children to reach abstract levels of thought which are often outside the realm of their experience. We have also noted that the problem of control becomes an overriding concern for teachers in slum schools and the extent to which the teacher's effectiveness is gauged by her ability to keep children quiet. Teachers in slum schools feel themselves powerless, caught between the demands of the principals and the counterforces of the classroom. In slum schools the experiences of teachers parallel the experiences of children and their families. Under the pressure, their perceptions of children become undifferentiated and they lose sight of relevance of the educational goals to the children's lives. Although all the problems spelled out above apply to the slum school and give them their special cast, this uniqueness is often an exaggerated reflection of what is wrong, to various degrees, in all schools.

Many children from disadvantaged groups tend to view adults as unreliable, the environment as unpredictable and hostile, lacking in reasonable controls and consistent support. The children's image of themselves is often negative, and typically they show poor ability to focus on tasks and specific subject matter contents. The areas of strength and competence of disadvantaged children do not correspond to the demands for intellectual mastery and competence of the school.

In his Task Force paper "The Slum Family and the Slum School," Minuchin notes that the slum school has developed a style of coping with its pupils which is a composite function of the tension of the neighborhood, the prevailing orientation of American education, and the teachers' perception of the children. Some aspects of the school's style of coping are discontinuous with the home, and some are not. The emphasis on focal attention is, for example, discontinuous with the children's previous interaction with their environment. The emphasis on external controls of behavior and the insistence on obedience, however, do mesh with and perpetuate the deleterious effects of their previous experience with many adults.

That the psychological position of the teacher in the slum school is far from enviable is strongly suggested by Minuchin:

The teacher, after some years in the system, usually feels extremely powerless, able to operate only along the lines that are drawn by an anonymous bureaucratic organization. Though the teachers have a certain freedom in their styles of teaching, they are pressured by the levels of achievement their children are supposed to have reached by the end of a year. They also feel very keenly the directives of the principal that in general "the class has to be controlled"—this is the major concern in the slum school. The problem of control gains an overriding significance for all the teachers in the school; the measure of teacher effectiveness is the quietness of his classroom. As he is graded by the principal in terms of his controlling ability, he is in some way at the mercy of the acting-out of his pupils. The teacher experiences himself as powerless between the forces of the principal and the counterforces of the classroom.

In general, the teacher, like the slum child and his family, does not have a sense of effectiveness. Though he may come out of teachers' colleges with ideas and attitudes organized around the individualized education of children, he tends to abandon these ideas very soon and become adapted to the needs of the slum school system. If he tries, probably ineffectively, to apply some of his best ideas about how to educate a child in the classroom, he finds himself labeled as a "weak" teacher. His class is singled out as noisy, and he is pressured into disciplinarian conformity. Then he finds that he is not so anxious, and that he is more effective. Any attempts he may have made to develop curiosity and exploration in the child frequently disappear. Caught between his inexperience and the system, which does not give supervision and help to new teachers, he takes a more experienced teacher for a model. He is captured by the dominant culture of the older teachers in the school. A fair number of these older teachers tend to be strongly controlling, and though the younger teacher may be unfavorably impressed by these qualities, he may learn that this is the quickest and most obvious way to control a class. His children respond to a familiar form of contact, and he is supported by the older teachers; he begins to feel safer. With his first lesson on classroom control the teacher is apt to start on a path of paying attention to external behavior and to ways of organizing it.

Most programs for helping denied children have been only tokenisms in the poverty program. Large sums of money and massive intelligence must be applied to change the nature of urban schools. While interdigitation of slum school programs with suburban schools will not free the urban schools from any of the present and general problems of education, encouragement should be given to any suburban and inner-city schools that are willing to undertake cooperative or collaborative school systems. Foster notes that unusual financing needs to be placed in this particular area.

Interdigitation of slum schools with suburban schools represents only one approach among many which have been developed to meet the problems of inner-city schools. In many instances radical changes in curriculum content, in teacher-pupil ratios, and in multidiscipline school staffing and availability of special services have been undertaken as ways of increasing flexibility through internal reorganization. Illustrations of change programs that are educationally based are the More Effective Schools Project and the Bank Street Public School Workshops Program in New York City.

Other kinds of innovative programs have been built into schools through cooperation with clinically trained specialists. One of these is conducted by the Philadelphia Child Guidance Center. Faculty of slum schools are invited to observe pupils in therapy whom they have selected to participate in family interviews. In this program the exposure of teachers to clinical analysis of behavior served as a catalyst for revising their perceptions about their charges. Another kind of program is the one conducted in Washington, D.C., as reported by Ruth G. Newman (1967). In this program, confidence is placed in continuous and regular consultation within the school as distinct from crisis consultation. Emphasis is placed on small group work to supplement one-to-one contacts, in strengthening methods of psychoeducational consultation by working with principles of a psychodynamic approach to learning borrowed from psychoanalysis, clinical psychology, and social casework.

Providing for Mental Health
in the Health Services

When consideration is given to the health services to school-age children it becomes obvious that the problems of fragmentation of services, lack of agreement on the unit and methods of treatment, and shortages of manpower plague this area as they do the other vital areas from which the school-age child requires services.

In a study entitled "Health of Children of School Age," the Children's Bureau suggests that the health professions have not paid sufficient attention to the fact that, with the decrease in incidence of communicable diseases and many acute illnesses of childhood, attention should now be given to the problems of psychological growth as well as to handicapping emotional conditions of childhood and adolescence. Material from the Children's Bureau points out that the expected figure of incidence of emotional disturbance for the year 1970 is 5.4 million (Lesser, 1964).

Though the Task Force did not deal with physical health services as such, we must note that many children of this country do without even routine medical care. The problem for the most part is poverty; however, the lack of a massive effort to change methods of delivery of health care is a crucial factor that must be recognized.

Yet, considering poverty and the lack of innovation in delivery of service as the only problems affecting health care could lead to the erroneous conclusion that children from working-class families and higher-income groups receive effective health services. While these groups are more able to make use of available service, the lack of integration of mental health concepts in health and medical practice affects them also—though to a lesser degree.

Health professionals have recommended various improvements for years, such as: early screening intervention; anticipation of problems and intervention in crisis situations; recognition of the mental health implications

159

of physical handicaps in the school-age child; the necessity for service when indicated, without being placed on a waiting list; advising the community of available service, achieving some coordination of local services as well as having and using centralized collection of health information on families. Although there may be instances across the country where mental health services are geared toward screening, early intervention, and various forms of education for mentally healthy development, for the most part psychiatric services as well as other health services are utilized to put out the fires rather than to prevent them from occurring.

In considering the problem of mental health care in the context of general health care, Task Force II looked from the vantage point of how to improve the distribution of health services to all children. We assume that mental health is an aspect of general health, and that the continued separation of services is no longer tenable. Therefore, we argue for efforts to further *integrate* health services rather than endorsing the development of separate facilities which are then difficult to coordinate.

In discussing the provision of health care, we have focused on the role of nurses, since, as a group, they constitute the largest segment of the health professions and are or could be most involved in providing health services to the school-age child. Our deliberations are based on Dr. Claire Fagin's paper, which reflects a review of existing literature on health services to school-age children, on Dr. Charlotte Keller's study of and visits to five facilities[12] providing health care to children in this age range, and on Task Force discussions of these topics.

Information was gathered out of which recommendations evolved on the problems of (1) identification of children in need of health care; (2) coordination, integration, and delivery of health services; (3) manpower problems and new careers; (4) hospitalization of school-aged children.

IDENTIFICATION OF CHILDREN IN NEED OF HEALTH CARE

It is difficult to comprehend the gap between knowledge and action in identifying children's health problems, since the school-age child is easily accessible for health supervision and service. The "Statement of the American Orthopsychiatric Association on the Work of the Joint Commission on the Mental Health of Children" (1967) reports two recent studies which highlight this gap between knowledge and action.

Under the auspices of Friendly Town, an Inner-City Protestant Parish in Cleveland, 932 children were given intensive medical examinations on a single

12. The Roosevelt Hospital Child and Youth Project; Maimonides Hospital Community Mental Health Center; Allegheny County School Health Project (Pittsburgh); Montefiore Bathgate Neighborhood Health Center; The Air Force Program CHAP: Children Have A Potential.

day, through the cooperation of the University Hospital. Most of the children came from families who were on public relief, most were Negro children. A few figures from this one-day survey are significant.

Of the 932 children, 111 were seriously underweight, 587 needed dental referrals, 150 had serious but correctible vision or hearing problems, 26 had severe neurological or endocrinological anomalies. Not only were these findings considered appalling by the examining physicians, who had all volunteered their diagnostic services, but it was found to be impossible to procure the needed corrective services, after elaborate attempts were made to follow through upon referrals.

In a second study carried through in Boston on 1,414 children, aged 4 to 6, and enrolled in an OEO Head Start Project in 1965, comprehensive diagnostic workups in five of Boston's teaching hospitals disclosed that 31% exhibited major physical defects or emotional problems of clinical significance. The brief report of this study[13] declares that "most striking of all was the high rate of emotional disturbance. Nearly 25% of all children had some sort of psychological difficulty, ranging from serious behavior problems to psychoses." The same report states that 28% of Job Corps applicants in Boston had substantial physical defects, "many of which were never diagnosed before."

While the two cited studies are suggestive, they may underestimate the actual magnitude of the problem. Adequate sampling techniques were not utilized and there is no evidence that case finding techniques were sufficiently exhaustive. At the same time, they give us something of a glimpse to hitherto unexamined and undiagnosed children. It cannot be an exaggeration to affirm that the children of the poor in the contemporary United States appear to do without even the most routine medical and psychiatric service. That up to 15–20% of the nation's children (this is the figure usually given for the proportion of families defined as "poor") may be plagued by untreated physical and emotional problems, appears to be a fairly safe conclusion (American Orthopsychiatric Association, 1967).

Despite the problems cited above, there are some questions about the use of early labeling of children as a result of some screening procedure. Such labeling might foster something akin to self-fulfilling expectations, thereby doing disservice to some children and possibly sabotaging positive programs. These questions notwithstanding, there seems at this time to be widespread agreement of the need for early screening and intervention. Ideas as to where this screening might be done include assessment centers as part of other community health facilities; developmental assessment as a requirement for entry into school; and milestone assessment scheduled routinely throughout the child's educational career. The objective of such programs would be the early detection of cognitive, functional, and organic malfunctions.

In addition to questions regarding "labeling" of children, early screening

13. *Medical World News,* Nov. 5, 1965.

also poses the problem of appropriate intervention when diagnosis is made. Unless rapid action can be taken in problem solution the advantages in assessment seem ephemeral at best. Some health services appear to be meeting the need for immediate intervention through alterations in concepts of treatment. These issues are obviously interrelated. We note that although one of the centers visited by Dr. Keller was well equipped to provide services in developmental assessment of children, the specific advantages of such assessments were not sufficiently demonstrated.

The school-age child is confronted with numerous life situations which have the potential of becoming times of crisis for mental health: birth of siblings, death of loved ones, illness and injury to members of his family, school entrance, school failure, divorce of his parents, precipitous changes in residence requiring readjustment to new circumstances. At such times children and families are particularly responsive to help. While the teacher may be the key person in the identification of the crisis situation, even the most sensitive and willing teacher can use support in helping the child. The availability of a health service team composed of school nurse, school physician, and guidance counselor or psychologist would enhance the school's effectiveness, provided that such a team was sensitized to the mental implications of these life events. For this reason it is recommended that:

a. participants in school health programs be cognizant of crisis situations affecting the school-age child and his family;

b. school health personnel initiate and participate in information and discussion programs aimed at primary prevention; planned programs with teachers, children, and parents which would deal with such areas as family living, human behavior, developmental characteristics and problems, patterns of learning, individual differences, etc., should be encouraged and studied;

c. school health personnel participate in investigation of known crisis situations through additional contacts with child, home visits, and consultation with family; and

d. when investigation indicates that services are required, they should be provided immediately with as little disruption of normal living as possible and therapeutically advisable.

COORDINATION, INTEGRATION, AND DELIVERY OF SERVICES

Coordination of services involves dealing with problems of freedom of action, initiative, experimentation, and power. Integration of services involving centralization of services in a neighborhood is even more subject to debate than coordination. It can be demonstrated that there is considerable fragmentation of health services to children as a result, in part, of the supposed value of independence and freedom.

Location of the service is also subject to considerable debate. Several recommendations were generated within this Task Force, although there was final agreement on the desirability of community-based total family services.

An analysis of the functioning of community mental health centers in the United States identified ten centers in which excellent integration of health and mental health services has been achieved. These centers use audio-visual techniques in novel ways, capitalize on fast and efficient information gathering and storage through the use of computer systems, and have achieved an informal and unconflicted collaboration between physicians in the health and mental health specialties (Glasscote, 1964).

One of the centers studied by Dr. Keller was equipped to serve an integrating function but seemed to serve only a coordinating one because it has not been feasible to integrate the new comprehensive health service with a previously established psychiatric service.

A true family service requires a comprehensive mental health approach. Models of such services are available for study in many communities, as stated before. Pending the establishment of such a service on a neighborhood basis, services could be obtained on a contractual basis. The Expert Committee on Mental Health of the World Health Organization suggests that some areas might benefit by the use of mobile psychiatric teams, comprised of psychiatrist, nurses, and social workers (*Programme Development in the Mental Health Field,* 1961). This kind of mobile team might come from the community mental health centers. Many community mental health centers provide services to the hospitals in their area via liaison psychiatric services. Such help could be provided to other hospitals from mental health centers throughout the country. Also, centralized service agencies which supply various businesses might provide information on how this can be managed so as to be of the most benefit to the greatest number of health agencies.

Though health services may originate in the school, treatment of the child should involve community resources. Treatment and service models should be comprehensive in scope so as to include the child, the family, the school, and the community. Effective service requires that the efforts of the various health facilities be integrated and that there be rapid and open communication between the helping persons and/or agencies. It can be assumed that electronic data processing will take care of much health information in the near future.[14] The usefulness of these techniques with interpersonal data has not yet been demonstrated. They should, however, allow far more time on people-centered activities as technical activities are

14. Editor's Note: In its final report, the Commission endorses such data collection but *only* if it is conducted on an anonymous basis, and only if there are a number of specified regulations within any such program that will safeguard the privacy of the individual. See *Crisis in Child Mental Health: Challenge for the 1970's* (New York: Harper & Row, 1970).

taken over by the machines. This is the kind of movement that should be encouraged in all situations involving health personnel. Release of time from technical and record-keeping functions should provide more time for interpersonal interaction. These interactions, however, should be planned on a community-wide basis. It is impossible to estimate the number of people involved in either the duplicating or the fragmenting of services. It is essential that all new plans be studied to determine levels of integration built into the programs.

In view of the above, it is recommended that:

a. participants of various health agencies be involved in planning programs in community health centers and that recipients of care be included in deliberations;

b. there be cross referral from school health to public health agency to hospital when necessary and so on as a child moves from one situation to another. This might be expedited by modifying manuals of various agencies (and professional organizations) engaging various kinds of health personnel to include reference to mental health functions and referral practices. Referral procedures must include notification of direct care personnel;

c. school health personnel assume a major role for coordinating health services for children under their jurisdiction;

d. all new health services should be planned as integrated services to families in a specific geographic area.

It is recognized that some centralized administrative pattern will be required to integrate services on a local level. In addition, *funding agencies should collaborate at the local, state, and national level to support, encourage, or require moves to integrate new and current services.*

Further, it must be noted that the traditional way in which health services are delivered does not reach a good part of the population which they are designed to serve. Only one of the centers visited by Dr. Keller reached out to the poor in offering services. While another used new methods to "advertise," a two-month waiting list was the discouraging result. There is wide debate in the health field as to how much direction and suggestion to give the potential patient regarding health care. A great many children and their families do not make use of so-called available services—they often seem to disappear from sight after the need for care has been identified. Public health nursing practices such as going to the patient to accompany him to the service, giving the patient enough encouragement to go alone, or providing service in the home are now viewed by some groups as methods which should be used more widely. Others see these methods as intrusion of privacy, taking over for the patient, and contrary to psychiatric principle.

Resolution of this issue involves consideration of the problems explored elsewhere regarding the unit of treatment, the concept of treatment, and who should treat. These questions require study and courageous trials to break down traditional practices that no longer meet society's health needs. The recommendations already made are relevant to delivery of services; in particular, those in crisis recognition, intervention, coordination, and integration.

PROBLEMS OF MANPOWER AND NEW CAREERS

Planning for future manpower needs must include consultation services presently needed, educational programs to ensure better prepared professionals in the future, and thoughtful proposals for new careers in the field of health.

Manpower in health services for school-age children is a severe problem which shows no signs of improvement in the future unless recruitment methods improve, types of personnel change, and concepts of treatment are altered. The decreasing numbers of pediatricians and general practitioners in relation to the child population are problematic even to those groups who can pay well for care. The magnitude of the problem for children of the poor has already been stated.

It might be said that the shortage of physicians is a real shortage as contrasted with the shortage of nurses, which can be considered only an artificial shortage. Real shortages create conditions which raise standards, working conditions, and salaries as well as prices in health care. Close to 300,000 registered nurses in this country are not practicing. Many of these nurses might be encouraged to return to work through liberalizing tax exemption privileges for working mothers, improving salaries and working conditions, and making provision for part-time employment.

Whether the present failure to make full use of available nurses is due to oversight, lack of information on nurse education, lack of information about the immediate availability of large numbers of nurses for mental health care, or factors such as status on the health team, it is obvious that the pattern must be interrupted so that community mental health needs can receive appropriate attention. However, some concern has been expressed about the small numbers of nurses entering the mental health field, and those concerned with manpower might well address themselves to means which will attract nurses to this area.

It is important to reiterate that most school-age children have some contact with physicians and nurses. Children are readily available in school, and many states have laws guaranteeing every child health examinations and care through the school system. The vast majority of public school systems in the United States having school health services are staffed with specialized school nurses or generalized public health nurses. Data indicate that school physicians and nurses, despite minimal mental health preparation, are being introduced to providing mental health care and are achieving favorable results. However, the evidence also indicates that the newly instituted mental health services in schools are made use of by immediate referrals which overtax the personnel provided (Albee, 1959).

The report of Gordon Liddle of the Interprofessional Research Commission on Pupil Personnel Services is specifically relevant to school health services. This Commission did a survey of pupil personnel services, including mental health services, in 20 school systems on the East and West coasts.[15] Liddle's group found that the strongest health services are moving toward full-time directors and nurses with baccalaureate and graduate education in public health. He also comments that nurses "are becoming increasingly involved in consultation with teachers, and involved in planning and participating in a comprehensive health education program. Sick rooms in these systems are being manned increasingly by sub-professional personnel and/or volunteers trained in first aid." Liddle further states that "administrators generally are coming to the view that it is wasteful of nursing talent and board money to hire R.N.'s to take temperatures, have children lie down, or take a sick child home."

We suggest that while certain aspects of this should be applauded, particularly in relation to recognizing the strengths of the prepared public health nurse, other aspects from the mental health standpoint must be critically examined. As nursing education emphasizes mental health preparation, nurses will bring with them the knowledge and skills to make the school health program an integrated physical and mental health service. Moving away from the child and family tends to deemphasize the importance of these aspects of school health. While there is no question that other personnel are able to take temperatures, check vision, keep records, and check schedules for immunization, certain aspects of the nurse-family interaction can be invaluable from the mental health and health guidance standpoint.

Many aspects of baccalaureate education of nurses enable them to be maximally helpful in implementing integrated mental health services. For example, formal classwork taught by the psychiatric mental health nurse instructor deals in detail with the reciprocal relationship between physical and mental health. In laboratory settings such as hospitals, homes, and clinics, student nurses are repeatedly able to observe behavioral signs of psychological distress and to discuss these with supervisors. Nurses thus become sensitive observers of people and should be utilized to a greater extent in primary and secondary prevention. Many features of the professional[16] nurse's education would serve the physician too in rendering him more useful as a mental health expert.

15. Personal communication to Dr. Claire Fagin.
16. Professional nurse—graduate of baccalaureate program in nursing.

With regard to the education of physicians the Task Force endorses the recommendations of the Expert Committee on Mental Health of the World Health Organization. The Committee points out that even where there might be a liberal supply of psychiatrists, certain mental health needs might be better met by persons concerned with comprehensive health care because of their specific functions within the community (Lesser, 1964). The Committee emphasized the necessity for postgraduate training for those physicians whose preparation has not been sufficiently rich in behavioral aspects of patient care. The report contains a list of recommended courses and the manner in which the theoretical knowledge can be used by the physician in his practice so that the training will be complete. Considerable information is given about the many opportunities available to the physician to engage in mental health work; methods of assessing his limitations; indications for referral to other facilities; and information about facilities to which he can refer his patients. It was suggested that some means be provided to cover the cost of instruction and also the cost involved in the physician's loss of time from his practice.

The Committee points out that the objective of the training is to enable the physician to become aware of his own attitudes, increase his ability for therapy with the mentally ill, and handle the emotional aspects of his patient's complaints. These objectives cannot be sufficiently stressed when we think of the physician's role with school-age children. It should be noted that the National Health Survey reports an average annual rate of 54.6 per 1,000 children between the ages of five and fourteen hospitalized, with an average length of hospital stay of 4.7 days (*The Role of Public Health Officers and General Practitioners in Mental Health Care,* 1962). Nurses and physicians coming in contact with children during such experiences could do much to promote mental health. Studies dealing with children in this age group point up behavior problems developing or increasing following operative procedures. With few exceptions, programs which prepare pediatricians and pediatric nurses are physiologically rather than psychologically oriented and need considerable strengthening in order that the usefulness of these professionals be maximized in the mental health area.

Available data suggest that some physicians who are providing physical health care are interested in participating in programs which will provide a service combining physical health care and mental health care; others are not, and when forced to participate by assignment, were measurably less effective (*Progress Report,* School Mental Health Project, 1966–1967).

Therefore, relative to the preparation of nurses and physicians to be utilized in the development of integrated health services, it is recommended that:

1. Federal support should be granted for baccalaureate education in nursing so that increased numbers of professional nurses will be available

to provide community health care which includes attention to mental health as well as to physical health.

2. Increased federal funds should be made available to physicians who wish to engage in comprehensive study of the behavioral sciences.

3. Since integration of services requires collaborative relationships among personnel, the educational programs preparing these personnel should include courses and experiences which will lead to the development of knowledge about each other and mutual respect.

4. Physicians and nurses who participate in the care of school-age children should be required to demonstrate understanding of normal developmental processes and an ability to recognize behavioral manifestations which indicate a psychological difficulty, and they should be able to demonstrate knowledge of intervening techniques.

5. Individuals who meet the above requirements, and whose functions include mental health counseling of children, should be provided with weekly consultation with a mental health specialist. The amount of time should be in direct ratio with number of children counseled.

6. Workshops should be encouraged for those now working in leadership positions in specialties other than psychiatric-mental health nursing and psychiatry, the purpose being to integrate behavioral concepts for all physicians and nurses who work with the school-age child.

7. The National Institute of Mental Health should maintain a registry of mental health specialists and mobile mental health teams available to provide services to interested agencies; and appropriate agencies should be notified by circular of the availability of these services.

As a way of ameliorating the severe manpower shortage many attempts are being made to train new workers in the health field. The centers studied utilized a variety of these workers in varying roles ranging from technical or administrative assistance to the principal agency worker in contact with families. The preparation for these new workers also varies enormously from brief in-service training programs preparing groups euphemistically called paraprofessionals to long-term programs preparing "new" professionals. The groups are quite different and pose very different problems. Paraprofessionals are very familiar in medical and psychiatric inpatient services. Their extensive use in outpatient services is one new feature. Actually nonprofessionals in inpatient units have usually been "indigenous" personnel, so this aspect is not new in practice. The *new* feature is the recognition that a "dead-end" job is not satisfactory to people and that career ladders must be built in to allow transition from one level of practice to another. There are possible dangers in both this idea and that of the new "professions." Not the least of these is the fact that the use and advancement of such workers is announced long before the field has indicated that there is a real possibility for this use and advancement. In reporting on the child development specialist, Lourie *et al.* (1967) state: ". . . we were not so successful in fitting these women into the existing system after they were trained. . . . The question is whether existing institutions are flexible enough to use people like this. . . ."

Regarding the briefly trained worker, two opinions remain diametrically opposed to each other. One view maintains that empathy is essential and that a minimum of training will render empathic persons capable of giving mental health services (Truax, 1967). The other position holds that a high degree of sophistication is required in terms of both training and personal qualities to ensure competent practice in this area.

Some supporting data have been presented for the use of paraprofessionals, but more exploration is necessary. Regarding new careers, therefore, we recommend that:

1. Prior to massive sponsorship of new paraprofessional, semiprofessional, or professional careers, there should be selected programs sponsored and studied over a five year period to determine:
   a. use of these personnel;
   b. length of time they remain in the position for which they were trained;
   c. satisfaction with position;
   d. effectiveness of program.

2. Criteria should be established for mental health workers or consultants which are broad enough to allow for a variety of disciplines, yet narrow enough to safeguard the consumer. These criteria should describe theoretical content areas and correlated clinical supervision but should not dictate the specific vehicle or modality of treatment.

3. Health services should be studied to identify aspects which can properly be performed by nonprofessionals.

HOSPITALIZATION OF SCHOOL-AGE CHILDREN

Of particular concern is the matter of hospitalization of school-age children for medical or psychiatric reasons. Pediatric units in the centers studied offered no innovations regarding visiting, planning, or crisis intervention. Research data reporting effects of hospitalization for the six-to-twelve age group are scarce. The following recommendations suggest themselves rather naturally from all of the previous discussion regarding health services:

1. Research should be encouraged to ascertain the effects of short-term and long-term hospitalization (for medical and surgical reasons) of the school-age child.

2. Liberalization of visiting should be built into law (as in England) and facilities for rooming-in of a parent should be provided.

3. Parental participation in hospital activities should be encouraged, and provisions for it should be built into accreditation regulations.

4. Day hospital treatment of children should be promoted and medical insurance companies required to allow appropriate compensation for outpatient treatment.

5. Large state-hospital-type facilities for children outside of the natural community should be discouraged in the strongest possible manner.

6. New criteria should be established for accrediting psychiatric inpatient units for children. These should include: size of unit; location in relation to child's natural habitat; kind and number of personnel; preparation and number of supervisory personnel; program of supervision; therapeutic philosophy and program.

Children Who Cannot Live
with Their Own Families

Youngsters who for one reason or another cannot live with their natural families have generally received inadequate care. This conclusion is supported by a position paper prepared by Task Force member Dr. Martin Wolins (see Appendix A). Wolins notes that the present inadequate state of foster care is perpetuated by misconceptions on the part of professionals as well as on the part of the general public, which is generally misinformed and whose attitude toward foster care is occasionally humane but often punitive. True, some children grow up passably well when institutional or family care is followed by adoption (Skeels, 1966); when certain combinations of child and foster family occur (Murphy, 1964); when institutions offer highly intensive treatment (Allerhand et al., 1966); but apparently children do not grow up passably well in foster homes (DeFries et al., 1964).

Kadushin, reviewing a number of studies of the outcome of foster care, concludes that 70 to 80 percent of the children in long-term foster care have grown up satisfactorily (1967, p. 411), but the conclusion seems too optimistic, given the data at hand. Murphy (1964), for example, designates 50 percent as satisfactory. Gil (1964) assesses 12 out of 25 cases as having achieved considerable realization of preadmission developmental potential. And even Meier (1962), whose results are most often cited as evidence for the positive outcome of long-term foster care, considers but 64 percent of her follow-up cases positive in the five dimensions evaluated.

The examination of a score of assumptions upon which prevalent practices of foster care rest leads to the conclusion that these assumptions are largely undocumented and mostly unfounded, and that some are simply incorrect. Present placement practices rest upon the conviction that access to agency services is reasonably well assured those who need them and that various supportive and supplemental programs (e.g., homemaker service, day care, financial aid, casework) substantially mitigate the need for placement. Further, the foster care system is built upon assumptions concerning the alternatives open to families in distress, upon notions of agency capability, and upon conceptions of children's attributes which do not withstand critical scrutiny. Large numbers of children are affected by erroneous perceptions of the realities of foster care. The difficulties are many.

The fact is that the road to service is tortuous. Many families searching for foster care fail to find it in time to prevent serious distress. Despite the charge to agencies that they must ". . . arrive at decisions . . . make recommendations . . . regarding (1) ways in which the child's needs can be met, (2) the kinds of help the child and his parents want, need, and can use . . . , (3) the services that may be required to supplement parental care . . . , (4) the point at which services should be given or terminated" (Child Welfare League-Children's Bureau, 1959, pp. 19–20), this takes place with much hesitancy and delay. A recent New York study shows that "although family problems were understandably at a critical phase at the time of placement, the data on family situations a year prior to placement indicated that these families (425 families in New York City), by and large, were even then functioning at a marginal level, and that they generally had experienced an abundance of problems and difficulties so severe that it might have been anticipated that further stress could not be tolerated" (Jenkins and Sauber, 1966, pp. 179–180). The point is that *no one did anticipate preventively*. Many of the children even attended school and their distress was not identified. The police referred five times as many cases, and the courts three times as many, as the schools.

Supportive and supplemental services do not come into operation for a very large number of known cases. Again, a quote from the New York study is more revealing than a statistic: "In another public assistance case with multiple agency involvements during the preplacement year, the investigation of the total family situation revealed a variety of critical problems" (Jenkins and Sauber, p. 152). Half of the 90 children from 48 families in which severe neglect and abuse occurred were receiving public assistance, and many of the families were known to social agencies.

A high threshold for admission to foster care which exists for reasons of philosophy and scarcity of resources does not necessarily lead to exertion on the part either of parents or of professionals to seek alternatives. The problem lies in the very high threshold of public tolerance of child neglect, so that difficulty of entry into care may mean only further deprivation of the child and *not* the use of other services. The punitive application of "suitable home" regulations in AFDC did not bring all disqualified children into foster care (although it did bring some); rather, it led some to starvation and malnutrition (see Bell, 1965).

It is difficult to know whether protective service agencies' staffs are callous, penny-pinching, aware of shortages in placement facilities, or theoretically committed to the "mother-child-at-all-cost" dictum. The point of the matter is that a very large proportion of the battered children's parents are known to social agencies prior to the final removal of the child. No action is taken until the case is *in extremis* (Jenkins and Sauber, 1966; Streshinsky *et al.*, 1966). If "separation anxiety" (on the part of professionals) is indeed the major block that the literature claims it to be, then it is well to note that Spitz, Bowlby, and Goldfarb (see Bowlby, 1951), who condemn separation above all else, have more recently been joined by Yarrow (1961), Seiden, and others who hold more moderate views. Seiden has even authored an argument entitled "The Salutary Effects of Maternal Deprivation" (1965).

Contrary to impressions conveyed by an extensive literature, we simply do not have sufficiently good guidelines by which to decide when an incapable family has so deteriorated as to require full-time substitute care for its children. Perhaps the best evidence for our uncertainty lies in the reluctance of judges to abrogate parental rights (Polier, 1958); to allow legally married parents to give their children up for adoption (Heller, 1966); and to decide between the unwed mother of a child and the foster parents who cared for him over a number of years (Wolins, 1963). It should come as no surprise that social workers also have considerable difficulty in making a clean, hard, guiltless decision when the possible continuum of parent-child relationships is artificially made so totally discrete. Given the inadequacy (quantitatively and qualitatively) of supportive and supplementary services, the family is either capable and cares for its own child or is incapable and others do so. The big gray area in the middle, given the trappings of capability and lacking its resources, is the ignored wasteland. Its magnitude is unknown.

Despite widespread belief to the effect that children who come into foster care are usually not sick, they may be sickened by the separation from their environment or by the bad foster care they subsequently receive, but initially, going into foster care is due to family incapability (74 percent) rather than to the child's emotional illness (16 percent) or to severe abuse (6 percent) (data from Jenkins and Sauber, 1966, p. 64). Similar conclusions are appropriate from a study by Maas and Engler (1959) of children in foster care, a smaller study by Boehm (1958), and a study of children in one institution by Elkin (1965) and in another institution by Wolins (1958, p. 221).

Given the major cause of placement—family incapability—it is not surprising that stay in foster care is by no means temporary for most children who enter it, or that it usually fails to lead to a return to the natural parents as some of the literature indicates. Maas and Engler (1959) estimated that some 60,000 children then in care would not return to their parents. Reviewing the nine communities in their study, they show 38 to 58 percent of the children then in foster care as likely to remain so, and another 16 to 32 percent as possibly being adopted but only if proper plans are made (p. 423). "In no more than 25 percent of the foster care cases . . . was it probable that the child would return to his own home" (Reid in Maas and Engler, 1959, pp. 379–380). A U.S. Children's Bureau study by Helen Jeter provides nearly identical data: "For nearly two-thirds (64%) of the children in foster care, the public agencies reported that the only plan was continuation in foster care" (Jeter, 1963, p. 87).

As to the usual assumption that the parents will be treated in order for the child to return to them, this is purely imaginary even in the most prestigious settings. For one thing, many families are already broken when the child is in placement. (Jeter shows only 19 percent of families complete.) For another, the impression of these services to families is generally unfavorable. Maas, for example, in summarizing his findings, writes that agencies relate so to the parents of children in foster care that if the parents are to change it will have to be by ". . . self-healing without the assistance of casework services" (reported in Maas and Engler, 1959, p. 5). Even more telling are cost data. Elkin (1965), in a cost study of one quite respectable institution, showed $8 per year spent in staff costs for service to an average child's family (cost per child: $4,600 per annum). Hylton's (1964) data on services in some of the best-known residential treatment centers in the United States are even more startling—1.1 percent of the cost of care was attributable to services to families of children under care (p. 181). There is always the possibility that the parents were receiving help elsewhere, but it is certainly not likely that their treatment *related* to that of the child. Under the present structure of services the treatment of several hundred thousand children in foster care and of their parents is simply not feasible, from the standpoint of personnel alone (Tollen, 1960, p. 12).

Closer scrutiny makes it apparent that foster care is neither temporary nor permanent; that treatment is an ideal which is not, cannot, and perhaps should not be realized for most children in care. No wonder, then, that some agencies are beginning to feel uncomfortable with this assumption. One of them has recently even come to the point of issuing a formal directive requiring a decision from its staff on whether the plan is for the child's return home or his retention in "permanent" foster care (West Virginia Child Welfare Manual Supplement, 1967).

Stability in foster care is not achievable under present conditions. Placing the child with a good family is no simple matter, and assuring constancy is nearly impossible. First, there is a chronic shortage of foster homes (Wolins, 1963, p. 35). The central cities and rural areas where most foster homes had originally been located are yielding ever fewer, by virtue of the population changes they have undergone. While these homes seem to be successful (Murphy, 1964, p. 591), the supply is drying up. The suburbs, where the agency naturally turns for a new supply, seem to yield less successful homes (Murphy, 1964).

Second, pressure induces changes in selection criteria. The greater the backlog of children waiting to be placed, the less likely are the social workers to follow their own criteria for determining suitability (Wolins, 1963). And, finally, the degree of withdrawal from the program and movement of children from one home to another indicates a basic deficiency. Maas and Engler found 36 percent of the children had moved two or three times, and another 27 percent had moved four times or more (1959, p. 422).

In the face of possible interparental conflict between natural and foster parents (see Wolins, 1963, Ch. II) and confusion in the child's identity resulting from changing foster families (Weinstein, 1960), the social worker involved is intended to provide stability and continuity. But he hardly lasts long enough in one job to do so. Turnover of staff in child welfare agencies is extremely high (Tollen, 1960; Hylton, 1964). In addition to much shifting in jobs, the high case loads make it not unreasonable to read of one-third of the foster mothers in one study ". . . that there have been times when they didn't know who their caseworker was" (Kadushin, 1967, p. 420, reporting a 1966 study by the Wisconsin Department of Public Welfare).

Contrary to the literature and the rather exhaustive criteria lists as to which children should and which should not be in foster homes or in institutions, social workers who make these decisions do not follow any set of consistent rules (Briar, 1963). The factor most closely associated with the decision to place a child in a given setting appears to be its availability in the agency where the worker is employed. Communities and certain religious constituencies have also been known to make these decisions on the basis of available facilities. For example, as family care was gaining favor nationally, some communities continued to rely on institutional care exclusively, quite untroubled by prevailing theoretical winds (Wolins and Piliavin, 1964; Maas and Engler, 1959). However, assuming the accuracy of trends in foster-family versus institutional placement recently predicted by the Children's Bureau, institutional placement should soon shrink to near zero, precluding altogether the need for embarrassing decisions.

Perhaps nothing is more unrealistic among all the assumptions about foster care than the idea that sufficient professional personnel can be trained (in our lifetimes!) to treat children and parents, find and hold foster families, and consult with and supervise institutional staff. Let us consider, for example, the utilization of social work shown by the Hylton study (1964). First, we should recall that only 1.1 percent of cost was devoted to work with families. Second, we should note that the mean cost of social work per child-year was about 10 percent of the total cost of care in these very expensive programs. Given a median total cost per child of some $8,000 per annum (at the time of the study), how many children could the work have been serving? Granted that in less intensive institutions, or in foster families, 20 to 25 children per worker may be tolerable, what are the implications when we speak of, say, 400,000 children? Is it reasonable to propose that social work allocate about one-third of its professional personnel to foster care alone?

ALTERNATIVE MODELS FOR FOSTER CARE

An alternative model for structuring foster care must be based on the reality that families need *varying amounts of assistance at different times*. For this reason child welfare agencies would do better to form a more flexible partnership with their clients than is the case at present. There is no need to create rigid boundaries between "home" and "elsewhere." If supplementary services ranged widely, for example, providing day care for four, six, ten, or twelve hours a day, if they could be used on weekdays or weekends, with opportunities for overnight care as needed, then the entire structure of supportive and substitutive services could better fit with what is actually needed at a particular moment, by a particular family. We can assume that with such flexibility, dependence on these services would be reduced, because there would be room for gradual change of responsibility for children. Such flexible procedures would require an acceptance of a social contract between family and community in which the degree of responsibility for the care of children would be primarily determined by the family, not by outside agencies.

Under such arrangements child care programs would increasingly take on the cast of socializing agents for normal children and shed their cast of treatment facilities for the sick.

It is necessary that child welfare agencies make more clear-cut decisions about the need for treatment and socialization. Some children need one, some the other; if well children whose families are in temporary distress are treated as sick (because there are no facilities for children like themselves), the "sick" population can be spuriously enlarged and many children who would require short-term care can be relegated to social limbo. If there is doubt about whether socialization or treatment is needed, it is best to opt for the assumption of normality.

Because children in the five-to-fourteen-year-old group need peer influence and peer contact, various group experiences for children hold great promise for socialization as well as for cure. Short-term and long-term group experiences (Hobbs, 1966; Feuerstein and Krasilowsky, 1967) can modify the behavior of disturbed children.

Socialization of children becomes more difficult as the child is withdrawn from the real world of the community. Educational and work programs acquire great importance in the socialization experiences of children with disrupted families. Therefore we must be more open to the idea of "child labor" than legislation dating back to 1924 allows (*except* for commercial agriculture, where exploitative, noncreative aspects of child work seem to endure). Through work, children can be exposed to the ways and values of adult society.

RECOMMENDATIONS FOR CHILDREN WITHOUT FAMILIES

The following recommendations grow out of the above considerations, and are taken from Wolins' paper. Their aim is to (1) spread the risks and burden of child-rearing by expanding the alternatives open to families; (2) strengthen the budding tendency for greater reliance on group programs; (3) increase the availability and shift the use of child welfare personnel; (4) increase knowledge about the need for foster services and the consequences of alternative solutions.

1. In conjunction with the newly developing family and child centers or the mental health centers (but preferably the former), establish and publicize a compact on the use of child care services with every family in the catchment area. Except in cases of proven inability by the family to make such a decision, the family should determine the amount of outside assistance it will receive. The family must be protected against the twin evils currently evident in some cases, namely: (a) being forced to care for a child even though the effort to meet his needs is beyond familial capability; (b) punitive removal of the child from a nonconformist family, even when the child's needs are being met.

Comments

a. Families desire to share in the rearing of their children to the limits of their self-perceived capability. Every effort should be made to enhance this capability and help them fulfill parental obligations. However, forcing families to exceed the limits of their capability is harmful to the children, to the parents, and, ultimately, to society. Easy access to the nonstigmatizing broad range of services of the type envisioned for the family-child center should serve to keep as many children with their natural parents as possible, but also permit a less drastic view of out-of-home care.

b. The center should have diagnostic, supportive, and minimal substitutive (e.g., day care, homemaker service) facilities only. More extensive substitution should be available elsewhere in the community but through center referral.

c. The flow of all cases in the center's catchment area should be through the center, and most out-of-home placements should be made within the area.

d. The families in the area may be expected to relate to such a center as they now do to the well-baby clinic or the public school. That is, *the primary image will be one of keeping the family and children well and together, with therapeutic and substitutive services available and accessible.*

e. The fee structure for such services should be tied directly or indirectly to disposable income. This may mean either that services are free to all and the budget is generated from taxation or, what is probably preferable, that a graduated fee for service structure is developed and supplemented with funds from general revenues.

2. A sizable proportion of children who leave their parental residence for substitute care cannot return to their families. Professionals involved must identify these children at the earliest possible moment, and be prepared to provide for them long-term familial or peer group substitutes. (Such a total displacement of the natural family is a drastic and painful procedure to be followed only when it is clearly in the best interest of the child.) The appointment of a legal guardian in such cases is advisable when the natural parents are incapable of assuming this responsibility (see Smith, 1955).

Comments

a. Evidence on the detrimental effects of children "in limbo" is so plentiful that action need not be delayed by any further doubts.

b. The assumption that every child—or even most children—will return to his parents is untenable.

c. Some action to implement this recommendation has already been undertaken, but the process must be markedly exploited. An example of a directive to this effect is the one issued by the West Virginia Department of Welfare.

d. A possibly desirable corollary to such a program of permanent quasi-adoption (shades of C. L. Brace! [1880]) is the appointment of a legal guardian for the child and the provision of fee-for-service social work on the guardian's demand, with payment for the social work services to be made by the agency. (See Piliavin, 1968, for the theoretical formulation of such fees for social work service.)

3. Extend the substitutive programs to take kinship and friendship patterns into account formally when it is necessary to place children, and make maximum use of such patterns while removing some of the economic and other burdens of placements from the relatives and friends involved.

Comments

a. Friends and relatives want to help when a family is in trouble; and they *can* help, but our present expectations are of an all-or-nothing type.

(For example, some public welfare departments will not accept close relatives as foster parents or pay them the usual rates. Rather, they will treat them as AFDC recipients if the taking in of a related child requires an income supplement.) Given relief from the economic consequences of caring for an additional child, and some supportive and part-time substitutive services (e.g., day care), friends and relatives should become a major resource.

b. While geographic mobility in this country is very widespread, the extent of mobility (between substantial catchment areas) among the least capable families is quite limited.

c. The center can function to extend the mutual assistance and friendship structure of its area and thus expand its resources for substitutive care.

d. Those children who truly need only a short-term substitutive placement (e.g., the mother needs surgery; a drastic housing change; intensive treatment of the child) should serve as a focus around which a relationship between the parents and the temporary family helpers (NOT FOSTER PARENTS) can be established. Geographic proximity and the center's emphasis on mutual help should be conducive to such a relationship.

4. Financial and other assistance should be given to the underdeveloped parts of the substitutive service continuum. Specifically, assistance is needed for: (a) day care and extended day programs; (b) full-range foster-care programs (see Recommendation 5 below); and (c) group-care programs (daytime only or full 24 hours) for socialization rather than treatment purposes.

Comments

a. There appears to be much danger (now *somewhat* abated by virtue of developments in day care and group homes) of a narrowing rather than a widening of program alternatives. Thus, either a family got its child into foster care or it received no substitute or supportive help; and when in foster care, the child nearly always went to another family. Greater emphasis on programs other than foster family care should reduce the frequency of these two "all-or-nothing" situations.

b. Massive expansion of day care for younger children, of after-school programs for the five- to fourteen-year-old children, and of all-day programs for mildly disturbed or unsocialized children should serve to help these children and their families and to reduce the flow into full-time care.

c. Persons responsible for helping families with their problems in child-rearing must have available for use (both in actuality and in their own awareness and predisposition) the widest range of alternatives. This means that decisions about the location of children who are to be away from their families (for whatever period of time) should *not* be made by agencies without the widest access to services. A community or an agency in which the range of programs is limited will inevitably end up with some very bad decisions.

d. Group programs with the primary object of child-rearing (socialization rather than treatment) should be encouraged particularly for pre-adolescents and adolescents. The extent of separation from the natural parents should range from all day during the work week only, to all day including weekends, to full-time care. These group facilities particularly should attempt to combine peer relationships, academic and work activities, and an ideology (see Recommendation 6 below).

e. In all these programs, while emphasis is to be upon normality, treatment should be available for those children who need it. Care must be taken, however, lest emphasis on treatment change the public image of the program from socialization for the well child to treatment for the sick one.

5. Public and certain publicly supported housing developments (for example, cooperative or condominium housing) provide an excellent but unused opportunity for the creation of an integrated supportive substitutive child care program. A large housing development should include specifically designated space for a day-care program, for foster children in short-term placements with a designated proportion of the resident families, and for a small residential group program. (See Lander and Birnbaum, 1964, for one possible arrangement.)

Comments

a. The number of available "foster homes" for short-term care can be markedly increased by providing space incentives and child care relief. Both of these are feasible under the above recommendation.

b. Grouping these families geographically yet mixing them into a normal housing environment will ease the delivery of professional services to them and provide opportunities for group action and exchange of ideas while at the same time keeping them integrated with a usual population.

c. Failure of a specific family-child relationship will not inevitably mean moving the child out of the area, since other families *and* a group program will be in the housing project.

d. The older "foster" children may be involved in the day-care facility as assistants to staff.

e. The group program may be organized either in family units (with varying ages, both sexes, and one or two hired "parents") or as peer group (youth group) units.

6. Rewriting of the Child Labor Act and of educational codes to permit (perhaps even to encourage) the integration of academic and "practical" education seems an urgent necessity. A child should be able to work *and* study from the time he has grasped the rudiments of relationships outside his family and the essentials of communication. (This probably means age ten or eleven.)

Comments

a. Foster children and other children from temporarily or permanently incapable families are woefully dependent upon the education and work world to provide them with access to social position and privilege, since such families themselves fail to serve their children in this respect. By separating work and education, we reduce the meaning of the latter and incapacitate the child for the former. They need to be temporarily and perhaps even spatially combined.

b. The setting where children may work should include a number of features allowing for identification, variety of choice, and progression of difficulty with increasing competence. A hospital, a large research facility, an airport, for example, may provide such settings. They incorporate reasonably clear ideologies (preservation of life, development of knowledge, speed and safety of transportation); a very broad range of adult models (from porters to chief surgeons and pilots); excitement as a built-in part of the enterprise; young people learning their jobs and older ones who already know them, thus giving a clear idea of progressive responsibility and its requirements in education and maturity.

7. Personnel is a major problem in foster care and in the supportive and supplemental services which may help prevent extended separation of children from their natural parents. Five steps are required:

a. Increase in status for those in our society who work with people as whole persons. If an increase in status requires more money, a national academy to recognize merit, or a change in national emphasis from purely physical to human resources, then these must be provided or established.

b. Introduce a new semiprofessional position: the Child-Rearer. (A better label is available in every modern language but English: *Vospitatel'* [Russian]; *Wychowawea* [Polish]; *Metapelet, Madrich* [Hebrew], are some useful examples.) This position will require courses and experience in child care which can be acquired at the junior college level. Persons with such training will occupy important positions in day-care centers, group-care programs, and as mothers' aides in certain supplementary services. They may also be employed as personnel in after-school and work education programs. In all instances they should, of course, be used under trained supervision. (Several training programs for such personnel already exist and may be used as models.)

c. Reexamine the use of professional personnel working on the adoption of normal Caucasian infants, the recruitment and selection of foster homes, services to children in permanent foster family care, and (out of foster care) in the review of eligibility for economic assistance. By using higher salary as an incentive, move staff to the mother-child centers, to supportive day-care programs, to intensive treatment arrangements whether in group care or foster family care, and to real work with families whose children are to return to them.

d. Under competent supervision involve foster parents in the formulation of agency policies and the recruitment of new homes. Move older and more experienced foster mothers (and fathers?) into positions of responsibility for child care in the homes of others by giving them supervisory and advisory functions vis-à-vis new foster families, and possibly by shifting to them the task of screening and approving new applicants. (Some work in this direction is already being done, for example, in Los Angeles.)

Comments

This recommendation would require a major paper by itself. I must, therefore, omit getting into details of the rationale and consequences of the proposals. Note that I am not proposing anything about the training of professionals. This is deliberate. The reasons for the omission are twofold: First, the proposal will undoubtedly be made by many others; and second, the functions and numbers of professionals in the kind of enterprise I envisage are insufficiently clear to me to allow honest recommendations, beyond the idea that getting there "firstest with the mostest" may be fine for the military but only half-right for child and family services. Accessibility and availability by all means, but also parsimony, seem advisable in the use of professional services.

8. There is a dire need for two kinds of information regarding foster care: how much is needed and for what types of children; and what the consequences are of various foster-care decisions. To meet this need three recommendations follow:

a. A national sample census of families is urgently required in order to arrive at a meaningful estimate of the numbers who need supportive, supplementary, and substitutive services. Initially such a sample may be quite small (on the order of one or two thousand); subsequent censuses should be enlarged to permit subcategories by area, SES, and other demographic variables. Conducted in a manner similar to the "Mid-town Study" (Srole *et al.*, 1962), such a census will be quite costly per case but not very expensive in total. It will yield information on incidence and prevalence of problems that are currently hidden and distorted by the service structure. We must continue to gather service statistics, but they are inadequate as data for program planning.

b. Several service and research centers should be established in various regions of the country with the primary objective of innovation and research follow-up. Foster-care decisions can and should be very clear-cut, and their consequences are knowable if a specific effort is made in that direction. Our experience with the usual service agency (public and voluntary) has been that, for various reasons, it does not invest sufficient resources in determining the consequences of alternative courses of action. The proposed centers should have exactly that as their primary objective. Secondarily, like the agricultural experiment stations, they should serve for demonstration and training.

c. Encourage feedback research in foster-care agencies through grants made specifically for this purpose. As noted above, agency decisions about children are not now modified by their knowable consequences. Such modification is necessary. (Mech, 1967, in a very detailed paper has outlined the nature of this problem and suggested some specific steps.)

9. Economic and administrative steps should be taken to improve the partnership between public and voluntary agencies in foster care. Voluntary agencies should be encouraged to extend the range of services available in each community and to formulate new approaches in the relationship between families and the social instrumentalities assisting them. Purchase of service agreements should be so drawn as to encourage experimentation and review with the intent that, ultimately, proposals of the cost-benefit type will be made by voluntary agencies both to public purchasers of services and to local funding bodies such as welfare funds.

Comments

a. Congressional testimony on the Social Security Amendments of 1967 provides numerous recommendations in this area.

b. The cost benefit approach to delivery of child welfare services is still in its most formative stages, largely by virtue of difficulty in describing the "benefit" component. (The cost component can now be calculated with considerable precision and relative ease. See Schwartz and Wolins, 1958; Wolins, 1962; Elkin, 1965.) The difficulties in the benefit component must be overcome by defining operationally the desired short-term and long-term results and linking them causally to certain agency actions. So far, agencies have not used this approach to programming and budgeting. They must be strongly encouraged to use it in the future.

Epilogue

The reader may have noted certain general principles which emerge in the many recommendations contained in this report. These principles were not put at the beginning of the report for a specific reason. They were not arrived at *a priori*, with recommendations then emanating from the general principles; rather, as we examined each problem area, and made our recommendations, we discovered that our thinking often propelled us toward the same general principles. Below follows a discussion which may be regarded, then, as a synthesis of our report. It is a synthesis on the conceptual level. Certain features of the foregoing report will be referred to, in order to illustrate the various principles.

Perceptions of the boundaries of psychological realities define the appropriateness of professional action. This principle is most eloquently illustrated in Task Force discussions of the most appropriate forms of psychotherapy for school-age children. It will be recalled that no agreement could be reached here, and that we concluded that at present there was no reason to recommend one form of psychotherapy to the exclusion of another. When the "sick" system, or the "disturbed" system, is seen as the child, individual therapy is recommended. When the system under consideration is broadened to include the family, the community, or any other larger subsystem, the intervention of choice changes to include the system *as defined*. It is fruitless to argue about alternative forms of therapy, putting one in competition with another; deliberations ought to be about the choice of systems for intervention because all else, even the last detail of recommendations, follows from the choice of systems. This principle will be unsatisfying to those who look for all-or-none recommendations, offered without doubt or ambivalence. Intellectually, however, it seems to be an undeniable truth: the choice of size and scope of systems determines the

184

intervention; recommended action can never be evaluated out of this larger context.

This principle inadvertently determined not only our choice of recommendations, where we could agree, but also what was discarded. For example, we have chosen not to favor sex education courses on a large scale because we could not think of concerns about sexuality existing separate from total cognitive and emotional growth on the one hand, and the broader curriculum on the other. We felt that an otherwise unresponsive and unpsychologically minded curriculum with either a course in sex or a course in mental health *attached* is a grotesque state of affairs.

The usually overused words "integration" and "comprehensive" appearing throughout this report are enlisted in the same spirit. For example, it appeared senseless to write recommendations about "mental health services in the schools" ignoring what to us appeared to be a truth, that mental health is part of the total health of an individual. Hence our criticism of fragmented programs, disjointed attempts at help, which often appear as *pieces from several different kinds of puzzles*, destined never to fit into a cohesive whole.

Phenomena which are continuous in nature are often made arbitrarily discrete; this is an undesirable feature of our policies toward children. The clearest example of this principle can be seen in our discussion of foster care. We have observed that in our society either children are seen as belonging in and with the family or they are seen as needing to be entirely out of it. There was a conviction in the Task Force that families need varying amounts of help at various times, and that the most commonly occurring reality may be need for *partial* help for brief periods of time. Also, in education, we raised the question of why the separation of children into age-homogeneous classes should be such an unquestioned practice, when so often chronological age does not correspond to psychological maturity. Development of an individual is a continuous phenomenon, and periods of growth spurt and moratoria are part of this continuity. It may well be that educational goals would be better served by grouping children according to principles very different from that of age homogeneity. We recommend a great increase in the *degree of flexibility* with which we act toward children. A rigid system cannot be responsive to the needs of people.

Our recommendation for increasing the community orientation in schools is in the same spirit of greater flexibility and responsiveness to changing needs. If we say "here is the community and there is the school," we have already dichotomized what belongs together, because in a very real sense the school *is* the community, an expression of its values, convictions, and goals. When we say "this is therapy and this is education," we are committing the same error of creating dichotomy out of an integral belonging. Therapy which is not educative or (good) education which does not lead to increased ego strength seems inconceivable in terms of the goals in each professional field. Our social institutions must begin to reflect unity where unity exists, and must cease creating artificial separations within which to exist, as in a self-created prison. Where separate institutional approaches are necessary, we recommend that there be semipermeable boundaries.

Children who do not fit into the mainstream of society or who have been excluded from it cannot be socialized by further exclusion from the mainstream of social realities. Children whose lives will require them to work and whose personalities would profit from working in realistic settings cannot be prepared for the world of work by exclusion from it. It was in this spirit that we recommended altering child labor laws. Boys who need to grow up to be men cannot gain nutriment for their evolving masculinity by being isolated from men and shut into a world of women. For this reason we recommended an increase in the number of male teachers. Children who cannot keep up with their group cannot learn to do so by being placed into a class of "educationally handicapped" or any other class, by whatever euphemism, which deprives them of information about and models for healthy development. We urged that special classes of various sorts be used only in the most extreme circumstances. We urged that children not be committed to state institutions and other places not suitable for youngsters and argued for the continued inclusion of deviant children in the mainstream of society. We argued for a *greater tolerance for deviance* on the part of everyone dealing with children. Our recommendation called for the development of community-based residential settings to take the place of state mental institutions.

Not only the content of services but also the method of delivery of services has a profound effect upon the recipients of the services. If children are hospitalized in ways that are incomprehensible to them or frightening to them, symptoms may be cured, physical health may be restored, but the method of hospitalization may leave a profound and deleterious effect. If fatherless families need public assistance, they may get the money, but the method of delivery of the public bounty may discourage the development of initiative, self-respect, and the wish to again take charge of one's destiny. Our discussions of the undesirable side effects of the method of delivery of welfare services illustrates this principle. If schools believe in the need for punishment, the manner of bringing discipline to bear on children's behavior can unteach what the disciplining is supposed to teach. We argue against the continuation of the bureaucratization of children's lives. Rules have to be comprehensible to children.

The preparation and subsequent treatment of professionals by their teachers and superiors affect not only their obviously measurable com-

petence but, more importantly, their way of perceiving their professional role. Poorly taught teachers may be competent in certain intellectual areas, but they cannot be good teachers in the sense in which we have described this ability. Teachers who cannot use their political power responsively in decision making about how schools should be run are also limited in their personal effectiveness with children. Adults who are not allowed to function autonomously and responsibly cannot impart such abilities to youngsters. Nurses whose duties deteriorate to bookkeeping or temperature taking cannot use their potential in early detection and program planning for prevention. We urge that a great deal of attention be given to *how* professionals are educated, not only with respect to obvious kinds of skills, but also in relation to the development of professional identity, sense of responsibility, autonomy, and connection with the *inner living* involved in performing any professional role in any helping or educative work. Our recommendation for the development of an Institute for Advanced Study for Educators partakes of this principle because the quality of teacher training and educational policy making so obviously affects what goes on between children and adults in classrooms.

Future policy making for the welfare of children will have to be based on more research evidence than is now available. On some of the most critical questions before us, for example the effectiveness of psychotherapy with different kinds of children, research evidence is very scarce. In the area of adoption and foster care, research efforts are hampered by poor information on the very level of help-dispensing agencies. All through this report sounds the refrain: much more data ought to be available on various aspects of child mental health. We wove recommendations for the initiation of research through all parts of this report; reiterating would be useless and rather like a list of complaints.

Appendix

POSITION PAPERS OF TASK FORCE II

Belmont, Herman S., M.D., "Common Denominators," June 1967, 5 pp.
————, "Introductory Material Concerning the Area of Psychological Disorders in Childhood from Age 5–12," n.d.
————, "The Psychotherapies of the School-Age Child," February 1968, 40 pp.
Biber, Barbara, Ph.D., "Developmental Characteristics in the Middle Years of Childhood," May 1967, 8 pp.
————, "Education and Mental Health in the Elementary School—Précis for Final Report," January 1968, 25 pp.
————, "Recommendations for the Functioning of the Elementary School in the Interests of Positive Development During the Middle Years of Childhood," June 1967, 27 pp.
————, "The School's Responsibility for the Mental Health of Children: Ego Strength and Individuality," June 1967, 3 pp.
————, "Steps Essential for Implementing an Expanded Concept of the School's Responsibility for the Education of the Elementary School Child," June 1967, 3 pp.
Engel, Mary, Ph.D., "Boys and Teachers—A Discussion of Certain Kind of Imbalance in Public Education," 1967, 18 pp.
————, "Summary of Conference on Special Education, Joint Commission on Mental Health of Children," July 10–11, 1967, 12 pp.
————, "Training in Clinical Child Psychology," January 19, 1968, 8 pp.
Fagin, Claire M., Ph.D., "The Nurse and the School-Age Child," 1967, 20 pp.
————, "Outline of Developmental Tasks of the School-Age Child," 1967, 6 pp.
————, "Providing for Mental Health in Health Services for Children in the 6–12 Age Group," January 1968, 71 pp.
Foster, Richard L., Ph.D., "The Search for Change," 1967, 8 pp.
Kohlberg, Lawrence, Ph.D., and Jean E. La Crosse, Ph.D., "Predictability of Adult Mental Health from Childhood Behavior," February 1968.

Minuchin, Salvador, M.D., "The Slum Family and the Slum School," 1967, 38 pp.

————, "Treatment and Services for the Disturbed Child," September 1967, 17 pp.

Minuchin, Salvador, M.D., and Jay Haley, "Broadening the Unit of Intervention: The Delivery of Services According to an Ecological Model," 1967, 108 pp.

Wolins, Martin, Ph.D., and Mary Jane Owen, "Foster Care Assumption, Evidence and Alternatives: An Exploratory Analysis," 1969, 71 pp.

References

Ackerman, N. W. *The Psychodynamics of Family Life*. New York: Basic Books, 1958.

Albee, G. W. *Mental Health Manpower Trends*. Monographs Series No. 3, Joint Commission on Mental Illness and Health. New York: Basic Books, 1959.

Allerhand, M. E., Weber, R. E., and Haug, M. *Adaptation and Adaptability: The Belljaire Follow-Up Study*. New York: Child Welfare League of America, 1966.

American Orthopsychiatric Association. "Statement of the American Orthopsychiatric Association on the Work of the Joint Commission on Mental Health of Children." 1967.

American Psychiatric Association. *Planning Psychiatric Services for Children in the Community Mental Health Program*. Washington, D.C.: American Psychiatric Association, 1964.

Bell, W. *Aid to Dependent Children*. New York: Columbia University Press, 1965.

Biber, B. "Integration of Mental Health Principles in the School Setting," in G. Caplan (ed.), *Prevention of Mental Disorders in Children*. New York: Basic Books, Inc., 1961.

——. "A Paradigm for Integrating Intellectual and Emotional Processes," in E. M. Bower and W. G. Hollister (eds.), *Behavioral Science Frontiers in Education*. New York: John Wiley and Sons, Inc., 1967. See also chapters 2 and 5.

Biber, B., Gilkeson, E., and Winsor, C. B. "Basic Approaches to Mental Health: Teacher Education at Bank Street College," *Personnel and Guidance Journal*, Apr. 1959.

Biber, B., and Winsor, C. B. "An Analysis of the Guidance Function in a Graduate Teacher Education Program," in *Mental Health and Teacher Education*, 46th Yearbook, Association for Student Teaching, 1967.

Boehm, B. *Deterrents to Adoption of Children in Foster Care.* New York: Child Welfare League of America, 1958.

Bowlby, J. *Maternal Care and Mental Health.* Geneva: World Health Organization, 1951.

Brace, C. L. *The Dangerous Classes of New York and Twenty Years' Work Among Them.* New York: Wynkoop & Hallenbeck, 1880.

Briar, S. "Clinical Judgment in Foster Care Placement," *Child Welfare*, 41 (1963), 161–169.

Carter, R. "How Invalid Are Marks Assigned By Teachers?" *Journal of Educational Psychology*, 43 (1952), 218–228.

Chadwick, F. E. "The Women Peril," *Educational Review*, XLVII, 109 (February 1914), 109–119.

Child Welfare League of America and U.S. Children's Bureau. *Child Welfare as a Field of Social Work Practice.* New York: CWLA-CB, 1959.

Clark, W. W. "Boys and Girls—Are There Significant Ability and Achievement Differences?" *Phi Delta Kappan*, 41 (1959), 73–74.

Crabtree, C. "Supporting Reflective Thinking in the Classroom," in J. Fair and F. R. Shaftel (eds.), *Effective Thinking in the Social Studies.* National Council for Social Studies, 1967.

DeFries, Z., Jenkins, S., and Williams, E. C. "Treatment of Disturbed Children in Foster Care," *American Journal of Orthopsychiatry*, 34, 4 (July 1964), 615–624.

Elkin, R. *Analyzing Time, Costs, and Operations in a Voluntary Children's Institution and Agency.* Washington, D.C.: U.S. Children's Bureau, 1965.

Engel, M., Marsden, G., and Woodaman, S. "Orientation to Work in Children," *American Journal of Orthopsychology,* in press.

Erikson, E. H. "The Problem of Ego Identity," in M. R. Stein *et al.* (eds.), *Identity and Anxiety.* Glencoe, Ill.: Free Press, 1960, pp. 37–87.

Feuerstein, R., and Krasilowsky, D. "The Treatment Group Technique," *The Israel Annals of Psychiatry and Related Disciplines*, 5, 1 (Spring 1967), 61–90.

Gil, D. "Developing Routine Follow-Up Procedures for Child Welfare Services," *Child Welfare*, 43 (May 1964).

Glasscote, R. *The Community Mental Health Center: An Analysis of Existing Models.* Washington, D.C.: Publication of the Joint Information Service of the American Psychiatric Association and the National Association for Mental Health, 1964.

Group for the Advancement of Psychiatry. *Psychopathological Disorders in Childhood: Theoretical Considerations and a Proposed Classification.* Vol. VI, Report 62, June 1966. New York: Group for the Advancement of Psychiatry, 2d printing, Apr. 1967.

Hamburg, D. A., and Lunde, D. T. "Sex Hormones in the Development of Sex Differences in Human Behavior," in E. E. Maccoby (ed.), *The Development of Sex Differences.* Stanford, Calif.: Stanford University Press, 1966, pp. 1–24.

Heller, E. "Applications by Married Parents for Adoption Placement of Their In-Wedlock Children," *Child Welfare*, 45, 7 (1966), 404–409.

Henry, J. *Culture Against Man*. New York: Random House, 1963.

Hobbs, N. "Helping Disturbed Children: Psychological and Ecological Strategies," *American Psychologist*, 21, 12 (Dec. 1966), 1105–1115.

Hollister, W. G. "Designing Curricula to Strengthen Ego Processes." Paper delivered at Conference of American Orthopsychiatric Association, March 1967.

Hylton, L. F. *The Residential Treatment Center*. New York: Child Welfare League of America, 1964.

Jenkins, S., and Sauber, M. *Paths to Child Placement*. New York: N.Y.C. Dept. of Welfare and the Community Council of Greater New York, 1966.

Jeter, H. R. *Children, Problems and Services in Child Welfare Programs*. Washington, D.C.: U.S. Government Printing Office, 1963.

Johnson, President Lyndon B. "Recommendations for the Welfare of Children." Feb. 8, 1967.

Kadushin, A. *Child Welfare Services*. New York: Macmillan Co., 1967.

Kagan, J., and Moss, H. A. *Birth to Maturity: The Fels Study of Psychological Development*. New York: Wiley, 1962.

Kagan, J., Moss, H. A., and Siegel, I. E. "Conceptual Style and the Use of Affect Labels," *Merrill-Palmer Quarterly*, 6 (1960), 261–278.

Knight, E., and Hall, C. L. (eds.). *Readings in American Educational History*. New York: Appleton, 1951.

Kvaraceus, W. C. "The Disadvantaged Learner: Some Implications for Teachers and Teaching." Paper presented at Sixth Work Conference on Curriculum and Teaching in Depressed Urban Areas, Teachers College, Columbia University, 1967.

Lander, B., and Birnbaum, R. *The Utilization of Subsidized Housing in Family and Welfare Services*. Lavanburg: Corner House, 1964.

Leacock, E. B. *Teaching and Learning in City Schools*. New York: Basic Books, Inc., 1969.

Lesser, A. *Health of Children of School Age*. Children's Bureau Publication No. 427, U.S. Dept. of Health, Education, and Welfare. Washington, D.C.: U.S. Government Printing Office, 1964.

Lewis, Hylan. "The Family: Resources for Change," in L. Rainwater and W. L. Yancey, (eds.), *The Moynihan Report and the Politics of Controversy*. Cambridge: MIT Press, 1967, pp. 314–343.

Lourie, R. S., Rioch, M. J., and Schwartz, S. "The Concept of a Training Program for Child Development Counselors," *American Journal of Public Health*, 57, 10 (Oct. 1967), 1758.

Maas, H. S., and Engler, R. E., Jr. *Children in Need of Parents*. New York: Columbia University Press, 1959.

Maccoby, E. E. (ed.). *The Development of Sex Differences*. Stanford, Calif.: Stanford University Press, 1966.

Mannio, F. V. "A Cohort Study of School Withdrawals with Implications for Mental Health," *Community Mental Health Journal*, 2 (1966), 146–151.

Marans, A. E., and Lourie, R. S. "Hypotheses Regarding the Effects of Child-Rearing Patterns on the Disadvantaged Child," in J. Hellmuth (ed.), *The Disadvantaged Child*, Vol. I. Seattle, Wash.: Special Child Publications, 1967.

Mech, E. V. "Decision Theory in Foster Care Practice." Paper prepared for the Practice Commission on Foster Care, Child Welfare League of America, 1967 (mimeo.).

Meier, E. G. "Former Foster Children as Adult Citizens." Unpublished doctoral dissertation, Columbia University School of Social Work, 1962.

Minuchin, P., Biber, B., Shapiro, E., and Zimiles, H., *The Psychological Impact of School Experience*. New York: Basic Books, Inc., 1969.

Minuchin, S., Montalvo, B., Guerney, B. G., Rosman, B. L., and Schumar, F. *Families of the Slums: An Exploration of Their Structure and Treatment.* New York: Basic Books, Inc., 1967.

Murphy, H. B. M. "Foster Home Variables and Adult Outcomes," *Mental Hygiene*, 48, 4 (Oct. 1964).

National Institute of Mental Health. *Outpatient Psychiatric Clinics, 1965.* Washington, D.C.: U.S. Dept. of Health, Education, and Welfare, 1965(a).

————. *Research Activities.* Washington, D.C.: National Institute of Mental Health, 1965(b).

Newman, R. *Psychological Consultation in the Schools.* New York: Basic Books, 1967.

Parsons, T. W., and Shaftel, F. R. "Thinking and Inquiry: Some Critical Issues," in J. Fait and F. R. Shaftel (eds.), *Effective Thinking in the Social Studies.* National Council for Social Studies, 1967.

Piliavin, I. "Restructuring the Provision of Social Services," *Social Work* (Jan. 1968).

Polier, J. W. *Parental Rights.* New York: Child Welfare League of America, 1958.

Programme Development in the Mental Health Field. Tenth Report of the Expert Committee on Mental Health, World Health Organization, Technical Report Series No. 223, 1961, p. 1461.

Progress Report, School Mental Health Project, 1966–1967. Allegheny County Health Department, Pittsburgh, Pa., 3–9.

The Role of Public Health Officers and General Practitioners in Mental Health Care. Eleventh Report of the Expert Committee on Mental Health, World Health Organization Technical Report Series No. 235, 1962. (See pp. 13–14.)

Rosen, B. M., Bahn, A. K., and Kramer, M. "Demographic and Diagnostic Characteristics of Psychiatric Clinic Out-patients in the U.S.A. 1961," *American Journal of Orthopsychiatry*, 34 (1964), 455–468.

Sanford, N. "The Development of Cognitive-Affective Processes through Education," in E. M. Bower and W. G. Hollister (eds.), *Behavioral Science Frontiers in Education.* New York: John Wiley and Sons, 1967.

Schwartz, E. E., and Wolins, M. *Cost Analysis in Child Welfare Services.* Washington, D.C.: U.S. Government Printing Office, 1958.

Seiden, R., "The Salutary Effects of Maternal Deprivation," *Social Work*, 10, 4 (1965), 25–29.

Simon, K. A., and Grant, W. V. *Digest of Educational Statistics.* Washington, D.C.: U.S. Government Printing Office, 1966.

Skeels, H. M. *Adult Status of Children with Contrasting Early Life Experiences,*

31, 3. Chicago: The Society for Research in Child Development, 1966.

Smith, B. M. "Evaluation of Exchange of Persons," *International Social Science Bulletin*, 7, 3, UNESCO (1955). (See p. 389.)

Srole, L., Langner, T. S., Michael, S. T., Opler, M. K., and Rennie, T. A. C. *Mental Health in the Metropolis: The Mid-town Manhattan Study*. New York: McGraw-Hill, 1962.

Streshinsky, N., Billingsley, A., and Gurgin, V. "A Study of Social Work Practice in Protective Services: It's Not What You Know, It's Where You Work," *Child Welfare*, 45, 8 (Oct. 1966), 444–451.

Tollen, W. B. *Study of Staff Losses in Child Welfare and Family Service Agencies*. Washington, D.C.: U.S. Government Printing Office, 1960.

Truax, C. B. "The Training of Nonprofessional Personnel in Therapeutic Inter-personal Relationships," *American Journal of Public Health*, 57, 10 (Oct. 1967), 1778–1791.

Vogel, E. F., and Bell, N. W. "The Emotionally Disturbed Child as the Family Scapegoat," in N. W. Bell and E. F. Vogel (eds.), *A Modern Introduction to the Family*. Glencoe, Ill.: Free Press, 1960, pp. 382–397.

Weinstein, E. A. *The Self-Image of the Foster Child*. New York: Russell Sage Foundation, 1960.

West Virginia Child Welfare Manual Supplement, "Selection and Use of Perma-nent Foster Family Homes," 1967, Sections 10400–10464.

Wilhelms, F. T. "Applications in Teacher Education," in *Mental Health and Teacher Education*, 46th Yearbook, The Association for Student Teaching, 1967.

Wolins, M. "Cost of Care in a Children's Institution," in E. E. Schwartz and M. Wolins, *Cost Analysis in Child Welfare Services*. Washington, D.C.: U.S. Government Printing Office, 1958.

———. *A Manual for Cost Analysis in Institutions for Children*. Parts I and II. New York: Child Welfare League of America, 1962.

———. *Selecting Foster Parents*. New York: Columbia University Press, 1963.

Wolins, M., and Piliavin, T. *Institution or Foster Family: A Century of Debate*. New York: Child Welfare League of America, 1964.

Woody, T. *A History of Women's Education in the United States*. Vol. I. New York: Science Press, 1929.

Yarrow, L. J. "Maternal Deprivation: Toward an Empirical and Conceptual Re-Evaluation," *Psychology Bulletin*, 58, 6 (1961), 459–490.

III

STUDIES OF ADOLESCENTS AND YOUTH

REPORT OF TASK FORCE III

Edited by Rita Pennington, M.A.

As the report of Task Force II has indicated, the middle years of child-hood can be a time of healthy emotional and mental growth if children are provided the care and services appropriate to their developmental needs.

Adolescence brings with it a new set of social and psychological tasks and the need for services designed for this stage of life. In the report which follows, Task Force III provides a portrayal of these developmental tasks and needs and an analysis of the changes which occur as the young person moves through adolescence to young adulthood.

—Editor

Members of Task Force III

Chairman: EDWARD JOSEPH SHOBEN, JR., PH.D.
Center for Higher Education
Foster Hall
State University of New York at Buffalo
Buffalo, New York

JUNE CHARRY, PH.D.
School Psychologist
Hartsdale Public Schools
Hartsdale, New York

JAMES P. DIXON, PH.D.
President
Antioch College
Yellow Springs, Ohio

W. EUGENE GROVES, B.A.
Past President
U.S. National Student Association
Baltimore, Maryland

FELIX P. HEALD, M.D.
Pediatrician in Chief
Children's Hospital of the
District of Columbia
Washington, D.C.

KENNETH KENISTON, PH.D.
Associate Professor
Department of Psychiatry
School of Medicine
Yale University
New Haven, Connecticut

WILLIAM C. KVARECEUS, PH.D.
Professor of Education and Sociology
Chairman of the Education
Department
Clark University
Worcester, Massachusetts

JOE P. MALDONADO, A.C.S.W.
Deputy Director
Regional Office of Economic
Opportunity
San Francisco, California

MORRIS F. MAYER, PH.D.
Executive Director
Bellefaire Treatment Center
Cleveland, Ohio

BERNICE MILBURN MOORE, PH.D.
Assistant for Community Programs and
Professional Education
Hogg Foundation for Mental Health
University of Texas
Austin, Texas

NORMAN E. ZINBERG, M.D.
Assistant Clinical Professor of
Psychiatry
Faculty of Medicine
Harvard University
Cambridge, Massachusetts

Acknowledgments

The Task Force wishes to thank Mr. Donald Eberly and Dr. Leon Bramson, who served as consultants in the areas of youth service. Mr. Philip M. Holland of the U.S. National Student Association was most helpful in the vital area of drug abuse. Special thanks and appreciation are extended to Mrs. Barbara Sowder of the Commission staff, and to Miss Lorena Jones and Mrs. Betty Bogan for their assistance in the preparation of this report.

Introduction

This report on adolescence and youth is composed substantially of working papers generated by Task Force members and material provided by contracts requested by the group.[1] In order to develop some uniformity in writing style and to keep the report to a reasonable length, some papers were necessarily excerpted, condensed, or paraphrased. In those sections of the report which are not based on position papers, I have tried to remain true to the thinking of the Task Force as it developed during the many Task Force deliberations.

As this report was not completed until after the research phase of the Joint Commission on Mental Health of Children had been dissolved, Task Force members were not able to give extensive study to the final draft before publication. However, all working papers were reviewed and discussed previously, as were the first two drafts of the report. The basic recommendations were hammered out at Task Force meetings, where consensus was reached on major issues.

As indicated in the report, the Task Force was well aware of the many areas that impinge upon the lives of adolescents and youth which need urgent attention. Under the limitations of time, however, the Task Force felt it necessary to set priorities which were within their own areas of competence and which they felt would be most facilitative of the normal development of adolescents and youth.

One final consideration should be emphasized. This hinges on the time lapse between the actual writings and deliberations of the Task Force and the final compilation of this material for publication. In the interim, a number of changes have occurred. Some, happily, are compatible with the proposals of the Task Force, such as the adoption of a lottery system for

1. For a list of working papers and contracts, see Appendixes A and B.

selection into military service. The drug scene has also changed considerably since the Task Force met to consider recommendations in this area. The Task Force is aware of the relative status of parts of this report. Had it been possible for them to convene in late 1969, there is little doubt that many of the proposals would be reformulated and tailored to the current scene. Since any changes would require the consensus of the group, I have not attempted to rewrite any of the recommendations in light of later legislative measures.

—RITA PENNINGTON, M.A.
Commission liaison to Task Force III

The World of Adolescents and Youth

Adolescence, as this Task Force has defined this stage of life, is not so much a biological or a physiological determinant as a psychological and social opportunity. This definition assumes that adolescence is not a fixed number of years, or a biological or cognitive measurement, but rather a possibility for an experience of psychological growth which *may or may not* occur after puberty. To be sure, the biological and physiological changes upon which the possibility of adolescent growth is founded are given by the human constitution. But if development other than physical, that is, emotional, ethical, and intellectual, is to continue through and beyond adolescence, then continual familial, educational, and societal confirmation and support of adolescent growth must be present.

The problems in living that trouble the inner selves of today's young, that separate the generations, and that create issues for the larger society are, in the judgment of this Task Force, the result of an interaction among three factors: (a) the instabilities of a human developmental stage, (b) the uncertainties of a world where cultural change is proceeding at an unprecedented rate, and (c) technological advance whereby man has radically and rapidly changed the nature of his environment. Today virtually everyone is directly affected by the tensions of international conflict, racial confrontation, economic disparity, the threat of nuclear war, and the breakdown in persuasiveness of old moral guides. It is widely felt, if only vaguely understood, that ours is a time of revolution—a time of more rapid and more far-reaching change than any before known in the whole history of our creative species. Following the shift from barbarism to civilization, our contemporary society has moved from what Lewis Mumford (1962) has called historic to posthistoric man or from what Kenneth Boulding (1964) has termed civilized to postcivilized society. Today's contrasts are startling.

In the United States, a little less than 10 percent of the population is employed in agriculture and still produces food in quantities that far outrun the nation's needs. Yet, starvation is a real and ugly problem in the contemporary world, but more because of our inability to solve economic and distributional problems than because of failures in production. Significant and dramatic changes have occurred also in the composition of the American nonfarm labor force. By 1900, farm workers were already outnumbered by those employed outside agriculture, but 57 percent of this larger group were in the so-called blue-collar occupations. By 1960, blue-collar workers were in the minority.

Thus, we are a major society which, having freed itself from the constraints of a preponderantly agricultural economy, is currently freeing itself from the constraints of predominantly muscular labor. Our breakaway technology, based on what it has become fashionable to call the "knowledge explosion," has enabled us to extract from the earth since 1910 about the same amount of metal that was mined throughout the existence of our species before that very recent date. It has written the entire history of aviation, from the first few minutes aloft over the North Carolina sand dunes to the current man-made satellites and lunar probes—all in less than 65 years. It has made possible the transplantation of such natural organs as spleens and corneas and created such mechanical and electronic substitutes for living tissues as the artificial kidney and the cardiac pacemaker. In less than three decades, it has released the power of the atom, broken the genetic code, and devised and refined the computer. The computer, in turn, has made possible systems engineering, taught us a great deal about the ways in which men think through complex problems, and substantially increased our capacity to predict the response of various defined populations to a wide range of issues and situations. In addition, the earth itself has become smaller. Changes in speed have virtually eliminated the once protective resource of distance.

This is the America that we are bequeathing to our young—a country with an ever increasing population, currently more than 200 million and expected to swell to 230 million by 1975 and to 250 million by 1980. This will increase the proportion of our people most affected by poverty and by the inequities which we have grafted onto minority status. Given the complexity of these harrowing problems and our slow pace to date in resolving them, we can anticipate a still more fertile soil for strife and conflict within the American community as our population increases. Within five years, about half our population will be twenty-five or younger. Interacting with the rate of social change, this state of affairs is almost sure to widen the gulf between generations. It is highly probable that the sheer mass of young people will sharply revise the tone and character of our historic mores and way of life.

We stand now at the threshold of a cybernetic age. Automation and computers have been steadily displacing the unskilled in our economic life; they are now beginning to nudge aside the machinist, the engineer, the auditor, the middle-level manager. Within a generation or two, cybernetic developments will probably put an end to work as the *focus* of life except for those people engaged in fundamentally creative activities. This is alarming when we remember the degree to which Western man has typically equated his self-respect with the economic enterprises that he has called "work," and when we recall the disruptive and distressing social consequences of mass idleness. Leisure for the majority is a mode for which there is no guiding experience in history. The difficulties are made more stringent by the probability that free time will be most abundantly available to those least equipped to capitalize on it as an opportunity for personal and social growth. New trends in biological and behavioral engineering permit manipulation of the genetic code and consequently a transmission of "instructions" which largely determine the nature and form of the subsequent generation. Telemetering and computer techniques also allow for the diagnosis and treatment of a variety of physiological malfunctions. These trends may be refined to a point where they can be used to control mental as well as physical processes in human beings. The problem of personal identity is likely to become complicated by the surgical transplantation of organs: Who am I if I live by virtue of another man's heart beating in my breast and see by virtue of another man's eyes fitted into my sockets? The availability and progressive refinement of chemopsychic drugs, conditioning techniques, and methods of propaganda suggest novel and extended powers of control over human conduct, just as the highly rationalized processes of systems engineering, applied to industrial and governmental management and to other social phenomena, suggest the increasingly efficient regulation of organizational affairs. Under these conditions, the individual, whose distinctiveness has been America's traditional touchstone of value, is likely to get lost in the search for manageable regularities and consistencies that make for orderliness, predictability, and efficiency. For many, the erosion of individuality is already in process. In addition, the enterprises of biological and behavioral engineering entail the making by a select few of the decisions which vitally affect the most intimate and personal aspects of life for the many.

The central impact of this modern life upon adolescents and youth is, thus, uncertainty. Because of the "new conditions" of the world, yesterday's experience cannot be the sole guide for today's behavior; and today's learning may not effectively anticipate tomorrow's challenge. For young people, then, the basic issue is how to live zestfully, humanely, and individualistically in a world that is increasingly crowded, fluctuating, and ambiguous.

Owing to the rate of cultural and technological change and the scale of their effects, today's youth face two major, but fluctuating, systems of relationships. One is the great and growing rift between the generations. The other is the relationship between young people and the official personnel of the society, such as political leaders, law enforcement officers, and educational and civic officials. As to the "generation gap," our concern is neither for the hegemony of adults nor for the notion that the only good society is one in which preceding generations pass on their particular store of wisdom to their grateful successors. Our concern, instead, is focused on three interrelated problems.

First, to what extent is the adult world accountable for the developmental difficulties of adolescence? There is a tendency for adults to become fascinated with the impulsiveness of youth—its wildness, its sexuality, its susceptibility to such new forms of experience as drinking and drugs may provide, its violence and unsubdued, unsocialized passions. This one-sided view of adolescent life may vicariously fulfill a number of adult frustrations and serve as a somewhat wistful commentary on the emptiness and regrets that color a surprising amount of modern maturity. It may also overemphasize events of minor significance and create less than necessary problems by defining a stimulus to which adolescents and youth must in some fashion react. It is at least conceivable that some of our social stress, as well as some of the experiential hardship in moving through the adolescent years, could be alleviated if adults were themselves less preoccupied with the "decadence and dangers" of today's youth.

Second, our concern for the so-called generational gap stems from the problem of how to provide continuity and stability at a time of whirling change in the cultural matrix from which all of us derive our basic humanity and much of our essential being. The solution is to winnow our traditions for what is wise and relevant, to capitalize *critically* on our past collective experience, and to maintain, in a truly modern form, a dialogue between the generations which will generate a humane combination of novelty and continuity. Major responsibility rests inevitably here with adults, who must consider revisions in their roles as mentors of the young and in their child-rearing practices to strike a more meaningful balance between the extremes of repression and laissez-faire permissiveness.

The generational gap seems important to us for yet another reason. To cope with the developmental tasks that are made more difficult by the uncertainties—often the grim and unjust uncertainties—of contemporary society, adolescents and youth must receive personalized support. Without such support, we cannot expect optimum development of our young. It is clear that postpubescent youngsters cannot properly be conceived of as children or absolved of responsibility for the consequences of their acts. But it is equally clear that they need room in which to err without being scarred for life by guilt, by crushed self-respect, or by the nature of their public records; and they require personal relationships within which they can reflect upon their experience and acquire more discrimination and sophistication in the quest for identity and a rewarding social role for themselves. This point must *not* be misread as a veiled recommendation for coddling or a wholesale extension of conventional clinical services. Rather, it states some of the preconditions under which the relations between the generations can be more cordial, more understanding, and more contributory to the building of a humanely generous society.

Focus on the adult role in the development of youth leads to two other considerations. On the one hand, there is a growing need for specialized services which, although they are not classically "clinical," nevertheless contain the elements of one-to-one helping relationships and the counseling process. On the other, there is a comparable need for greater speed and flexibility in the creation of institutions that are responsive to the changing character of adolescent problems. In this context we have examined such possibilities as those pioneered by Margaret Rioch at Chestnut Lodge, the evolution in some urban school systems of teachers' aides as either volunteers or on a paid basis, and combinations of such enterprises as the Big Brother program and the "psychiatric companions" conceived jointly by Wesleyan University and Middletown State Hospital in Connecticut. Without intending to decry either expertise or professional status, we find these rather differently oriented ventures promising because they are rooted in relational warmth, moral concern, and social commitment. In short, they impress us as possible ways of injecting personalized caring into a world that is increasingly rationalized, systematized, and depersonalized, and this factor seems essential if relatively specialized services are to find a social context in which they can, in significant ways, facilitate desirable forms of development.

The second major system that is changing for today's youth is their relationship to the official personnel of society. With almost half the population twenty-five years of age and younger, it seems clear that youth will either exercise increasing influence on the social decisions that affect us all or increasingly and understandably become more alienated, less contributive, and more a source of disruptive dissidence in public affairs. Two broad matters seem paramount here. One is the meaningful involvement of adolescents in properly influential roles in the community—the question of lowering the voting age to eighteen or nineteen is only one of several topics to be considered. Of interest also are the ways that current methods of enforcing social rules—by police, by school officials, by the military and others—and the differential distribution of the military obligation affect such developmental processes as self-definition, attitudes toward authority, social commitment, and identification with the historic values of American life. It is quite probable that widespread moralistic tendencies in our society find expression in the enactment of essentially unenforceable laws. Realistically, patterns of enforcement are the concern of a socially aware public which eventually sees that the laws are changed. The professionalization of police power makes self-esteem and police career advancement basically a matter of technical competence, rarely leavened by developmental concerns and which, when interacting with moralistic laws, leads episodically, and not very beneficially, to raids and crackdowns on youthful enterprises involving sex, alcohol, marijuana, or hallucinogens, or such political behavior as sit-ins, protests, or picketing.

The central point is twofold: on the one hand, the patterns of law enforcement are inconsistent; on the other hand, they are discriminatory, penalizing youngsters for activities that are openly engaged in and enjoyed by their elders. This but adds to the mistrust and misunderstanding that presently rifts the relationship between generations. The question of drugs is one illustration. There is a growing tendency among the American people generally to use pharmacological agents as a device for altering the dimensions of consciousness. Aspirin, with its dulling of pain, is the most common example of this trend. The widespread use of tranquilizers, sleeping pills, and such stimulants as Benzedrine is rather more dramatic and telling, though probably less significant, than the annual outlays for nicotine, alcohol, and caffeine. It is little wonder that the adolescent finds a troubling hypocrisy in the condemnation of marijuana expressed by his elders as they sip their third preprandial cocktail. Further, laws now on the books and taken often as a basis for prosecutions are badly out of phase with knowledge about the drugs in question. The linking of marijuana to the addictive narcotics, for instance, makes no sense biochemically, psychologically, or socially. Modernization of the relevant statutes and a more accurate and vigorous campaign of public education about marijuana, the hallucinogens, and narcotics seem very much in order. One can argue more forcefully and cogently for the wise control of pharmacological agents if one is discriminating and informed about the drugs being considered. Hypocrisy, panic, and a kind of anti-intellectual brutality in both the existing laws and many patterns of their enforcement strike us as relevant factors in the current discussion of increasing drug usage.

The official personnel of any society include those in the educational system. Since the school is the only social institution that universally reaches young people, the Task Force has particularly concentrated on the ways in which education can simultaneously retain its proper emphasis on cognitive development and the facilitation of skills, and yet contribute more effectively to the growth of those nonintellective and more personal traits through which society attempts to prepare people for significant, satisfying, and contributory roles in the human community. Several questions of educational policy are considered in this light. Education has become a right and a requirement in the United States through the twelfth grade or the sixteenth year of age. Yet the emotionally disturbed are in many ways deprived of that right and opportunity. What kinds of legislation and what kinds of modifications in public policy can rectify this situation? Many segments of the school-age population, advantaged as well as deprived, find that the educational experience has little relevance to their potential careers or, indeed, to the environments in which they live or to which they aspire. How can the membranes between school and community be made more permeable so that school learning can be experienced as more germane and productive in relation to the meaning of contemporary citizenship, the diversity of people to whom one must relate, and the social conditions under which youngsters actually live? Regardless of the likelihood in the future of extended and enforced leisure, there is evidence that work represents both a highly educative source of experience and, for many persons, a necessary step toward economic self-sufficiency and self-respect. The present child labor laws, originally drafted for the most humane reasons, are currently impediments to the dovetailing of work and education in ways that could facilitate growth for large numbers of adolescents and youth. How can these laws be revised to maximize the educational significance of work opportunities and to equip young people with marketable skills from the exercise of which they can derive some pride and self-esteem?

The processes through which teachers are selected, trained, certified, employed, and retained tends to curtail rather sharply the range of adult models to which young people are exposed through their school careers. Are there ways in which, in spite of the extraordinary burdens which it already carries, the school can provide more scope in the relationships it affords during the adolescent years? This query is related, of course, to questions about reducing the barriers between school and community. If, in their educational experience, high school and college students become more involved in the affairs of the larger society, they are more likely to meet, to come to know, and to be instructed by a greater variety of adults who function as models—either to emulate or to reject. The Task Force has also been impressed by the rapidity with which such agencies as community mental health centers, child guidance clinics, etc., can become outmoded. In not entirely satisfactory contrast, some community action councils and indigenously developed community facilities have shown a good deal of agility in adapting to the changing nature of the local groups to which they are responsible. It seems probable that the loose but explicit coupling of school systems with teams of mental health consultants concerned with personal development rather than pathology and with the school environment as a stimulus to growth toward greater self-determination and social sensitivity might provide a basis for a useful institutional model.

Although secondary schools and colleges must retain their proper focus on education, there is abundant evidence that cognitive development extends the capacity of people to cope more effectively with the world in which they live, including the phenomenological world, and that school and college environments inevitably exert a shaping effect on the attitudes, including the self-attitudes, and the values of young people. A major question is that of how intellectual training can be made more relevant to the human condition and how the influences of the school and college environments can be directed more effectively into desirable channels. It is probable that from about the seventh grade on, youngsters themselves should take a progressively greater hand in the planning of their educational experience; and second, as a result of the interaction between school officials and their associated team of mental health consultants, the domain of the school should become progressively broader, involving parents, businessmen and industrialists, artists and scholars, and political and civic leaders in meaningful ways. Again, we are concerned with increasing the relevance of academic experience at all levels to the world beyond the classroom and playground, relating the sequences of personal development more closely to the processes and people that determine the contours of both our communal and our private lives.

Finally, none of these issues can be considered without recognizing the great diversity of the population of adolescents and youth in the United States. The newly menarchial girl and the young woman of twenty-two are very different from each other; so are two fourteen-year-old boys, one of whom lives in a Harlem tenement and the other in Shaker Heights or Beverly Hills. The activist, the hippie, and the aspirant to a Madison Avenue advertising firm may all be undergraduates on the same Ivy League campus. Though members of recognized minorities, the Mexican-American in Austin or Santa Fe is likely to differ markedly from his youthful Puerto Rican counterpart in Spanish Harlem. Ample provision must be made, therefore, for a commensurate variety of efforts in the service of our heterogeneous population of young people. The programs and facilities successfully developed for one group may fail if applied to another; and if we give more than lip service to the value of pluralism, the very criteria of appropriate service may differ widely from one group to another.

Finally, we insist that the adolescent experience be made available to all. In Western societies as late as the eighteenth century, and in many societies even today, the transition from childhood to adulthood has been early, brief, and coercively controlled by inflexible rites of passage or apprenticeships. Until very recently, adolescence was an experience largely reserved for the extraordinarily privileged or the extraordinarily lucky. One of the unique psychological achievements of industrial and postindustrial societies has been the gradual opening of an opportunity for a real adolescence to a great number of less privileged and less talented young men and women, with all of the rich possibilities for continued development this opening brings. It seems clear to us that American society must take vigorous steps to grant to all its youth the right to developmental experiences appropriate to the adolescent years. The cultural and social deprivations, the discrimination, the lack of opportunities for imaginative thought and experimentation, the pressures toward conformity and a yielding to conventional authority must, in our judgment, be strikingly reduced to allow for the personal autonomy, the expansion of the self, and the unfolding of individuality which are requisite to this stage of development.

The Tasks of Adolescents

Given adult and societal confirmation that supports without smothering, adolescents will develop into emotionally sound, ethically responsible, and cognitively rational human beings if they have not been irreparably handicapped by childhood. But without this backing, the development of the adolescent may be derailed, foreclosed, or distorted—as evidenced not only in the more obvious forms of personal and social pathology, but equally important, in a constriction and restriction of human potentialities for fulfillment, independence, integration, and usefulness. Our chief concern in thinking about the years between childhood and adulthood in American society is that, even today, so few young Americans are given the opportunities for a *real* adolescence, and that so many, for one reason or another, are not supported in their efforts to move ahead to a more complex, more responsible, more autonomous adulthood. Our culturally lengthened adolescent period, now so void of adult roles, is no more a guarantee of optimal development than is privileged status. Many middle-class young are forced into an early, superficial adult mold without experiencing the fluctuations of this period which are so necessary if one is to arrive at the threshold of adulthood with a new stable definition of the self. For many of our disadvantaged youth, this adolescent period is virtually nonexistent, as evinced by the following recollection of a Chicago woman:

I never was a little girl. I never were. I always was grown up. I started cooking when I was seven years old and I was doing housework and taking care of smaller kids under me. I just got married early and regretted it afterwards, but what could you do about it? I was a mother at 14 so this is just all I know . . . (Holden and Jackson, 1967, p. 9).

This Task Force takes exception to the traditional view that the adolescent experience is largely a recapitulation and working out of the themes

211

of childhood. What happens in adolescence is important in its own right—a fortunate adolescence can do much to repair the damage of an unfortunate childhood. The preadolescent years are enormously important in defining where the adolescent begins, how much he has to work with, and what issues he must work on. Some boys and girls arrive at the teens so crippled by the experiences of childhood that only the most devoted remedial efforts can begin to undo the damage; others reach adolescence with such abundant inner resources that only the grossest deprivations can finally detain their development. But most are in between these two extremes, resourceful yet troubled, eager to grow up yet rather afraid to, and in need of the confirming presence of an understanding but not smothering environment.

With adolescence—an age that Erikson (1959) wryly says lasts "from puberty to maturity"—the psychological mechanisms which normally maintain emotional reactions within a reasonable range swing so erratically that in each case it is necessary to decide whether the conditions require psychological treatment. No one would wish to institute therapy with young men or women whose painful struggles are moving them closer to an understanding of themselves or of their relationship with the external world. But for other individuals, hard to distinguish from their fellows, the general confusions of adolescence mask a diffusion and despair not characteristic of a developmental phase, but indicative of emotional disorder. This differentiation of normal developmental crisis from emotional disorder, this ability to pick out disturbance but to avoid potentially weakening or infantilizing interference, must be the underpinning of what we call the preventive service.

In this summary of the tasks of adolescence, we will not be speaking of the statistically typical adolescent in American society, or for that matter in any society. Rather, we will be describing a concept of adolescence at its best. For despite the infrequency with which this ideal is attained, it constitutes the standard by which we have judged the adolescent experience in our society. But however much cultural expectations revolve around this ideal, societal conditions do not permit adolescents of all class and ethnic groups the same chance to approximate this ideal. There may be little difference in the internal dynamics of the adolescent period among ghetto, Appalachian, or Westchester County youth. However, for each of these groups, there is variance in the assessibility of the forms through which the tasks of development can be accomplished, and the readiness of opportunities by which the adolescent experience can be made most profitable. Thus, under existing conditions, the attainment of this ideal adolescence may be extremely difficult—if not impossible—for many of our youth.

First, we will consider some of the *intrapsychic changes* which occur if adolescent development is not foreshortened or frustrated; second, we will touch briefly upon the *changes in interpersonal relationships* and feelings about them by which the adolescent experience is achieved and which are the external manifestations of its successful unfolding. Third, we will describe some of the major *human characteristics* which in some sense should begin to emerge as adolescence ends. These three perspectives on adolescence—intrapsychic, interpersonal, and characterological—inevitably overlap and complement one another: our separation of them for purposes of presentation is in no way intended to deny their continual interdependence.

INTRAPSYCHIC CHANGES IN ADOLESCENCE

Adolescence can produce profound changes in the internal structure and organization of the personality. First and most frequently discussed by educators and those professionally concerned with the intellectual development of the adolescent is the child's capacity for "rationality," which can be greatly extended during the postpuberty years. As Inhelder and Piaget (1958) have suggested, the physiological onset of puberty coincides roughly with the emergence of new intellective and cognitive abilities. The adolescent becomes capable for the first time of deductive and systematic thinking, of constructing ideologies, utopias, and models of reality with which he compares the world around him. At the same time, his historical sense expands greatly, so that both the distant past and the far future acquire increasing psychological immediacy for him. If encouraged and supported by his environment, the adolescent can develop his cognitive abilities in constructive and rational ways. Concomitantly, he can develop a capacity for planning, for the mental rehearsal of alternate paths of action, and a capacity for guiding his behavior according to long-range purposes.

As the adolescent achieves a new range, agility, flexibility, and adaptability of mental processes, lessons of the past, both personal and collective, can be applied with far more sureness to present and future events. Personal, interpersonal, and societal options, sometimes learned from others, sometimes learned from books, are rehearsed first in fantasy and then often in actual behavior. He develops new loyalties to individuals and existing groups, as well as new allegiances to different ideas, inclusive goals, and synthetic ideologies. It is in adolescence, then, that the intellect "cuts loose" from the concrete events of daily life and becomes a powerful force, for better or worse, in the governance of daily behavior.

In this process (which is at best an extension of rationality and at worst a flight into unreality), the adolescent normally vacillates between romantic, highly intellectualized theory building and impulsive daily behavior which may bear little relationship to his high ideals and theories. Profound alternations in self-esteem and self-conception routinely result from the adolescent's heightened capacity to compare his own and others' behavior in terms of an ideal which grows increasingly intense. The newfound ability to theorize, to range freely across time past and future, and to imagine a world that does not exist produces both new tensions and new possibilities. His imagination of the world as it might be frequently alienates him from the world as it is. His capacity to envision a future radically different from the present makes it possible for him to construct for the first time a world of fantasies that may serve not merely as goal and ideal, but as refuge and cocoon in times of acute stress. Moreover, at the same time that the adolescent becomes aware of and embodies in his behavior the separation of the cognitive and the ideal from the actual and the behavioral, he gradually begins to learn through experimentation, "role playing," and the tentative trial of ideals in action to join fantasy with reality, imagination with action, and utopia with personal purpose. At best, as adolescence proceeds, the youth learns to tolerate more forgivingly the unbridgeable gap between ideal and fact while strengthening his bonds to both.

Closely related to the extension of rationality is another aspect of adolescence which we may term the humanization of conscience. The morality of the very young child is generally unreflectively assimilated from the stated and unstated views and assumptions of adults, especially his parents. Increasing age brings about a spontaneous restructuring of experience and an increasingly autonomous and complex moral development. With adolescence, the moral edicts and prescriptions of parents and the adult world come under critical scrutiny, as does the congruence between adult precept and practice. Especially at this period, adolescents become aware of the often radical discrepancies between what others tell them to do and what others actually do themselves—and no one is more likely to be the object of bitter criticism in this regard than parents. But however preoccupied the adolescent may seem to be with exposing the clay feet of his former idols, he is also in the process of reexamining his own internal values and codes of behavior, a process which frequently involves a need to reject totally and vociferously the simple morality he assimilated as a child, and those from whom he acquired it. The adolescent makes conscious, examines, criticizes, and selectively reassimilates the values of his parents and of his culture. Like all adolescent developments, this "rejection of the childhood superego" can be highly ambivalent, involving both intense and often bitter rejection and recrimination and a simultaneous search for ethical support and moral confirmation.

The wide view of the world, made possible by our mass media, extends the adolescent's growing awareness of the gap between the real and the ideal to the world beyond his family. He begins to see that this discrepancy applies not only to individuals but to institutions. Institutional "hypocrisy" has become a familiar cry among the activist and hippie subcultures. One study (Silverstein et al., 1967) indicates that alienated youth "are particularly sensitive to the many value and action disjunctures which they feel have developed within American society. Not only are ethical and moral codes frequently violated, but they believe that those who often vehemently espouse these codes are at the same time the most frequent violators. In this sense, they feel victimized by a general lack of social idealism among those of the establishment. . . ."

In a time of rapid social change, it is inevitable that youth will do much more than unreflectively accept the morality of the parental generation; in a time of revolutionary historical upheaval like our own, adolescents must more than ever scrutinize, reflect upon, and selectively both reject and accept the values of the previous generation before they can be made an integral part of the emerging adult self. Speaking of this process, Silverstein and his associates state that the alienated youth whom they interviewed feel "it is their right, and indeed their *obligation*, to subject the values and rules of the received culture to skepticism" (italics added). They "view themselves as neither immoral nor amoral. On the contrary, they view themselves as highly moral, or at least concerned with moral issues and with developing ethical philosophies. But they do reject the notion that laws embody morality. They reserve the right to decide this question for themselves." Whether disadvantaged youth similarly scrutinize and criticize the values of the larger society from which they are excluded is still open to question. Hyman Rodman (1963) suggests that the disadvantaged develop a "lower-class value stretch," which broadly includes the general values of the society; but, in the process, they either stretch the values or develop alternative values as a means of adjusting to their deprived circumstances. However, the development of such a value stretch in no way relieves the disadvantaged adolescent from coming to terms with the dominant society's values and of integrating the outcome into his emerging self.

When this process occurs, whether in the privileged or the disadvantaged, its frequently distressing symptoms—turmoil, apparently irrational rejection of parental values, and routine conflict with the adult world—are evidence of an often agonizing movement from primitive childhood morality to a more complex adult ethic. Ideally, the child's motivation to avoid guilt is gradually replaced by the adult's determination to live up to his own highest standards. In this process of ethical development, the automatic rules of childhood are replaced by a more articulated, graduated, and complex hierarchy of personal values and purposes. Ideally, whether these values are religious or non-religious, the evolving ethic is humanized. The adolescent recognizes and eventually accepts the fact that the ethical and responsible life is not simply a matter of "obeying the rules," but a matter of being one's best self. He learns to forgive himself and others for the fact that no one is ever quite his ideal self.

This evolving and different definition of the self is a product of the interaction of the physiological change of adolescence and the resultant shift in the individual's social role. Thus, adolescence inevitably requires a new attitude toward the life of the impulses. Especially for boys, but also for girls, the onset of puberty is marked by an influx of new sensations, desires, physical changes, and fantasies. The sexually maturing adolescent must learn to modulate, control, and yet be able to express freely his desires for sexual gratification, love, and intimacy. Equally important, adolescence brings with it new capacities and impulses for violence—capacities made more threatening to both the adolescent and the adult world by his physical, sexual, and intellectual maturation. In a variety of respects the adolescent must learn to live with impulses that are both quantitatively and qualitatively new, and for which no childhood experience, however ideal, can ever have totally prepared him. New impulses, feelings, and capacities must be integrated into a sense of self, a conception of ethical responsibility, and an extension of rationality, all of which during adolescence are shaky, ambivalent, and incomplete.

It is around the issue of the control and the integration of impulse that the most dramatic and socially disruptive alterations of behavior can take place during adolescence. Compulsive sexual activity, often heavily laden with the remnants of childhood preoccupations and fantasies, can alternate with periods of asexual asceticism; rage, fury, violence can be suddenly superseded by peaceableness, self-restraint, and saintlike gentleness. These apparently unpredictable alternations, however bedeviling and anxiety-provoking to adults, should not be seen simply as expressions of the perversity and irrationality of the adolescent, but also as a part of a normal dialectic of development in which impulsive action and excessive self-control alternate in ever narrowing cycles, eventuating at best in the slow development of a capacity to substitute flexible internal controls for the external controls of childhood.

It is crucial to emphasize, however, that integration of the impulses requires more than control and self-regulation. Equally important are release and freedom—of learning to express both sexuality and anger without guilt or anxiety when the occasion demands. Because they are highly visible social problems, uncontrolled sexual and aggressive impulsivity command immediate social attention. Of equal weight in the balance of human suffering are the less visible problems of sexual inhibition and over-control of anger, both of which lead not so much to violent acting out as to lives of quiet desperation and incapacitation. As the following example indicates, the psychological residue of early training does present obstacles, for even those adolescents who advocate sexual freedom. One woman interviewed by Silverstein and his associates in their study of alienated youth describes her relationship with a former boyfriend:

When we slept together, I didn't enjoy it too much. . . . And [boyfriend] was always bogged down in guilt and stuff like that. And he'd always say, "Well, how did you feel about it?" And I'd say, "Great." He'd say, "Oh no, stop repressing it baby. You feel guilty."

A Puerto Rican adolescent in the same study views his tendency toward aggressiveness as a reaction to a humiliating pattern of passiveness that he claims is common among lower-class Puerto Ricans:

Well, I think I have a little thing about this, a theory: it's Puerto Ricans in general, the lower class people. You know, there's a phrase in Spanish which means shit-eaters. This, I think, is typical of some Puerto Ricans; it's a trait that they have. They take a lot, you know, of shit from people and they don't know how to talk back. A lot of people think it's just because of the English bit, you know, but it's not. In general, they're like that. They kind of take it and then just eat themselves up. . . . You know, they must get sad or something, but they don't speak out. And this is what I mean by passive sort of thing in the society. That's why I became—with people—I became passive, because I couldn't speak out when I should have. . . . I think it was a trait from my parents. Oh, what they used to do. I think about it now, and it's a disgrace. You know, they used to go into a store and they'd get gypped or something. They'd leave, you know, without saying anything. And then outside I'd say, "Why didn't you say something?" And they'd say, you know, that they didn't want to start trouble. So maybe, you know, it's a complicated thing about being passive.

As the adolescent learns to modulate and control sexuality and aggression, he must also move toward an adult life in which the capacity for guilt-free sexual activity and unanxious expression of appropriate anger will be crucial for his well-being. If adolescence goes well, the frequent terror of the early adolescent at his "uncontrollable" passions does not lead to massive self-restriction and inhibition, but evolves into a capacity to incorporate these passions and the energies that derive from them into personally and socially acceptable activities and relationships.

Finally, adolescence involves major changes in the complexity, definition and coherence of the self. The childhood self is largely defined by the parents and other key persons. It reflects, in a relatively uncomplicated way, the immediate world of crucial persons to the child, and is based on relatively simple identifications with these people. The adolescent self, in contrast, must be broadened, redefined, reexamined, and reintegrated—on the one hand made consistent with the adolescent's new capacity for rationality, the humanization of his conscience with the integration of his impulses, and on the other hand reconciled with the socially available possibilities for work, love, and play in modern society. This process, brilliantly described by Erikson as the development of identity, involves and includes all of the changes we have previously discussed. It entails the integration into actual life of emerging cognitive abilities and potentials; it involves the integration within the self of new values, ethics, and purposes; it requires a capacity to live with one's sexuality, aggressiveness, instinctual life, fantasies, and drives. Above all, it involves a movement away from the simple mirror-like view of the self which originated in childhood to a new, more integrated, more autonomous, and more individuated sense of self, involving uniqueness, independence, and self-identity, and also relatedness, interdependence, and involvement with others. Those theoretical views which interpret the "self" as the simple obverse of the perceptions of others seem to us not to reflect "normal" development, but rather the fact that normal development has not occurred.

During adolescence, psychological pain, distress, worry, fear, confusion, shame, and guilt are probably more intense than during any other stage of life. (To be sure, some adolescents show few outward signs of inner turmoil, and a few may actually be able to weather adolescence with little subjective storm and stress.) In later life, most of us find it difficult to recapture the painful feelings of our own adolescent periods; we can recall the events and perhaps infer the distress, but an affective amnesia protects us from reexperiencing the emotions. This amnesia is among the many factors that make it difficult for the old to understand the young. But for most adolescents, no matter how calm, cocky, and composed on the surface, this stage of life involves times of intense psychological pain. Never before or after in life does the conscious gulf between actuality and aspiration, between the "real me" and the "social me," and between the feeling of loneliness and the need for love loom so wide or seem such a bottomless pit of despair.

The inner experience of the adolescent, then, reflects the changes and tensions of this period. The key words to describe the full adolescent experience in Western societies are terms that suggest a movement between polarities: ambivalence, alternation, conflict, tension, inconsistency, dialectic, and so on. When these characteristics are absent from both the behavior and the subjective experience of the adolescent, we may suspect that something is amiss, and have reason to ask whether the adolescent experience has not already been foreclosed or thwarted.

CHANGES IN INTERPERSONAL RELATIONSHIPS

The beginning of adolescence is marked not only by obvious physiological and physical changes and by the emergence of less obvious cognitive capacities, but by a series of new interpersonal and social interactions. The emergence of primary and secondary sexual characteristics requires that the adolescent begin to come to terms with himself as an adult and as a sexual being. Similarly, new cognitive capacities enable him to attain an expanded and qualitatively different intellectual approach to the world, to construct models of the future which will guide his behavior, and to contrast the actual with the ideal. But at the same time, the attitudes of parents, teachers, and friends toward the adolescent change, and often change drastically. A new distance develops between the postpubescent youth and his family, as if to recognize not only his developing sexuality but his imminent entry into the adult world. New social expectations make themselves felt in schools, with peers, and with adults. Moreover, the impossibility of achieving within his family any complete or lasting satisfaction of his new impulses, values, and cognitive abilities serves to propel the adolescent away from his family toward friends, peer groups, and—eventually—toward adulthood.

Thus, the chief interpersonal tension in the development of early adolescence involves a gradual movement away from childhood dependency and immersion within the family toward ever greater involvement with the extrafamilial world. This process of emancipation is generally fraught with internal, sometimes unconscious, tension, trauma, and conflict which is not always visible. But whether conscious or unconscious, acted upon or merely felt, the normality of ambivalence around the issue of dependence and independence should be emphasized. Almost without regard to the actual behavior and attitudes of his parents in permitting him increasing freedom, self-control, and autonomy, the adolescent himself is torn inwardly between his desire for independence and his usually less conscious but equally powerful wishes to remain a child, to be cared for, and to avoid the many deprivations and conflicts that adult life seems to entail. The provocativeness of adolescents toward authoritarian parents and the extreme rejections by youth of reasonable parents and admirable parental standards can be understood only in the context of the adolescent's own profound ambivalence. Indeed, it is often precisely through the acting-out of this ambivalence in alternations between provocative self-assertion and childlike requests for succor that the adolescent gradually becomes able to emerge from his family. Although this pattern is common to all class segments, the age at which it occurs may vary. Among the lower class, loss of parental control occurs at late childhood or preadolescence—owing either to parental abdication or to the revolt of the child. This pattern should be juxtaposed to that of the middle class, in which adolescence is the socially accepted and expected period for revolt.

Much of the real provocativeness of the adolescent is related to this ambivalence about inner independence and outer freedom. He may continually clamor for recognition of his "real self" but be quite unable to express or define that self. He often demands self-determination, but almost as often resents or refuses to exercise whatever freedom he is granted. He needs to be heard by others, but is often unable to listen to them. He may at times be blindly hostile to all authority, "needing" to have tyrants and despots to prove his independence. And he may expect others to have a degree of understanding, tolerance, and patience of which he himself is as yet incapable. In all these ways, the adolescent creates and perpetuates his reputation as one with whom it is impossible to live.

To draw a sharp chronological or even theoretical line between early and late adolescence is clearly impossible. Not only do individuals differ enormously in their rates of psychological development, and not only do varying sets of social circumstances and opportunities make the timing and meaning of adolescence different in various sectors of American society, but the distinction itself between early and late adolescence is only a relative one. Nonetheless, this distinction is meant to suggest that one of the ways we recognize the "successful" progress of adolescence is by a gradually decreased preoccupation with issues of emancipation, independence, and autonomy from family, coupled with a slow growth in concern with questions about the future, the integration of self, the development of a sense of social role and personal purpose—a gradual shift that is by no means automatic or guaranteed by the passage of time, much less by physical growth. It requires at each step a social environment that can willingly confirm the adolescent's movement toward adulthood, just as it requires of the adolescent a process of struggle, both intrapsychic and interpersonal. If such environmental support and confirmation are present, whether from parents or others (and ideally from both) sometime in mid-adolescence there will be an increasingly explicit preoccupation and experimentation with issues of identity and role that were less salient in the immediate postpuberty years.

Two of these issues seem to us of special importance in late adolescence: the related questions of self-definition in the wider world and the capacity for intimacy, including sexual intimacy, with the opposite sex. As Erikson has noted, until the boundaries of the self are delineated, intimacy poses the threat of engulfing and being engulfed, and mature love relationships remain secondary to the effort "to find one's self" in and through the other. In this sense, identity precedes intimacy. But especially for women, and for many men as well, identity development itself is inextricably bound up with relations with the opposite sex, with fantasies about marriage and family, and, most specifically, with a growing sense of adequacy and comfort in one's sex role. In modern American society, most late-adolescent girls see relationships with men as a primary way (and often as *the* primary way) of achieving identity and fulfillment in life. Although for late-adolescent boys, vocational concerns over "what to do with my life" generally assume greater conscious importance than issues of intimacy, love, and marriage, the nonvocational (and in some ways more fundamental) aspects of identity development at this stage have much to do with a developing sense of maleness which is usually tested and consolidated in increasingly intense relationships with girls. Thus, for both sexes, the achievement of intimacy with others parallels the development of a sense of personal identity. This is aptly illustrated by the following statement from a young college dropout in New York City:

Right now, I think is a time in my life when I've got to get away from every-thing. Like I don't think I'm ready for a relationship or anything. . . . If one came along I would probably take it. But I don't think I'm really ready just yet. I think I've got to know . . . I've got to know what I'm selling. I've got to know who I am. (Silverstein *et al.*, 1967).

Occupational and marital choice, both crucial issues in late adolescence, are not only intrapsychic and intimately interpersonal matters, but are also related to what and who is actually available in the societal, cultural, and historical framework into which the adolescent moves. For those privileged few who confront a world of virtually limitless possibilities, with doors opening in every direction, the central problem will inevitably be the difficult question (which is nonetheless a luxury) of choosing wisely be-tween the many options available. But in sharp contrast, for those whose position in the social and historical landscape condemns them to continu-ing inferiority, social inadequacy, and exclusion, the options are only two: to accept social rejection, cultural inferiority, and historical degradation in a pattern of self-destructive overcontrol and passivity, or to lash out violently and often irrationally against the institutions, the culture, and the legacy which condemns them to inferiority, deprivation, and humiliation.

In late adolescence, then, the relative importance of achieving emanci-pation and psychic independence from family tends to diminish, and in its place, issues of psychosocial and psychohistorical identity come to the fore. It is as if once relative inner and outer freedom from family control and dependency has begun to be achieved, the question of what to do with this freedom becomes central. At this point the adolescent turns from his family, and from the negative past of breaking and resolving his bonds with childhood, to the more positive task of defining himself, his future relationships, and his place in society. At this point in life, what society *really* offers him (not what it professes to offer him), what honor, merit, dignity, respect, and reward, makes all the difference.

THE OUTCOMES OF ADOLESCENCE

Central among the qualities which emerge is the capacity for com-mitment, engagement, loyalty, and fidelity. When we speak of the capacity for commitment, we are primarily referring not to an unquestioning ac-ceptance of the world as it is, but to the commitment to certain values, people, purposes, groups, goals, and strivings, to a set of imagined pos-sibilities, some of which are within the realm of partial attainment, to a set of values and ideals relevant to the evaluation of action and intent, and to enduring relationships with other people, to groups, and to institutions, and to the purposes these serve.

In the modern world, especially for the more talented, privileged, and sensitive among today's youth, commitments will often be fluid, open, and to a certain degree provisional. Indeed, the dizzying pace of social change and the fundamental unpredictability of the future means that increasingly, commitment to specific roles, traditional values, and existing institutions will be replaced by commitment to a set of general purposes, overriding values, historical possibilities, and styles of human relationships. To be able to make such commitments without undue inner conflict and ambivalence, and to act in their service, seems to us a defining characteristic of the psychological adult.

Underlying all other commitments, we believe, is a certain quality of commitment to self—not to the selfish pursuit of personal pleasure, but to a basic sense of one's own value, founded on a realistic assessment of one's capacities, potential usefulness, and real and possible achievements. Not to be confused with vanity, narcissism, or false pride, this proper sense of self-regard is not so much a matter of ranking oneself relative to others (How good am I?) as of developing an awareness of one's own actual strengths (What am I good at? Who am I good for?). It involves a willingness to be one's self, an effort to become more truly what one is, and a conviction that, in the end, *one is a self that is worth being.*

Without a sense of one's own strengths and potential usefulness, commitment to all other people and purposes is difficult, ambivalent, and often self-defeating. Such a commitment to self is made possible by familial and societal experiences and opportunities which enable the adolescent to test and define his real strengths and weaknesses, assets and liabilities, providing realistic opportunities for achievement and dignity. It is undermined by forces that convince the individual of his inadequacy and worthlessness, or that deprive him of realistic avenues of achievement, enjoyment, and dignity.

Especially in an achievement-oriented society, such as modern America, commitment to a task is a central value. The meaning of the task will vary from man to man, and man to woman—maintaining a home, rearing healthy children, satisfying job standards, achieving a life's work, writing a poem, running a lathe. But however the task is defined by individual purpose and social opportunity, the late adolescent ideally turns from the question of what to do with his life to actually doing it; and in this turning, work is of crucial importance. What society defines as productivity is too narrow a standard for commitment here, for many of our dissenting youth groups may devote themselves to work considered neither productive nor useful by traditional cultural standards. An extreme example of this is the young Negro in Watts who told Martin Luther King and Bayard Rustin to go back where they came from, for their method of commitment to the civil rights movement was ineffectual. This youth boasted that *his* method was working, and as he held up a match, he stated, "This is our manifesto and it's winning" (Rustin, 1968). Other groups reject work as a de-humanizing force in modern American society. One alienated youth in the East Village, New York City, stated, "It's the fact of not being yourself which is unbelievable—to me—oppressive. You can't be yourself in an office. Certainly the only time you might strive for that is on a weekend; but then it's too mannequin, too distorted, too grotesque" (Silverstein *et al.,* 1967). On the other hand, activist youth tend to avoid institutionalized careers and look with favor upon academic careers—at least so far as the academic career is able to provide them with "freedom" (Flacks, 1967). For the adolescent, however, the crucial task is the capacity to take upon oneself the achievement of competence in work, whether competence is defined in personal and idiosyncratic terms or, more commonly, in terms of the existing roles and rewards of postindustrial society. Further, commitment to a task entails commitment to activity that furthers it, even when the task is by definition endless. Phrased differently, as adolescence ends, the gap between grandiose purpose and puny accomplishment that characterizes many adolescents is narrowed, and the adult is able to turn to the fulfillment of specific tasks.

Another area of commitment is interpersonal, which we would define as the capacity for mutuality, that is, for entering into intimate reciprocal relationships in which the real needs and characteristics of each are centrally important to the other. For most, this capacity is concretized in marriage, where the complementarity of the sex roles is combined with a profound identification of each marriage partner with the other, with the other's welfare, and with the generation of a new family. But for others, this same capacity for mutuality is actualized primarily in friendship, in work, and in shared play. Interpersonal commitment involves the ability to relate to others, not despite their differences, but because of their unique individuality, which includes both their similarities and their differences from one's self.

The concept of commitment also entails a concern with the welfare of the wider community and, above all, care for the next generation. In adolescence, youth first feels itself part of a wider community and its historical tradition; in adulthood, this feeling is translated into activities consistent with and facilitative of the development of others. Increasingly, for Americans as for citizens of other nations, the relevant community is no longer the nation but the world. And in a time with cataclysmic possibilities for world holocaust, commitment to the next generation will increasingly involve, especially for the most historically conscious of American youth, a commitment to the avoidance of worldwide outbreaks of violence. But for most, commitment to the community and those who embody its future will be most concretely expressed in a capacity and willingness to bear and rear children thoughtfully and lovingly.

Finally, in a striving society that rewards and praises hard work, it is especially important to recall that one of the attainments of adolescence should be the development of the capacity for invigorating play. The future will bring increased opportunities for leisure, for recreation, and for enjoyment. It is too easy to forget, in a society that has not fully renounced the legacy of puritanism, that one of the tasks of adolescence is the development of a capacity to be childlike rather than childish, to live zestfully as well as purposefully, to be able to engage oneself fully with the world and with one's fantasies and passions, and to be capable of free, buoyant, exuberant, and spontaneous pleasure. In the absence of play, tomorrow's adults may be moral, virtuous, and responsible, but they will also be driven, compulsive, joyless, and grim.

THE RIGHT TO AN ADOLESCENCE

Although these are the characteristics by which we would try to distinguish the adult from the adolescent, we recognize that no adult ever possesses all of these qualities in full, and that they are approximate criteria, rather than a definition of what any one individual can ever be. Furthermore, we see a danger in separating adolescence too radically from adulthood by listing its "achievements" as we have done. As we have noted, adolescence does not end, but rather it simply fades away; and we must add the further qualification that adulthood does not mark the end of development, but a beginning of a lifetime of further development, intrapsychic as well as behavioral—none of which has yet been adequately studied or understood in our youth-oriented society. Especially for those most privileged, talented, and sensitive, adolescence in some sense may never end at all; the self is never finally consolidated or fixed, and commitments may not only be provisional, open, and fluid, but may involve a deliberate effort to retain and elaborate the flexibility, intellectual intensity, historical consciousness, sensitivity to the inner and outer worlds, and ethical passion which characterize adolescence at its best. Many of our alienated young understand this possibility for continued self-expansion and feel that it is "immoral to 'turn off' emotionally, to fail to grow, learn, experience, and fulfill oneself" (Silverstein et al., 1967). However, there is a difference beyond physiology and social role between the adolescent and the adult. What was latent becomes at best actualized; what was "mere" fantasy is ideally transmuted into the mainsprings of behavior.

Although we can outline provisionally the hallmarks of a "successfully completed adolescence," we cannot provide criteria for "mental health" during adolescence itself. The concept of "mental health," slippery and elusive during all other stages of life, is almost useless during adolescence, except perhaps as it describes the overall direction of development. The adolescent routinely exhibits "symptoms" that only reflect the routine trials of growing up, but which—were they to occur in later adulthood—would rightly be deemed ominous. Violent swings of mood and behavior, feelings of depersonalization and estrangement, hypomanic flights of ideas and frightening feelings of inner breakdown—all can be merely the signs of routine inner turmoil, and need not bode ill for the adolescent's future.

But the problem is complicated because some adolescent feelings and behavior are in fact ominous. Adolescence is the stage of life when a whole series of self-destructive and socially disruptive adaptations first make their appearance. Separating these ominous developments from the normal difficulties of adolescents is an important task, though not an easy one. In the end, the skilled adult who attempts to differentiate the ominous from the normal must fall back on developmental criteria, attempting to judge whether the adolescent's behavior reflects the routine turbulence of forward movement or the agitation of truly blocked development.

But even the most experienced clinician finds such differentiation difficult. And in our experience, the greater his experience, the more reluctant he is to label, characterize, and "diagnose" adolescent behavior. Untold harm is done by adults who attach to some transient aspect of the adolescent's behavior a self-confirming label like "delinquent," "schizophrenic," "homosexual," or "psychopathic." The vulnerable adolescent, already confused as to who he is, may seize upon even such negative rubrics in a despairing effort to be *someone*. Many of the disturbances of adolescence that endure into adulthood are the products of a similar interaction of the adolescent's hunger for self-definition with the adult world's thoughtless willingness to label him on the basis of a single act or episode.

The goal of all interventions with adolescents, then, should be to strengthen and confirm *them* in *their* development. Some adolescents may need special help; but the purpose of this help should not be to "cure" them of their "illness" (much less of their adolescence). Rather it should be to restore to the adolescent his capacity to proceed in his growth without special help. Too much help can be enfeebling, just as too much understanding without respect can be undermining. Even today, much of what passes for "counseling" short-circuits adolescence by undercutting the questioning, rebellion, and search that necessarily and productively should accompany the adolescent experience.

As more adequate "special help" becomes available for American youth, that help must seek to intensify, deepen, and in many cases prolong adolescence, rather than simply to hasten the passage to adulthood.

Mental Health as a Quest

Whether poor or affluent, the adolescent and youth of our time are indeed children of anxiety. Owing to the paucity of recorded attitudes which characterized earlier periods of our culture, comparisons of these eras with our own are fraught with possible errors. However, there are indications that today, because of the intensity, massiveness, and rapid pace of social change, the young's connections with previous generations, although far from severed, are rather more tenuous than has been true at any other period of our history. Further, today's youth lack the previously held, generally unquestioned, assumption that the future was predictable, secure, and stable. If there is much that is exciting, humane, and fraught with possibilities for human good in the modern world—and there certainly is—there is also a dark and ominous side, distinctive to our era, in which our young people live and move and have their being. Today's adolescents are seldom given, and would find it hard to accept, the reassuring myth of a predictable future. Indeed, the adolescent culture itself changes rapidly—the beatnik, the Peace Corps generation, the hippie, the New Left—all have followed themselves in rapid succession, with a concomitant shift in the focus of the adolescent identity. Thus, as the Group for the Advancement of Psychiatry (1968) has noted:

. . . Some of the manifestations of adolescence are not only specific to, but are partially caused by, the culture. Comparative anthropological considerations are useful to give perspective, to alert us to the arbitrariness and contingency of much of our cultural handling of adolescence, and even to offer possible alternatives and modifications. The biology of puberty is universal, but human reactions to puberty always occur within a particular culture, and adolescence becomes fully intelligible only through an awareness and understanding of the culture which surrounds it.

226

Task Force III has defined the societally important problems of adolescence and youth as essentially a function of the interaction between the instabilities of a developmental period and the instabilities of the historical era which happens to be our own. Under rather stringent limitations of time whereby priorities had to be set, this Task Force was pressed to the belief, as we reviewed the evidence, that the course of development in our youngsters from pubescence to adulthood would be most facilitated by a critical examination of the human environment that so critically shapes them. This emphasis on aspects of the social process and patterns of contemporary culture, as they affect youth, is not intended to denigrate the traditional clinical concerns of diagnosis, treatment, and facilities for psychiatric care. *We look upon these concerns as crucial.* Rather, it was felt that a greater understanding of the adolescent in the world today, by both adults and youth themselves, would result in less derailment and disturbance among adolescents, would help keep the young on a normal path and aid in preventing those first steps toward emotional illness. Once those first steps have occurred, this Task Force stresses the importance of *readily available* facilities—which are presently lacking—for all the segments of our youth population, in order to prevent the more serious and crippling effects of severe mental illness.

Against a reading of the contemporary environment, traditional concepts of mental health, although they retain a basic validity, lose a good deal of their vitality and relevance. Indeed, absolutism in the field of mental health is not merely imprecise and inflexible, but potentially destructive, particularly in dealing with adolescence. This critical human phase, halfway to full social status, is a formative period in which trial and error are a major part of the developmental process. Any monolithic and absolute view of mental health which seeks to apply uniform and moralistic standards to all developmental phases may consequently label for life an adolescent who, in the process of identity formation, is attempting to determine whether this situation, behavior, or way of thinking is really a part of his true self. In its very nature, the concept of mental health is subjective: it is a culturally determined idea, a product of social choice rather than an observable phenomenon. Because the idea is not objective, mental health is in one sense a mirage. Yet for all its seeming nonexistence, it is difficult to do without this concept—more for pragmatic reasons than for philosophical ones— as there is a limit to the amount of diverse behavior that any known society can value or tolerate, and certain observable responses like schizophrenia violate many accepted social mores. It is this inescapable mingling of necessity and amorphousness in the concept of mental health which accounts for much of the confusion about it that is endemic in our time.

The common belief that mental health is in parallel with physical health, and that mental illness is as definable, tangible, and biological an aberration as physical illness, has tended to foster psychological determinism[2] and to deemphasize the crucial human element of choice. Biological growth is a process that occurs in nature and can be observed, and while it can be interfered with, there is very little choice involved. Man does not choose how many fingers or livers he will have. On the other hand, much psychological growth *is* a matter of choice. Each choice a person makes, or chooses not to make, affects his development and results in potential changes in his mental being. His choices are not unlimited, nor are they irrevocable. Although an individual is not consulted about parents or place of birth, he can change his mind about jobs and marriage, and his *flexibility affects the development of his personality*. Similarly, his psychological growth depends quantitatively and qualitatively on the choices made by those who compose his external environment. Every day a child's parents and teachers make large and small decisions about his education, the values of his society, and how he is to learn them. In James Gould Cozzens' (1957) evocative phrase, the psychological growth of a human being can be described as a "decision tree"—the decisions made by a person and those close to him then branch to certain alternatives and preclude others.

The parsimony and the absolutism of the medical profession permeates both the field of mental health and the conception which the lay public has of mental illness, as well as the value system underlying notions of treatment, definitions of adjustment, and so on. Efforts, both lay and professional, to differentiate between physical and mental illness have, in general, only confused the issue.[3] To understand how monolithic standards of health,

2. The argument against absolute standards of mental health depends greatly on the principle of psychological choice, and thus we must consider psychological determinism as it affects the workings of the mind. To many psychoanalysts, this doctrine is the scientific basis of psychoanalytical theory and its definitions of regularity. Others feel, on the contrary, that a rigorous determinism is literally inconceivable. A third view, which dissents from both extremes and sees reality as something of a paradox, states that the ego (a psychoanalytic abstraction for a coherent series of mental operations) can make choices. The active part of the mind attempts to reach a reasonable decision about the evidence it is given, as if it were responsible and free. But in recognizing the reality of internal and external conditions, the ego accepts the limitations of its own choices, and makes workable decisions that are continuous with what has gone before. Robert Waelder (1960) describes this process: ". . . enough regularity exists in life to make rational action possible but not enough to make the future a foregone conclusion."

3. In recent years a number of professionals, most notably Dr. Thomas Szasz, have argued that because the physical-mental analogy is inaccurate, there is no such thing as mental illness. It is unfortunate that this error has had widespread acceptance in our culture because "proper" psychological performance is more a matter of opinion than of fact, and improper performance, with certain exceptions, is only slightly less vague a notion. But the exceptions are precisely where Szasz and his supporters go astray. Whereas illness implies deviation from clearly defined norms derived from the structure and function of the human body, nevertheless, in malfunctions like schizophrenia there can be no doubt that something is "wrong," that there is a deviation from a norm—in short, that a person is sick. Because the

including mental health, retain their force in the contemporary world we must understand the values of the doctors, and in particular the difference in values between those engaged in physical medicine and those who concentrate on emotional difficulties. Health, mental and otherwise, is an obsessive concern in our brawling, success-loving society, and doctors play a potent social role that affects almost everyone. Thus, the private values of doctors, and their interpretation of their role, exert an enormous influence on both the development and the persistence of the attitudes held by the mass of people in our society. Specifically, medical doctors believe that it is good to understand a patient's psychological condition if it is relevant to his physical complaint; otherwise it is secondary. They also feel that physicians should judge and direct in many situations and that only the patient's consciously stated feelings need interest the doctor. Psychoanalysts, on the other hand, believe that it is good to have an extensive understanding of a patient's psychological state and its connection with all his life experiences, but feel they should not, in their professional capacity, morally judge or direct their patients. They contend a patient's unconscious feelings exist simultaneously with the conscious feelings they may oppose, and must be taken into account. This emphasis on understanding has great importance, because an extensive understanding of a patient's psychological state and of its connection with all of his life experience is, in fact, the basis of psychoanalysis as a therapeutic technique. This belief in the benefits of understanding begins with the analyst himself, for the more he knows about himself, the better prepared he is to treat patients. For the analyst it is relatively easy to discover how a patient is similar to other people. In an interview or two, he can usually acquire a fair idea of the conflict dominating the patient at this particular moment. But if he is genuinely to determine how this person's history and particular conflict differ from other people's—in other words, how he is unique—he must devote careful, searching consideration to as many of the patient's thoughts and feelings as possible, and then form a coherent whole that will stand for this one human being.

This is the doctrine of inclusion. Despite protests to the contrary, the other specialties of medicine work mainly by exclusion. A series of possibilities is considered until either a diagnosis is reached or factors dangerous to the health of the patient have been eliminated. Some unusual findings can be overlooked if the main pathognomonic findings are negative. Physicians are parsimonious: if one diagnosis can explain everything, they will use it,

---

schizophrenic cannot function in our society, his disturbance is comparable to physical illness. By denying that so profound a disorder as schizophrenia is a form of illness, and preferring to consider it only as a problem in living, Dr. Szasz not only derails the public's belief that physical illness and mental illness are alike, but he dislocates everyone's understanding of less severe failures in adaptation adjustment.

but they move from one isolated possibility to another until they discover what is wrong, and then treat that. A patient may turn out to have a gall bladder ailment that the physician cures, but the backache remains a mystery. The physician still feels secure because he has taken care of "the trouble." It is impossible to separate emotional reactions in this way, for they are all part of the total individual. To understand any one emotional response, it must be examined in the light of the whole personality and cultural background. In discussing psychoanalysis—perhaps the most searching form of introspection yet devised—one can even say that there is no difference between diagnosis and treatment. The analyst's knowledge and understanding of himself is the treatment. Only at the end of the analysis is our knowledge inclusive enough to give a complete picture.

Once every individual is considered as a coherent whole, a unique entity, he cannot be characterized through any one set of standards. Inclusion is a comprehensive sociopsychological method, and everything pertaining to the patient must be considered: age, biology, family, clan, culture, humanity. In this perspective any standard of mental health becomes variable, and the meaning of illness, in the sense of disease, becomes obscure. What is paranoiac in a middle-class white suburban teen-ager may be nothing of the kind in an adolescent Harlem Negro; the habit of melodramatizing anecdotes may mean something different in Puerto Rican ghetto youth than it does in a seventeen-year-old middle-class Caucasian girl who wants to be an actress. But we are not merely saying that it is bad to think of people as stereotypes, for that is just another value judgment. Pragmatically, inclusion means that while some general standards of mental health are hard to do without, we must see each individual as a whole, instead of comparing him with others to find out what is wrong.

It is exceedingly difficult for people to accept the constant tolerance dictated by ambiguous individual standards. It is much more gratifying to pursue definite, unambiguous standards for "better" mental health with missionary zeal. Thus, psychological treatment is not only constantly entangled with the physical-mental analogy, but with moral preoccupations as well. Since physicians assume there is essentially one correct way for a particular organ to work, the proselytizers of mental health often apply the same yardstick to a person's psychological condition. People consult psychiatrists because they want to get better—meaning, as author Harold N. Boris has pointed out, that up to now he has been sick. More specifically, the patient wants to find out whether he is bad, and can help himself become good, or is sick, and cannot. In seeking psychiatric treatment, people fail to realize that their motives—how they *want* to deal with the world—are going to be identified and described; instead, they want prescriptions for "good" or "better" ways of being. Unhappily, the popular idea of mental health—an ideal state of inner peace and social adjustment—has grown uncritically out of conventional morality, and it describes what ought to be rather than what is. To speak of ambiguity, to distrust absolute, specific standards, seems amoral to the clergyman, police, parents, teachers, and physicians who now crowd the ranks of the mental health world. Once specific rigid ideals for behavior have been imposed, it is inevitable that similar strictures should be imposed on feelings. When these ideals are applied, patients, parishioners, the poor, and especially children are expected to demonstrate *proper* modes of feeling as well as action. These mental health goals become incongruous, even absurd, when inflicted upon disadvantaged groups. Instead of looking objectively for the ways that people can live more comfortably with themselves and others, the mental health evangelists insist that poverty is their first order of business. Somehow their marvelously expanded concept of mental health will get the poor off the streets and off welfare, miraculously curing their troublemaking impulses and transforming them into quiet, unobtrusive, and healthy citizens.

Another distortion, of a similar kind, appears when one thinks of a person's relationship to himself and to the life style that is currently touted as "healthy." No single set of psychological defenses or responses can be equally effective in every phase of an individual's life. Equally so, though a person's mental state can be observed at any moment of time, it does not remain the same over a period of time. But even though character can change and develop, flexibility is limited by the distinctive style that begins at birth. In each phase of life, heredity and development up to that point will either unite or conflict with the culture that surrounds an individual. For example, a superbly well-coordinated boy, always orderly and obedient to the rules, became a fine athlete and leader in high school. By the age of forty, however, the attitude toward life that had suited him so admirably in adolescence was less successful. Not only was he past the prime of his physical power, but the rules he had adhered to so strictly in youth turned out to be more ambiguous in adult society than they had been in school. There is similar incongruity in the case of an old man in a busy hospital ward who sat aloof, neat, and unruffled in the midst of geriatric chaos. The doctors found his cool but responsive dignity a refreshing contrast to the whining, depressed, demanding world of the old and sick. Yet the gallant old man's family wanted nothing to do with him. For the isolation and detachment from his surroundings that the doctors considered such a successful way to age had made that same man, as a young adult, chary of intimacy, and detached from emotional responsibility. What had been neurotic in the young man made the old man comfortable about himself and at ease with the outside.

On the other hand, the aging athlete had been, by any standard, a healthy adolescent; any suggestion of therapy at the time would have been idiotic. Freud (1937) warned against one of the serious disservices that psychoanalysis may have done our culture: to strengthen the myth of maturity, which assumes that a human being can successfully adapt to *all* the vicissitudes of life and social change, as if such capacity were infinite. Even Erik Erikson, whose concept of a life cycle has added brilliantly to our understanding of the relationship between psychoanalysis and culture, subtly gives the same impression. No slave to psychoanalytic orthodoxy, Erikson has made a fresh elucidation of the libido theory of child development, and has shown how early phases may persist in the competent adult. Yet even as he clearly states that individual development is nonlinear and variable, that it continues throughout life and is not fixed in childhood, he implies that if various factors are moderated within the framework of the culture, healthy people have it made all the way. This is a discomfiting implication to those who mistrust inflexible concepts of mental health. In order to work, such concepts must be precise and literal, eschewing the qualifications, doubts, and indistinctness of many human responses. By insisting on an absolute notion of right and wrong, such a concept, moralistic and righteous, confines man within unrealistic strictures. Adolescence is the clearest example of this dilemma, because at this time of life a person is halfway between childhood and adulthood. Neither the adolescent nor our culture can tolerate such straddling, and we need to remind ourselves often that adolescence is not a disease but part of growing up. A young person's nature is one of incessant contradiction, and the pendulum swings wildly from subjectivity and rebellion to objectivity and the need for adult understanding. In the presence of so much erratic turmoil, it is no small achievement to let adolescents know that they are adolescents (and all that this word implies). By facing a fact—that adolescence is limited by time and is also subject to variation and change—we forgo moralistic ideals of mental health. To avoid being overcome by impotent hopelessness, we strive for a neutral pragmatism.

Adolescence contributes to the formation of an individual human being in two important ways. First, out of emotional chaos, the youth distills a sense of all his different potential selves, but instead of accepting any one of them, he creates his own sense of self. Judged by specific standards of society, this sense may be unstable; but it is nonetheless committed to the preservation of society, and to his own relationships with others. In rejecting conventional standards of mental health, we try not to make the youth's acceptance of traditional values the criterion by which we evaluate his emerging identity. But we *do* look for some development of values; if an adolescent winds up in a mental hospital or a criminal gang, he violates the boundaries of psychosocial achievement. Second, through the process of "ritualization,"[4] as it has developed through childhood and into adolescence, the youth acquires in the adolescent period an ideology, a coherent

4. Ritualization is Erikson's (1966) term for a mutually accepted interplay between at least two persons who repeat it at intervals and in recurrent contexts, and which must have adaptive value for the ego of each participant.

framework of values and ideals, and a structure to ideas. Thus the individual learns what he must do to live reasonably in society. According to Erikson (1968), "Much of youthful 'demonstration' in private or in public represents a dramatization of a spontaneous search for new forms of artful or ideological ritualization invented by or for youth itself." The search of young people today has an even deeper significance because our culture itself is dedicated to change, in technology and in less well-defined areas. The search for ritual, for ideological form, is an attempt to counteract the meaninglessness and vagueness of existing conventions and values. Because our society permits considerable deviation, we omit the formalized steps from one phase of life to another that would be taken in a highly formal society. As a result, we place great unconscious importance on psychological processes that are orderly throughout life, one developmental step following upon another.

In the very ritual delineated for adolescence, we see how young people experiment with development, and thus how misleading a specific ideal of mental health can be for them. The adolescent's naïveté-cynicism is like the infant's trust-mistrust, but it is strongly influenced by the outside culture. He feels that all previous dissenters have compromised, but what it is that he must keep pure is never clear.

When we say that human strength is a process, just as ritualization and "mental health" are processes, we come to the crux of our argument. Different historical periods emphasize different conflicts, which in turn create different crises and solutions. Human strength depends on the new crisis, which exposes new strengths and new weaknesses. In sum, we have a complex network of checks and balances in psychic equilibrium with a shifting culture. For want of a better name, we call this total process (not one part of it) mental health, which permits perpetual ambivalence and ambiguity, and still allows for spontaneous action.

But this view clashes with some of man's most primitive fears. Life is frightening, and people long for definition, not namelessness. Rituals are not standards, and in our time even psychoanalytic objectives are culturally *promoted* as mental health. This very promotion is what renders absolute criteria for mental health imprecise and, in fact, ruinous. Whether the standard is "love thy neighbor," "to thine own self be true," or "work and love," once it is fixed as a concrete goal demanding uncritical religious belief, rather than a relative, limited, and variable concept, it leads by the way of disappointment to rage and, ironically, to the destruction of these very principles of human strength we are attempting to uphold. As Michael Oakeshott (1963) has remarked, "To try to do something which is inherently impossible, is always a corrupting enterprise."

This enigma is not at all new to psychoanalysts. In the 1890's Freud wrote, "We have found a therapeutic method, abreaction, which caused each hysterical symptom immediately and permanently to disappear when we had succeeded in bringing clearly to light the memory by which it was provoked" (Breurer and Freud, 1936). Forty-two years later, he cautioned, "The first step towards attaining intellectual mastery of our environment is to discover generalizations, rules and laws which bring order into chaos. In so simplifying the world of phenomena, we cannot avoid falsifying it" (Freud, 1937). By 1937, then, not only had Freud left his earlier certainty about mental health far behind, but he felt it necessary to emphasize the curious paradox discussed in this essay: the process of searching for mental health may become an end in itself. The search can be ennobling if we choose to *struggle*, but it is demoralizing if we believe that the ultimate goal is an ideal society of people who will be "healthy" all their days. For Task Force III, then, "mental health" is a process, a struggle, and a *quest* rather than a relatively static state of being. The mentally healthy individual thus becomes one whose private life is evaluated against such somewhat vague but still highly meaningful concepts as integrity, authenticity, and self-determination, and whose relationships with others may be judged in the light of such notions as effective intimacy in love and friendship, contributory participation in the affairs of a community, and the breadth of his sympathy with others whose background of experience differs from his own. A capacity to shape one's own destiny is, therefore, as important as a capacity to adapt and to adjust to rapidly altering circumstances, and a measure of zest in coping with the shifts and stresses in the contemporary environment is a germane touchstone of mental health. Viewed from a developmental angle of regard, the particular behaviors that fulfill the criteria implied by these terms are likely to change—often rather markedly—with both the stages of life and the conditions of the environment.

To understand the process whereby people live and struggle together, devise sustaining rituals, maintain fairly stable social groups, and care about each other seems bleak against the vision of Utopia. But this understanding can achieve spontaneity and aim at bringing recognizable order out of potential chaos. As Erikson (1966) points out, it is impossible to prescribe ritualization because it is pervaded by the spontaneity of surprise. "It thus depends on that blending of surprise and recognition which is the soul of creativity, born out of the abyss of instinctual disorder, confusion of identity, and social anomie."

Professionally, we know that we cannot always make such concepts work, but *we can strive toward social education.* We must find meaningful ways of presenting not only to our children but also to adults the true nature of the human animal, and demonstrate how difficult it is to try to keep society's standards reasonable and flexible without sacrificing the ability to act spontaneously. This is equally true of our eating habits and our sexual ones, our parental concerns and our pedagogical ones. It is true that our concept of human strength establishes only an uneasy equilibrium and denies the comfort of a continuum. But those in the helping professions must try to dissociate themselves from goals they know are excessive, for when we expect too much of ourselves and of others, we are continually disappointed. Because people must understand this above all, it is the professionals' job to teach it.

Quest Through Societal Involvement

AN ADOLESCENT EXPERIENCE FOR ALL

As never before in history, our national climate is conducive to the creation of a new type of adolescence, one in which the majority *could* experience the expansion, autonomy, and growth that is potentially implicit in this stage of life and which is so crucial to the assumption of a rewarding and responsible citizen role. But, to varying degrees—depending upon ethnic and class membership—our adolescents and youth today find themselves in a state of limbo. The community at large regards them as neither children nor adults. Yet, this large and increasing proportion of our population is growing ever more biologically mature at an earlier age.[5] Coinciding with this early physical maturity is the greater sophistication of today's adolescents and youth. Never before have so many in this population segment been so well educated, so aware of the world historical events, and so ready to participate in the realm of societal undertakings. Correspondingly, at no other period have adolescents and youth been so excluded from the adult world or so alienated from the roles which their previous counterparts shared with adults. Whereas previously work or apprenticeship provided some interaction between the adolescent and adult, today's world of work has become increasingly age-graded and specialized and is seldom tailored to the skills, potential, and creativity of youth. It is often irrelevant to a future adult working role, devoid of meaningful interaction between persons of

5. Menarchy in American girls now typically occurs at age 12.5, rather than at age 14+, as in previous eras. Boys are also exhibiting sexual maturity at an earlier age (Tanner, 1962, p. 153).

236

the younger and older generations, and characterized by a status which implies the immaturity accorded to youth by society. Yet, the youthful worker, like the older worker, is expected to assume a mature, responsible work role, to pay his taxes, and so forth. Perhaps even more than the student, the youthful worker is expected to serve his country, whether it be an era of military crisis or of peacetime, and if his conscience should dictate otherwise, he—like the student—is penalized. Whether worker, scholar, soldier, or unemployed, youth are denied adult privileges but expected to assume adult responsibilities. Until recently eighteen-year-olds weren't allowed to vote, yet all states legally sanctioned the selective service system. In many places, the youthful soldier who is expected to die for his country cannot legally buy alcoholic beverages until he is twenty-one and the college student who is expected to behave largely according to adult standards cannot prove he is capable of doing so because *in loco parentis* still regiments his life. In short, the larger community has yet to create a meaningful place for today's youth. The idealism, the hopes and longings so characteristic of the young today, can generally be expressed only "outside the establishment." Such expressions, having few roots in culturally sanctioned values—at least as far as youth's inclusion is concerned—meet either with punitive measures or with disapproval or are ignored by the adult world.

Our review of the facts about American youth today leads us to the conclusion that far too small a proportion of Americans have available to them the societal resources requisite to the full unfolding, differentiation, and individuation of personality during adolescence. Far too often, the years that follow puberty lead only to self-restriction, rigidity, and constriction, to premature foreclosure, and to the uncritical assimilation of the childhood world and its unexamined assumptions about self, family, and society.

Our primary concern, then, is that the impediments and obstacles to adolescence are still too numerous in American society. These impediments include cultural and social deprivation; overt and subtle discrimination; unimaginative, coercive, or simply inadequate educational resources; the absence of opportunities for imagination and experimentation; irrational pressures toward conformity to peer groups and adult authority; and the far too prevalent assumption by adults that all adolescent criticism of the older generation is perverse, trivial, or unworthy of a hearing. Few adults attempt to analyze the motivations underlying the varied, often desperate, dissent of today's adolescents and youth. Thus, most adults are either unaware of or unempathic toward such phenomena as the agonizing search among affluent youth for ideals and values which seem worthy of commitment and which promise to alleviate social injustices or of the desperate quest for personal identity and societal respect among young Negro radicals. Equally so, adults are oblivious to the crippling effects of passivity and insensitivity characteristic of many youths. The older generation has yet to grasp the fact that youth today have no place to go, no culturally sanctioned roles which they find satisfying, few means of redress for wrongs, and no channels through which their idealism can become incorporated into social reality. But if adults are unaware of youth's agonies they are equally unaware of their skills—of the great potential which lies in this untapped pool of manpower. To avail ourselves of this potential we must listen to youth's ideas and capitalize on their creativity, energy, and talents. Rather than tell youth how things should be—no matter how well intentioned such vestiges of authoritarianism may be—we must allow them the freedom to explore, to participate, and to help plan the world which we share together.

To romanticize adolescents would overlook the existence in every youth of enduring childishness, underlying dependency, systematic provocations, and often obstinate unwillingness to accept the responsibilities of maturity. Earlier biological maturity is not necessarily followed by earlier emotional maturity and, in fact, may add to the problems inherent in trying to reach emotional maturity. However, we doubt that adolescent ambivalence is solely responsible for the foreshortening and derailing of adolescence. Some degree of responsibility also lies within our families, which before and during adolescence promote anxieties, fears, rigidities, and guilts that make further development difficult; within our educational system, which too rarely touches, much less strengthens or consolidates, the adolescent's capacity for rationality, ethicality, sentience, and moral passion; within our social institutions, which perpetuate injustices that deprive many in American society of any possibility of a constructive adolescent experience. Most frequently, the responsibility for the failure of adolescence lies with the vicious interaction of all these forces, especially among that large minority of young Americans who are simultaneously deprived familially, educationally, and societally. Thus, we wish to emphasize those actions, public and private, which might better guarantee for all young Americans the possibility of an adolescent experience.

Adolescence is, of all later stages in life, that which can most readily permit profound reorientation of intrapsychic and interpersonal life. A benign, responsive, and confirmatory environment can enable an adolescent to undo vast damage done in earlier childhood, to heal the wounds of parental inconsistency, ignorance, or neglect, and to move beyond the handicaps of his past to a responsible and satisfying maturity. Adolescence can provide those lucky enough to have a second chance an opportunity to move away from the malignancies of family pathology, social disorganization, and deprivation. All too often, those who need this second chance most are precisely those who are denied the opportunities. We still know too little about the precise way in which the adolescent can, with a favorable and supportive environment, free himself from the scars of childhood. But we know enough to be certain that American society today does far too little to support the self-renewing capacities of its youth, and we insist that Americans have the right to such an adolescence.

ADULT-YOUTH DISCONTINUITIES

We believe there is a growing "generation gap," an alienation between youth and adult with a lack of mutual trust and respectful involvement with each other. Channels of communication between generations tend to be choked off by misunderstandings, and attempts at communication often take the form of demands for unconditional surrender. In a song that is a manifesto of the rebellious young, Bob Dylan answers the older generation's insistence on the essential rectitude of its view and ways with an ultimatum.[6]

While much has been said about alienated youth, there has been insufficient emphasis upon the alienated adult who cannot or will not tolerate, accept, and integrate himself with the younger generation. We emphasize this in the belief that the adjustment of the adolescent to the society is an oversimplified and hazardous goal. The adolescent, as any individual, must be allowed more freedom to adjust the society to himself. He must even be *encouraged* to have more of an impact upon the society through meaningful involvement with the older generation.

These principles apply to all institutions and groups—as much to the hippies, the acid heads, the protesters, the disillusioned, and the bored of the middle and upper classes as they do to the delinquents, the drug addicts, the rebels, the dropouts, and the unemployed youth of the disenfranchised classes. But they are tenets that can generate a maximum effect in the relationships between adults and adolescents because adolescence is a time when identity and social involvement are often in crisis and always in the making, a time of heightened feeling and intensified potential for change. Yet, too often alienated and intimidated adults abandon the adolescent at the crucial time, thereby forcing the adolescent to "give up" to society or to "drop out." Rather than fostering adolescent withdrawl into futile, self-destructive antisocial subcultures, or forcing youth into revolutionary poses to achieve social change, we must do our best to open up society to them. We must give them a voice in the world we share. We must be prepared to hear and to be influenced, much as we wish to be heard and to influence. Under existing conditions, youth have few sanctioned meaningful channels for active involvement and participation in our society. Youth are demanding entrance into the world we have labeled "for adults only." We must give them legitimate roles to play.

6. In his song, "The Times, They Are A-Changin'."

DIRECTIONS OF YOUTH

The Negro

The directions which society offers become an either-or alternative—either withdrawal, through drugs or passivity, or "acting out" through protests, riots, rebellions, and the like. The "normal" channel of participation is lacking.

These either-or behaviors, in fact, may reflect differently expressed manifestations of an underlying wish to change our society. Among small minorities of both disadvantaged and affluent youth, there is a pervading belief that our society is not worth redemption. The more affluent who are of this opinion may simply "drop out," turning often to drugs and seeking a group isolation within a hippie community, or may channel their energies into the activities of the New Left. Others may withdraw from society to lesser degrees, as we will note later. In contrast, the destructiveness inherent in the black radical movement grows ever more intense, ever more persuasive to desperate and disenchanted black youth. The black radicals have become as distrustful of moderate Negro leadership as of the white power structure. One young radical, upon being interviewed, stated to a member of this Task Force:

... The riots mean to the black man in America that if he can't win his freedom, his equality by peaceful means, he will have to turn to something else. He'll have to resort to violence. And the Declaration of Independence gives him that right. It says that when a government doesn't give the governed what the governed demand, then they have the right to change that government by whatever means is necessary. Burn it down, if necessary.[7]

Like his fellow radicals, this youth spoke only of bringing it down, no word of plan, future, or what he wants. Yet, it is certain that he wants respect and a share in power. When he says his situation is desperate and that he is on the train to death, he means to convey that this very recognition gives him strength to fight and offers a reason for fear from "honky." He becomes angered when white men speak of the Negro's difficulty, because he does not want pity and help; he wants out. Out where the strength derived from his slow but now fully realized recognition of his plight—total dependence on an unfaithful and destructive enemy, the white man—will magically repair the economic and educational damage of centuries. If he allows himself for one minute to want their help, he is dead because then he is right back in the same dependent bag from where he started. He thus

7. Paper prepared for the Task Force by N. Zinberg, "The Negro Adolescent."

tends to reject existing Negro leadership and the best intentions of white liberals.

The changes in the philosophy of black radicals have brought about corresponding changes in the outlook of many whites. During the years of nonviolent protest among the Negroes, the whites were unable to project their own feelings of black rage, dirty lust, and foul violence that are an intolerable and unacceptable part of their own psychic striving. But when Negroes began to riot, the old stereotype of the Negro as the wild, uncontrolled one was again revived. Instead of guilt, the whites experienced fear, a fear at least partly due to their own repressed feelings. Once the Negro exhibits a sense of power and willingness to use violence, many whites, relieved of their sense of guilt and out of their fear, must "resist" the terrible Negro. This need to resist amounts to license to express and act on anti-Negro feelings. Such whites, like those police who fear the Negro, feed the radical's image of strength and potential destructiveness. The black radical feels at least that he is respected. The liberal Jew, on the other hand, becomes the black radical's target for hatred because he cannot bear the Jew's wish to be accepted into the establishment, and his insistence on offering a concept of slow integration of "passing" as a way out for the Negro.

Erik Erikson proposed a concept of identity that helps explain this reaction. Identity is different from identification with a particular individual. All of us, in growing up, *uncritically* assume the mannerisms and attitudes of key people. This collection of identifications during adolescence begins to coalesce or synthesize into a coherent identity; we can then think of ourselves as people with multiple facets rather than trying to decide who we are among seemingly disorganized and unrelated parts. Even this more synthesized view of ourselves has a negative as well as a positive aspect and is an amalgam of how we view ourselves along with how we are viewed by those with whom we identify. In this view of identity, therefore, an essential ingredient is our understanding of how the outside culture in which we grow up views us. Also our value system, in part, would be based on that of the culture in which we are reared.

The black American adolescent has the same basic struggle attaining identity formation as anyone else but with certain additional hardships. His world view includes, inevitably, common values such as: a child should have a chance for health care and education; women are also people; time and space have invariable limits and regularity; and many others. That these values are basically part of the Negro's identity is evinced by the fact that many Negroes who have gone to Africa with the Peace Corps or otherwise realize sadly that, in spite of the brotherhood conferred biologically, they are closer to the spirit of whitey. Hence, the positive identity of the Negro reflects the view of the world held by the dominant white majority and pulls him toward them. The view of himself, however, includes their views of him, and in this culture, unfortunately, this is indeed a poor image. The negative identity—the collection of debased self-images—would then have to be accepted if he accepts this tug toward white responsibility. It is only if he uses the negative identity as an alternative rather than a concomitant and says yes, he is black and ugly, potent and destructive, untrustworthy and shifty, that he can stand up. If he accepts the white view of himself from their vantage point, he is nothing. If he accepts the same view but changes the vantage point, he makes his identity a thing of pride.

But a vital part of the Negro radical position, of the new identity, springs from a faith in the black people—that is, the soul brothers, a concept entirely irrational to white ears. It is the "soul brothers" who will bring about the downfall of the present system, and it is this mystic faith in the commonality of the black skin which provides a base of solidarity. Radical leaders hope to channel the free-floating aggression of the Negro community which is often released within the group, and they think the group solidarity derived from *black* will be very different from the loose confederation of the weak and rootless derived from *Negro*. The present emphasis upon group solidarity disposes of the white argument that the Negroes are crippled by breakdown in family structure, poor education, cultural disadvantages, and economic deprivation. It provides a faith that they have good stuff in them, that they are not rotten all the way through, and that what they might not be able to do individually, they can do as a group. Above all, it says to the whites, "We don't need *you*."

The lack of understanding of individual psychology prevents some workers from understanding the range, depth, and complexity of the psychological position of the American adolescent Negro who feels pushed into a radical position from both sides of himself and from both the black and the white worlds. We should be able to see the sense in their plight, their protest, and their actions—which does not mean that we must accept it— and plan our programs accordingly. This will be hard on many whites whose attitudes, rooted in the Protestant ethic and in prejudice, do not readily permit receptiveness to wide-ranging social programs designed to alleviate unjust conditions and give the Negro dignity.

But even if programs such as family allowance, negative income tax, job retraining, new schools, reform of welfare laws, slum clearance, model housing, medical assistance, etc., were promptly enacted—all of which would be beneficial—these would not be enough. Short-term programs would need to be devised which capture the imaginations of the radicals and pull them in willy-nilly. These programs must challenge them and offer them, at least in part, some of what is implicit if not explicit in their position. First would be more specific political enfranchisement. The radicals must be given considerable political and social responsibility for programs— including the running and planning of specific programs. There may be many fiascoes, but at least we can learn by working together, and the main lesson learned may be virtually one of national survival. Working together means that the whites should offer sympathetic and controllable expertise, not overriding and controlling domination.

The Alienated

While the alienation of our more affluent youth cannot be attributed to the same type of disadvantaged circumstances as that among Negro radicals —whether these circumstances be poverty, discrimination, or both—it seems evident that our institutional structure has produced a profound sense of social and personal emasculation of many middle-class youth. This conclusion was borne out by a survey commissioned by this Task Force in which a representative group of 33 alienated youth, ranging in age from seventeen to twenty-five, who resided and participated in the bohemian East Village community of New York City frankly expounded upon their experience of growing up in middle-class Americana. Although these young people are above the average in terms of education and family income, they are not typical of middle-class young people; considerable involvement in art, for example, and the decision to come to the East Village are in themselves atypical. Nor are they typical "hippies." However, they may well be "representative" of both the middle-class conformist youth and the hippies in the sense that both have taken the route of passivity.

These youth differ from other middle-class youth in that they have left home and their relatively secure economic circumstances. They have moved into an impoverished bohemian area and have limited themselves to a way of life in which impoverishment is equated with a more noble state of man. They are representative of a transitional group, and of many "troubled" middle-class youth who have not yet made the decision to become déclassé. We believe this group of youth is extremely sensitive to the demands, norms, and pressures of the middle-class life style. The frustration, disappointment, and conflict that result from the opposition of conformative and alienative pressures undoubtedly affect a very large number of middle-class young people. These pressures appear at maximum intensity among this interview sample, who, in this regard, may be seen as amplifiers of the major problems of their generation. They can be regarded as "instruments"—thermometers, for example—that can be used to diagnose the cultural conditions facing their generation. However, in so regarding them, the fact should not be obscured that the process of measurement often entails a certain amount of wear and tear on the measuring instrument. Frustration; confusion about one's identity; anxiety and an inability to think realistically about the future; disturbances in relationships with elders and with peers; inability to make the transition between adolescent and adult roles; the conviction that the world of the American middle-class is unsatisfactory and stultifying to the spirit and mind, that a life of poverty is, for different reasons, unsatisfactory and stultifying to the spirit and mind; and that American society offers very few legitimate alternatives to this unhappy choice; and a feeling of impotence to change an uncongenial world for the better—these are some of the consequences of being sensitive to the social and cultural climate in which middle-class young people find themselves. It is a working assumption of the Task Force that such "symptoms" affect a great number of young people in our society, even though they may not experience these symptoms in the same intensity, or describe them with the same fluency, or so stubbornly resist—at least for the moment—the lures of the not-so-bad job or the not-so-bad marriage as is characteristic of our sample.

As these 33 young people discussed their experiences and attitudes, several consistent patterns of responses emerged. First, there is a rather complex rejection of the dominant values of middle-class America. For example, *materialism* is rejected by these youth, thus their withdrawal into a community where financial interests are of secondary importance and poverty, although at times physically uncomfortable, is seen as socially and spiritually ennobling.

In addition, there are repeated comments about *ritualistic conformity* perceived as ever present in the behavior of the adult generation. These youth see their elders as essentially unfulfilled and reason that this failure to explore one's basic potentiality lies in their tendency to opt for economic and social security without sufficient efforts directed toward achieving a higher level of individualistic attainment. The world they experience is seen as populated by compulsive social, political, and economic robots who will in all probability remain "underdeveloped" for the balance of their lives. Hence, these youth imply that for them to adapt to this form of social participation will therefore deny them the opportunity to explore maximally their own potential, or put another way, this potential is not afforded viable alternatives for its own development.

Closely related to this pattern of conformity is the observation that society is replete with individual and institutional *hypocrisy*—a belief we have already commented upon. Furthermore, these youth point to the *irrelevance* of the content and substance of social institutions in which their participation is required, especially in the educational world where, as students, they were ill prepared for the present and future realities of contemporary life. Although many of these youth continue their association and contact with schooling, they do so in unhappy ritualism.

Just as educational systems are regarded as dead-end and spiritually decimating experiences, they see middle-class family life as essentially *pointless*. They believe that members of the middle class are too deeply involved in an overconventional behavioral style, so much so that humanistic interests and objectives, again critical for individual development, are totally absent. This is found fully developed in their discussions of sexuality and drug use, both of which they regard as necessary for human potentiality and growth.

In sum, these youth have substantially withdrawn from conventional middle-class community life and gravitated to the bohemian life style and milieu. To a large extent, this withdrawal is fairly complete, although obviously not total. For some, this pattern is an act of defiance and anger; for others it is an attempt on their part to sever their dependent ties at home and embark on an independent course of social and personal development. Although this may appear as fundamentally dysfunctional—that is, socially discontinuous and therefore maladaptive—it might also be suggested that their course of action is basically a preparation for social and personal competence in the future. During a period in which resolution of personal identity may occur, these youth are exploring a number of viable social alternatives, among which is their own interest in participating in creative and artistic endeavors.

Of course, this process of independent exploration has several risks. For some it may trigger profound identity confusion as well as social disorientation. Much of this depends upon the conditions and social experiences with which they will be confronted while they are engaged in the process of withdrawal. Most of these experimenters will in all likelihood return to the social community of their origin, perhaps picking up the threads of middle-class life—a bit depressed, anxious, and discontented by this final option. Along the way, some may by chance have enjoyed a vitalizing and salient experience, and in those cases, the move for independence will have been useful for their growth. However, since the communities to which they have gravitated are not organized to deliver this revitalization, it would appear that this would occur in only a very few cases.

For many, bohemianism may be a disillusioning experience, defined by them as a retrievable error. And in some cases, it may lead to severe disturbance and profound disorientation. Aware of the hazards of premature prognostications, we would guess that most of these youth will return "home" without suffering any of the significant difficulties which are often thought to emerge in "retreatist" communities such as the East Village. In this regard, however, our information is incomplete, and further inquiry concerning the possible dangers and benefits is needed before more reliable predictions can be made. Recent descriptions of hippie communities across the country have emphasized a number of sources of potential difficulty among youth entrenched in these subcultures; yet more objective inquiry is still necessary.

Finally, we regard as unfortunate the current sociological research that so far has failed to provide us with more comprehensive and circumstantial observations of middle-class community life. A somewhat one-sided view of this community was offered by those youth who have been socialized into it and who have, if only temporarily, rejected further participation in it. Whether their conceptions of economically advantaged community life offer us a usable index of its substance and nature remains problematic. Nevertheless, it seems evident that any institutional structure producing so profound a sense of social and personal emasculation as these youth express requires careful evaluation. Competent and fully developed youth require competent communities which foster, or at least permit, their continuous growth.

The Activists

Many have dubbed this the "generation of protest." This appellation seems fundamentally incorrect when applied to the vast majority of students at most colleges. Only small minorities have been actively committed to political or societal change, even at those colleges and universities where student protests, political activity, and dissent have been most publicized. In fact, protests over the quality of food served in student cafeterias may be a more common issue than that of American involvement in Vietnam or civil rights. In general, the rule is student conformity or indifference, and the exception is student activism or protest.[8] However, those who share the views of the activists are increasing in number. The attitude of the activists toward the school and society is expected to become more prevalent in the years ahead.

Although both the alienated and the activists comprise only a small percent of their age cohort, they are an influence—far greater than their numbers would imply—on the vast majority of their conforming peers. Together they are a major force which is helping to shape and color the idiosyncratic character of the current generation.

But despite the relatively small numbers of students involved in demonstrations, protest activities, and the like, the phenomenon of student protest and dissent preoccupies not only the general public but much of the time and energy of college administrators. This Task Force feels that the nature and meaning of most student dissent is grossly misunderstood, not only by

8. It was the conclusion of a group of Fellows at the Center for Advanced Study in the Behavioral Sciences which held several seminars at Stanford University between December 1967 and April 1968 that less than 10 percent of a given student body is actively involved in initiating activist demonstrations on campuses ("Student Protests . . . " , 1968).

The National Student Association reported that there were 221 major demonstrations involving 38,911 participants or 2.6 percent of the enrolled student body of the college students from January 1 to June 15, 1968 (*New York Times*, Aug. 27, 1968).

the general public (who must depend upon often unreliable information in the mass media), but even by many of those administrators who deal directly with students. For example, it is widely thought that student political and societal activists are "misfits" who are in some way rebelling against parental authority. In fact, activists are drawn from among the most academically talented, idealistic, and committed of today's college students. They generally come from politically active and liberal families whose values they are not rebelling against but rather *implementing*.[9] Activists are strongly committed to traditional American ideals of justice, equality, and democracy, as well as faith in human nature and the efficacy of human action. Thus activists tend to believe that through human efforts the American Dream can be realized for *all,* and that the discrepancies between ideals and actions can be eliminated. Activist students want to improve their country—and they want to begin by improving the one institution that is closest to them, the college itself.

This Task Force finds little reason to be disturbed over the occurrence of *orderly* student protest and dissent, which seems to us in the best tradition of citizens' involvement in the political process. We are more concerned that so relatively few students are currently involved in the critical examination of the present policies and future directions of our society. We are more distressed that lawmakers, administrators, and the general public so often fail to appreciate the nature and promise of today's student political involvement, and seek to curtail, restrict, or limit the active involvement of today's college population in the crucial national and international problems that beset our nation. An attitude of uncomprehending opposition and efforts to sabotage student activism are detrimental to the development of a mature and responsible political attitude on the part not only of activists but of their less active classmates. Activists, frustrated by the deafness and restrictiveness of those to whom they address themselves, are tending toward more and more desperate efforts to draw attention to their causes. Finally, they may move outside the realm of democratic political discourse and activity. The apathetic student is further convinced by the public reaction to his dissenting classmates that any effort on his own part to work for an improvement in his community or his society would be destined to failure, and that he had, therefore, best devote himself to the pursuit of grades, popularity, and material success. In this way, rigid opposition to and incomprehension of the often legitimate com-

9. In fact, the occurrence of student protests or organized efforts to hasten social change is strongly correlated with the academic quality and prestige of the colleges where such activities occur. Parents of activists are largely from the upper-middle class and as a group place greater stress on involvement in "intellectual and esthetic pursuits, humanitarian concerns, opportunities for self-expression, and tend to deemphasize or positively disvalue personal achievement, conventional morality, and conventional religiosity" (Flacks, 1967; Smith, 1968).

plaints, demands, and proposals of student activists serve to push activists toward extremism and nonactivists further into conformity.

Neither of these outcomes is consistent with the traditional American conviction that citizens be encouraged to inform themselves about major public issues, take positions with regard to these issues, seek to persuade others of the validity of their convictions through legitimate avenues, and attempt to change and improve American society. Nor does an attitude of opposition to student political and societal involvement help prepare students, many of whom are already voting citizens, for responsible involvement in the life of a democratic society. Therefore, encouragement should be given students to discuss all current issues, on and off campus, and to take positions and legitimate action concerning a variety of issues from the governments of the university communities to international foreign policies, knowing as they do that they speak only for that particular organization of which they are a part, and not for the university, or school. High schools and colleges should encourage and facilitate students to become knowledgeable about and involve themselves in local community issues, as well as in state, national, and international policies. Thus academic and extra-academic concerns in the community surrounding the school should be discussed in the context of disciplined academic inquiry within the classroom. High schools and colleges should provide a forum for speakers of a variety of persuasions, beliefs, and faiths regardless of their "controversiality." In so doing, it is imperative that schools defend the right of free speech in general, not the particular right of some partisan group with a vested interest in one position. Zealous student activists of all persuasions must respect the rights and freedoms of other students, and speakers. And colleges must be prepared to defend the rights of minorities of students who hold views unpopular with their fellow students, with faculty members, with administrators, and with those responsible for the overall governance of and support of the school. In all political activities, civil disobediences, breaches of peace, etc., students who are subject to civil action should not be subject to disciplinary action by the school for the same offense. Where existing civil laws do not apply, the school must have the right to establish its own standards of intellectual integrity, attainment, and decency within the school. Whenever possible, student publications should be self-governing, and when feasible, financially independent; in addition, they should be limited in their freedom of expression only by the laws that govern the press in the United States. Thus, this Task Force feels that high schools, colleges, and universities ought to encourage this "generation of protest" by meeting with and listening to students who present demands, grievances, and concerns. Vigorous and controversial debate is the most powerful device that a nation possesses in training its students for democratic citizenship.

All Youth

Owing to the enormous diversity in America's youth, no one characterization is adequate to comprise the Negro radicals, the alienated, the activists, and those in the majority conforming population, whether working, in the military system, or in school. However, as previously indicated, each of the many segments of youth in our society aids in setting the tone and direction of our current and future generations. What do these varieties of young share? What is there that is, within varying degrees, common to all, from which we can draw some thoughts that will help us in understanding, reaching toward, and learning from this ever increasing portion of our population? Many of these ways of thinking or of doing things are characteristic of only a particular segment of today's youth, but the *tendency* to act and react in this manner drifts down in varying degrees to the other divisions of the young.

Indeed, youth today do not feel as divided as our discrete categories would indicate. In fact, one central tendency, different for this generation than for others, is that of an overwhelming identification with the peer group, rather than with elders, a particular class stratum, or an organizational structure. Today's adolescents and youth tend to form alliances among themselves, not infrequently in opposition to sanctioned authority and in protest against traditional forms of social organization. They do not have clearly defined leaders and heroes, but rather their identification is, first, to their own particular small group and, second, to the larger youth movement. A division of two or three years may constitute a real change in a way of thinking, or an approach to a goal, and therefore, there are distinctions made within the segments of youth themselves, for example, between the old New Left, the New Left, and the new New Left, as well as between seventh graders and ninth graders. Youth's leaders must move rapidly to make their impact in a brief period, before they are "dated" and outworn. Psychologically, this tendency is partly responsible for the generation gap, as the ideologies of previous generations are viewed as depleted or irrelevant. Thus it becomes possible for the adolescent of any class or ethnic group to view an older person of any class or ethnic group, regardless of the older person's higher position on the status scale, as simply a "stupid old man," and in confrontations this epithet is often liberally applied.

Another tendency, which is somewhat in conflict with the latter trend, is the ethos of personal development, a part of which is an emphasis on openness to all new experiences and interactions. Thus, many youth are not willing to accept a fixed end—say, at the termination of adolescence— in their search for their inner identity. Rather, they feel that their "true identity" is in constant flux, and indeed, they feel *obligated* to continue to "grow," that is, to continue to change themselves, to reform and establish a new identity regardless of the arrival of adulthood, but always in the context and light of the changes in the world. Personal growth and the development of a real identity is thought to be achieved through eliminating all of one's "hang-ups," and therefore, one aspect of this generation is their stress on being psychologically free and capable of interacting with anyone, or in any situation, no matter how alien the other person or situation may be. Thus, they are capable of involving themselves and identifying with groups which might be normally outside their realm of experience, such as the peasant in Vietnam, the poor in America, and the nonwhite the world over. The relationship that really counts is the one that is face to face. The goal is to truly "be oneself" at all times, and to be capable of relating to *all* others in a direct one-to-one relationship. This is in contrast to the thesis of "playing the game" and manipulating others in order to advance oneself which is the modus operandi in so much of upwardly mobile America. Whether in individual or group situations the tactic used is that of confrontation. The object is to meet with the individual or group of opposing views, and to discuss the issues. It is felt that both individuals or groups are *obliged* to meet with the other. Many demonstrations by student groups and others can be explained as a result of anger caused by the failure of the adult world to meet with a particular youth group over a particular issue. Thus, many youth feel justified in using disruptive tactics to bring their grievances to the attention of adult authorities.

As a part of psychological freedom, the adolescents and youth today strive to move away from the Puritan tradition of the Protestant Ethic. To be able to express oneself without inhibition is a primary goal, particularly if one can do so creatively. The desire to have the ability to enjoy life colors much of their actions. In this age of affluence for many of our young, work is chosen for its quality and enjoyment rather than for purely pragmatic reasons. In this age of the "pill," sexual relationships are chosen for their meaningfulness, and exploitative relationships, sexual or otherwise, are disapproved. To be able to enjoy sex without fear or guilt is a concomitant of the capacity to "be oneself."

Another attitude which today's youth possesses to a varying degree, depending upon the population of which he is a member, is that of expecting a person to live his life according to his professed values. The current generation is very aware of the gap between principles and actions that pervades American society, and as a result, they search, in their personal life, for "authentic" relationships and commit themselves to act out the social and political principles that they feel are right. It has been suggested that today's youth are not confronted with a greater gap between deeds and words than other generations but, rather, that this generation is confronted with an internal ambivalence within the parental generation (Keniston, 1968). Many parents today, who were raised under a Victorian ethos themselves, have reared their children in a more permissive and more humanitarian way as a result of the historical period during which they lived. Women's suffrage, the Depression of the thirties, the New Deal, etc., effectively discredited the values of the Victorian period. However, to rear one's child in an atmosphere of self-determination, as opposed to the un-questioning obedience expected in one's own childhood, is difficult at best, and children are particularly sensitive to the discrepancies between avowed and unconsciously held values. Thus youth today perceive the values that their parents purport and the values from which their actions are derived, just as they perceive the disjunction between our national creed and our nation's policies. They insist on closing both gaps—that between personal deeds and words, and that between institutions' professed guides and their actions.

A final characteristic that links most of our youth population is their continual cognizance of the world in which they live. Their awareness and acceptance of the pace of social change is hinged to their distrust of en-during leaders, and to their view that today's problems may not be answered by yesterday's wisdom. They perceive the world as a global village and react to events in Southeast Asia as keenly as they do to events in Cleve-land, Ohio. As one of our task force members has stated: "In post-modern youth . . . , identity and ideology are no longer parochial or national; increasingly, the reference group is the world, and the artificial subspecia-tion of the human species is broken down" (Keniston, 1968). In contrast to those who have invented the machine and view it with awe or hate, today's youth take it for granted. High-speed travel, the communications media, and the Xerox are part of the culture into which they were born, and are regarded as necessary parts of the environment. Affluence, how-ever, may determine the degree of attainability. For example, the Princess telephone in the ghetto may be the counterpart of the summer trip to Europe in the suburb. The conveniences of the technological society are not opposed. What is resisted is the relegation of mankind to a secondary place, and the consequential dehumanizing of the environment—the de-personalization, the commercialism, and the devaluation of human relation-ships. Hence, youth, who have never had to "adjust" to the machine in the same manner as their elders have had to, perceive the technological society as the norm, but object to its debilitating effect on the human spirit.

This Task Force finds these trends encouraging. What may appear as real innovations in the "style" of youth in today's world may prove to be necessary conditions for existence in the world of tomorrow. Interna-tional rather than national social class or familial identifications, a continual flexibility and capability of personal growth, and a movement away from violence and toward the humanization of our world society could well mean the difference in quality of life in the twenty-first century and, indeed, could well mean the difference between life or destruction for the human species.

THE NEED FOR YOUTH TO BE INVOLVED

At this point in time—within our body politic—we are a society that places more importance on selling cigarettes and automobiles to adolescents than to understanding what the adolescent needs relative to the process of becoming a responsible adult in the community (Duhl, 1968). We wonder: What has happened to the kids today? but we do not think through our own question. We fail to look at and examine the social framework and the social structure within which our young people must grow and learn how to be adults. We often rely on past traditions, forgetting that many of the ways in which adolescents used to learn what being an adult was all about have all but vanished. As the self-sufficient family unit of the pioneer days became less useful, as the small town yielded to the megalopolis, and as the period of time that adolescents and youth remain in school lengthened, the old avenues for learning adult roles largely disappeared. We have failed to provide new ways because we have not yet recognized that the old ways, for the most part, no longer exist.

In contrast to many societies, rigidly defined steps toward adulthood have never been part of American culture. The fit between school and work, adolescence and marriage, and parenthood and citizenship, for example, has generally been quite loose. Nonetheless, patterns did exist in the past and, for many, were healthy and regular steps toward adulthood. Today, it is more difficult for youngsters to see the link between their present life and their adult future. Few sons are apprenticed to their fathers to learn a trade, as in the past. In fact, few children actually see their parents or other adults at work. Children develop a concept of work and of many other adult roles almost totally from the world of fantasy—from television, the movies, or comic books. Adolescents seldom work or participate with adults in any project or undertaking.

Essentially, adults and youth move in two separate worlds with little interaction or real opportunity to learn from each other in a *mutual* way. In addition, there are fewer opportunities for youth to interact with children or younger adolescents, with elderly adults who represent the grandparent generation, or even with one another where differences in social and cultural backgrounds exist. Segregation by age, social class, and ethnic membership is becoming characteristic of American life, greatly limiting the opportunities for genuine interaction and involvement between individuals and groups. Such separation denies the adolescent the experiences needed to learn some of the fundamental relationships of life and weakens the pathways through which he learns how to be a responsible adult.

Our national affluence has played a great part in lessening the opportunities for youth to participate in meaningful ways in our society. As we have grown more prosperous, we have tended to share this affluence with our young, and to provide them comforts and possessions in a quantity and style unknown to earlier generations. Today, we pride ourselves that our young are better provided for than we were as children. We tend to think our teen-agers should be happy because they "have it better" and are freed from responsibility for a longer period of time than those in their parents' generation. But, in reality, we have disenfranchised our youth. We have "provided for" them and, at the same time, given them little or no responsibility in a period when the traditional routes of learning adult roles are disappearing. We have cut them off from bona fide participation in our mutual society until they assume, with little or no rehearsal, the roles of wage earner, spouse, parent, and citizen. We thus train for adulthood and responsibility by excluding youth from the adult world and the exercise of responsibility (Musgrove, 1964). Unwittingly, we have removed youth from all the worlds of adult concerns, and excluded them for increasingly longer periods of time. As the roles and responsibilities of being an adult become more and more complicated, we allow fewer and fewer opportunities for the young to test themselves, to observe, and to get the feel and understanding of what it means to be a marriage partner, a parent, a taxpayer, and a concerned citizen.

The kind of pathways to adulthood and responsible community membership which our society provides is integrally involved with the identity process of the adolescent. Identity formation is an unconscious mental and moral process, which *cannot be acquired alone.* Those persons who can undertake responsibility and have gained maturity have worked through their own identity. As Erikson (1968) states, ego strength "emerges from the mutual confirmation of individual and community, in the sense that society recognizes the young individual as a bearer of fresh energy and that the individual so confirmed recognizes society as a living process which inspires loyalty as it receives it, maintains allegiance as it attracts it, honors confidence as it demands it." The crisis of identity is concomitant with the emerging capacity for commitment on the part of the adolescent. This commitment is twofold. It involves commitment to one's self, that is, a conviction that one is a self that is worth being. It also entails a dedication to values worthy of that self, that is, commitment to particular roles, to existing institutions, and to persons and relationships that embody these values. Such commitment and identity formation is made possible only when the family and society provide experiences and advantages which enable the adolescent to test and define his real strengths and weaknesses, his assets and liabilities, and real opportunities for achievement, for growth through mistakes and failures, and opportunities for involvement. The trying-out process, involvement in a task, and communication with persons of varying ages, races, and classes are the human pathways to responsible adulthood.

Essentially, this Task Force feels that we need to allow *youth a much greater degree of participation in our society.* As we have stated previously, we must grasp the fact that youth today have no culturally sanctioned roles which they find satisfying, few means of redress for wrongs, and no channels through which their idealism can become incorporated into social reality. We have a large number of youth who are strongly motivated and possess many skills; yet, they cannot find a place to use their skills or to act on their motivations. If we want and expect a good deal of adolescents, we must match our desires and the opportunities we actually provide our young. If we want adolescents to learn about work and what it means to be a wage earner, we must involve them in real work. If we want youth to behave responsibly, we must give them responsibility and hold them to it. If we want young people to learn judgment, we must involve them in situations where they hear adults exercising good judgment and allow them to learn by participating. We must listen to youth, just as we want youth to listen to us. And if we want young people to learn, we must be willing to learn from them. Thus, a fundamental requirement for building new pathways toward adulthood is to provide genuine communication and dialogue and meaningful interaction between age groups—between adolescents and children, as well as between adults and adolescents. Many of the boisterous demands of youth today are legitimate requests for entrance into the world of adult concerns, and for entrance into the areas of society which directly affect their lives. Both the 1950 and the 1960 White House Conferences on Children and Youth emphasized the principle of youth taking responsibility as partners with adults in identifying and solving national, state, and local community problems. At this point the question is not: Should youth be involved? Rather, it is: *How* can youth be more meaningfully involved?

CHANNELS FOR ACTIVE INVOLVEMENT

Much of the recent youthful dissent expressed through sit-ins, draft card burnings, campus turmoil, protest marches, and other demonstrations ·is, in effect, a demand that youth be let into society and allowed to have a hand in determining policies and activities that affect their own lives. Decisions are made daily at all levels of school and political governments involving rules that the young are expected to follow. Yet, their voices are seldom heard at the policy-making level. We must find ways to hear these voices, and we must act on *just* grievances. Youth must have a legitimate hearing and legitimate channels to voice their views without resorting to attention-getting disruptions.

The 1968 Presidential campaign showed responsible and sophisticated youth action and gave evidence of the increasing numbers of young people who are actively involved and care in a very personal way about moving to effect change through established democratic processes. Young people seize the opportunity to exercise influence and power which are denied them under normal conditions. For example, Youth Patrols in Negro ghetto areas have helped to control riots and keep peace. A study by the Lemberg Center for the Study of Violence has indicated that these Youth Patrols, whose members include dropouts and those with criminal records as well as recent rioters, have been effective in reducing or stopping violence in a majority of cases (*Washington Post,* Apr. 3, 1969). Large numbers of these Patrolmen previously participated in disorders, throwing Molotov cocktails one night and walking the streets trying to restore order the next. Although this may appear to be inconsistent behavior, it is understandable when viewed as an example of the need of young people to be recognized and to have an influence on their world. It has been suggested that youth will reverse their response to authority, changing from rebels to peacekeepers, when persons with power and prestige request their assistance under circumstances and in a manner which youth interpret as reflecting a high regard for their worth. The use of youth's affirmative response will continue at least as long as they are able to elicit respect from authorities (White and Fishman, 1967).

However, it must be stressed that all adult-youth interaction is not as simple as it sounds. Opportunities for participation by adolescents and youth must be *real* activities in the *real* world. Many current youth programs are viewed as "Mickey Mouse" activities and thereby rejected by the young. Thus, youth must have a genuine opportunity to be heard and to effect change. Many adults view such involvement as a threat to the existing social order. Because their identity and security are involved in it, adults have a vested interest in maintaining the status quo. It is difficult for most adults to allow the young to test adult ideas and values, and it is relatively easy to label differing opinions of youth as immature and inappropriate. On the other hand, a small fraction of today's youth do not want to be part of the existing society because they feel the social institutions are corrupt and must be destroyed, not merely changed. In still other instances, youth leaders, whose power has been based on resisting adult power, oppose genuine opportunities to work with adults and others. In almost all cases, youth find it necessary to test the authenticity of the opportunity and the trustworthiness of adult leadership.

At the present time, conflicting demands are made on adolescents in many areas of life. They are expected to behave responsibly but at the same time are denied real responsibility. Legally, they are considered adults at different ages for different purposes, depending upon their state of residence. Typically, adolescents can leave school at age sixteen but cannot work at most jobs until age eighteen. The legal marriage age shows a wide variation by sex and residence, ranging from age fourteen to age twenty-one.

As a general principle, this Task Force endorses the concept of lowering and making consistent the age limits at which adolescents can legally participate in societal functions. We believe this general principle is one that will draw adolescents and youth into society. Ideally, this legal integration into society would occur after approximately age fifteen.

Participation in the Political Process

Although we believe adolescents should be part of adult institutions and be allowed opportunities to participate according to their individual abilities, we realize this principle will take a long time to become a reality.

In order for youth to truly play a part in the nation that shapes their lives, they must be able to express themselves through the political process. Today's generation of eighteen-to-twenty-one-year-old youth is better educated than previous generations. They have more information at their disposal, and a more sophisticated grasp of the issues. At this age the ability to understand new ideas and comprehend increasing complexities, and to adapt to them, is great, or greater than it will be throughout the rest of life. It is seldom recognized that the impulsiveness and intolerance for ambiguities, so often cited as characteristics of youth, are tempered by a tolerance for new ways of perceiving events and relationships, and an ability to adapt to a rapidly changing technological society. Both of these abilities, which may not be characteristic of those older, are valuable contributions to the overall political system. The kind of skill needed for intelligent voting is not interpersonal competence or occupational-technical expertise, but an understanding of the meaning and consequences of the issues that are raised in an election and an ability to perceive certain basic personal characteristics of the candidates. Having a fresh view, youth, in many instances, may be able to do both of these better than many adults. Eighteen-year-old youth have the skills necessary to participate effectively in regular political processes, and they deserve fair treatment under the law. By this age, youth are sufficiently socialized in the norms of the society and have learned the theory of political process through high school courses. The years between high school and age twenty-one are crucial for the formation of patterns of activity that last throughout life. Not only will youth benefit, but so will our nation—by including youth's view in the political system. Three favorable consequences will emerge from the eighteen-year-old vote: obtaining higher overall voting participation by the registered electorate when habits are formed young; involving the more activist youth in the normal political process so they feel it is responsive to their needs; and the broadening of the perspective of the electorate during a time of rapid social and technological change.

Participation in the World of Work

Whereas excessive work and work at young ages are not desirable, some orientation toward and involvement with work on the part of middle and late teen-agers plays a necessary and constructive role in the transition to adulthood. For the vast majority of Americans, one's sense of worth is directly tied to one's ability to compete effectually in the job market. This capability, or the lack of it, affects all other relationships. Many of our youth are not adequately equipped to compete in the job market even when they complete high school. For those who drop out of school, the chances that they will lead psychologically satisfying and competent working lives is drastically reduced.

Owing to the increased birth rate after World War II, there has been a rapid population growth among all teen-agers in this decade. More than half of the total labor force increase between 1961 and 1968 was made up of young workers under twenty-five years of age. The unemployment rate for teen-agers (ages sixteen to nineteen) seeking work is the highest for any group in the nation. The nonwhite teen-age rate exceeds that of whites, and the female nonwhite teen-ager is the most unemployed. At the same time, the nonwhite adolescent population has shown the most rapid rise, a trend that will continue into the 1970's before declining. Between 1965 and 1975, the nonwhite labor force aged sixteen to twenty-four will increase 52.7 percent according to projections, and the greatest increase will be among nonwhite women (*Manpower Report of the President*, 1969). It thus appears that the already acute youth unemployment problem will be further magnified, particularly for nonwhite teen-agers.

Although the needs of school dropouts, juvenile delinquents, and disadvantaged youth are particularly severe, all youth would benefit from an earlier involvement with the world of work. Indeed, youth themselves have begun to seek this involvement. There are increased numbers of young people going to college, and proportionally more college, as well as high school, students are working.

Involvement in the world of work, however, does not necessarily mean actual job experience. Rather, this Task Force feels that through the educational process and related experiences (for example, boys' clubs), adolescents should be able to gain a greater understanding of the role of work, of theories of work, what kinds of work exist, what opportunities are available, what kinds of education and training are necessary for what types of jobs, and some understanding of what it means to be a family wage earner. In this age of specialization, we have increasingly made one man's work incomprehensible to another, and have made most work invisible to youngsters. By junior high school, students should have an awareness of the give and take of the job market, and should have begun formulating some thoughts as to their individual place in this market. During high school, students (especially those outside the college preparatory curriculum) should be able to acquire a salable skill, while at the same time preparing themselves for the fact that they will need to take post-high school training, and probably eventual reeducation and retraining in their lifetime. Such programs should emphasize the ability to cope with change, while at the same time attempting to match the individual and his particular interests and talents with the complementary occupational "family." For both adolescents and preadolescents, our aim should be increased familiarity with and knowledge of a variety of work experiences, on both a theoretical and a practical level.

Wherever possible, opportunities for real work experience on both a volunteer and a paid basis should be expanded. In order to effectively do this, it will be necessary for the child labor laws to be reevaluated within the context of the present and the future work world. The Child Labor Act was enacted for the most humane reasons, many of which are still valid today. Whereas standard legislation, such as minimum wages and hours of work, should of course apply to working minors, child labor laws need to be reexamined in the light of today's world and should not serve as a means to discriminate against the young and their adequate vocational preparation. Rather, a more careful balance needs to be made between adequate protection against harmful and abusive working situations and maximum opportunity for work and work-related experiences for adolescents and preadolescents.

The Concept of Service

The way that youngsters learn what being an adult is all about has changed in the past several decades. But then, so has the potential role that youth are able to play in our society. Better physical health care has meant healthier adolescents. Wider coverage by the mass media has meant more rapid dissemination of information and better-informed children and youth. They are better educated, and have a more sophisticated grasp of the issues facing the nation. Although many middle-class teen-agers are overscheduled, the time available for leisure pursuits has increased. In short, today's youth have the time, the vigor, the knowledge, and the inclination to question our society. And many seek to become involved, both in the questioning and in possible answers or solutions.

Yet, opportunities for creative work and service for the young are severely limited. Chances for meaningful service have not kept pace with the increased number of capable youth who seek such involvement. In its deliberations, Task Force III of the Joint Commission discussed at least three major ways in which youth could become more constructively and meaningfully involved in service to the nation. First, as already outlined, the expansion of actual job experiences and work-related learning processes, particularly in the human service areas, will increase the opportunities for youth to become more knowledgeable about and to contribute to the solution of particular problems and conditions, on both a practical and a theoretical level.[10]

Second, there is the vast area of service in which the job to be done is the major concern regardless of monetary return, if any. The Peace Corps, VISTA (Volunteers in Service to America), and the Teacher Corps, among other groups, are tapping youth's skill, manpower, energy, and interest in solving national and international problems. There are a substantial number of other less well-known organizations which are currently engaging great numbers of youth in service programs designed to improve or change the world around them.[11] Whereas today's youth are disillusioned with many of our society's imperfect institutions and skeptical as to their prospects for their reform, there are unpublicized numbers who do not withdraw from society and do not engage in direct, impassioned, and militant attacks against the established institutions, but work for social change through service.

Two simultaneous trends have heightened the development of the service concept. One is the increased economic and occupational focus on the human services area; the other is an increased resentment among those humanistically inclined toward the growing emphasis on intellectual technology and expertise (Lipset, 1968). Thus, many are opposing the lack of individual identity in an IBM card environment and are reacting against

10. In this context, it may be noted that the trend among many of our young college graduates and college dropouts is to seek work which they consider to be meaningful and personally satisfying as well as offering them monetary and materialistic rewards. In a society which increasingly offers an adequate financial return for those properly equipped with a skill, such considerations as the general philosophy of a particular company or organization or its involvement in social issues are beginning to outweigh salary, wage, or fringe benefit considerations. For some youth, they far outweigh material rewards.

11. The National Commission on Resources for Youth, Inc., prepared for the Joint Commission on the Mental Health of Children a detailed study of some 45 youth participation projects which focused mainly on secondary-school-age adolescents. There are a number of programs on most college campuses in the nation. Of particular relevance are the several thousand college student volunteers in state mental hospitals (Kohler, 1968).

a society that is emerging as cold, impersonal, and dominated by large bureaucracies. The young of the sixties asserted their faith in values that represented what is both individual and human. This has found expression in the projects mentioned above, which include the demand by many college undergraduates today for more involvement in and contact with the "real community" as contrasted to the campus. In line with this trend an increasing number of colleges throughout the nation are granting college credit for community work (National Student Association, n.d.). The Task Force heartily supports this trend.

Task Force III endorses the expansion of opportunities for service, both during school years and afterward, and feels that the country is ready for a nationally coordinated program along these lines. The Task Force, therefore, supports the "Youth Power Act" of 1969 as introduced to Congress by Senator Hatfield and co-sponsored by Senators Mathias, Percy, and Saxbe.[12] The purpose of this bill is to supplement and increase service and learning opportunities available to our young people, and establish a National Youth Service Foundation and a National Youth Service Council. Its goal is most succinctly stated by Donald J. Eberly of the National Service Secretariat as follows:

We must ask our young people to engage themselves fully with the war on poverty, on disease, on illiteracy, on pollution. We must make it possible for every American youth who wants to serve his fellow man to do so. Black or white, rich or poor, from north or south, east or west, from slum or suburb, village or farm, from the school, the college or university, our young people are needed.

They are needed in our schools as tutors for young children. They are needed in our hospitals and clinics to assist doctors and nurses.

They are needed in our courts to work with youth who have started off on the wrong foot. They are needed as friends by old folks living alone, by the mentally retarded and the mentally ill. They are needed in our forests and open lands, to protect and conserve them. They are needed to respond to natural disasters, at home and overseas. They are needed to build new towns where there will be no discrimination, no illiteracy, no pollution, but opportunities for all to move with confidence into the 21st century.

Already the organizations exist to make this program possible. We shall ask the nation's schools, hospitals, churches, labor unions, businesses and industries, civic organizations, governmental departments at the local, state, regional and federal levels to provide opportunities for young people to serve.

We shall ask private citizens, foundations, profit-making organizations and, as necessary, Congress, for funds to provide the yearly subsistence that will be needed to feed, house, transport and give a living allowance to each young person in service.

12. *Congressional Record,* Vol. 115, No. 64 (Apr. 22, 1969). See Appendix C.

We shall ask our colleges and universities, labor unions and industries to organize training and information programs so that each young person will be able to find the challenge he wants and will be able to meet that challenge ("Directory of Service Organizations," 1968).

Subsistence allowances would allow youth to serve on a full-time basis and would not limit participation to persons who could afford to volunteer their time. The object is to expand opportunities so that no young person is denied a chance to serve. At this point, large-scale pilot projects in youth service are needed to provide empirical data for research; to determine how many young people in a given area would volunteer and the potential for accomplishment of the program; to work out the interrelationship of youth service to such areas as education and labor; and to define the jobs to be done.

Another area with potential for the expansion of opportunities for youth service is work-study programs serving off campus and in civic service activities. Such programs are multipurpose, allowing the individual to earn money for his formal education, test career possibilities, and serve his community.

The third way in which youth could be effectively involved in our society is through their becoming a contributing part of adult institutions. A major adult role is that of community service in which the person gives his time and efforts for little or no monetary return. His motivation may range from enhancement of his prestige to working toward an ideal of world betterment or simply the recognition of a task that needs to be done. Adolescents and youth should be involved in this process when they are as young as possible. At least by age fifteen, adolescents should be invited and *encouraged* to become a part of most adult institutions—particularly in those activities, programs, services, projects, etc., that are designed to affect the lives of youth. They should be a part (not represented by an adult) of police boards; draft boards; school boards and various school committees; employment training groups, various institution-community bodies including human relations councils, and social service groups, especially those which deal with juvenile delinquents; and in mayors' offices, city councils, and other local political authorities. Youth should be allowed to gain entry to such groups by the same means as adults; that is, by volunteering, by appointment, by authentic invitation, or by election. Although the degree of participation by youth may be determined by the particular institution and community, one general principle follows here: participation must be real—the opportunity must be for a genuine voice and influence. Youth need to be involved in the planning, decision making, implementing, and subsequent responsibility in all community services—especially in those institutions which have an impact on the lives of young people. The goal must be to plan *with* youth, not *for* youth.

Finally, youth should be involved in the evaluation of all projects aimed at serving youth. This principle of evaluation by the target groups themselves, especially by patient groups, is all too often overlooked. The result is ignorance—we simply don't know how our subject reacts to the program or the effectiveness of the service. Specifically, we suggest that government projects dealing with youth should not be funded without a built-in system of evaluation by the youth themselves, and that this principle should be adopted at all levels—local, state, and federal.

The Draft

In its discussions the Task Force recognized that a major problem for young men in their quest for societal involvement is the uncertainty of the draft. At the present time, many young males cannot plan their futures or their careers, not knowing when and if military service will be required of them. The majority cannot participate in youth service projects, since they feel that they will be drafted instead. Those who do not desire or cannot afford a college education have a greater likelihood of being drafted. In order to allow young people to plan their futures, to be able to participate in youth service projects, and to experience their society as one humanely concerned with problems of equity, Task Force III urges the adoption of the reforms in selective service recommended by the Burke-Marshall Commission (Report of the National Advisory Commission on Selective Service, 1967), a liberalizing of the definitions of conscientious objection, and a lottery system of selection that distributes the obligation of service equitably across all segments of society.

Our World Is Mutual

Today's adolescents mature physically at an earlier age. They are more sophisticated and they have more knowledge. But they are still adolescents, and they do not necessarily mature emotionally at the same rate as they mature physically. One of the major tasks of adolescence today is to learn how to handle this disparity between biological and emotional maturity in a period when society is raising the age at which an adolescent is recognized as an adult. As these gaps between physical maturity, emotional maturity, and social readiness widen, there are greater conflicts for today's young than for those who moved through adolescence even a generation ago. Many adolescents want no part of the adult world, or the people in that world. Many adults want no part of adolescents. But like it or not, our world is mutual, and adolescence is the time to venture into the adult world, to learn by doing, and not to be forever branded by a mistake or misjudgment. There is no easy counter or simple solution to youthful dissent and rebellion, but a way to begin is to stop being so fearful of the young. In particular, we must bring them into our society and let them make their own mistakes. That is one of the things that youth is all about—that one can make a mistake and learn more *from* it than one must pay *for* it.

Quest Through Education

The developmental tasks of the adolescent are difficult, often confusing, usually traumatic, and sometimes never achieved. Patterns of emotional ties with parents must be broken or rearranged; social roles, sex roles, occupational roles, and citizenship roles must be learned. Standards of conduct need altering so that the rigid rules of the child may become the ethical morality of the adult. A beginning framework of values requires formulation which permits the individual to function freely and securely within himself and with others.

School, with its structure for learning and its housing of the peer group, is second in importance only to the family as an avenue through which the adolescent's search for identity occurs. If the school is a place where the adolescent can explore varieties of interests, abilities, and roles, secure in the knowledge that he will be stopped from being harmful to himself or to the school society, then many of the developmental tasks can be completed with relative ease. If the school is lock step in curriculum and discipline, where rules and expectations are made for the convenience of the faculty with little regard for the developmental abilities and emotional capacities of the adolescent, then we will have from this school many graduates who will have learned either conformity or rebellion—but very little about themselves. Young people from the latter school may never become "mentally ill" in the sense that they need hospitalization or even therapy. But, depending on other factors in their lives, the school may have added sufficient stultifying influence to inhibit their effectiveness as husbands or wives, parents, workers, or members of society.

There is no intent here to imply that the schools have the sole responsibility for the mental health of adolescents. Mental health, or even degrees of adaptability and adjustment, are dependent upon many factors.

264

The individual's own physiological equipment, the family into which he was born, and the neighborhood in which he lives are all fundamental to what the person will become. But among the important pieces in the puzzle that configurates a person's life is the school which he attends for twelve developmental years. The child or adolescent does not view his school years as a transitory period of preparation for life. School *is* his life. It is the reality of the here and now. For the student, many of the satisfactions and frustrations, goals worth working for, meaningful strivings, and feelings as to self-worth are formed and bounded by school experiences and expectations. Unless other life aspects are too devastating, education can significantly help the adolescent to wend his way through these years, gaining insight into the positive and contributing person he *can* be. The youngster with borderline adjustment in other life areas can be influenced, for better or for worse, in his ability to cope with later life experiences through his years of school experiences. If we are to help improve the mental health of adolescents, then we must concern ourselves with the educational environment.

THE CHANGING ROLE OF EDUCATION

The vital role of the school in the life of a young person today is relatively new to contemporary society (Kimball and McClellan, 1966). Education has changed from a peripheral position to a central one for today's youth. It is the major bridge for the child and adolescent to move from the nuclear family to a place in the larger social structure. School has always been one of our society's major socialization agencies for youth. Learning the customs, mores, values, and contradictions of our culture is a gradual and unconscious part of our educational system. Moreover, schools have always housed a peer group. What young people learn about themselves in interaction with others their own age in this structured situation varies considerably from the learning that occurs with family or chosen friends. Schools have also been the institution through which child and adolescent learn not only skills and knowledge but also a great deal about their own abilities and interests.

Previously, however, if a youngster failed in school, was rejected by the school peer group, or learned more about the school's contradictions than about society's values, there was little cause for concern. There were other avenues through which a youth could find acceptance, a place, and a role. Family, relatives, neighborhood friends, church groups, etc., could replace the adjustment experiences which failed in school. Academic degrees were not necessary to find adequate employment, and status did not necessarily accrue from one's educational level.

Today, barely 20 years later, education has assumed a far greater significance. The burden of responsibility that has fallen on education as a result of our complex technology, increased population, and mobility seems only vaguely understood in many sectors. Education is rapidly becoming the only avenue through which an individual can assure himself of employability. Today, if an adolescent fails in school, many occupational roles are closed to him. His productivity, in both economic and human terms, may never be achieved. Hence, parents and school are no longer required to pressure a young person to succeed in school. Adolescents are putting this pressure on themselves. The dropouts, or the seemingly unmotivated, are no exception. When standards are unrealistic for the individual, or a meaningless curriculum is the fare day after day, or the anxieties and tensions of pressure become unbearable, the "sour grapes" rationalization of not caring is a momentarily effective (though in the long run self-defeating) way of resolving conflicts.

The increased stress on education, as well as the increased length of time put in school, has added considerably to the influence of the school peer groups. Whether a young person is in the "in group" or the "out group," or is a "fringe loner," the adolescent accumulates many attitudes about himself, about his acceptability to others, and about the role he must play to be acceptable to someone or some group. Assessing peer reactions and soliciting some peer support seem an essential part of adolescent growth in our society. Seeking independence from one's parents, and establishing a separate individuality, is a lonely and scary business if no friends are around to support one. With each generation having to establish its own nuclear family, the adolescent breaking of familial ties to the extent of finding one's own identity is basic to healthy growth. In our mobile society, where the extended family and stable neighborhood groups are becoming extinct, the school has become the pivotal point around which peer groups are formed. Success or failure in school, teacher approval or disapproval, the amount that one is in trouble with the disciplinary powers, all become hallmarks of an adolescent and, to a large extent, determine the peer groups to which he finds himself acceptable. Peer groups today are becoming as homogeneous as some academic groupings. The "hoods," "squares," or "eggheads" are bounded by a reputation which they must live up to, often heartbreakingly so. The lonely student, with no peer support, is even more restricted in his means for identity search.

Schools have traditionally paid little attention to the social groups formed within their walls. Teachers have generally assumed that young people will find their own medium and that peer group relations are outside of the bailiwick of educational concern. What is not generally recognized is the extent to which school atmosphere, teacher attitudes, and school activities can influence the way students view and assess one another. The interaction between the teacher and the peer group, as well as the interaction among peer group members, both inside and *outside* the school, has an impact on the learning that goes on in the classroom.

Thus, education has become heir to far greater responsibilities than in times past. Our youth are more dependent upon education today as a road to their future, not only in the realm of intellectual development, but also in their groping to find social roles and to become emotionally integrated human beings.

Certain aspects of the school situation are particularly pertinent to the emotional development of adolescents. These spheres of influence, which are a natural part of the school environment, are discussed in the following sections.

The Reward-Punishment Balance

Every school has its unique atmosphere. At one end of the spectrum, it may be rigid, restricting, and demanding, or at the other end, it may be overly permissive and laissez-faire. Neither atmosphere aids the learning of self-control and self-direction that adolescents need in later adult life. The school atmosphere, which results from the attitudes of administrators and teachers toward young people, is generally transmitted through the organized systems of discipline and privileges found in the school. Where access to the legitimate privilege and reward system set by the school is denied, the peer group may set up a counter-reward system. Thus, how a student achieves esteem and acclaim can explain the motivation of many students. To be accepted for admission by an Ivy League school may give a student high status in one school; the student who returns from the juvenile court facility after having received his credentials as an adjudicated delinquent may be equally honored in another school system.

The understanding that there are two types of discipline—constructive and destructive—and that privileges often produce the desired results better than discipline is not often remembered in our schools. The *only* purpose of discipline for youth should be educative. Young people need to learn self-control, respect for others, and the rules and regulations that make living within a society a successful enterprise. Constructive discipline does just this, without demeaning, degrading, or debilitating effects upon the individual. Standards of conduct and limitations of behavior should be clearly understood and discussed by the student body. But detention, suspension, or expelling a student should not be the only means through which adolescents are encouraged to adhere to the rules. Adults often forget that inconsistent discipline, or discipline administered without permitting a young person the right to his defense, can produce untoward effects. As the Committee on Adolescence of the Group for the Advancement of Psychiatry (1968) has stated, "It is possible, then, that our social forms are not as well suited for training children to become adults, as for training them to be successful children."

Systems of privileges in schools have seldom been employed to foster socially desirable behavior. A substantial amount of psychological knowledge indicates that reward-learning is more emotionally facilitating and has more positive effects on adjustment and behavior than does punishment. Yet, teachers and administrators almost universally adhere to punishment as a means of inculcating certain behavior in our young. This fact should have some sobering implications for our teacher training programs.

Educational institutions across the country traditionally have a limited type of reward system—the honor roll for grades and some athletic or extracurricular activities recognition. The reward may or may not carry any special privileges within the school, but the approving attitudes of teachers carry much meaning for those who do, or do not, make the grade. There is no quarrel here with recognizing those who are capable and sufficiently motivated to receive such recognition. But there are other worthwhile characteristics and qualities that should be rewarded. Human beings are enormously diverse in their characteristics and talents, and adolescents may contribute to or have the capability of contributing to their school and community in a variety of ways that are infrequently recognized. The reward systems within schools should be expanded to recognize authentic talent, creativity, and contribution to the school or society. These could range from an award for special services to the school, in which an individual contributes time and effort in a special project, to a simple statement in the school assembly that a particular student has helped to organize a boys' drill team in an inner-city area. The key is recognition. When an adolescent is recognized for something he does well in one area, he is apt to try harder in the areas in which he does not do as well. The reward system must be based on *authentic* performance, however, or the entire system loses its meaning. All responsible students in junior high and high school should be awarded certain privileges and freedoms within the school, regardless of their academic achievement or test scores. It is possible that the students who make high grades are rarely the disciplinary problems because of the greater recognition and approval they receive.

All schools must not remain institutions that give rewards and satisfactions to only bright, academically achievement-minded students; continue to be tolerantly disinterested in the plodding conformer; and persist in being punitive to those students who rebel against a system where they can find no place for themselves. In order to serve the broad spectrum of adolescent needs, and consequently the ultimate needs of society, schools must recognize the diversity of human creativity and accord sufficient rewards to aid in drawing the adolescents so concerned *into* the society, rather than forcing them out of society.

The Influence of the Teacher

A fundamental influence on the student is the classroom teacher. What a student learns, how he learns it, and the way in which he perceives and measures himself in the learning process is largely teacher-determined. An adolescent's future is seen as very dependent upon his educational performance today. If a young person can, and does, successfully learn what a teacher teaches, then parents, school, and the student himself tacitly assume that he will be a successful adult. If a student cannot, or does not, learn, he is viewed as a likely future failure. These assumptions may or may not be correct, but the impact on the emotional life of an adolescent is very real. The tensions and anxieties that ensue can be overwhelming.

All students within the normal range of intellectual functioning can learn in varying degrees if the expectations are realistic and the material is so presented that the student is enabled to learn. The important role of education today in the lives of our youth places a great burden on teachers in what and how they teach. These responsibilities have been recognized in recent years, but we are far from the mark in preparing and facilitating the teacher's ability to execute these responsibilities. Many teacher training institutions are improving, and importantly so, the education of teachers in subject-matter areas. But how these subjects can be taught to the differentially able and motivated students is not yet broadly learned. Teachers need to understand that certain kinds, and levels, of education are appropriate for students with certain backgrounds and abilities. (The diversity of the curriculum within the school, which is also a basic factor in meeting varying needs, is discussed in a later section.) With the narrowed avenues through which adolescents can proceed to adult functioning, education cannot afford to close its doors to any student.

Teacher influence does not end with the teaching of knowledge and skills. Teachers are viewed, by child and adolescent alike, as symbolic of the larger adult world. As such, they may become models to be admired and emulated. Or they may become just the opposite—to be disliked and mistrusted. The perception a student has of a teacher will, to a degree, be colored by his past experiences with teachers and adults in general. The way a teacher responds will either confirm or alter a student's prior impressions of the adult world. It is in interactions with adults that adolescents attempt to understand the values of the society into which they are growing. It is against this backdrop that youth accept, reject, or revise but develop a value system of their own.

In addition, teachers have an influence on the peer group formations within the school. Teachers can make an adolescent accepted, or they can exclude him, or they can make the others in the class begin to dislike him

—not always by rejecting the student themselves. Sometimes the very students that the teacher rejects are the ones that the other students like, and vice versa. This process of student-teacher interaction and resultant peer relationship is complicated and varies with class, personalities, and age levels.

Every adolescent generation has a need to question, and modern-day youth have even more impetus and reason to query their elders than in the past. Adolescents today know more, have more issues to which to react, and have more uncertainties to produce anxiety. Teachers are instrumental, either for good or for ill, in the adolescent's task of defining and acquiring values. A teacher's attitudes toward questioning and his ability to understand the adolescent's need to disagree, dissent, or voice antiestablishment views are fully as important as what a teacher says in the classroom about standards and ideals. Permitting and encouraging young people to question and meditate about the society of their elders, in an atmosphere where student and mentor view each other as respected human beings, aids in helping the adolescent to constructively arrive at his own identity and will more nearly ensure the continuance of our democratic world. In order to perform this function, teachers need to understand a good deal more about the adolescent and his world than current teacher training provides.

Teacher influence reaches further. Adolescence is that period between childhood and adulthood where the individual attempts to integrate what he was in the past with what he will be in the future. The adolescent is a personality in transition, and as such is very vulnerable. Superficially, however, these youth appear just the opposite. They often seem dogmatically opinionated, stubbornly headstrong, resistant to adult guidance, and closed to adult advice. As a group, adolescents are more frustrating for adults than youngsters at any other developmental stage. Once an adolescent begins to withdraw or rebel in earnest, he is almost unreachable. For this age group, prevention is the surest method of treatment for emotional and social disturbances.

Teachers cannot become therapists, nor should they. But they can become people who understand the developmental dynamics of the age group with whom they work. Disinterested, unmotivated, rebellious, or hostile adolescents in the classroom are saying some very important things about themselves. The basic difficulties may result from the home, and special school service personnel should be available to contact the parents; however, teachers and school policies can compound the difficulties or serve as a source of alleviating some of the student's distress. To respond to the unmotivated student with increased pressure, or to react hostilely and punitively to the angry student, can only push the young person further into the negative stance already developing. Understanding these students, and helping them to find a meaningful and recognized role in school society, does *not* mean that standards and limitations of the school are ignored. Young people can take, and learn, a great deal from discipline, providing teachers do not also look upon them as criminals and the school does not throw up walls of frustration at every turn.

The influence of the teacher and the quality of the relationship between teacher and student are particularly crucial to disadvantaged adolescents who are easily shaken off the educational ladder. Studies have indicated that a low performance expectancy on the part of many teachers serves as a self-fulfilling prophecy for the disadvantaged. Teachers can and do use psychological tools and tests to reinforce and justify their low predictions. Just how much home background information should be fed into the classroom is largely determined by how the teacher will use the data. Whereas an enlarged view of the "total" student is generally useful in the teaching function, such information is of dubious value if it is employed to explain away failure to learn. Background data should aid teachers, administrators, and special school personnel to help the student to learn, rather than serving as a means to project failure and limited objectives.

The teacher's essential role and function is not therapeutic; nor is it to indoctrinate middle-class values. The unique and essential feature of the teacher's role is to educate—to develop the cognitive processes. The school is a unique opportunity for learning to take place and rational powers to be developed. In this role, the teacher functions by motivating, by guiding the learning activities toward selected objectives, and by evaluating the product and the process of learning. But the teacher cannot carry out these functions unless he is *authentic*.

There are three kinds of authenticity that are crucial for all learners, but which are particularly critical for the disadvantaged. First, substantively the teacher must be knowledgeable or expert in his field. Teachers of history must be historians; teachers of science must be scientists; teachers of mathematics must be mathematicians. The local school authorities in the public school system of a large eastern city were recently heard to complain about "1,200 vacancies." When asked, "Do you really have 1,200 uncovered classrooms?" they answered, "Of course not, but we do have 1,200 marginal teachers." How does it feel to be a marginal teacher and how does it feel to have a marginal teacher?

Marginal mentors, poorly equipped for teaching in a given field, exude an insecurity that is contagious. Uncertain teachers run the risk of producing uncertain students. It is questionable that third-rate teachers can produce first-rate scholars. Students—white or nonwhite—know a subject-matter expert when they meet one. They are sensitive to expertise and scholarship, and they resent the insecure and the make-believe scholars.

Second, the teacher himself must serve as the living symbol and the embodiment of his goals and his subject matter. There are teachers of English who invite their class to enjoy their first experience in reading *Julius Caesar* or who invite their class to enjoy some lyric verse—never having enjoyed either, even when they were forced to include these courses as a part of their "major" in college. The intellectual model is a rarity in the American high school. We do not need to look at the distribution of test scores in teacher-preparation institutions and departments of education. All we need to do is to inspect the intellectual behavior and reading habits of secondary school teachers who seldom exemplify the goals they are trying to sell in their classes. Recent studies confirm the height of teacher reading to be in the zone of the *Reader's Digest* (Graves, 1966). When a history teacher states that he has two young historians in his classes, you can be sure it is because he has been more than a teacher of history. It is because he has been thinking, talking, and acting like a historian.

Third, and most important, as we have pointed out earlier, the teacher must ring true in his interpersonal relationships with his students. There are two kinds of fears which dominate inner-city classrooms. Many teachers in deprived areas fear their students, particularly Negro students. These teachers are also afraid of bright students who challenge them and who find the correct answers via routes other than those promulgated officially by the teacher. The current trend to place police personnel in secondary schools reflects the basic fear relationship now visible in many American classrooms.

Special School Service Personnel

America's increasing population and enlarged educational responsibilities are daily compounding the problems schools face in providing for *all* of their students. By the nature of their preparation and responsibilities, teachers have a commitment to the group which overrides concerns for any one individual. Junior high and high school teachers are subject-matter-oriented. Their job is to educate. But this is not an easy directive. Teachers discover, very early in their careers, that not all students learn at the same rate or in a uniform manner, and that some students present particular difficulties in learning or adjustment that are beyond the scope of understanding by the classroom teacher. Teachers cannot be given the background training necessary to analyze the many varieties of individual differences which have important implications for the education of that student, but they can facilitate learning if they are aware of what is involved for a particular student.

Special school service personnel are concerned with the *individuals* in the matrix of the school groups. Young people who show learning difficulties or who have problems in social and emotional adjustment are revealing some variety of handicap in their development toward adulthood. The depth, degree, and causes of these problems can vary considerably. The deviant behavior of some students can be reflective of educational frustrations. The difficulties of others are reactive to deeper emotional disturbances. Some students need only more thoughtful planning, programming, and remedial help; others require more persuasive counseling or therapy for themselves, and perhaps their families.

Detecting, diagnosing, and recommending avenues for remediation or treatment are the responsibilities of the special school personnel. However, to deal only with the individual child or adolescent, and not with his environment, is grossly ineffective. It is time that the knowledge of teachers be combined with that of allied professionals. Working together *within a school setting,* counselors, psychologists, and teachers, among others, can develop a truly viable educational experience for youth. Teachers and specialists can pool knowledge to establish more flexible classes, aid in designing curriculums, and discuss the applicability of the disciplinary system involved. For example, psychological knowledge of cognitive growth and levels of conceptualization should be basic to designing curriculums for students with particular social backgrounds and academic abilities. Information from guidance personnel concerning new occupations and needed technological skills could prove extremely beneficial to whole groups of adolescents. The reading specialist should alert the school to the levels of comprehension of students and help teachers in providing pupils with appropriate material. There is no attempt here to list all of the specialists who could or should be involved in developing education into both a group and an individualized enterprise. Whatever specialists, other than the occasional consultant, are deemed necessary in a particular school district, these special personnel must be a part of the permanent school staff.

For an additional reason, all special school service personnel need to orient their services to teachers as well as to individual pupils. According to recent studies there are more than 11,000 full-time guidance counselors in the nation's high schools; but there are also about 9 million high school students. The implication is that individual pupil counseling will have little impact on the incidence of failure, school leaving, and social-emotional problems of youth, judging from the number of cases that can be handled in individual counseling situations by the number of available personnel. In order to effectively work together, a mutual relationship of trust and respect needs to exist between teachers and personnel workers. Many social workers, psychologists, and guidance workers could make their influence felt on a schoolwide basis by conducting group therapy sessions for staff and by creating opportunities for individual counseling of staff members. At the present time, barriers to this broadcast role exist both in the concept the teacher may have of the specialist and in the special personnel worker's concept of his own professional role. Whatever the role that is attributed to him by others, the specialist is the one who sets the limits of his wider potential role. Most frequently these limits are placed too low.

Teachers and special school personnel working together are instrumental in planning for their special student body. The diversity of communities and students requires individual planning for each school. Today, no educational models can be established to be uniformly applied to all. The social and cultural backgrounds and intellectual capabilities of students in a school district vary across the country, and the district itself may have a completely new population in three or five years. What might be excellent education in one district would be flat and meaningless in another.

Finally, we must state that special personnel may be reminders of the inadequacies and malfunctioning of an overcrowded and inefficient school agency. They may represent the community's gesture to repair the wear and tear of an inadequate curriculum, of bigness and impersonality, of overworked or poorly trained teachers, and of the cultural discrepancies between home and school. It is not enough to keep providing more and better personnel services in a valiant and expensive effort to prop up the classroom; it becomes imperative to shift the focus of the personnel services and to attack the basic causes that result in a demand for these services in the first place. The chief goal of school and student personnel services should not be simply more and better services; it should be the elimination or solution of the school-community problems that create the need for such services.

Curriculum Reform

The concept of the comprehensive school, which provides for varying interests and abilities of students, is historically a part of American tradition. Unlike European schools, our high schools developed under the philosophy of educating *all* students, regardless of background and intellectual proficiency. The intent was to provide common democratic experiences and understanding, and to offer both academic and vocational courses of study through which students could proceed according to their own ambitions and abilities. This educational theory of the comprehensive school has continued through the years. But planning and providing the programs needed has become more difficult with the increasing population, the accumulation of knowledge, and our technological development.

Accelerated curriculums with greater complexity of content have made educators acutely aware of individual differences in students' learning ability. Academic course offerings no longer consist of a series of subjects taught at the same level and in a uniform manner. Many students who desire the academic road cannot manage the accelerated pace or absorb the depth of understanding possible for top students. In many cases, schools have initiated homogeneous groupings or track systems to meet differing student abilities. Unfortunately, educators have been prone to tackle the problem of individual differences in learning solely through the organizational method of grouping students rather than considering *how* students learn and *what* should be learned by young people of varying ability. In most instances (the exception being the accelerated courses in math and science offered in high school), the subject matter taught to the less able students is a watered-down, slower-paced version of what the brighter students are receiving. Teachers of the less able students are seldom given help in understanding what concepts could profitably be mastered by the students, through what means of learning this might be accomplished, and how to achieve the maximum learning situation for the individual student. The result is an inferior education (not only less broad in scope) and usually boring and meaningless education for masses of our youth.

In trying to assist these youngsters, many teachers and special school personnel suffer severe job frustrations. Lacking a comprehensive and balanced curriculum, the best they can hope to accomplish is to persuade the disinterested and failing pupil to return and to adjust to what is basically an unsatisfactory and unpromising learning situation. A major and primary prerequisite to effective learning at all levels is a balanced and varied curriculum. Under present curriculum conditions, indications are that the holding power of the public schools has probably reached its peak—graduating about 60 to 70 out of every 100 persons seventeen years of age annually.

Students, as well as parents, teachers, administrators, and special school personnel, should be involved in the process of differentiating and broadening the curriculum. As stated earlier, it is a basic recommendation of this Task Force that adolescents and youth become involved in all processes and institutions which impinge upon their lives. The learning process, in general, and curriculum reform, in particular, are examples of such involvement. Students, including those in junior high, should become *one* part of the process of curriculum revision, contributing such input as what subject matter they consider meaningful for the present and for their future.

One danger to slow-learning students is that the curriculum will be so modified and thinned that the adolescent will spend most of his time with the jigsaw making doorstops or with reading materials one level above the comic book. Courses that take on a practical and utilitarian complexion and that prepare youth only for a rote and standardized occupation can be so lacking in the intellectual and ideational area as to degrade and demean a student's self-concept. Curriculum content is a specific area whereby a student's goals and objectives can be severely limited. A youngster who is placed in a special class is usually powerless to do anything about it.

A particularly difficult area in curriculum reform is that of vocational preparation. In its enthusiasm for the benefits of education, our society places the emphasis on the importance of a college education. Thus, the student who is basically not interested in college is found with the dilemma of being considered a second-rate future citizen if he chooses vocational courses. However, a low percentage of schools provide vocational courses within the comprehensive high school, other than the usual home economics and business education (Conant, 1967). Through expanded federal funds, vocational schools have been established in many areas, separate from the academic school. Considering the responsibility our democratic society places on the individual to function in citizenship roles, as well as occupational roles, isolating the academic and vocational is a highly questionable procedure. Recognizing the inherent danger of such a separation, many schools have devised programs for students whereby they spend one-half day in the academic high school and one-half day pursuing vocational study in another school. This practice can also present difficulties for the student in the limitations or disruption of peer group contacts.

But there are also other difficulties that are arising in the attempts to provide vocational programs. In our increased technological society, vocational schools are looking for the able and talented just as are the academic schools. Years ago, the student who could not succeed academically was "shuttled" to the courses in business and shop. Today, even in a junior high or high school, business and shop teachers do not want students assigned to their courses who are not motivated or do not show some ability along the lines of their instruction. Vocational schools are becoming very selective in the students they admit to their programs. To an extent, this attitude has merit in that no student should be "shuttled" just to get him out of the academic orbit. But while the academic teachers are making some effort to meet varying levels of abilities, our vocational educators are becoming more selective. The student who cannot succeed in either the academic or the vocational, by virtue of his background or abilities, is caught in a no man's land in our educational maze. Vocational education is a very important road through which many of our adolescents can find themselves to be adequate and effective human beings and prepare themselves for adult roles. Not all adolescents can develop skills to the same level of proficiency, but each student can develop some skill if taught correctly. Ideally, an individual should be able to leave the educational system with a marketable skill at the terminal point chosen by the person, without closing the door to future progress and development. In reality, we are far from this goal. Recognition of this fact, and of the importance of occupational instruction for scores of youth, should be a major concern of educators and citizens.

A final comment must be made on curriculum and its impact on the emotional health of adolescents. Many young people charge that school courses are meaningless and are far removed from the real world. A related charge is that students are counseled or required to take subjects that "look good on the record," but do not necessarily help them in gaining knowledge needed for their future occupational or citizen role. What, or whether, a youth learns seems irrelevant or artificial to many young. The reality of such charges must be carefully weighed in redesigning curriculums and subject content.

AREAS FOR CHANGE

Up to the time that Russia jarred Americans awake to education, no one thought to consider that we regarded education as a stepchild institution in our society. How teachers were trained, what they taught, or how they regarded youth was given scant attention. Teachers were second-class citizens in both salary and status. When the focus of attention turned on education, educators were ill prepared to meet the challenge. In the last half-decade education has been under bitter attack from many fronts. Teacher training programs have been criticized as inadequate. Certification requirements are regarded as inflexible, as either too stringent or too ambiguous. New curriculum materials have flooded the educational scene. Parents, in local school districts, have been angered by too high or too low academic standards, or too much rigidity, or too much permissiveness. And finally, taxpayers in several areas, feeling the weight of too much or too unevenly distributed taxation, have failed to support necessary school bonds.

The overriding need in the field of education today is for unifying leadership. Every aspect of education requires attention. Teacher preparation programs, continuing teacher education, certification requirements, reciprocal certification of teachers between the states, distribution of financial aid, and advisory services to local school districts with especially difficult and complex educational problems are among the most outstanding. The current arguments among professional educators and commissions as to who should assume the leadership in the various educational areas is not our concern here. The fact is that the individual states have the legal responsibility, and as long as it is so invested, they have the moral obligation to perform leadership functions for the educational progress within the state. State boards of education, with their advisory counsels, and departments of education have the responsibility to provide the impetus for the improved education of teachers and students within their boundaries. There are varieties of ways the states have of serving such a leadership role. Among the methods are: (1) changes in educational requirements, both in teacher certification specifications and in local school responsibilities, (2) teams of visiting consultants to teacher training institutions and to local districts, and (3) distribution of funds according to the needs of the individual districts. The following areas for educational changes in practices and programs are limited to our concern for the mental health of youth.

Certification and the Stage of Development

Teacher certification requirements should be revised in line with current knowledge of the developmental needs of children and youth. We firmly believe that young people grow as whole individuals. The learning processes cannot be separated from the biological and psychological processes occurring in a particular chronological age range. To stultify one is in some measure to inhibit the growth of other facets.

Professional educators and educational psychologists have been acutely aware, for many years, that conceptual learning and emotional readiness for learning are dependent upon the developmental stage of the youngster. The primary school child differs considerably from the elementary child in thinking and emotional processes. The same is true of junior high as differentiated from high school boys and girls. The notable changes, at certain stages of growth, in the cognitive-emotional system of the human organism require teachers who are aware of, and prepared for, the developmental characteristics of the students they teach.

With few exceptions, state boards of education have retained the broad, general categories of elementary and secondary certification for the teaching of basic subjects.[13]

Such broad categories of requirements indicate that our education of teachers lags badly behind our knowledge of the developmental and educational needs of children and youth. The majority of our nation's teachers (physical education teachers as well as academic) seem not to have been educated to this understanding of conceptual development. Holt's (1964) observations of the lack of knowledge of teachers in what children are ready to learn and the resulting emotional reaction of the youngsters should provoke serious thought for those who train teachers, or who can influence teacher training.

Considering only the stage of adolescent growth, the teacher training requirements for these boys and girls seem based on no discernible logic. Most states certify teachers kindergarten to grade 8 or grades 7 to 12. The overlap in grades in which elementary or secondary teachers may instruct

13. Only four states accredit teachers separately for junior high and high school, while a total of ten states require some type of extra preparation for kindergarten and primary teaching. Elementary certification generally includes K–8, although there are some variations. Some states specify K–9, a few limit 1–6, others permit K–12. Secondary certification permits teaching in grades 7–12. Special subject teachers (music, art, and physical education) are certified upon completion of a training program which ranges K–12 in all states except two.

often results in poor education and confusion. No wonder the junior high schools of America are considered the no man's land of education! The orientation of an elementary teacher to children is quite different from that of a secondary teacher to the adolescent. Neither is beneficial to the junior high student.

The early adolescent is just entering the stage of formal operational thinking. Learning, for these students, is often a sporadic and uneven process. It requires a knowledgeable teacher to discern when the learning steps need to be retraced and more associations made between the concrete and the abstract. Moreover, many students entering junior high have imperfectly developed their skills in reading and mathematics. The teaching of skills, as well as concepts, needs to be in the repertoire of the junior high teacher.

Junior high boys and girls require relationships with teachers that are deeper than their high school counterparts, but which permit more independence than is required of the elementary child. The early adolescent will, on one day, feel very confident and in control. The next day, he is beset by doubts and uncertainties. Such extremes of behavior may be more apparent in some of our populations than in others. Those whose family cultural values conflict with those of the school may find the transition from early to late adolescence particularly confusing.

The systems of privileges and discipline must be quite different between junior and senior high. The differential expectations in ways of self-control, self-direction, group planning, and self-government require knowledgeable and experienced teachers. To train teachers in a 7 to 12 program, without differentiating the stages of adolescence, neither promotes good education nor contributes to positive emotional growth.

Certification and the Teachers of Exceptional Children

The category of exceptional children is generally used to include the physically handicapped (orthopedic), mentally retarded, emotionally disturbed, and brain injured. Each of these groups of children presents quite different educational and emotional problems. Teachers of any of these disabled or disturbed youth require attributes of empathy, understanding, and a sensitivity to the needs of others. They also need, in large measure, an objectivity and sense of reality which leads each child to grow to whatever next level he can attain. In order for a teacher to utilize his own personality effectively in interaction with his students, he needs a basic understanding of human adjustment, combined with the knowledge of the specific problems of the differentially disabled or disturbed. The teachers who are to work with these special children need thorough instruction in curriculum, materials, and procedures applicable to specific groups.

The need for specialized training programs for teachers has largely gone unrecognized by state boards of education. Fifteen states certify teachers for physically handicapped and mentally retarded classes, and only six states require special training for teachers of the emotionally disturbed. There are no states which specify the need for additional training for teachers of brain-injured children. Special education certificates, which are unspecified as to area, are conferred by four states.

Certification requirements for teachers of exceptional children should be established in all states according to specific areas of preparation. Existing certification requirements and training programs need to be evaluated and such information used to guide new programs. Letters of recommendation from the faculty of the training institution regarding the personal qualities of the applicant and his relationship to the teaching of exceptional children should be a part of the certification requirement.

Special School Service Personnel

The contributions that specialists can make in our schools are expanding and increasing as we understand more about the concept of the "whole" individual. Universities and colleges generally are not yet giving close attention to the breadth of skills and knowledge required for special school service personnel. In many cases, the "specialist" in the school is a former classroom teacher who has acquired a semester or two of additional education in some specific field.

State boards of education have perpetrated the inadequate preparation of school specialists. In the majority of states, no recognition is given to many of the special school service personnel through certification. The certification in itself might not be important, but specifications by the state have implications for training and do influence the attitude of local school boards in their employment practices.

State boards of education should encourage the development or revision of training programs in universities and colleges for school specialists, and local school districts should be made aware of the importance of special personnel on their staff. Financial aid should be provided if required. In addition, certification recognition should be given to all special school personnel.

Teacher Training

Teacher training institutions must face up to their responsibilities in the selection as well as certification of the beginning teacher. The introduction of sensitivity training, group therapy, and counseling as an integral part of the teacher preparation program may begin to meet some of these

needs. But more attention needs to be given to the problems of early identification, selection, and admission of young people into the teacher training
program.

The Practicum. In spite of the many studies that have been undertaken
to identify teacher characteristics that are closely related to effectiveness of
teaching, the review of research in this area is more disappointing than
definitive. The research reports show little or no consistent relation between
any teaching characteristics and teaching effectiveness. Nevertheless, Gage
(1966) has offered five teaching behaviors as "desirable" on the basis of
correlational or experimental evidence of their relationship with desirable
outcomes or aspects of teaching. These include: warmth, cognitive organization, orderliness, indirectness, and ability to solve instructional problems.
Gage defines these characteristics as follows: *warmth* means "the tendency
of the teacher to provide emotional support, to express a sympathetic attitude, and to accept the feelings of pupils"; *cognitive organization* includes
a certain kind of intellectual grasp of subject matter that takes the pupils
beyond rote learning and knowledge and provides "relevant ideational
scaffolding" that distinguishes new materials from what has already been
learned and integrates it at "a level of abstraction, generality, and inclusive-
ness" going beyond the learning material itself; *orderliness* refers to "the
teacher's tendency to be systematic and methodical in his self-management";
indirectness places emphasis on student talk and initiative and tries to move
the learner from a passive to an active role by enabling him "to discover
ideas and solutions to problems rather than merely receiving them from
the teacher"; and, last, the *ability to solve instructional problems* includes
the teacher's "ability to solve problems unique to his work in a particular
subdivision of the profession."

What becomes obvious in recounting Gage's "desirable" characteristics
of teaching behavior is that they cannot be learned on a college campus
and in college classes; they must be learned in the classroom through
practice with live students. This calls for a close union of campus with
classroom in the preservice and inservice training of teachers. The outstanding and pervasive recommendation that was heard in the four regional
conferences for student teachers and beginning teachers of the disadvantaged sponsored by the National NDEA Institute for Advanced Study in
Teaching Disadvantaged Youth (1967) conducted in 1966–67 was the
need for more emphasis on the practicum aspects of teacher preparation.
The young teachers stated that the practicum including observation, demonstration, and participation should begin much earlier and should constitute
the solid core of their training. They further stated that the bulk of the
teacher training time should be spent on the actual scene, and that the
schools themselves should become the college laboratories. Beginning in
the freshman or sophomore years, students should work as teacher aides,

teacher assistants, tutors, and the like through school- and community-based programs.

Such early practical experience has an additional advantage in the selection of teachers. Currently, many students do not know how they will react in the classroom as a teacher and are not sure of teaching as a career until they go through the practice teaching experience. Early involvement in the classroom area will allow student teachers to explore other career options before they have invested so much time and money that they cannot switch their career goal, and may allow students in other fields to determine if teaching could be a career possibility for them.

The quality of the practicum will depend upon three factors: the development of the "clinical professorship" in which the action-theory competencies will be enjoined by instructors who have one foot on campus and one foot in the schools; clear conceptualizations of the teaching-instructional processes which serve as guiding principles to be tested out; and systematic supervision and discussion focused on certain specific materials and experiences that constitute the curriculum. Using the practicum as the core of teacher preparation, other aspects of teacher training such as educational measurements and evaluation, educational sociology and philosophy, child development, etc., can take on greater relevancy. In a sense, all other areas should spoke off or spin off from this basic and continuing learning experience with children in their school and classroom.

Too often the beginning teacher is hired on his first job and left adrift with only the informal supervision of his more experienced colleagues in the faculty room to help him master the complex responsibilities of his own classroom. A student teacher generally has one school semester of practice teaching, which may be spent in one classroom or in several classes of different grades. The requirements vary among training programs, but during that semester a supervising professor from the university or college usually observes the student three or four times. The remaining student experience comes from observing the regular classroom teacher and engaging in whatever teaching he is permitted by that teacher.

This kind of practicum leaves much to chance in the training of a neophyte teacher and has many limitations. The regular classroom teacher may or may not be an adequate teacher; or he may have an excellent grasp of his subject matter but pay small attention to differential learning needs, or to the attitudes he is fostering in his students. He may be a warm and responsive person, but lacking in his ability to explain concepts adequately. He may be none of these, contributing nothing in positive learning to the student teacher.

The supervision provided by a professor from the training institution also may be limited, not only in the amount of time such a supervisor can give the student in the public school setting, but in background knowledge and experience, as Conant (1963) has observed:

Practice teaching is often under the supervision, as far as the teacher education institution is concerned, of a person who has not himself or herself been active as a teacher for years. In the case of secondary school teachers, the person may never have taught the subject in question and never have been prepared to teach it.

The concept of the process of acquired knowledge, followed by a period of supervised application, is almost as old as the medical profession itself —all professions dedicated to serving human needs are coming to recognize that internship experience is a vital part of learning. Teachers not only serve the learning needs of youth, but establish atmospheres and environments that have lasting effects.

Designing an internship program for teachers presents considerable difficulties. Unlike other professions, few people have been trained in education with the breadth and depth of knowledge required for a supervisory role. Within education, we have not trained a level of "professional teachers" who could serve supervisory roles. This is not to say that we have no good teachers. There are no doubt thousands of very excellent teachers across the country. No matter how fine, few of them have had the requisite breadth of background to prepare them as supervisory educators for interns. The general requirements of a professional teacher would be:

1. Knowledge of subject content.
2. Familiarity with varieties of materials and methods of instruction.
3. Knowledge of ways in which subject content, materials, and methods could be utilized for the differential learning needs of students.
4. Knowledge of cognitive development and learning processes.
5. Understanding of emotional development, and of the particular characteristics of the age range of students with whom they are concerned.
6. Understanding of the community in which the school is located, as well as understanding of the socioeconomic and cultural differences of the student population. The professional teacher must be able to aid the student teacher in his understanding of the adolescent at home, among peers, and in relation to the majority society.

Professional teachers should be employed by individual school districts or shared by several districts depending on size, and should function within the school setting. Their major role would be supervisory, although they might teach a class or two, according to circumstances. There are numerous ways in which programs to train professional teachers could be established. A variety of models should be tried in differing local circumstances and evaluated in local terms. The following suggested approach seems logical and efficient in that it utilizes existing agencies.

State boards of education, in conjunction with representatives from teacher training institutions and accrediting agencies (regional and national) could devise certification requirements for a special professional teacher certificate. The universities and colleges throughout the state would be invited to submit a proposed course of study for students to meet these criteria, and local school districts would be advised that such programs were being offered. Following the firm establishment of the concept and position of the professional teacher, internship programs could be incorporated into state certification requirements.

Continuing Education of Teachers. The general practice in most states is for teachers to continue their own education if and as they choose. Inducements for taking courses are provided by many local school boards in increased increments for additional credits. Small attention is paid to the type of course taken; and there is seldom awareness as to whether the teacher and, therefore, his students have profited. The sporadic and miscellaneous investment in formal education courses during the school year by teachers seems, at best, useless. It can be actually harmful by reducing the teacher's time for his own class preparation.

The need for continuing teacher education is becoming more vital as knowledge continues to accumulate at an astounding rate—knowledge not only in scientific and technological subjects but in the social sciences in new ways of observing and responding to human behavior, etc. Inner-city schools present particular problems for teachers who have had little contact with, and little understanding of, minority groups. Learning how to reach these students to enable them to learn is no small task. How to stimulate children to learn, and how to provide for all students at their individual level of understanding, is a skill that most teachers need help in developing. To ignore the fact that teachers need continued learning in ways to provide for their students is to cut at the very core of education.

Several types of programs have been tried, none with astounding success. All were well conceived and theoretically sound, but in all cases, teachers were asked to give after-school or vacation time to attend courses. Criticism is often leveled at teachers because of the reticence to use off-school hours to attend meetings and courses. Not all off-school hours represent free time. Conferencing, grading papers, devising tests, making out report cards, lesson planning, etc., represent considerable blocks of time in a teacher's work day outside of school.

It is doubtful that any continuing education programs will work unless offered *during the school day.* Attending an educational seminar, at scheduled times, should be in place of classroom time. Such an arrangement would mean that students would be excused from school occasionally, for example, half a day, twice a month. What the teacher would gain from his own education, to pass on to his students, should more than compensate for the class time lost.

As a part of continuing education programs, educational seminars should be held within circumscribed geographical areas, for teachers from several school districts to exchange ideas and to learn from resource people. While the content of these courses would be different across the country, according to the particular needs of the teachers and their students, there are three areas that seem basic. Stated in general terms, these are:

1. Discussions of new knowledge within the teacher's own, and allied, subject areas.
2. Discussions of teaching methods to better facilitate learning and motivation.
3. Discussions of the socioeconomic, cultural group which predominates in a district—and the resulting values, goals, and pressures on students.

Since continuing teacher education has a history of failure, such educational seminars should be tried as a pilot project. State boards of education, in coordination with the United States Office of Education, should initiate programs in this direction. Universities could be invited to submit a proposed program of seminar offerings for teachers, in conjunction with a school district or districts. Federal monies would be required to reimburse the professors for their participation. The contribution of the school districts would be to release time for teachers.

THE DISTURBED OR DELINQUENT ADOLESCENT IN SCHOOL

At the same time that schools today face ever increasing and shifting enrollments, it is estimated that 2 to 3 percent of our children and youth suffer from mental illness and another 8 to 10 percent from serious emotional disabilities. It is also estimated that 11 percent of all children will be referred to juvenile courts for an act of delinquency (excluding traffic violations) prior to their eighteenth birthday. The FBI in its *Uniform Crime Reports* estimated that 1.2 million children under eighteen were arrested by police in 1963. If we add to all those disturbed children, who remain passive and manifest mainly silent symptoms of their maladjustment, the overt aggressive norm-violating group, we will be dealing with a minimum of 10 percent of the school's population,[14] and depending on the socioeconomic-cultural forces as well as on the tolerance of local authority (parents, teachers, and police) to deviancy, the school and community may need to give special attention to a third of its clientele.

The hospitals, the specialized service of the children guidance clinics, the detention centers, the training schools, and the jails offer limited diag-

14. A review of studies completed for the Joint Commission indicated that 10 percent of elementary school children are identified by teachers as having behavior problems serious enough to require clinical attention (Glidewell and Swallow, 1968).

nostic, treatment, and placement opportunities for these large groups of youngsters. More and more the schools and the police, two universal agencies, will be called upon to shoulder the responsibility for helping the emotionally disturbed and the socially maladjusted.

There is currently a strong movement for the school and the classroom to accept a greater responsibility in the total treatment program for emotionally disturbed and delinquent children. This movement may be strong enough and the circumstances may be severe enough (we have many disturbed and disturbing youngsters to be served and too few mental health specialists to serve them) to precipitate the school—whether it be ready or not—into a central role responsibility with the mental health specialists providing supportive service on a marginal basis.

In mobilizing community forces for prevention and control of juvenile delinquency, the social planner intuitively looks to the school as a major —if not central—resource. The schools have almost all the children of all the people. They receive the child early and maintain a close and intimate relationship with him for an extended period of time; they have trained personnel to deal with children and youth; they aim to develop integrated and socially effective citizens; they are found in every community; and they still enjoy the active support of the community at large.

The temptation is ever present to make of the school an omnibus agency to serve any and every community endeavor. Yet the school, as one agency, cannot hope to be everything to every child. The school is not a hospital; it is not a clinic; it is not a community warehouse for disturbed or disturbing children and youth; nor is it an adolescent ghetto or limbo. The unique and special role of the school is to be found in its teaching-learning function aimed at agreed-upon objectives.

Keeping in focus this unique and special function and recognizing the fact that most of the adolescent's difficulties stem from forces and antecedents outside the school, just what can be expected of the school staff in community programs aimed at curbing delinquency or alleviating emotional disturbance? What is the potential role of the classroom teacher, the school administrator, and the school counselor? In answering these questions, we shall attempt to list the major problems and issues that face the staff and the clientele of the secondary schools.

The school picture of the delinquent and disturbed youngster, as reported in the controlled studies, has generally revealed him standing in bad school posture, if not in educational bankruptcy. His report card shows many failures; he is overage for his grade; his attitudes toward school are negative and heavily charged with hate; he changes schools frequently; he is caught and squeezed in the academic vise of a book-centered curriculum for which he has little intellectual orientation and interest, with the result that he becomes the teacher's worst motivational problem; he intends to leave school as soon as the law will allow, or sooner; and he is frequently truant in a temporary recess from his unsatisfactory, frustrating, and degrading school situation. While he represents a severe headache to the school, the school represents an even greater headache to him.

The exact nature of the school's roles (there is more than one role pattern) in prevention and control of deviant behavior will depend upon a clear differentiation among the varieties of children and youth that can be found along the health- and norm-violating spectra. We need to differentiate, in program planning, between the delinquent whose major behavioral determinants stem from factors under the skin, i.e., those who show some pathology, and those delinquents whose determinants can be traced to dictates in the culture and subculture, i.e., those whose superego is delinquency-identified. (The reader will, hopefully, note the implied false dichotomy.) Most troubled youngsters represent a mixture of types. In particular, the school's preventive and treatment program must be planned with reference to the locus of the antecedents of disturbed behavior. More often, these antecedents are to be found *outside* the domain of the school.

The school can make its contribution in prevention and control of maladjustment at three operational stages. The "good school" will make its primary (or basic) contribution by becoming a "better school." At the second stage, the school can help to prevent emotional disturbance and delinquency by spotting and helping those youngsters who are exposed or vulnerable to maladjustment and who may be sparking signals of future difficulty in living within themselves and within legal norms. At the third stage, the schools can aid in the rehabilitation of those youngsters who are already emotionally ill or delinquent and who may be on probation or parole by working closely with police, probation, court, and clinic.

Recognizing that deviant behavior exists on a continuum, educational provisions will need to be made on at least three levels of operation. Some disturbed and delinquent pupils on this continuum can work best in a regular school-serving classroom with a skilled instructor who has adequate supervision from the principal and other school personnel. Other students on this continuum of behavior can best function in a classroom which is a serving and collaborative agency working closely with a child guidance clinic, a private therapist, or a mental health consultant; and still other youngsters who are more disturbed will need the help of a collaborative-serving classroom perceived as a clinical tool which may be a part of a hospital, special school, or residential treatment center. But in all these three levels of classroom, the teacher cannot relinquish his responsibility or his autonomy. He maintains his unique responsibility for the cognitive development of the pupil-patient. The teacher does not capitulate in behalf of understanding and empathy his pedagogic role and responsibility. Empathy is no substitute for pedagogy.

Making a Good School a Better School

The United States Office of Education in its report on delinquency and the schools made to the President's Commission on Law Enforcement and Administration of Justice called attention to three major deficiencies of schools that may contribute to delinquency:

1. The educational enterprise is not meaningfully related to the real world outside—the world of employment, changing social conditions, etc.

2. The school does not present itself as a model of the pluralistic society. Groups are kept apart by ability, race, economic class. The school isolates. It excludes.

3. The school often does not prepare youth for mature life; it infantalizes them. Kids learn largely through imitation. Therefore, they have to be presented with a model of future expectations. The school must allow the exercise of self-responsibility and opportunity for decision making to prepare youth for adulthood.

The answers to the following questions will suggest specific practices which will implement the general ideas and philosophy expressed in this chapter. The school system that incorporates most of these practices is likely to become a constructive force in the prevention and control of undesirable behavior.

1. Does your school know its individual pupils?

2. Does your school program meet the needs of individual pupils?

3. Does your school carry on a continuous program of curriculum revision and planning?

4. Does your school offer an organized guidance and counseling service to all pupils?

5. Does your school-community alert the teacher to telltale signs of potential or beginning delinquent behavior?

6. Does your school make available special services to aid the teacher in understanding and adjusting pupils?

7. Does your school conduct frequent guidance conferences in regard to the better understanding and adjustment of pupils with problems?

8. Does your school see that every child of school age attends school regularly and that the curriculum is of such value that he desires to continue learning either in school or out of school?

9. Does your school offer a work-study program for certain youth who will enter the world of work on leaving school?

10. Does your school aim to develop children who are effective family members now and who will be effective parents later?

11. Is your school concerned with the social and moral growth of the pupils?

12. Is there an organized health and nutritional program in your school?

13. Is the emotional climate in your school conducive to learning and wholesome pupil growth and development?

14. Does your school utilize the most effective teaching methods in assisting pupils to learn?

15. Does your school have an effective class size?

16. Are the new teachers adequately prepared to take their place in the modern school?

17. Does your school carry on a planned program on in-service training of staff personnel?

18. Does your school assign the most competent teachers to classes in high-delinquency areas and in underprivileged areas?

19. Does your school maintain a close contact with every child's home and neighborhood?

20. Does your school offer many and varied activities in its after-school program to engage the child in worthwhile pursuits?

21. Does your school make available its plant and equipment in an all-day and year-round school-community program?

22. Does your school consider its learning outcomes and goals in terms of desired changes in behavior?

Quest Through Therapy and Special Services

In order to plan preventive and therapeutic steps in working with the adolescent, it is important to bear in mind that, aside from the cultural and parental pressures experienced at this age, there are also the pressures resulting from normal psychological realignment. Psychologically, adolescence is probably the most complex maturational phase in the normal individual's development. Its complexity is probably most dramatically reflected in the psychological reliving of every stage of childhood. The reliving process, itself, calls for a new adjustment to the basic conflicts in order to reach adulthood. Early adjustments are abandoned and new ones structured. An aspect is not worked through just once and a final solution reached. Various solutions are tried; each may be abandoned and a new approach attempted. As a result, the normal adolescent presents a very confused picture to those working with him.

The adolescent experiences most of his feelings with great intensity. He responds with great fervor to anything that has any meaning to him; if he likes football, he is an enthusiastic football fan; if he likes to study he does so with intense dedication; if he likes to be alone, he is a confirmed hermit; if he is a hippie, he is religiously so; if he is delinquent, he is wholeheartedly so. However, he is also intensely responsive to all stimuli. What he is totally invested in during one hour, he may be indifferent to in the next because a new stimulus has superseded the former one. Provided it has real meaning, any inducement is responded to with the whole emotional self of the adolescent, or with an equally all-encompassing repression of his emotions.

Because of the force of his feelings, as well as his unsureness of his own self-identity, the adolescent is extremely sensitive to the response of others. He is easily hurt by others, disappointed in others, or fearful of others, often for seemingly minor reasons. He also reacts just as totally to slight, positive experiences. As a result, he develops strong friendships and strong admirations, but frequently shows poor discriminatory power in evaluating individuals. Since the person he loves or admires most is also the person who can hurt him the most, he may abandon intense relationships or hero worship with the same facility with which he initially established them.

There is no symptom of the disturbed adolescent that does not in one way or another fit into the category of normal adolescence; it is the degree, the crippling, and the unchangeableness of the symptoms that should be the criteria for evaluating whether the individual's behavior is that of a normal adolescent or indicative of something at least potentially going awry. Such disturbances as depression, hypochondriasis, antihypochondriasis, fantasy, and sexual problems may be an indication that the adolescent is being sidetracked in his normal development.[15]

Many more adolescents could profit by therapy if the opportunity were provided. However, punishment rather than therapy is often the means of dealing with those who manifest maladaptive behavior, on the assumption that punitive measures will automatically prevent a recurrence of certain behaviors. In a less severe form, the punishment may be only condemnation. In either case, there is no thought of treatment or aid. If a youngster drops out of school, adults are prone to evaluate this action as poor judgment. If the adolescent turns to drugs, arresting the source of the drug supply and the drug user is presumed to be a sufficient preventive measure. If the youth does not manifest his behavior primarily in antisocial or asocial areas but rather struggles with experienced depression, irritability, confusion in his goals, and chaos in his value system, he may be tolerantly smiled upon or unsympathetically censored for his immaturity, his attention-getting devices, his laziness, or his irresponsibility. Eventually, he may become psychotic because help was not available early and the strain became too much for him to maintain any effective integration. The troubled youth who expresses himself in antisocial acts will, in all likelihood, be eventually diagnosed as "delinquent."

The goal of therapy with the young adolescent is to facilitate a sorting out of his chaotic thoughts and feelings so that these can begin to fall into some unity. Therapy is indicated when the normal psychological process of adolescence is blocked in its effectiveness. If the barrier is due to a neurosis, the neurosis must be treated. However, very few adolescents

15. For a more detailed analysis of the psychological symptoms of disturbed adolescents, the reader is referred to a separate volume prepared for this Task Force by Irene Josselyn, M.D., *Adolescence* (New York: Harper & Row, 1971).

are disabled by a neurotic crystallization. Rather, most troubled youngsters are blocked because they can find no nuclei around which to begin to build a cohesive self-identity that represents maturation rather than a perpetuation of childhood. For this reason, the goal of most therapy with the young adolescent is that of helping him tolerate and profit by his developmental state so that he is free to constructively try out a variety of character and personality constellations, internal guides, and ways of dealing with reality. In many instances, the function of therapy is to prevent crippling rather than to correct disorders. The threat of actual crippling may be evident; the task is to prevent its occurrence.

Concern for treatment of the unique developmental and sociopsychological problems of adolescents is a recent development in the United States. This concern, however, has become increasingly acute because of the increase in the numbers of adolescents and a more sophisticated awareness of mental health problems. Facilities are taxed beyond capacity, as indicated by the large number of waiting lists reported. Yet a satisfactory solution is not likely to be found in merely providing increased numbers of facilities with sufficient staff and funds. For it is not possible, at present, to evaluate definitively the effectiveness of varying treatment methods with the adolescent population. Perhaps our emphasis should be not on increasing numbers of facilities but rather on increasing the ways to avoid the need for these facilities. This includes more emphasis on the need to work within existing educational and family institutions in the spirit of community psychiatry. This includes services to schools, special "crisis" centers in the community, family therapy intervention at home, and so forth.

However, although we wish otherwise, preventive measures applied now will do little or nothing to aid adolescents already in need of specific treatment services. And although the need for such services may be greatly diminished by preventive measures, we will continue to have adolescents and youth who will need help in staying on or returning to the path of normal development. This report gives little more than an overview of current treatment facilities and therapeutic methods provided for adolescents. Even this brief description, however, is clouded by the general lack of satisfactory statistical data.

Before discussing some of the problems in evaluating various treatment programs in order to determine "what works" for the adolescent, we must call attention to a factor that has an effect not only on evaluation and diagnosis, but on who gets treated and what type of treatment they receive. That factor is social class or income level. Global measures of mental health and sociopsychological adjustment have, by and large, found the highest concentration of maladjusted individuals in the lowest social stratum. When differentiated by diagnoses, the more severe cases are located most frequently among those persons in the lowest income groups.

In this respect, little is known about the adolescent population. Some studies have found that the maximum rate of disorders for all ages is in the adolescent group; however, their material has not been analyzed by age *and* social class. The well-known New Haven study of Hollingshead and Redlich found that lower-class adolescents contributed less than their share of patients, that is, they received less treatment than could be expected from their numbers in the total population. Such a finding is not surprising, however, in view of the fact that other studies of psychiatric treatment of children and adolescents in public clinics have found that middle-class children are more frequently deemed "good treatment cases" and receive most of the treatment whereas poor children receive mostly diagnostic and testing services. Among the adult population, social position has an effect on the type of treatment received, and although there are fewer studies on children, those available do indicate that psychotherapy is ordinarily not considered the treatment of choice for disadvantaged children and adolescents. There is some evidence that lower-class persons may be diagnosed as more disturbed than middle-class persons with essentially the same records. In addition, patients in the lowest socioeconomic strata are more likely to drop out of treatment on their own volition, and are less likely to profit by traditional therapies.[16]

The disadvantaged adolescent is most often referred for treatment by schools and courts, and thus enters treatment through a coercive process. This limits his chances for successful treatment, as outcome is greatly affected by the individual's view of the treatment process and his anticipated view of the results. The more favorably he anticipates the outcome, the more likely the treatment process will be a success.

Finally, disadvantaged teen-agers may tend to display symptoms of their disturbance in overt antisocial behavior. Hence, they are more likely to be placed in penal or custodial institutions, where opportunities for psychological treatment may be minimal. In the following discussion of facilities and therapeutic methods, the lower-class adolescent has not been singled out as a separate population; however, his needs in both of these areas are acute.

Problems in Evaluation and Diagnosis

Many investigators view juvenile delinquents as being emotionally disturbed. Others point to the incidence of retardation in both mentally ill and delinquent populations. Physical handicaps are often complicated by retardation and/or emotional disturbances. The consequences of such multiple factors for treatment outcomes are not clearly delineated at present.

16. For an overview of studies see the paper prepared for the Task Force by R. Pennington, "Mental Health Services as Related to the Lower-Class Adolescent."

The inadequacy of present classificatory schemes—especially for child-hood psychiatric disorders—continues to be an obstacle to both effective treatment and the evaluation of such treatment.[17] Kramer (1966) has emphasized the need for adoption of a standardized examination which will indicate the presence or absence of psychiatric disorders, the degree of im-pairment, and the identification of persons who will benefit most from certain types of services.

Present thinking about mental health problems reflects a much more complex conceptualization than that which gave rise to the construction and use of the facilities, discussed later in this chapter, in which effective treatment was expected to result merely through the administration of medicinal or psychiatric remedies. The more popular current view recog-nizes the importance of the total milieu; consideration must be given to the total environment of the patient. Environmental factors are now seen as having an impact on the entrance into treatment, on the progress of some treatment modes, and on the facilitation or hindrance of post-treatment outcomes. Greater attention is being given, therefore, to family therapy or counseling. Also, a greater emphasis is being placed on the community as a therapeutic agent. There is a recognition that traditional cultural attitudes toward mental illness must be changed and that efforts should be made to educate parents and members of the community in both preventive and treatment techniques.

Professionals also need to be more adequately trained to deal with adolescent problems, and research is needed to construct a more coherent theory of adolescent psychology. The advantages adhering to the use of professional and nonprofessional multidisciplinary teams seem well estab-lished; some means is needed, however, to effect a greater coordination among the members of such teams. Environmental factors within institu-tions require study to determine how the institutional atmosphere may be utilized to enhance treatment outcomes.

Further research is needed on: (1) the relationship noted between class membership and the etiology of certain neuropsychiatric disorders and mental retardation; (2) the reported differential correlations between sex, class, and/or ethnic membership and delinquency and psychopathology; and (3) the higher incidence of juvenile delinquency and/or psycho-pathology reported among some socially disorganized areas and among some lower-class populations and the related diagnostic question of whether or not class value systems exclude some delinquent behavior from the cate-gory of emotional disturbances.

17. The Clinical Committee of the Joint Commission was very aware of the need in this area. For a detailed discussion, the reader is referred to their report, especially to the paper by Dane G. Prugh, M.D., "Psychosocial Disorders in Childhood and Adolescence: Theoretical Considerations and an Attempt at Classification." This report will appear in *The Mental Health of Children: Services, Research, and Manpower,* Harper & Row, 1973.

The present disorganized state of treatment services, the shortage of facilities and professional workers, and the more complex conceptualization of the factors affecting treatment compound the problem of evaluating the effectiveness of treatment methods and services. Even if these factors were lacking, however, a definitive evaluation of treatment of adolescents—based on an intensive, individual basis—would not be possible. Some of the problems involved have been stated before (U.S. Dept. HEW, 1955), and a review of recent literature[18] yields many of the some complaints—e.g., a paucity of controlled research which will differentiate the effects of various types of therapy on different types of disorders; a general lack of standardized criteria for evaluation which would permit the averaging of a large number of studies; and an overlap in diagnoses previously noted.

Treatment Methods

Psychotherapy continues to be the preferred method of treatment directed at the individual adolescent diagnosed as emotionally or mentally disturbed. There is general agreement that conventional therapies must be modified for adolescents, and there is a particular need for new approaches to disadvantaged adolescents. More comparable studies are needed on what type of treatment works with adolescent patients with a certain type of diagnosis, and to differentiate these results by socioeconomic levels. Hospitals, as well as residential treatment centers, are placing a greater emphasis on total milieu therapy. The therapeutic value of continuing the education of these adolescents is recognized, and the trend is toward an educative program based on individualized needs and capacities. An unresolved question is the debate as to whether all-adolescent or adult-adolescent wards are best suited to the needs of hospitalized youngsters. A related area involves the general hospital which has become a major placement arena for the community mental health centers and has become increasingly important as a treatment setting for the adolescent. Wards set up for adults have become predominantly adolescent wards, a practice that has given rise to problems of rebellion against idleness and rules.

Adolescence actually represents two phases of development rather than one. Broadly speaking, early adolescence refers to a stage in which childhood patterns of adjustment are abandoned, and attempts are made to establish new patterns of problem solving. In late adolescence new patterns become crystallized with some fluctuation back to older patterns. Treatment methods can vary for these two groups. As the theory of adolescent psychology is developed, further distinctions in adolescent needs must be determined.

The mentally retarded population receives somewhat diverse treatment,

18. Paper prepared for the Task Force by B. Sowder, "The Question of Effective Treatment for Adolescents."

depending upon the degree of retardation. A large percentage of the severely or moderately retarded institutionalized population is still being housed in large facilities which are not conducive to positive treatment outcomes. Current trends for educable adolescent retardates are toward social-vocational habilitation and toward prevocational and vocational training as well as treatment. Because of poor diagnosis and dispositional procedures, many emotionally disturbed youngsters are placed in facilities for the retarded.

In the case of juvenile delinquents, rehabilitation training is stressed, and attempts are being made to implement primary prevention. Returnee rates at training schools have been found to be correlated with the size of the institution—i.e., the returnee rate increases as the child population of the institution increases. Foster care and group homes have been found feasible in some cases, but successful treatment appears to be dependent upon effective and meaningful diagnosis, upon the placement operation, and upon treatment programs designed to fit the need of each *type* of delinquent.

Physically handicapped adolescents are in need of more psychiatric care as an adjunct to the specialized educative training and vocational training which are, at present, the central treatment emphases.

PATTERNS OF TREATMENT SERVICES

Care facilities and treatment services for children, adolescents, and youth are drastically inadequate. If the current trends in the use of psychiatric clinics and mental hospitals continue, approximately 1.2 million children and adolescents will receive care in such facilities by 1975 (Rosen, Kramer, *et al.*, 1968). However, there will be about 8 million youngsters under eighteen in need of help.[19] A well-planned reorganization of existing facilities and services would aid in alleviating some of the present problems. The proliferation of services stemming from the development of new diagnostic categories has created not only long waiting lists but also a mismatching of populations and a duplication of services (Sonis, 1964). There is also a lack of coordination between referral sources and existing treatment agencies (Rosen, Bahn, *et al.*, 1965). To answer the drastic need for more staff, it seemed to members of Task Force III that the mental health field must move away from the classical one-patient-one-mental-health-professional form of treatment, into other forms of service delivery. The use of nonprofessional workers in all areas seems a necessity. One particularly promising approach is the use of adolescents and youth to work with their peers in need—a concept which we endorsed previously (see p. 258). The trend toward community psychiatry is another approach which should be encouraged, particularly for the teen-age population. Readily accessible service

19. This is based on a 10 percent estimate of need. See p. 285.

is a must for this age group. Drop-in clinics and emergency and counseling services in neighborhood areas, courts, hospitals, detention centers, and correctional institutions are acute needs for youth. The following is a cursory overview of existing patterns of service.

Child Guidance Clinics

As a preventive measure, child guidance clinics apparently have not been successful in reducing the incidence of mental illness or juvenile delinquency, according to follow-up studies conducted in all parts of the world. However, fully satisfactory studies are lacking. Where new centers are developing, there are insufficient personnel and a lack of public support (Soddy and Ahrenfeldt, 1967).

Outpatient Clinics

Outpatient clinics, too, have failed to meet the needs for which they were intended. Of 53,000 adolescents served in such clinics in the United States in 1962, two-thirds received no treatment; most simply had admission and diagnostic interviews. Withdrawal occurred in one-third of the cases, referral to other agencies in another third, and one-third were eventually terminated by the clinic without referral elsewhere (Rosen, Bahn, *et al.*, 1965).

Community Mental Health Centers

A survey of eleven centers suggested that none came close to meeting the needs of all the emotionally disturbed children within its area. Some provided virtually no services for youngsters. Five provided no inpatient facilities, and such services were limited in the other six. Outpatient facilities were inadequate in all these centers (Glasscote *et al.*, 1964).

Adolescents Away from Home

A substantial number of children and adolescents in this country live away from their homes in institutions, foster homes, and group homes. Although the goal should always be to keep the adolescent within his family and community, it is not always possible to avoid placement away from home. Some youngsters just cannot live in their own homes without damage to themselves or to their environment. Placing the adolescent outside his own home may have a damaging developmental effect. However, the tendency to keep adolescents in their families beyond the endurance level is only partially caused by fear of the consequences of separation. More often it is caused by the dearth of appropriate facilities, by the geographic location, and by the particular bias of the adult authorities (Briar, 1963). For the overwhelming number of adolescents with problems, placement is not the method of first choice. Nevertheless, if placement is effected with professional competence and provides a range of appropriate resources, it can offer some adolescents the only possible way toward maturation. If these conditions are not met, placement can be another destructive experience.

Foster Family. Placement for adolescents in foster families has been fraught with many problems. Success of foster home living is based on the child's ability to develop a quasi-filial relationship with the foster parents; he is expected to accept the foster family and respond positively to their daily interaction, their patterns of living, their culture, their affection and controls. Since adolescents find it hard to accept the demands and controls of their own parents, for the adolescent separated from his home the adjustment to another family is often impossible (Hoffman, 1963). They test the foster family beyond endurance, challenge their authority and competence, or refuse to respond in any form. Foster parents, angered and frightened by this attitude, may retaliate in kind or give up and return the youngster to the agency.

Nevertheless, virtually every child welfare agency in the country can report some striking successes (Rabinow, 1964). The chances for success are greater if the youngster entered the foster home early and grew into adolescence there. Yet even under these circumstances, adolescents often have to be removed from foster homes because foster parents "cannot meet the violent expression of adolescence" ("Foster Family Care for Emotionally Disturbed Children," 1962). What goes for the "normal" adolescent is, of course, even more pertinent for the disturbed adolescent.

Not only has the number of children cared for in foster families increased sharply over the past decades, but an increasing proportion of these children show serious signs of emotional disturbances. At the same time, the number of applicants capable and willing to accept these children within their family has been decreasing. There is thus a serious crisis in foster care for which a solution must be found (Garrett, 1966).

The largest number of children in foster family care are supported by public agencies (see Table 3). This number has been steadily increasing since the beginning of this century and is continuing to grow. Unfortunately, the case loads and staff in many public agencies do not permit the intensive care urgently needed by emotionally disturbed and socially unstable adolescents in foster care. Financial responsibility for public foster care continues to rest mainly with the municipality and the states, although recent legislation has increased federal participation. However, some legislation has been invalidated by punitive stipulations.

It has been suggested that foster care be reevaluated owing to the number of psychological disorders reported in foster care case loads (Eisenberg, 1962). However, institutional care is not likely to be adequate in the future, and aggressive children are frequently shunted aside. Reformatories have been unable to rehabilitate such youngsters. Foster care, therefore, is an alternative which should not be ignored. Many of the difficulties reported could be alleviated by aiding foster parents in coping with their role. There is a shortage, however, of caseworkers as well as good foster homes and educational facilities.

Table 3.—CHILDREN IN FOSTER FAMILY CARE (INCLUDING GROUP HOME CARE)

YEAR	TOTAL	RATE PER 1,000	PUBLIC AGENCY	PERCENTAGE OF TOTAL	VOLUNTARY AGENCY	PERCENTAGE OF TOTAL
1960	158,900	2.4	117,800	74%	41,100	26%
1965	207,800	2.9	162,800	78%	45,000	22%
1966	219,900	3.0	172,400	79%	47,500	21%
(Projected)						
1970	247,100	3.4	202,600	82%	44,500	18%
1975	302,100	3.9	255,600	85%	46,500	15%

SOURCE: "Foster Care of Children—Major National Trends and Prospects," U.S. Department of Health, Education, and Welfare, Welfare Administration, Children's Bureau, 1966. (There is no breakdown by age.)

Group Homes. During the past decade, a promising new facility has been developed to bridge the gap between foster homes and institutions. Group homes are residences in the community in which about eight to twelve adolescents of the same sex live under the supervision of adults. This arrangement allows adolescents who are neither acceptable candidates for foster homes nor in need of institutional or hospital care to maintain ties with the community until they can function in their usual living situation. Group homes may be *enlarged foster families* which differ from foster homes in the greater number of children served, staffing, and financial reimbursement; or small *institution-type units*, which differ from traditional institutions in their smaller number of residents, fuller use of community life and resources, greater flexibility in designing programs for individual children, and greater emphasis on group interaction (Gula, 1964).

The group home can be used as a "halfway home" for teen-agers after residential treatment, or as a preventative measure for adolescents who must be removed from their home environment before residential treatment becomes a necessity. All children and adolescents should be kept as near as possible to a normal living situation within the community. Once the adolescent is removed from his community the problem of reentry becomes magnified. Thus, group homes can prevent excessive institutionalization in cases in which the parent-child relationship cannot be adjusted and can allow the youngster to return to the community before treatment is completed. Group homes also can serve severely disturbed adolescents who cannot adjust to the intensive group-living process of the institution. In addition, group homes could become effective as temporary living facilities for adolescents with a variety of developmental difficulties which may not be particularly abnormal, but which can drive the youth to more extreme actions. Indeed, there are some presently existing semigroup homes which have been set up by church groups and other interested persons just to fill such a need. The adolescent runaway is a recurring problem in our society. The counseling opportunities, dialogues, group discussion, and temporary group living experience of the group home could be an effective tool in setting the adolescent back on the normal developmental track before his course has veered too far.

Although the number of children residing in group homes in this country is small, the use of the facilities is growing. The dearth of sufficient and adequate child care staff affects the group home development as it does practically all placement facilities. For this relatively new form of placement, it is of importance to develop "specialists." The group home worker must handle many crises as they occur, make instant decisions, and play a vast variety of roles. In addition, a new ingredient must be added to the training of both professional and nonprofessional staff for group homes. The utilization of the small living group experience for educational, recreational, and therapeutic purposes is an added dimension. This is particularly important for treatment, as all members of the environment may play auxiliary roles in the treatment process (Crocker, 1955).

Adolescents in Institutions. There is a danger in writing about placement opportunities for adolescents, because it assumes a certain need for placement and encourages the idea of "more of the same" type of placement possibilities. What we really need are new ways to avoid the placement. This is particularly true when discussing adolescents in institutions. As long as we tolerate the use of institutions for children and adolescents, they will continue to exist. Although many have noted the adverse effects of total institutionalization, we have yet to engage our resources and know-how in determining other alternatives.

According to the 1960 census, there were 305,325 children in institutions of all kinds (exclusive of private boarding schools), of whom 156,228 or 51 percent were age fifteen years or more (see Table 4). From Table 5, however, it is apparent that nearly 80 percent of all children institutionalized because of social or emotional maladjustment are fifteen years or older. Before a parent or a social agency decides to send a child or preadolescent to a training school or a mental hospital, the child's pathology usually has to be more incapacitating and overwhelming than that of the rebellious adolescent. Universally, the adolescent dominates nonadult institutions.

The following are the main types of existing institutional care available for adolescents:[20]

1. *Day-care centers:* A number of communities and states are currently experimenting with programs for children and adolescents who can return to their own homes at night and over the weekend. A number of these day-care programs utilize guided group interaction for adolescents at work or adolescents with school problems. Programs in Newark, New Jersey; Louisville, Kentucky; and California operate on this basis.

2. *Project Re-ED:* Programs have been developed in connection with schools and universities which emphasize the educational and deemphasize the therapeutic task with certain types of disturbed children. These children and adolescents stay in the institution during the week and return to their families on weekends. Certain types of mental health classes are available to parents. Project Re-ED in North Carolina and Tennessee is an attractive approach that is achieving results equal to traditional programs, as reported in the research literature, at a cost per child substantially lower than for most intensive residential programs and in a shorter length of stay—an average of seven months as opposed to two years. As a model for other programs, this approach has much to offer.

3. *Dependency institutions:* About 15,000 adolescents live in institutions of this kind. Since many of these children have emotional problems, there is a tendency to refer to such institutions as treatment centers, although they are typically without appropriate treatment programs, facilities, or services. Some of these provide vocational and social experiences to youngsters who do not require more intensive treatment. There is no doubt of the need for a facility of this kind within the total range of services to the adolescent in placement.

4. *Boarding schools* serve mainly the middle- and upper-class child. Unfortunately, no statistical, diagnostic, or evaluative reports are available to enable us to analyze the role of the boarding school with respect to the disturbed adolescent. Apparently these schools absorb a number of emotionally disturbed and maladjusted youngsters who, in other socioeconomic groups, come to the attention of social agencies, clinics, and courts.

5. *Institutions for the delinquent:* Correctional institutions care for adolescents to a far greater extent than do other types of institutions. In 1961, 98 percent of the youngsters who were incarcerated were adolescents.

Delinquency is a manifestation of social and psychological maladjustment which is different from various other emotional disturbances in the type and degree of acting out (Peck, 1959). All maladjusted children suffer

20. For a more thorough discussion see the Task Force paper "The Adolescent in Placement," by Morris F. Mayer.

Table 4.—Children in Institutions, by Age and Type of Institution, 1960

WELFARE

Age	Homes for dependent and neglected children		Homes for the aged and dependent		Homes for unwed mothers	
	Number	Percent	Number	Percent	Number	Percent
Under 5	5,965	8.4	294	11.8	1,084	38.5
5–9	18,191	25.7	473	18.9	79	2.8
10–14	31,860	44.9	540	21.6	137	4.9
15–19	14,709	20.7	958	38.3	1,335	47.5
20	167	0.2	236	9.4	178	6.3
Total	70,892	100.0	2,501	100.0	2,813	100.0

PHYSICAL DISABILITIES

Age	Homes and schools for the blind		Homes and schools for the deaf		Other homes and schools for physically handicapped		Tuberculosis hospitals		Other chronic disease hospitals	
	Number	Percent	Number	Percent	Number	Percent	Number	Percent	Number	Percent
Under 5	54	0.9	160	1.4	767	16.9	1,123	23.9	349	20.8
5–9	1,945	31.1	2,684	24.0	1,361	29.9	872	18.5	496	29.5
10–14	2,342	37.5	4,137	36.9	1,605	35.3	812	17.3	429	25.5
15–19	1,797	28.8	3,997	35.7	739	16.2	1,522	32.4	342	20.4
20	108	1.7	229	2.0	77	1.7	370	7.9	63	3.8
Total	6,246	100.0	11,207	100.0	4,549	100.0	4,699	100.0	1,679	100.0

CORRECTIONAL

Age	Training schools for delinquent children		Detention homes		Diagnostic and reception centers		Prisons and reformatories		Local jails and workhouses	
	Number	Percent	Number	Percent	Number	Percent	Number	Percent	Number	Percent
Under 5	48	0.9	213	2.1	—	—	42	0.1	23	0.2
5–9	428	1.0	573	5.8	8	0.7	—	—	13	0.1
10–14	12,209	27.5	4,093	41.3	316	25.7	95	0.3	522	3.1
15–19	31,316	70.6	4,988	50.4	904	73.6	19,377	68.3	12,535	71.2
20	365	0.8	37	0.4	—	—	8,851	31.2	4,465	25.4
Total	44,366	100.0	9,903	100.0	1,228	100.0	28,325	100.0	17,598	100.0

MENTAL DISABILITIES

Age	Mental hospitals and residential treatment centers		Homes and schools for the mentally handicapped	
	Number	Percent	Number	Percent
Under 5	417	1.9	4,473	5.7
5–9	1,860	8.5	15,232	19.4
10–14	5,210	23.7	26,564	33.9
15–19	11,682	53.1	27,610	35.2
20	2,817	12.8	4,454	5.7
Total	21,986	100.0	78,333	100.0

SOURCE: U.S. Department of Health, Education, and Welfare, Children's Bureau Publication No. 435, *America's Children and Youth in Institutions: 1950–1960–1964* (1965).

TABLE 5.—PROPORTION OF ADOLESCENTS INSTITUTIONALIZED BECAUSE OF SOCIAL OR EMOTIONAL PROBLEMS, 1960

	TOTAL	15 YEARS TO 21 YEARS	PERCENTAGE OF TOTAL
Training schools	44,366	31,681	71.4
Detention homes	9,903	5,025	20.8
Diagnostic and recreational centers	1,228	904	73.6
Prisons and reformatories	28,325	28,228	99.5
Local jails	17,598	17,000	96.6
Mental hospitals and residential treatment centers	21,986	14,449	65.9
	123,406	97,287	78.9

SOURCE: See Table 4.

from a combination of conflicts, some of a social and others of an intra-psychic nature. To a certain extent, the definition of "juvenile delinquency" is socioeconomic. The adolescent of the lower socioeconomic group is placed on probation or sent to a correctional institution. The adolescent of the middle and upper socioeconomic group is returned to his parents, who consult a specialist in child and adolescent behavior. The delinquent who comes from a disadvantaged environment is a product of cultural conflict in addition to the conflict of his ego with his impulses and the demands of society.[21] The latter conflict is one he shares in common with all the nondelinquent disturbed children in treatment centers.

In some institutions, particularly the psychiatrically oriented ones, the cultural conflict may be completely ignored or treated as though it were a part of the intrapersonal conflict. The socially underprivileged delinquent, who understands neither the value system nor perhaps the language of the adults in such a situation, is then frequently given up as "untreatable," "unreachable," "void of superego," etc.

In other institutions, particularly the training schools, not enough attention is given to the intrapersonal conflicts of the disturbed delinquent. The whole emphasis is on conditioning and retraining without regard to the inner tensions determinative of the maladjustment.

The amount of recidivism among such "trained" delinquents is very high. The training school's attitude to the recidivist is often one of desperation or even cynicism. Thus, the delinquent is often abandoned by the training school as well as the treatment center. He may be sent to a more

21. This point has been made particularly succinct by Rubenfeld in *Family of Outcasts: A New Theory of Delinquency* (1965).

custodial, more punitive institution without the resources to treat his personality problems. Because of the lack of facilities, he may be thrown back into his home, where he finds himself in the social chaos in which he failed in the first place. He is then doomed to probable repetition of failure. The term "corrective institution" raises the question: Corrective of what? The adolescent who has been committed to such an institution returns to the community, where others assume that he has been adequately punished for his acts and will refrain from committing other such acts. The chances are that he has learned not to refrain from delinquency, but rather to correct his past errors that led to detection.

Society recognizes that juvenile delinquency is the forerunner of adult criminal behavior, but does not adequately consider how to avoid this transition. Juvenile courts, probation officers, institutions, and parole officers that could be described as contributing toward a positive rehabilitation program are in the minority, as far as the national programs are concerned. Because the delinquent frequently becomes the adult criminal, society increasingly becomes more angry and punitive toward the juvenile, rather than accepting the viewpoint that early constructive handling of juvenile delinquents might decrease adult crime.[22]

6. *Mental hospitals:* The available data do not permit our distinguishing statistically the children in residential treatment centers from those in hospitals (Table 4). A number of hospitals have established excellent treatment facilities for a limited number of adolescents. These hospitals serve as pioneers in research and in the practice of residential treatment. Other hospitals have reluctantly developed adolescent wards in which therapeutic attempts are thwarted by inadequate facilities, inability to control intake, undifferentiated grouping, etc. Sometimes the adolescent who is relatively intact is thrown together with a psychotic youngster who cannot benefit from group living. State hospitals are in particular need with the apparent rise in adolescent admissions to adult-oriented wards.

A part of the problem seems to be the unavailability of appropriate post-hospitalization facilities. Youngsters are discharged either too late or too early. They are kept beyond the time when they need the medically oriented hospital facilities, and/or they are discharged into settings in which the other services they need are not available. In spite of the improvement that many have shown in the hospital, they are often doomed to failure in the post-hospital environment.

7. *Residential treatment centers* are a transitional place not only in the child's life but also in the child's treatment process. They are part of a continuum of treatment which normally starts before placement in the

22. For a more in-depth discussion of juvenile delinquency and the court system, see the separate volume completed for the Task Force, *Adolescence*, by Irene M. Josselyn.

treatment center and continues upon the termination of treatment in the center. Sometimes, as indicated, hospitalization precedes the treatment center. Other forms of placement, day care, group home care, foster home care, visiting at home, may also be a part of the individualized program for the child at the treatment center.

A residential treatment center which cannot provide for the medical and protective care that an adolescent may need during a psychotic or psychotic-like breakdown cannot serve the more seriously disturbed adolescent. Such breakdowns do occur quite frequently in the emotionally sick adolescent. They need to be handled matter-of-factly through temporary hospitalization without "giving up" on the patient or declaring a state of emergency each time a breakdown occurs. Hence, residential treatment centers and mental hospitals must have a close relationship. The organizational auspices under which a treatment center operates are much less significant than the cooperative arrangement and the availability of a variety of services.

The adolescent who comes to residential treatment usually has worn out a number of psychotherapists, caseworkers, and physicians. He has failed in social interaction and in education. The assumption is that psychotherapy has been tried and has failed outside the residential treatment center. In residential treatment, psychotherapy is only one part of the treatment services given to the child and may not, at times, be the most relevant part. The children who come to treatment centers may not be accessible to any form of direct psychotherapy until their total life and social attitude has been modified at the treatment center.

Residential treatment is the integrated and coordinated method of rendering physical, educational, social, and emotional care of the child who could not adequately develop without such coordination. The whole program is the treatment. The therapeutic organization of the adolescent's day and the therapeutic utilization of all his relationships are the essence of residential treatment. Because of the cost factor, however, such programs are available to a limited number of adolescents.

Summary

There is a pronounced lack of mental health programs specifically designed for teen-agers. Many child guidance clinics take only preadolescents. Hospital programs are seldom aimed at the special needs of the adolescent population. There is a lack of staff in almost all facilities, and the cost of most care is prohibitive to a family of "average" means and impossible for those of low income. Each year a large number of adolescents pass through a variety of institutions, the majority of which provide little approaching adequate treatment or rehabilitation and many of which in themselves create disturbed youngsters. The percentage of teen-agers admitted to state hospitals and correctional institutions is increasing. Resident patient rates as well as admission rates of youth to state mental hospitals are continuing to increase in spite of the current emphasis on reducing the hospital patient population. Outpatient and after-care service is lacking. Adolescents are in need of mental health services at every level from prevention and early treatment to service for the severely psychotic youth. Such drastic need cannot be met unless we turn our enormous resources and know-how toward the problem and recognize it as one of national importance, not only for today's world but also for the world of tomorrow.

SPECIAL SERVICES

Some groups of adolescents and youth have particular needs because of their particular problem (for example, suicidal tendencies) or because of the particular phase in their life cycle (for example, college students). The Task Force turned its attention to some, though by no means all, of these special services required by our youth.

Mental Health in American Colleges

At a time when 54 percent of all American high school graduates go on to college,[23] American colleges are beginning to expand their mental health facilities at a rapid rate. Even at English and European schools, where American infatuation with psychiatry is a standard joke, the real need for counseling the college-age group has led to the introduction of college psychiatry. The international recognition of need is the more remarkable because it comes despite the remnants of attitudes that consider psychological disturbances shameful and despite the extreme shortage of adequately trained personnel. But the rapid expansion of mental health facilities in America has not led to the enunciation of clear principles as to what the prime objectives of college mental health programs should be. Much more than mere recognition of need or expansion of services is required if these clinical facilities are to become an integrated part of the total college experience.

One measure of the present muddle of college mental health services is seen in the results of the only large survey attempted of such facilities, made by the American College Health Association. Dr. Allen Frank, chief of the Psychiatric Health Service of the University of Colorado, who conducted the study, notes:

There is much confusion as to what is diagnostic and what is treatment service among doctors, and what is counseling and advising among the non-M.D.'s. Nobody seems to be willing to say when student counseling becomes a

23. U.S. Office of Education, 1968 figures.

sort of therapy, long or short. In order to obtain a valid picture of just what psychological services exist in the colleges and who participates in them, someone would have to visit each and every college and study the individual situation. Our questionnaire supplied us with little worth-while data.

At present, the American College Health Association lists only 62 schools which maintain a definite psychiatric health service: these constitute less than 3 percent of the more than 2,200 colleges in the United States. Many other colleges—an undetermined number—retain a psychiatrist for such emergencies as psychotic breaks or suicide attempts. Yet almost all colleges provide some form of counseling service—vocational, social, philosophical, theological, or emotional. Indeed, all of the colleges surveyed indicated that they see the process of socializing their charges as part of their job, and thus accept in principle a responsibility for providing some kind of counseling.

The movement to add some form of more psychiatric- or treatment-oriented service to traditional student counseling began after 1945, when the custodial role of the American college began to break down under the great influx of veterans. This breakdown has continued without interruption. It is in this situation of "decustodialization" that psychological facilities began to be opened. Yet, paradoxically, at the very moment of such a much needed beginning, the seeds of conflict between college administrators and newly formed psychological services also begin to emerge. Whereas once it seemed there was not enough psychological awareness on campus, it now seems there is too much—too much because the college tries to use clinical facilities as the sole means of remedying its longstanding disinterest in anything but the student's intellectual development. This misuse of clinical and counseling services puts the counselor in a special bind. When he complies unselectively with administrative requests for action, information, and intervention, he finds himself going beyond his professional competence; but when he refuses such requests, he may seem ineffectual.

No one doubts that college and university administrators need all the help they can get. Drugs, sex, war, suicide, career decisions, political activism, or just plain apathy or restlessness: all the difficulties faced by the college-age group demand hard decisions and clear positions that most colleges have avoided. Understandably, colleges look all over for help with these problems, and it is not surprising that they turn to the psychological counselor as the one who may really have the "answers."

But colleges can get only a small fraction of the help they need from any kind of individual psychological counseling. To be sure, a great deal may be contributed by psychological theory to an overall understanding of the student's stage in life; but at the level of disciplinary and educational problems, the administrator's appeal to the psychiatrist amounts to a cop-out. The counselor, for his part, knows full well that his contact with the patient gives him an intensive view of only one facet of that patient's life, a view that only rarely permits the prediction of total behavior. After interviewing a student, the counselor may know much of what the latter *feels*, but the relationship between feeling and behavior is complex and indirect. Administrators, on the other hand, are not so much interested in what the student feels as in what he *does*. It follows that if a mental health service is to develop into an effective part of an integrated college experience that promotes intellectual, ethical, and emotional development, both administrators and psychological counselors must be clear about the strengths and limitations of each other's (as well as their own) vantage points. No one denies the necessity for an interrelation between clinical psychological services and administrative services in a college. But the degree in which these functions can conflict to the detriment of the student has not received adequate attention when planning the role of college mental health services. In large part, this particular lack of clarity reflects only one visible aspect of American colleges' more general failure to think through the problem of the impact of the college experience upon students.

To use the mental health facility as a college's sole response to the fact that students are more than recipients of grades, potential disciplinary problems, or budding academic scholars is a major evasion of the primary responsibility of the faculty and administration for the overall development of students. Integrating mental health services in college life at many levels should not be interpreted as license for others to wash their hands of everything but the student's cognitive and intellectual development, labeling all other emotional and moral issues "psychological problems" and dumping them in the laps of counselors and therapists. On the contrary, one of the chief objectives of any sound counseling service with a clearly defined relationship to the rest of the college should be the development of increased sensitivity at all levels of college life to the issues of student development. Thus, in addition to (a) providing adequate *treatment* for psychologically disturbed students, mental health facilities should be designed to (b) assist the college community as a whole in its task of *facilitating* student development within the college experience, and (c) play a major role in the creation of institutions and a college climate that will help in *preventing* serious emotional disturbances.

In the exercise of its facilitative function, a college mental health service teaches the student and the administrator about late adolescence and the stages of development, about the relationship between the routine turmoil of this stage and real emotional disturbance, about the intimate nexus between the educative experience and the process of growing up. Ideally, this teaching enhances and helps to integrate the explicit goals of most colleges (variously stated in college catalogs as concerning the development of intellect, ethical sense, responsibility, sensitivity, character, independence, emotional maturity, and so on) with the actual impact of the college experience. To be sure, colleges are not psychological "therapeutic communities"; that is, their primary goals are not to correct faulty development but to stimulate, support, and confirm normal development. And ideally, all members of the college community should contribute to this development. In different colleges with distinct traditions and community structures, the contributions of the counseling services will inevitably vary. But the counselor should always be a member of a team concerned with the overall problems of the student experience in college, and not an isolated dumping ground for those already deemed emotionally disturbed, nor an adviser on uncomfortable but essentially administrative decisions, nor a covert adjunct to the dean's office or the campus police.

For a mental health service to function as a genuine facilitative influence on the entire college atmosphere requires both from the college administration and from the potential mental health service a demonstration of potentiality that neither has indicated so far. The college would need to commit itself to the formation of a mental health service with no less zeal than it commits itself to its chemistry department. The decision to commit capital funds and to raise money for the equivalent of endowed chairs for a mental health service would be the first, hard, necessary step. The *ad hoc* committees that would have to be formed to supervise appointments in this area would find their job as demanding as the choice of any other senior professor, and at first they would feel hampered by concerns about their capacity to select people in this vast and ambiguous field of mental health.

It is just around the issue of demonstrating available standards for such selection that the mental health profession itself has not demonstrated its potential. To be sure, there has been no chance to date to operate from the position of security and influence outlined above. But surely we also need more clearly stated positions from college health officials that show not only that they understand the students, their time of life, their position in the college, and the problems connected with these, but also that they can communicate this understanding to the students, faculty, and administration. Further, this capacity to understand the key issues would move toward the development of that intellectual and emotional maturity spoken of so warmly by college catalogs and would not be a sterile business leading to a few learned papers. The mental health service must show that this kind of understanding germinates a dialogue in the college among students, faculty, and administration.

"Communication" and "meaningful dialogue" are the essence of the facilitative function, no matter how tarnished and hackneyed these phrases have become. We cannot expect *answers,* either from the mental health service or from anyone else. We can, however, expect understanding of the differing positions of the students, faculty, and administration. The facilitative function is epitomized by a recognition that by the nature of their life positions, faculty, students, and administrators must differ, but that this differing does not preclude people of good will talking with one another and, if not resolving their differences, at least learning to recognize and live with them. Differing positions are inevitable, but the way they are held and expounded is not. Marijuana is the perfect example. Its use is against the law, so the colleges' position can have little give. But how colleges convey this position to students can narrow the gulf that divides the generations. Students neither expect nor want to be joined by the faculty or the administration. The professor or the dean who smokes pot may get a few days' quick popularity, but he will soon lose student respect. A mental health service must show that talking with each other can produce an atmosphere conducive to learning at all levels, and it must show that they can facilitate this learning. And the colleges must give mental health services a chance by offering them a firm base of operations and a respect for the importance of their efforts.

The preventive function of college mental health problems includes, but goes beyond, adequate academic and nonacademic counseling. It should above all create and support a network of personnel sensitive to student responses, able to detect true disturbance and yet to tolerate without anxiety unusual ambiguities in student behavior. It should help sensitize teachers and administrators to the impact on the student of the pressures and inconsistencies found in the college environment, and to the importance of the ability of adults to tolerate these changing ambiguities of students, without themselves feeling ineffectual or becoming unreasonably authoritarian.

The implementation of a solid program designed to prevent emotional difficulties and provide services that affect the school's positions on important matters requires both a change in the school's traditional orientation and a great leap forward by college health practitioners. If colleges should commit themselves to these carefully selected, tenured positions equipped with built-in status, the next concern is how to use them. At first glance it seems obvious that the voice of someone knowledgeable about the psychosocial state of the students, both individually and in groups, could add an important dimension to many faculty committees. Things as disparate as the design of dining rooms, parietal hours, character of grading policies, student participation in administrative decisions, housing, and a wide variety of others should take the students' time of life and current cultural condition into account.

However, even after the first two steps are taken—influential mental health practitioners are provided and those selected are appointed to these vital faculty and administrative bodies—the problem of just how to integrate mental health understanding into the college community remains. As stated before, the mental health specialist offers no answers. He should know full well that what Erik Erikson says, "At different historical periods, different conflicts are emphasized which lead to different crises and different resolutions," is equally true for the mini-history of college generations. But each college, with its own tradition or history, attracts students and faculty with interests more or less consonant with that school, and these groups with their built-in biases speak for the school. On any committee the mental health specialist can only contribute one point of view; he cannot represent the college. If he is good, and if his field comes through with more and better research leading to clearer concepts, he will be a sound and influential member of committees.

But he and the school must know his limitations. His knowledge about what to do with vast problems like drug use or grading is far from total or exact, and in addition his very role imposes restrictions. Confidentiality, which will be discussed under problems of treatment, is a broad issue. For example, if a health service official abuses the theme "we've seen a patient who," this can be provocative—the faculty and administration will want more exact information which cannot ethically be provided. And often a generalization from an individual case seems more convincing than it turns out to be; however, the health official can show the rest of the faculty and administration trends both in this particular student body and in the general culture. He can educate them about how people work, constantly dispelling the myths and misconceptions about "normal" human functioning and "mental health" that pervade our culture. This sort of education provides knowledge that each can use in his own way and makes no effort to turn each faculty member into a counselor and therapist. The mental health worker, in his turn, must be willing to be educated, not just into the traditions and molds of that particular college, but also into the complexities of sound education.

In no sense do the preventive activities of the mental health specialist conflict with his treatment function. Although as a practitioner he is employed by the university, his loyalty is to his patient. When working with his colleagues to affect the college institution so that the sorts of conflicts that breed emotional difficulties can be headed off, he has no individual patient responsibilities; the college is his patient. This may seem obvious, but in this ambiguous and complex area of mental health the rights and interests of the individual are recognized as always paramount. However, the individual does not exist in a vacuum. While in one sense many problems are viewed as intrapsychic, it is rare for their presentation not to include interpersonal involvements that may be of great consequence to the patient. Decisions which deny the patient his legal rights or violate the confidentiality of the doctor-patient relationship must not be made under the guise of protecting the patient's "best interests." The essence of a preventive function for a college health service is to assure the college community that the patient's rights and interests are paramount. Without that, no effective treatment service is possible.

The treatment function of the mental health service is the easiest to describe per se, once it is clear how dependent any treatment is on the adequacy of the college environment in facilitating the student's development and in detecting and preventing emotional disturbance. Very few American colleges provide realistic preventive services; even fewer pay more than lip service to the goal of the total college experience. And even with regard to the provision of direct treatment, very few American colleges have constructed a mental health service adequate (in terms of manpower, staffing, facilities, and mandate from the administration) to the mental health needs of their students. Indeed only 25 percent of American colleges today provide adequate facilities to care for the *physical* health of their students.[24] Offices, consulting and testing rooms, and group and seminar rooms needed for college mental health service are nonexistent on most campuses, at the same time that colleges must compete for woefully scarce adequately trained mental health personnel.

The experience of those few colleges with adequate mental health facilities is that between 10 and 20 percent of all college students will avail themselves of such services at least once during their college career. Adequate staffing, therefore, means enough personnel to interview all students soon after their initial contact with the mental health service, and to treat (in individual or group therapy) those who require more extended care. Inadequate staffing means that students cannot be helped when their problems are acute; it leads to long waiting lists, and it promotes among students the accurate presumption that help is not available when they need it. Not only does this inadequacy help convince students that no aspect of the college community will come through when they need it, thus broadening their breach with the adult world, but it clogs treatment facilities with those students who can and sometimes prefer to wait. The result is, of course, that only a small portion of the whole student population is served.

When we speak of adequately trained staff, we mean personnel thoroughly familiar with the problems of this age group from both clinical and theoretical points of view. Staff should know psychodynamics and developmental theories, and should have adequate clinical experience, which includes a background in severe psychopathology and organicity.

The definition of adequate training can lead to foolish, unnecessary, and doctrinaire arguments, as can be witnessed in the controversy between

24. American College Health Association (25 percent of colleges cover approximately 50 percent of the total student population). Personal communication to the editor, 1968.

the American College Personnel Association (nonmedical) and the American College Health Association (medical). The American College Personnel Association maintains that because work with student developmental crises requires the services of those interested in the psychology of normal development rather than emotional problems, the proper people to treat students are not psychiatrists but one or another of a variety of nonmedical psychological counselors. The M.D.'s insist that they are as interested in normal development and prevention as the next fellow, and should not be limited to serious emotional illnesses. But in the midst of this feud, neither organization has been able to spell out standards of general competence in the field of late-adolescent psychology. This is a real loss in the field, where more than the usual training in child or adult work is required to make the careful clinical differentiations between the normal crises of adolescent development and the symptoms of more ominous emotional disturbance, and where therapeutic helpfulness requires a special ability to feel and communicate respect for the integrity and strengths of the student without denying him the right to be vulnerable, weak, dependent, or even at times "sick."

The college-age group is, in general, relatively healthy from a mental health point of view; for example, few students require long-term hospitalization for mental illness. Furthermore, those students who do experience acute crises and require emergency hospitalization (and who then receive adequate care) generally recover rapidly and are soon able to resume their college careers. Every mental health service should have available to it the facilities for emergency short-term hospitalization and treatment for those students who experience acute disturbances. Close liaison should be maintained between college mental health personnel and hospital authorities. In some cases, the college infirmary—when there is one—can be used to good advantage to provide a short-term sanctuary for students in acute distress without "committing" them to a specifically psychiatric facility and to the enduring self-perception of being "mentally ill" which such hospitalization can entail.

One of the most crucial issues for any counseling service is confidentiality. All student communications must be absolutely guaranteed privileged. A single break in confidentiality (and here the swiftness of the campus grapevine exceeds any electronic miracle) reduces the counselor's usefulness to the student. This demand for absolute confidentiality creates impossible conflicts when the counselor doubles in brass as a dean and has police functions, or even if he is only an instructor giving out grades. How can a student talk to someone as a dean, instructor, or faculty representative one minute, and as a counselor-therapist the next minute?

Certain restrictions help, particularly in small schools where overlap of functions may be an absolute necessity. Mental health workers should not act as consultants to the administration on individual students whom they are counseling. All mental health records must be closed to *all* college and noncollege personnel, even when these agencies have the written consent of the student. It would be naïve to believe that all students who grant written "consent" to government investigating agencies, future employers, etc., to consult college mental health records do so "voluntarily," since failure to grant such consent is known to mean automatic disqualification from a desired position. If advisory opinions on a student's capacity to function are requested of mental health service workers, separate interviews should be arranged with someone other than the student's counselor or therapist, and their evaluative purpose explicitly explained to the student.

Because these safeguards are often not observed, and because of the frequent lack of clarity on the distinction between counseling, teaching, and policing functions, confusion is common. At one school, for example, a student pointed out that to go to a psychiatrist, he had to be referred by the dean of students. "Can you imagine," he said, "going up to him and saying, 'I'm a mental health problem'? So I don't go, because he would never forget it." Another school's psychiatric services complained that little use was made of their doctors for the kinds of conflicts about homosexuality, abortions, drugs, and cheating on exams that were reported by psychiatrists of other colleges. Cursory investigation revealed that this school required a medical excuse for any unusual situation—leaving school, missing an exam, dropping a course, etc. Medical reports were sent to the dean or the administrative board as recommendations upon which the administrator could act as he pleased. Furthermore, once such a procedure occurred, a "bar" was put against the student's record which, if he dropped out, prevented reregistration until he was cleared by the health service. Given this arrangement, students were understandably unwilling to go to psychiatrists for counsel, since they saw them as only another arm of the administration.

The student population's capacity to trust the mental health service will stem in large part from the service's quality of function, its probity with regard to confidentiality, and its capacity to know and understand students and their culture. In this last regard, ill-advised and ill-informed comments by mental health workers on problems affecting student culture tend to make the mental health service a laughingstock, not a trusted ally of the student in his struggle toward maturity. But for the college mental health service to be truly effective in both its preventive and its therapeutic roles, encouragement and support must also come from the rest of the college community. Although some students are self-referred, just as many may need advice and encouragement to seek counseling from teachers, administrators, student advisers, house parents, deans, and others who work closely with them. Such liaison and collaboration between mental health

workers and other student workers is essential in detecting signs of psychological difficulties in students before they become severe, and in encouraging disturbed undergraduates to consult the mental health service.

In addition there should be opportunities for consultation between
students and counselors about situations in which the former may not see
themselves as having trouble. Although some students find it easier to
present their *own* problems by beginning with, "I have a friend who . . . ,"
there are many other students who really do worry about their friends.
Where can a student turn when he sees his depressed roommate give
away prized water skis? Is there a known and used structure at his school
for such situations? Once a suicide attempt actually occurs, the procedure
is usually clear; but to whom does one turn before it occurs? If a student
goes to a dormitory headmaster or faculty member who has only a hazy
picture of the scope and availability of psychological services, whether
he receives help or not, he becomes dependent upon the vagaries of that
adult's personality. A student who is privately worried about masturbation
should not have to talk to someone who insists that his presenting complaint that he can't study is merely related to poor "study habits."

We are prepared to suggest a number of guidelines for adequate mental
health services, and a number of recommendations to bring such services
into being at the vast majority of American colleges where they do not
presently exist. The first guideline would be for mental health workers
from a variety of disciplines and backgrounds to collaborate in the same
service. The practice of separate facilities staffed by clinical psychologists,
other counselors, social workers, or psychiatrists seems to us wasteful and
unnecessary. It reflects no particular responsiveness to the mental health
needs of students, but merely an inability to overcome vested professional
rivalries and jealousies. Furthermore, it deprives the members of each profession of contact with other professionals, perpetuates conflicts between
services, creates insoluble problems of jurisdiction (e.g., where to draw the
line between "severe" and "not severe" disturbances), and causes understandable conflict in the minds of students as to which services they might
best consult.

Furthermore, a clear separation should always be made between police
and teaching functions, including assignment of grades, and counseling
functions. The diverse traditions of American colleges provide a plethora
of community structures that make possible many different combinations
of advisement units—freshman advisers, resident masters, tutors, and
various other counselors. But it is crucial, we believe, to provide clear
definition for the specific functions of each role and to avoid the fusion of
counseling and treatment with grading or policing functions in the same
staff person with regard to any one student.

Another area of confusion which badly needs clarification concerns the *amount* of psychological service available to students. If long-term therapy is available, are there limits on time or number of hours? For a college or university service to limit itself to diagnostic procedures or short-term therapy is, of course, acceptable and often necessary, given extreme shortages of staff, space, and funds; but the student, his family, the counselor, the faculty, and the administration must all know exactly what is meant by "short-term therapy." Administrators often oppose the provision of long-term therapy to students because of its expense. But when a student is in serious trouble, these same administrators sometimes expect the school psychiatrist or counselor to assume complete responsibility for him. Furthermore, unless available services are clearly defined, a vast potential for disagreement and disappointment extends to students and sometimes to their families. If a student sees a college counselor or psychiatrist a few times, but is then referred to a private practitioner, this student's future treatment has been undermined unless the school's policy has been spelled out in advance.

In the same way, the position of the mental health unit in regard to campus activities must also be clearly defined. If clinical facilities are to be an integrated part of college life, and are to make a contribution to the productiveness of the college experience with regard to student development, then counselors should have active advising and innovating functions in relation to a multitude of social and psychological issues which capture the student's interest. Many campuses, for example, have groups which volunteer in mental hospitals, tutor retarded or disadvantaged children, and participate in worthy community activities of many kinds. Mental health workers can help educate such students and can even at times stimulate new projects. But if their functions are not clearly defined, they can find their advisement functions in conflict with other aspects of their own roles or of the school's policies. If mental health workers join closely with administrators in preparing policy decisions on mental health-related topics (e.g., drug use, regulations concerning sexual behavior, dropouts, underachievement, etc.), this conflict can generally be avoided from the start. Too often, however, consultation occurs long after policies have been made: counselors are called in to clarify a decision or clean up a mess which could have been avoided with early cooperative consideration. Such conflicts rarely work to the student's advantage.

To say that a college's policies with regard to these matters should be hammered out in advance does not mean that they should be rigid. On the contrary, areas of discretion should be clearly allowed. The more room allowed for judicial discretion the better the chance for sophisticated, individualized attention to each particular student. At times, rules are useful for those who need rules; but they don't *have* to be applied to those who don't. Yet whatever the rules, the final responsibility for decision should be unambiguous. There is only sophistry in a dean's saying to a psychiatrist, "Yes, it's my decision, but you have the 'answer,' " or a counselor's telling a student after several personal interviews that he will be forced to report his stealing to the administration (although of course he won't tell the police).

Above all, schools and mental health workers must learn to recognize the nature of the beast. John Dewey pointed out that you can't stuff learning into children in schools. Neither can you stuff maturity into college students. You can only create conditions that are less likely to interfere with growing up, and more likely to confirm tentative steps toward maturity. If we expect a vibrant, dynamic, committed student body, then we must give up hopes for their smooth, untroubled passage into adulthood. Psychological intervention is worthwhile at the right time—indeed, many counselors think that occasional nudges at tough times may be even better than continued treatment—but it does not replace living. Nor should counseling interfere with this age group's struggle to grow up.

This list of desiderata is currently met in only a small number of American colleges. That the opportunity to obtain adequate mental health care be extended to include *all* college students seems to us of urgent national importance. The availability of such care can help prevent the consolidation of pathological patterns that might seriously jeopardize the individual's chances for productivity and satisfaction in later life. And students whose psychological growth has been blocked or impeded by internal conflicts or environmental stress can frequently be assisted to move forward by very occasional consultations with mental health personnel while in college. But when such consultation is not available, the same students frequently develop symptoms or antisocial behavior patterns which, once established, are less easy to deal with. It is particularly important to provide such services to our college youth before they have made major commitments to career, life style, and marriage partner; in working with college students, a very little goes a long way.

To implement these objectives, considerably more active intervention by federal and federal-state-community programs, as well as greater initiative and investment by the colleges in mental health activities, must occur. Federal support for the actual construction of mental health facilities for the comprehensive health care of students would require Congressional action. However, the construction of physical facilities, important as it is, must take a very distant second place to massive efforts to provide adequately trained manpower.

First and foremost, then, a number of training programs, specifically in this broad area of college mental health, for qualified workers from a variety of fields—psychiatry, psychology, educational and vocational counseling, social work, selected nonprofessionals, and so on—should have priority. Fellowships at both pre- and post-doctoral levels will be needed far beyond present levels not only for basic training in minimal therapeutic skills (i.e., supervised group and individual psychotherapy, psychological and organic diagnosis, basic psychodynamic theory with special reference to adolescence, psychological testing, consultation, teaching, etc.) but for extensive training to implement the more far-reaching preventive and facilitative services recommended. To establish and maintain such programs and to see that the manpower trained does not cluster around a few "prestige" schools will require thoughtful (and expensive) legislation.

As more and more states and communities accept the principle that they must supply higher educational facilities for as many of their citizens as can make use of them, provision must be made for states and communities to join with the federal government in creating programs made available for an area or region rather than a single school. There is precedent for this in existing educational programs: already a number of geographically related colleges have arranged to share faculty and facilities, both for economic reasons and to avoid redundancy. But regional or cooperative college mental health facilities must be more than isolated regional clinics for disturbed students—mental health shopping centers which have no impact on or relationship with the college communities where their student clients spend the *other* 167 hours a week. An area mental health facility could easily become simply an outpatient consultation, diagnosis, or treatment center, unless it is clearly understood in advance and provided for in legislation that preventive and facilitative services must be supplied to and accepted by each participating school. This more extensive concept of mental health, as involving not merely therapy of the disturbed, but prevention of disorder and—most important—facilitation of growth in the context of the college experience, must be built into each project in advance.

This community pooling of resources might be equally useful for groups of small private schools, junior colleges, and community colleges, since most small colleges alone lack the physical, financial, and manpower resources to supply a wide range of mental health services. But here we must question the attitudes of not just the small colleges but almost all of the large colleges and universities as well. To be sure, to set up physical and manpower facilities of the magnitude advocated here requires government assistance and goes beyond the capacity of even many of the largest and richest schools. But how hard have American colleges even tried on their own? Have the colleges done their part in allocating resources, placing mental health programs high on priority lists for fund-raising, or recruiting the best available staff for mental health facilities? At which colleges has the essential interest in the overall emotional well-being of the student been treated with the same openhandedness as the college's effort for his intellectual advancement? If colleges expect federal and other governmental aid, they will themselves have to give more than lip service to their own health establishments.

Because the available services at most schools are so sparse and the recognition of the need for such services so new, our temptation has been to dwell on services that were needed the day before yesterday. This should not be construed to mean that a service emphasis precludes an equal interest in research. In this ambiguous, difficult, hardly formed field, not to assess carefully and in every way its validity, not to suggest improvements and changes, or not to try to understand better what we are doing is sheer lunacy. For instance, something as generally accepted as the use of group and individual psychotherapy for this student group offers unlimited areas for experimentation and research. Surely we cannot abandon hopes for a more effective, less costly, and less time-consuming treatment so early in the game.

The list of unstudied or inadequately understood problems is endless. Most of the things mentioned above have hardly been examined: the total college experience, preventive services and case finding, crisis intervention, adolescence as a developmental phase, the experimental establishment of a variety of college settings, to name but a few. In all of these areas, there is not only too little research at present, but existing research is often poorly coordinated, supported by competing rather than cooperating agencies, and inadequately conceptualized. Furthermore, it is striking that American universities themselves, who spend many millions of dollars annually in studying the intellectual, psychological, and athletic development of prefreshman applicants, have almost universally failed to establish comparable programs to study the development of these same students once they are admitted.

Thus, while increased federal funds are urgently needed to assist individual colleges and universities to examine in greater detail and depth the many problems about which present ignorance is so extensive, federal, state, or other public intervention should not be a substitute for the active involvement and support of research on student development and student mental health by colleges and universities themselves. In particular, we believe it desirable that every college, large or small, devote systematic attention to the study of its own effects upon the psychological development of its students, to an investigation of the routes and pathways currently used by distressed students in seeking help, and to a frank evaluation of the adequacy of existing facilities for the facilitation of development, the prevention of psychological disorder, and the treatment of serious disturbance when it occurs. Granting of federal research funds to institutions which show little independent interest in understanding student development should be the exception rather than the rule.

Existing federal funding of research in the area of college mental health and student development is extremely haphazard and uncoordinated. Grants currently rejected by one federal agency may be enthusiastically accepted by another; some research-supporting bureaus insist upon cross-institutional comparisons before funds can be granted, while others make no such requirement. Furthermore, few public funds are available for well-conceived theoretical and clinical studies, despite the fact that the most important hypotheses about adolescent development have been derived from precisely this kind of research. Thus, any expansion of federal support for research on student mental health should go hand in hand with increased efforts at specifying the policies of existing agencies that concern themselves with investigations of students (particularly the Office of Education and the National Institute of Mental Health).

As different agencies have different interests, one inevitably will end up supporting a project not of interest to another. While competition should scrupulously be avoided, an emphasis on a variety of approaches to a problem could be healthy as long as everyone—the other agencies, the government bureaucracy, the potential investigators, the professional community —knows the regulations. At the moment, however, highest priority must be given to seeking a liberalization of existing policies, particularly as regards clinical and theoretical investigations.

But far more important than federal monies for the promotion of research, the facilitation of student development, or the prevention and treatment of psychological disorders is the imperative need for a greater, more explicit, and more tangible recognition that the emotional state and moral development of the student are central to his college experience. If this principle is neglected, mental health facilities financed will merely be an evasion of the responsibilities of higher education. Students are growing, developing human beings, not disembodied intellects; they live in a stage of life and during a period of history when stress, turmoil, tension, and conflict are routine rather than exceptional. To do justice to students themselves, to the next generation in American society, American colleges and universities must move rapidly toward granting the opportunity for the emotional and moral development of the student equivalent to his intellectual formation.

Suicide by the Young

On face value, the statement that suicide is a leading cause of youthful deaths is misleading. Youthful suicide is about one-half of 1 percent compared to 1 percent for adults per year. Actually, the recent prominence of suicide is due to a notable shift in mortality trends over the years. Improvements in sanitation, medical care, and pharmacology have all but eliminated many infectious diseases as major public health problems. With the decline in mortality from infectious diseases, the relative importance of chronic diseases and violent deaths, such as suicide, has increased. Although the rate for youthful suicide has risen since reaching a low point in 1954, it is still lower than it was in the early part of this century and considerably lower than during the peak Depression years.

Still, on balance, suicide at younger ages has assumed a relative importance as a leading cause of death. It is the second leading cause of death among the college population and ranks consistently high among other young age groups. Suicide, which is directly related to advancing age, is virtually nonexistent under age nine, rare between ages ten to fourteen, but increases in frequency about seven- to eight-fold between fifteen to nineteen, and more than doubles again in frequency in the twenty- to twenty-four age group (U.S. Dept. HEW, 1966). On a worldwide basis, suicide among young persons has been on the upswing since the early fifties.

Attempted suicide by adolescents occurs much more frequently than committed suicide, and has been estimated to be as high as 50 attempts for each successful act. Girls attempt suicide more often, but there are about three boys to every girl who actually take their own lives. Nonwhite rates are lower than those for whites; however, there is a recent tendency for the nonwhite male rate to rise. Other young groups with high rates are Indians and Puerto Ricans.

The reasons for all suicide are as yet undetermined, but it is especially difficult to understand among the young. Socioeconomic status does not appear to be a relevant factor, as the distribution of suicide is about the same in all class levels. College students, however, appear to be at greater risk of suicide than their nonstudent peers. Rates at several English schools, as well as those at three American universities, have been found to be substantially higher than the corresponding rates for the nonstudent populations.[25] The literature on suicide indicates a relationship with multiple child-parent(s) separations, parental ambivalence, broken homes, and other such factors which lead to the loss of a love object or of love. Further love-object loss is frequently cited as the precipitating mechanism in adolescent suicide attempts. Social isolation is the most important factor between those young who attempt suicide and those who commit suicide. It appears that those who believe there is someone in their environment who will answer their "cry for help" attempt to take their own lives, whereas those who are substantially cut off from adults and peers give little opportunity to be rescued from their fatal act.

Those who work with adolescents and all relevant mental health personnel must be alert to the signs of suicidal thoughts. The potential suicide almost always gives indications of his suicidal fantasies before undertaking

25. For a more detailed analysis, see the Task Force paper "Youthful Suicide," by R. H. Seiden.

the act. Overt and covert indications include obsessional concern with issues of life and death, giving away treasured possessions, ending cherished relationships, conspicuous purchase of the instruments of suicide, and most overt of all, actual threats of suicide. Also indicative of the possibility of suicidal feelings are the characteristic symptoms of intense depression—depressed affect, loss of interest in the outside world, sleep and appetite disturbances, and so on. Often it seems that the adolescent resorts to a suicidal act only after all of his indirect and direct announcements for help have gone unnoticed by everyone in his surroundings.

Public information on the subject of suicide would be a major help in deterring young deaths by such a means. All who come into constant contact with the young—parents, teachers, counselors, and others—should be made aware of suicidal symptoms; and adolescents themselves should be aware of where they can go for help. The best defense against self-destructiveness in colleges and high schools is a climate respectful of individual differences and the diverse rates of student development, a faculty and administration sensitive to the individual needs and characteristics of students, and opportunities for open communication. For those adolescents and youth in acute distress, there must be some facility which can aid the individual in getting through the period of crisis. In all cases, the individual's situation must not be ignored or played down—he must have help beyond the crisis period.

Use of Drugs by the Young

There is no doubt that experimentation with drugs by preadolescents, adolescents, and youth has increased enormously during the past few years, and that peak rates of drug use have yet to be attained across the nation. We view with alarm the apparent trend of drug usage by increasingly younger students. Research concerning the motivations of those who experiment with drugs has only begun. But enough is known already to indicate that the stereotype of the young drug user as a confirmed "hippie" or "head," a person profoundly alienated from the values of American society and dedicated to the pursuit of pleasure, is applicable to only a small proportion of student drug experimenters. Some who are termed drug "users" have discontinued all experimentation. The majority, we believe, experiment with drugs in the hope that the psychoactive agents will assist them in the resolution of their personal problems, intensify their encounter with experience, with art, and with their fellows, and perhaps solve a few of their "hang-ups" in the process. The concentration of student drug users among the most talented and searching students at the most selective colleges in America points to a possible relationship between the often unremitting demands of American higher education and student effort to find intense and meaningful experience outside of recognized institutional paths.

Scientific evidence as to the long-range physiological, genetic, and psychological effects of marijuana and the other hallucinogens is at present inconclusive, although there is mounting indication of enduring physiologic and genetic changes. With an unknown minority of users of the more powerful hallucinogens, immediate effects include adverse reactions like panic states, transient psychoses, and in a few instances, more enduring psychotic states. Similarly, prolonged use of the hallucinogens seems related (whether causally or co-symptomatically is not clear) to changes in values and psychological orientation such that some users abandon long-range goals in favor of more short-range and inwardly focused preoccupations. To the convert to drugs this reorientation of values and goals is of course one of the prime benefits of the drug experience: he has seen through the "games" which society asks him and his fellows to play. To the members of this Task Force, however, these benefits seem highly questionable, the more so because they are not the products of the "natural" experience of the individual, but of a chemically induced state with unknown physiological sequelae.

The one thing that is amply clear is the legal status of drug use. The possession of marijuana, for example, is a felony punishable under the Federal Narcotics Act and under the narcotics acts of many states. State and local authorities have frequently shown their determination to apply with great vigor laws that lump marijuana with the truly addictive narcotics. A growing number of students have already experienced the full impact of these laws, and with consequences that have been severely damaging to them and their futures. At the same time, the prosecution of students for the possession of marijuana has had no noticeable effect in diminishing student use of hallucinogens. On the contrary, the existing legal status of marijuana and the hallucinogens probably serves to increase student drug use in two ways. First, marijuana is not a narcotic, despite its classification with narcotics in various legal statutes. Students scornful of laws based on incorrect information tend to flaunt such laws in a misguided protest against ignorance and hypocrisy. Second, even the casual student pot smoker now finds himself involved in serious criminality for the commission of an act whose actual effects have not been shown scientifically to be as deleterious as those of alcohol or tobacco. In at least a few students, there ensues a process of increasing involvement with illegal activities, often involving other more dangerous hallucinogens. The thrill of the illicit and the sense of rebelling against laws based on ignorance and misinformation both add to the lure of the use of drugs.

Laws that classify marijuana and other hallucinogens with the addictive narcotics are clearly based on serious misinformation. There is no evidence that the hallucinogens are physiologically addictive, although like any psychoactive compounds, they may sometimes lead to psychological dependency. Nor is there any clear-cut evidence of a causal relationship between the use of marijuana and the use of addictive narcotics. Current laws governing the use of marijuana are therefore based on an incorrect assessment of the facts, and in that measure, require early modification.

At the same time, however, claims of the benefits of drug use have received no systematic substantiation, despite the messianic fervor of the advocates of Psychedelia. We know of no study that demonstrates that the unsupervised use of any hallucinogen leads to an improvement in the behavior, creativity, capacity to love, insight, self-understanding, or mental health of the individual involved. The only undeniable consequences of drug use are two: first, a certain proportion of drug users are left with a subjective conviction that they have experienced an enlightenment whose behavioral consequences and actual nature is extremely difficult to spell out, even for them; second, a proportion of users of the more powerful hallucinogens experience strong and sometimes violent adverse reactions. Some studies are beginning to indicate the damage that can be caused by some hallucinogens. Given the absence of demonstrable positive effects, the presence in some individuals of clear adverse reactions, and the possibility of long-range physiological changes induced by drug use, the Task Force can see no ground whatsoever for the legalization of marijuana. The argument that alcohol and tobacco are also deleterious does not seem to us to justify adding a new family of harmful drugs to the list already available. At the same time, we can see where new and immediate scientific knowledge is needed about the various hallucinogens and their long-term, as well as short-term, effects.

The problem of the use of hallucinogens is a part of a wider and more long-range problem concerning the use of psychoactive compounds by the American public. The enormous proliferation of such drugs, both natural and synthetic, has already shown its positive promise in the relief of the symptoms of acute mental illness, in the alleviation of pain, in the lifting of depression, and in the lessening of anxiety. Yet the same drugs, which properly used can alleviate suffering, can create untold hardship and distress when used without supervision. Student misuse of amphetamines during the past years has resulted in frequent psychiatric hospitalization; misuse of barbiturates leads to addiction far more dangerous than that of narcotics and to chronic changes in personality. The same antipsychotic drugs which have helped many seriously disturbed Americans resume normal lives have the capacity to produce severe and incapacitating side effects. Furthermore, the day of the mind-altering drug has only dawned: hundreds of synthetic compounds with narcotic, hallucinogenic, antipsychotic, energizing, tranquilizing, antidepressive, and other properties

have been synthesized and are being tested. Other drugs, far more frightening, are known only to those concerned with biochemical warfare. Already,
60 percent of the prescriptions filled in America involve psychoactive
drugs; and we see no end to the manufacture of new drugs, many of
which are or will be easy to produce with minimal chemical knowledge,
starting from supplies that are difficult to control.

In the long run, then, while governmental efforts to control the manufacture and sale and use of psychoactive drugs deserve high priority, even
higher priority should go to efforts to educate tomorrow's adults about both
the potential medicinal effects of the mind-altering drugs and the extreme
hazards that attend their unsupervised use. We would anticipate that within
the next decades, the problem of public education for the use of mind-
altering compounds may assume a prominence comparable to that currently
held by issues concerning sexual behavior.

American colleges, high schools, and junior high schools should undertake, with the assistance of the Food and Drug Administration, informed
medical sources, and educational organizations, continuing programs of
education concerning the use and abuse of psychoactive compounds including amphetamines, hallucinogens, barbiturates, narcotics, tranquilizers,
alcohol, and tobacco. Discussion of drug use and abuse should be a routine
part of health education programs at all levels in American schools.

In the end, however, we doubt that the solution to the problem of
drug abuse is to be found in legislation, or even in efforts to inform
students of the actual dangers of misuse of drugs. Rather, we would view
student drug abuse as a symptom of the absence of exciting alternatives,
options, and purposes in American school life. In this regard, the student
drug user is a witness against the school he attends, and a witness against
our society. He attests to a growing-up experience which provides nothing
more captivating, thrilling, or enticing than the heightened perceptiveness
of the marijuana high; he is a symptom of a society in which many of the
most talented, perceptive, and gifted must seek life's meaning entirely in
the inner recesses of the mind and the eye.

The Mental Health of the Disadvantaged Young

Of the 25.7 million poor in the United States in 1968, it is estimated
that 3.5 million were between the ages of fourteen and twenty-one ("OEO
Budget Call," 1969). Probably another 400,000 poor are between twenty-
one and twenty-four.[26] They daily face deprivation so severe that they must
choose between enough to eat and other essentials of life. The stress of
economic deprivation exacts other tolls: broken homes, learning difficulties,
delinquent behavior, and poor health. Not only does the world of the poor

26. Unofficial estimate, OEO, personal communication.

draw to itself the physically weak and mentally ill, but that environment contains stresses and ambiguities conducive to mental illness.

The best of the recent antipoverty programs are built on the strengths of the poor—their human resources of pride, dignity, and humor honed in the struggle for survival. The better programs also recognize that the poor face a number of problems so crucial and interwoven that attack on several fronts is required. Concern for their mental health is vital if 6.1 million youth are to survive their struggle against poverty and become productive rather than destructive or noncontributing citizens.

Going beyond a description of conditions, there are two basic questions which arise in the consideration of the mental health of disadvantaged adolescents and young adults. How does deprivation affect mental health during the growing-up process? What problems deter the provision of mental health services to disadvantaged youth?

How does deprivation affect mental health during the adolescent years? If adolescence is viewed as a developmental period during which self-identity and a meaningful relationship with the surrounding society are established, the difficulty confronting disadvantaged youth in achieving the tasks of adolescence should be apparent. The environment he knows and the self-concept he has learned have ill prepared him to interact effectively in socioeconomic strata other than his own. The relationships he establishes within his environment, the roles with which he masks his damaged self-esteem, and the meanings he attaches to his experiences may be well integrated in terms of his life circumstances, yet regarded as maladaptions by those whose values are nurtured within the middle class.

Some concepts of mental health which relate to the developmental tasks of adolescence and to the achievement of competence during the school years include:

1. The ability to adapt to one's environment.
2. The ability to perceive reality accurately.
3. The ability to manage stress healthfully.
4. The ability to stand on one's own two feet.
5. The ability to learn.
6. A feeling of well-being.[27]

1. The deprived youth lives in an environment characterized by unemployment, crowded and unsanitary living conditions, commercialized vice, and sickness. To adapt to such a destructive and negative environment is hardly desirable. Yet it is likely that he is trapped there by the lack of transportation facilities, by housing discrimination, by language barriers, by simply not having enough money to move elsewhere. To survive, the poor youth must adjust to some of these circumstances. He may learn to avoid

27. The relationship between mental health and achievement of competence in school has been developed by Bower (1966).

trouble if he can, but to fight if he must. He will learn to communicate in the language patterns which he daily hears, even though his school penalizes him for substandard speech. Many of the adaptations demanded by the hostile environment in which he lives result in behaviors and attitudes which cause those in more fortunate circumstances to reject or patronize him. Adaptation jeopardizes his chances for escape from poverty.

From a mental health point of view, the task of the deprived youth is to escape from his environment or to find a means of changing it. The first alternative requires that he find some route upward in socioeconomic status. Education has traditionally provided upward mobility for the healthiest and strongest of the poor. But as education becomes a *sine qua non* for employment, the years of education required are increased and the curriculum becomes more academically oriented. The disadvantaged learner may find this route is closed to him.

Increasingly, the youthful poor are demanding a change in their environment, are stubbornly refusing to adapt to it. Perhaps they see upward mobility as a sociological myth; perhaps they are so alienated by the rebuffs of the larger society that they prefer to re-create their own environment rather than reject it. Among the militant, "I live in the ghetto, the slums," is almost a boast. In short, they wish to adapt their surroundings to their needs.

This seems an adequate starting point for a mental health program. The environment must be modified if the cycle of poverty with its associated incidence of mental illness is to be interrupted. This would appear to be a complex and interrelated process in which adaptation *to* the environment must proceed in conjunction with adaptation *of* the environment. Certainly mental health professionals can learn from and simultaneously be helpful in this process.

2. The disadvantaged youth's perceptions of reality have been shaped in the crucible of poverty. His view of life may be stark, pessimistic, and fatalistic. He knows a great deal more about sickness and death, about pain and hunger, about violence and tragedy, than the sheltered youth living in comfortable suburbs. Perceptions of the harshness of the poverty environment perhaps constitute a threat to mental health, since it discourages hope and fosters despair.

However, the perception of reality is also curtailed by the poverty community. Deprived youth have too few opportunities to explore other environments, to view the range of society, and to know how people in other socioeconomic circumstances live. The view provided through mass media is often distorted. Consequently, their ability to realistically plan for upward mobility is limited.

Many compensatory education programs begin with expanding the experiential background of disadvantaged children. Often this means visiting a farm, riding on an escalator, talking with a policeman, or the like. Mental health programs for the poor may require equally simple beginnings. The poor and the mental health professionals involved in such programs will need to know about each other, will need a common ground of reality for communication to be established.

3. The most debilitating and cyclical aspect of poverty is the unremitting state of deprivation and stress. To survive, the poor must establish an emotional equilibrium that can upright itself after each crisis. When no money can be saved for tomorrow's emergencies, the adolescent knows that his broken arm, his need for new clothes for school, the breakdown of the family car, all precipitate financial crises. Healthy adjustment is usually evaluated by "middle-class concepts involving such principles as impulse control, responsibility, and goal commitment" (Chilman, 1966). Often the disadvantaged adolescent has learned to manage continuing stress and recurring crises by abdicating responsibility, by concentrating on immediate goals, and by releasing impulsive behavior.

A deprived childhood inadequately prepares the adolescent for the choices he must make. The poverty environment acquaints him with prostitution, vice, and dope addiction, and illustrates few rewards for virtuous behavior. Any offer that promises easy money is difficult to refuse when deprivation and insecurity are a way of life.

The accommodation of continual stress and frustration is not a desirable state. The youthful poor are finding new ways to handle frustrations. One way is protest. The larger society should not be fearful of lawful protests, but should accept this as a healthy substitute for apathy. We all take action against inequities, although most of us are less direct. The crucial point is that protest be heard, that the poor find a means of productive and meaningful action within the law. In order to do this, the laws must be responsive to demonstrated needs.

4. The literature of poverty which makes frequent reference to generations of welfare recipients implies that "hard-core" poor prefer being on the public dole or feel such support is their birthright. This is true, if at all, of only a few. Most feel like the impoverished head of a family who described accepting public assistance as selling her citizenship. Adolescents need to have opportunities to demonstrate their self-sufficiency before they are caught in the cycle of hopelessness and defeat.

Such programs as the Community Action Arm of the Office of Economic Opportunity, the employment projects for subprofessionals, and the youth training and employment programs are seeking to do just that. These programs seek to effect not only changes in individuals, but also and more importantly, changes in institutions. For today's disadvantaged adolescent needs not only to learn the skills and attitudes which will enable him to be independent, but he also needs standing room and a share in the responsibility of our technological society.

5. Some crucial findings regarding poverty have had far-reaching

effects on education. One is that the deprived child enters school with a severe disadvantage which is seldom compensated for in the traditional school program. Preschools for the disadvantaged are insufficient. An enriched and individualized instructional program is necessary at least throughout the primary grades.

Typically, during a ten-month school year, the disadvantaged youngster progresses seven months in reading grade placement as measured by standardized reading tests. The deficit is cumulative. When he reaches tenth grade, the disadvantaged adolescent is probably reading at the seventh-grade level. Since much of his secondary education depends on language facility, he is severely handicapped in all academic subject areas. Today many school districts are expanding funds provided under Title I of the Elementary and Secondary Education Act to improve reading instruction for disadvantaged youngsters. Special reading teachers, a variety of instructional materials, enrichment experiences, and subprofessional aides are typical components of such projects. These programs are costly. However, project beneficiaries generally progress a full month for each month that they participate. That is, they progress in reading at a normal rate for children of their age.

If support for compensatory education programs can be obtained, we can be hopeful that education will provide a more realistic opportunity system for the disadvantaged. Both the local resources available to the schools and the federal funds provided under the Economic Opportunity Act and the Elementary and Secondary Education Act are entirely inadequate to meet the needs for compensatory education.

Many problems of the disadvantaged impinge on the ability to learn. Thus, guidance counselors, psychologists, psychiatrists, nurses, and school social workers need to observe and work with the children and advise the teaching staff. A close working relationship must exist between the mental health facilities and the school.

6. The young adult who has lived a life of deprivation and insecurity knows that the satisfaction of basic needs for survival is fundamental to a feeling of well-being. He does not take food and a place to sleep for granted. But self-esteem, self-respect, may require something more.

The young person needs to feel that he can become an effective, respected, contributing member of society. He must be hopeful of achieving a realistic, believable goal. He needs to know that there are opportunities and systems by which he can achieve success. Everyone needs a purpose and hope. In groping toward our goals, we discover what is realistic, we reshape our dreams, we sharpen our plans. Most people fall a little short of their goals, but they grow in the climbing. One of the most pernicious effects of poverty is the stunting of goals. The deprived child has few close associations with successful individuals. His school experience seems to tell him that he should not aim too high. He is advised to enroll in vocational courses. He knows he is in a class for less able learners. Such circumstances do not encourage a feeling of well-being. We speak of motivating the disadvantaged adolescent, but too often we want to determine what those motivations should be. All people must be allowed to measure their achievements against some vision of what the future can hold for them. They must believe that there is a way up and out, a better life that they might achieve. Given a ladder, they will do their own climbing.

What problems are involved in providing mental health services to disadvantaged youth? Any enterprise that seeks to improve the mental health of disadvantaged youth must be based on an understanding of the environment in which those youth live. Community forces which work against mental health should be identified, as well as community resources which can support a mental health program. Understanding of the social milieu is also essential to diagnosis of individual problems.

Making and maintaining contact is difficult. The inaccessibility of mental health services to many poverty neighborhoods and the dearth of services for youth are major problems. A number of community health programs have established contact with children and their families by providing services at the elementary school site. Similar programs in collaboration with secondary schools are rare and limited in scope. However, the adolescent may be reached through a program serving a younger sibling.

The low-income parents associate the clinic with problems, with waiting long hours only to be referred to another agency, with seemingly unsympathetic personnel, with communication difficulties created by barriers of language and social distance. They are reluctant to submit their children to this setting and may do so only when pressured by the school or court. These agencies usually refer youth to mental health services when they can no longer cope with problem behavior. Parents may express their hostility by refusing to participate in family therapy.

Mental health professionals have discovered that they cannot serve the poor by remaining in their offices. Increasingly, they are going into the homes of their clients to work within the family setting. The indigenous subprofessional is extraordinarily helpful in establishing and maintaining contact with disadvantaged families and in encouraging them to use available services. Usually, the poor have been shunted from agency to agency, each with its waiting list and each with its interview and evaluation procedures. The concept of neighborhood multiservice centers offers one solution. Another lies in a team of workers representing several different agencies.

Appropriate therapeutic methods for working with low-income groups are being explored by mental health practitioners. Role playing, peer group, and family therapy sessions are frequently employed with disadvantaged teen-agers. Being available and accessible so that the youngster can drop in when he perceives a crisis in his life is very important.

One obvious reason that many agencies experience difficulty in reaching the poor is that they do not ask the poor how to go about it. If a community is to become concerned about mental health and to use services, that community should be involved as much as possible in planning the mental health program. The opportunity to be genuinely involved in a worthwhile project may be more beneficial to mental health than the services to be provided.

Adolescents are especially eager to be involved in programs concerning them. They are also especially wary of programs which other people develop for their benefit. Channeling their youthful energy into the development of a mental health program may seem to some a facetious suggestion, but its advantages are many: a greater likelihood that they will utilize the services; involvement in activities which are meaningful to the larger community; participation in a program which should involve all age levels and both professional and nonprofessional personnel; and the consequent growth in self-esteem and understanding.

High school students, dropouts, and young adults can assist not only with clerical work and custodial and gardening tasks, but also in some contacts with clients. They can talk with other young people who are waiting for appointments, provide baby-sitting service, help older people, show new professional staff members around the neighborhood, contact youthful clients to remind them of appointments, and help train other adolescent aides. The last is important. Professionals are often inaccurate in assessing what an aide does or does not know, and they are sometimes impatient about explaining.

In this section we have attempted to show that the young adolescent has multiple and complicated problems to solve. Thus, the role of his particular environment is to provide multiple forms of assistance to him. The antisocial or disturbed young adolescent manifests his disturbances by responses and behavior that are exaggerations of typical adolescent patterns. His behavior is evidence that he is overwhelmed either by the task of bringing order out of his emotional turmoil or by the chaotic relationship between his internal confusion and his evaluation and response to the external world. He needs assistance in achieving his multiple tasks, assistance in any way he will accept it, if he is to reach an optimum self-fulfillment in the adult world. No single discipline, no single social institution, has the tools to provide the essential help; all must contribute from their area of competence.

Quest Through Institutional Revisions and Reforms

SUMMARY AND RECOMMENDATIONS

In a very real sense, the state of youth is a reflection of the state of the world. The functional environment of today's young people is not only one in which change is king; it is one in which it is easy and understandable to perceive the winds of change as blowing from all quarters in ways that are confusing to the intellect, disruptive of old values and credal guidelines to conduct, and threatening to one's security and very existence. Many have documented the intense impact of modern technology on our social life and morals; still others have analyzed such phenomena as urbanization, the fouling of the nest of nature in which man lives, the revolution of rising expectations all across the globe's face, or the fears bred of developments in nuclear weaponry or the techniques of biological and chemical warfare. We need only remind ourselves that the adolescents and young people of our time are indeed children of both affluence and poverty, and whether poor or affluent, they are children of anxiety. Because of the intensity, massiveness, and pace of social change, their connections with previous generations, although far from severed, are rather more tenuous than has been true at any other period of our history. If there is much that is exciting, humane, and fraught with possibilities for human good in the modern world—and there certainly is—there is also a dark and ominous side, distinctive to our era, in which our young people live and move and have their being.

Against this reading of the contemporary environment, traditional ideas of mental health, although they retain a basic validity, lose a good deal of their vitality and relevance. In a fundamental fashion, "mental health" is socially defined; the attributes of the mentally healthy person are those which are looked upon as desirable, productive, and usefully appropriate in the tissue of values, beliefs, and behaviors that define the norms of our interpersonal and communal life. For Task Force III, this line of thought led to a scrapping of any absolutistic ideas of mental health, a grave doubt about the applicability of the conventional medical model to the solution of our central human problems, and the substitution of a kind of psychological equivalent of the old Quaker ideal of a fusion of "the inner light" with "the sense of the meeting." The mentally healthy individual thus becomes one whose private life is evaluated against such somewhat vague but still highly meaningful concepts as integrity, authenticity, and self-determination, and whose relationships with others may be judged in the light of such notions as effective intimacy in love and friendship, contributory participation in the affairs of a community, and the breadth of his sympathy with others whose background of experience differs from his own. A capacity to shape one's own destiny becomes, therefore, as important as a capacity to adapt and to adjust to rapidly altering circumstances, and a measure of zest in coping with the shifts and stresses in the contemporary environment is a germane touchstone of mental health. Viewed from a developmental angle of regard, the particular behaviors that fulfill the criteria implied by these terms are likely to change—often rather markedly—with both the stages of life and the conditions of the environment. "Mental health" is a process, a struggle, and a quest rather than a relatively static state of being.

The Task Force therefore recommends that involved professionals initiate a vast effort toward social education to counter the present monolithic and absolutist view of mental health which applies uniform and moralistic standards to all phases of human development and makes mental health the parallel of physical health. Our shifting culture requires instead a view which permits perpetual ambiguity and allows for spontaneous action, a view which recognizes that we have a complex network of checks and balances in psychic equilibrium which may not meet the American ideal of perpetual health as an ultimate goal (see pp. 226–235).

In the light of these considerations that touch upon the state of the social and political world and which define mental health in such a fashion, it was inevitable that the Task Force define the societally important problems of adolescence and youth as essentially a function of the interaction between the instabilities of a developmental period and the stabilities of the historical era which happens to be our own. Under rather stringent limitations of time, whereby priorities had to be set, this Task Force was pressed to the belief that the course of development in our youngsters from pubescence to adulthood would be most facilitated by a critical examination of the human environment that so critically shapes them. This emphasis on aspects of the social process and patterns of contemporary culture, as they affect youth, is not intended to give secondary importance to the traditional clinical concerns of diagnosis, treatment, and facilities for psychiatric care. *We look upon these concerns as crucial.* Rather, it was felt that a greater understanding of the adolescent in the world today, by both adults and youth themselves, would result in less derailment and disturbance among adolescents, and would aid in preventing the first steps in the direction of emotional illness. Once such steps have occurred, this Task Force stresses the importance of *readily available* facilities—which are presently lacking—for all segments of our youth population.

The making of this critical examination, however, is terribly complicated by the ever more apparent division in American society. When one looks at youth, one finds inevitably a wide spectrum of persons, not only along the usual dimensions of age, sex, and age-graded role, but in terms of such polarities as haves and have-nots, Caucasian majorities and colored minorities, the poor and the affluent. In their striking differences, these groups not only define different populations for those concerned with the mental health of our country; they also reflect new and sometimes puzzling coalitions and bonds of sympathy—for instance, the identifications formed by significant numbers of young people from advantaged and white backgrounds with their disadvantaged and black compeers. Such identifications certainly reflect a broadening of the base of human sympathy, but they also often indicate a rejection of traditional behavioral styles, values, and rules that order social life. Programs designed to facilitate mental health as it is conceived here must, then, give appropriate attention to not only a highly heterogeneous population of adolescents and youth, but also to the relatively new ways in which groups within this age bracket tend to form alliances among themselves, not infrequently in opposition to traditional authority and in protest against traditional forms of social organization.

The Task Force was concerned about the lack of leeway allowed adolescents for trial and error, for making mistakes and learning more from them than they pay for them, and by the difficulty of removing the label once the youth has been pigeonholed. Whereas adolescents and youth must not be absolved of responsibility for the consequences of their acts, it is necessary that they be given room in which to err without being scarred for life by guilt, by crushed self-respect, or by the nature of their public records and that they be given personalized support within which they can reflect upon their error or misjudgment and acquire more discrimination and sophistication in the quest for identity and a rewarding social role for themselves. Untold harm is done by labeling for life an adolescent who, in the process of identity formation, is attempting to determine whether this situation, behavior, or way of thinking is really a part of his true self. By attaching to some transient aspect of the adolescent's behavior a self-confirming label like "delinquent," "schizophrenic," "homosexual," or "psychopathic," we may add an enduring dimension to the disturbances of adolescence. The vulnerable youngster, already confused as to who he is, may seize upon even such negative rubrics in a despairing effort to be *someone*.

The goal of all interventions with adolescents should be to strengthen and confirm *them* in *their* development. Some need special help; but the purpose of this help should not be to "cure" them of their "illness" (much less of their adolescence). Rather it should be to restore to the adolescent his capacity to proceed in his growth without special help. Too much help can be enfeebling, just as too much understanding without respect can be undermining. Adolescence must not be short-circuited by undercutting the questioning, rebellion, and search that necessarily and productively should accompany the adolescent experience. As more adequate "special help" becomes available for American youth, that help must seek to intensify, deepen, and, in many cases, prolong adolescence, rather than simply to hasten the passage to adulthood.

Until very recently, adolescence was an experience largely reserved for the extraordinarily privileged or the extraordinarily lucky. One of the unique psychological achievements of industrial and postindustrial societies has been the gradual opening of an opportunity for a real adolescence to a great number of less privileged and less talented young men and women, with all of the rich possibilities for continued development this opening brings. Adolescence is, of all later stages in life, that which can most readily permit profound reorientation of intrapsychic and interpersonal life. A benign, responsive, and confirmatory environment can enable an adolescent to undo vast damage done in earlier childhood, to heal the wounds of parental inconsistency, ignorance, or neglect, and to move beyond the handicaps of his past to a responsible and satisfying maturity. Adolescence can provide those lucky enough to have a second chance an opportunity to move away from the malignancies of family pathology, social disorganization, or deprivation. We know too little about the precise way in which the adolescent can, with a favorable and supportive environment, free himself from the scars of childhood. But we know enough to be certain that American society today does far too little to support the self-renewing capacities of its youth, and we feel that American young have the right to such an adolescence.

The Task Force therefore recommends that American society take vigorous steps to grant to all of its youth the right to developmental experiences appropriate to the adolescent years. The cultural and social deprivations, the discriminations, the lack of opportunities for imaginative thought and experimentation, the pressures toward conformity and a yielding to conventional authority must be strikingly reduced to allow for the personal autonomy, the expansion of the self, and the unfolding of individuality which are requisite to this stage of development see pp. 211–225).

Never before have so many of America's adolescents and youth been so well educated, so aware of world historical events, and so ready to participate in the realm of societal undertakings. Correspondingly, at no other period have so many from this population segment been so excluded from the adult world or so alienated from the roles which their previous counterparts shared with adults. Whereas previously work or apprenticeship provided some interaction between the adolescent and adult, today's world of work has become increasingly age-graded and specialized. Those jobs open to youth are often irrelevant to a future adult working role, devoid of meaningful interaction between persons of the younger and older generations, and characterized by a status which implies the immaturity accorded to youth by society. Yet, the youthful worker, like the older worker, is expected to assume a mature, reponsible work role, to pay his taxes, and so forth. Even more than the student, the youthful worker is expected to serve his country, whether it be an era of military crisis or of peace, and if his conscience should dictate otherwise, he—like the student— is penalized. Whether worker, scholar, soldier, or unemployed, youth are denied adult privileges but expected to assume adult responsibilities. In most places, the youthful soldier who is expected to die for his country cannot legally buy alcoholic beverages until he is twenty-one and the college student who is expected to behave largely according to adult standards cannot prove he is capable of doing so because *in loco parentis* still regiments his life. In short, the larger community has yet to create a meaningful place for today's youth.

Unwittingly, we are training for adulthood and responsibility by excluding youth from the adult world and the exercise of responsibility. The old avenues for learning adult roles have largely disappeared, and we have failed to provide new ways because we have not yet recognized that the old ways, for the most part, no longer exist. We need to allow *youth a much greater degree of participation in our society*. Youth today have no culturally sanctioned roles which they find satisfying, few means of redress for wrongs, and no channels through which their idealism can become incorporated into social reality. We have an increasingly large number of youth who are strongly motivated and possess many skills; yet, they cannot find a place to use their skills or to act on their motivations. If we want adolescents to learn about work and what it means to be a wage earner, we must give them responsibility and hold them to it. If we want young people to learn judgment, we must involve them in situations where they hear adults exercising good judgment and allow them to learn by participating. We must listen to youth, just as we want youth to listen to us. And if we want young people to learn, we must be willing to learn from them.

The Task Force therefore recommends that the age limits at which adolescents can legally participate in societal functions be lowered and made consistent. Ideally, legal integration into society should occur around age fifteen. Adolescents should be invited and encouraged to become a part of most adult institutions, particularly in those activities, programs, services, and projects that are designed to affect the lives of youth. They should be a part of police boards; draft boards; school boards and various school committees; employment training groups, various institution-community bodies including human relations councils, and social service groups, especially those which deal with juvenile delinquents; and in mayors' offices, city councils, and other local political authorities. Entry should be gained by the same means used by adults; that is, by volunteering, by appointment or by authentic invitation, or by election. The opportunity presented must be for a genuine voice and influence in the planning, decision making, implementing, subsequent responsibility, and evaluation of all community services—particularly in those institutions which have an impact on the lives of young people. The goal must be to plan *with* youth, not *for* youth.

As a first step toward involving youth in more meaningful roles, the Task Force supports the lowering of the voting age to eighteen.

The Task Force supports the Youth Power Act of 1969 (see Appendix C). The purpose of this bill is to supplement and increase service and learning opportunities available to our young people, and establish a National Youth Service Foundation and a National Youth Service Council. The object is to tap youth's skill, manpower, energy, and interest through the service concept. Thus, opportunities for young people to serve would be opened in the nation's schools, hospitals, churches, businesses, civic organizations, governmental departments, and the like. Subsistence allowances would allow youth to serve on a full-time basis and would not limit participation to persons who could afford to volunteer their time.

In order to allow young men to participate in youth service projects, to allow them to plan their futures and their careers knowing if military service will be required of them, and to allow them to experience their society as one humanely concerned with problems of equity, the Task Force recommends the adoption of the reforms in selective service recommended by the National Advisory Commission on Selective Service, "In Pursuit of Equity: Who Serves When Not All Serve?" (Feb. 1967); a liberalizing of the definitions of conscientious objection; and a lottery system of selection that distributes the obligation of service equitably across all segments of society. In addition, we endorse an enlargement of educational and training opportunities in the armed services and the development of more effective procedures for restoring young people to civilian life after military service.

The Task Force recommends that adolescents and preadolescents become familiarized with and involved in the world of work to a greater degree. Through the educational process, boys' and girls' clubs, and community services, youngsters should be brought into contact with adults with various job skills and with various work settings. By junior high school, students should have an awareness of the give and take of the job market, what kinds of education and training are necessary for what types of work, and an understanding of the role of work. Ideally, high school students should be able to acquire a salable skill. Vocational counseling services in both junior high and high schools should be expanded. Combined work-school programs should be increased to allow more opportunities to earn money in order to stay in school.

To aid in reducing the youth unemployment rate, high school graduations should be staggered over the year to facilitate absorption into the labor force.

The Child Labor Laws should be reevaluated in the context of the present and future work world to allow greater dovetailing between work and education. A more careful balance needs to be made between adequate protection against harmful and abusive working situations and maximum opportunity for work and work-related experiences for adolescents and preadolescents. (For discussion of above recommendations, see pp. 257–258.)

This Task Force finds little reason to be disturbed over the occurrence of orderly student protest and dissent, which seems to us in the best tradition of citizens' involvement in the political process. We are more concerned that so relatively few students are currently involved in the critical examination of the present policies and future directions of our society. We are more distressed that lawmakers, administrations, and the general public so often fail to appreciate the nature and promise of today's student political involvement, and seek to curtail, restrict, or limit the active involvement of today's student population in the crucial national and international problems that beset our nation. An attitude of uncomprehending opposition and efforts to sabotage student activism are detrimental to the development of a mature and responsible political attitude on the part not only of activists but of their less active classmates. Frustrated by the deafness and restrictiveness of those to whom they address themselves, activists are tending toward more and more desperate efforts to draw attention to their causes. Finally, they may move outside the realm of democratic political discourse and activity. The apathetic student is further convinced by the public reaction to his dissenting classmates that any effort on his own part to work for an improvement in his community or his society would be destined to failure, and that he had, therefore, best devote himself to the pursuit of grades, popularity, and material success. In this way, rigid opposition to and incomprehension of the often legitimate complaints, demands, and proposals of student activists serve to push activists toward extremism and nonactivists further into conformity.

The Task Force therefore recommends that junior high school, high school, and college administrators and teaching personnel take positive steps to aid students in accurately informing themselves about major public national, international, and local issues; encourage students to take positions with regard to these issues; and encourage students to persuade others of the validity of their convictions through legitimate avenues. Appropriate officials should meet with students and listen to their demands, grievances, and concerns. In all cases, channels must be established to allow legitimate hearings of student views, and action must be taken on just grievances. Increasingly, students should be involved at the decision-making and policy level.

Schools should provide a forum for speakers of a variety of persuasions, beliefs, and faiths regardless of their controversiality. In so doing, schools must defend the right of free speech in general. Zealous student activists of all persuasions must respect the rights and freedoms of other students and speakers. The schools must be prepared to defend the rights of minorities of students who hold views unpopular with their fellow students, faculty members, administrators, and those responsible for the overall governance of and support of the school.

In all political activities, civil disobediences, breaches of peace, etc., students who are subject to civil action should not be subject to disciplinary action by the school for the same offense. Where existing civil laws do not apply, the school must have the right to establish its own standards of intellectual integrity, attainment, and decency within the school.

Student publications should be self-governing, and wherever possible, financially independent; and should be limited in their freedom of expression only by the laws that govern the press in the United States. (For discussion of above recommendations, see pp. 246–248.)

Although today's adolescents mature physically at an earlier age, and are more sophisticated with more knowledge at their fingertips, they do not necessarily mature emotionally at a rate parallel to the physical growth. One of the major tasks of adolescence today is to learn how to handle this disparity between biological and emotional maturity in a period when society is raising the age at which an adolescent is recognized as an adult.

The Task Force therefore recognizes that research is needed to devise ways to aid the young in coping with biological maturity while striving to achieve emotional maturity. Specific research is needed on sex differences in this area, and its relationship to early and late adolescence (see pp. 262–263).

In the last two decades, education has changed from a peripheral to a central position in the lives of the young. As a result of our complex technology, increased population, and mobility, education has become the major avenue through which the individual can assure himself of employ-ability and a productive future. Thus, school roles, both intellectual and social, have become increasingly important. In the groping for social roles and identity formation, many aspects of the school situation have an impact on the emotional development of the adolescent.

One example is the school atmosphere, which results from the attitudes of administrators and teachers toward young people and is generally transmitted through the organized systems of discipline and privileges found in the school. How a student achieves esteem and acclaim, whether through the legitimate system or the peer group system, can explain the motivation of many students. A substantial amount of psychological knowl-edge indicates that reward-learning is more emotionally facilitating than punishment, and that it has more positive effects on adjustment and be-havior, yet the systems of privileges in schools have seldom been employed to foster socially desirable behavior. In order to serve the broad spectrum of adolescents' needs, schools must recognize the diversity of human crea-tivity and accord rewards to more than the bright academically achieve-ment-minded student. Authentic talent, creativity, and contribution to the school or society other than that in the intellectual area should be recog-nized within the school system. Currently, some schools reward outstanding athletes or members of the student political body. Such rewards should be expanded to include all areas of human creativity and talent when authentic contributions are made both to the school and to the local com-munity.

The teacher is a fundamental influence on the student. What a student learns, how he learns it, and the way in which he perceives and measures himself in the learning process is largely teacher-determined. However, we have yet to facilitate the teacher's ability to teach those who are dif-ferentially able and motivated. Teachers have an influence as a role model, and influence peer group formations. They are instrumental, either for good or for ill, in the adolescent's task of defining and acquiring values. The quality of the relationship between teacher and student is particularly crucial to disadvantaged adolescents and to those young who are emotion-ally disturbed or antisocial. The teacher's essential role is not therapeutic; it is to educate—to develop the cognitive processes. In so doing, however, the teacher has a tremendous influence on the emotional development of the adolescent.

Every aspect of education requires attention—teacher preparation pro-grams, continuing teacher education, certification requirements, curriculum reform, and distribution of financial aid, to mention just a few. However, the overriding need is for unifying leadership. Since the individual states have the legal responsibility for the educational process within the state, the Task Force felt state education boards must assume the leadership function.

The Task Force therefore recommends that state boards of education revise teacher certification requirements in line with current knowledge of the developmental needs of children and youth.

State boards of education should establish certification requirements for teachers of exceptional children according to specific areas of preparation. Letters of recommendation from the faculty of the training institution regarding the personal qualities of the applicant and his relationship to the teaching of exceptional children should be a part of the certification requirement.

State boards of education should initiate the necessary steps leading to the establishment of professional teacher and internship programs.

State boards of education, in coordination with the U.S. Office of Education, should invite universities, in conjunction with local school districts, to present proposed programs for continuing teacher education as pilot projects.

State boards of education should establish certification requirements and encourage the development of revision of training programs for school specialists.

Teacher training institutions must place greater emphasis on the practical aspect of teacher preparation. The bulk of the teacher training time should be spent in the school rather than in the college classroom; and beginning in the freshman and sophomore years, students should work as teacher aides, teacher assistants, tutors, and the like through school- and community-based programs.

Students, as well as parents, teachers, administrators, and special school personnel, should be involved in the process of differentiating and broadening the curriculum. In general, from the seventh grade on, students should be more involved in all aspects of the educational process including that of policy making.

Schools must be involved as cooperating agencies within total community action programs. Thus, students, parents, and community agencies will have greater involvement in the selection and training of teachers, in curriculum reform, and in the establishment of programs for the mental health of both pupils and teachers. (For discussion of the above recommendations, see pp. 264–289. For a series of questions pertinent to the education of emotionally disturbed or delinquent adolescents, see pp. 288–289.)

In order to plan preventive and therapeutic steps in working with the adolescent it is important to bear in mind that aside from the cultural and parental pressures which he experiences at this age, pressures resulting from normal psychological realignment are also occurring. Adolescence is probably psychologically the most complex maturational phase in the normal individual's development. There is no symptom of the disturbed adolescent that does not in one way or another fit into the category of normal adolescence; it is the degree, the crippling, and the unchangeableness of the symptoms that should be the criteria for evaluating whether the individual's behavior is that of a normal adolescent, or indicative of something at least potentially going awry. Many of those who are manifesting maladaptive behavior are assumed to need punishment which will automatically prevent a recurrence of such behavior. They may drop out of school; the evaluation by adults is that the young person is manifesting poor judgment. They take drugs, and the limited preventive measure of arresting the source of the drug supply and the user of the drug is presumed to be sufficient. In addition, the adolescent who does not manifest his behavior primarily in antisocial or asocial areas, but rather struggles with consciously experienced depression, irritability, confusion in his goals, and chaos in his value system may be tolerantly smiled upon or unsympathetically censored for his immaturity, his attention-getting devices, his laziness, or his irresponsibility. Eventually the former group will be diagnosed as "delinquent" because they have come to express their problems in that fashion. The latter group eventually may be psychotic because help was not available early and the strain became too much for the individual to maintain any effective integration.

Concern for treatment of the unique developmental and social-psychological problems of adolescents is a recent development in the United States. This concern, however, has become increasingly acute because of the increase in the adolescent population and the marked rise in the numbers of teen-agers being admitted to state hospitals. The *Report of the Committee on Clinical Issues* of the Joint Commission on the Mental Health of Children (1969) stated:

> The admission of teen-agers to the state hospitals has risen something like 150% in the last decade. . . . Instead of being helped, the vast majority are the worse for the experience. The usual picture is one of untrained people working with outmoded facilities within the framework of long abandoned theory (where there is any consistent theory), attempting to deal with a wide variety of complex and seriously sick youngsters and producing results that are more easily measured by a recidivism rate that is often 30 to 50%, and occasionally higher.

All facilities are taxed beyond capacity. Public clinics can serve only a fraction of the numbers referred to them, and private residential care is available only to those whose parents are in the higher income brackets. Those with middle incomes frequently feel lost in between—with incomes too high to receive service at some public clinics, they cannot afford private care for their youngster. However, poor adolescents receive the least care, and are more likely to be placed in penal or custodial institutions rather than in treatment facilities.

Many child guidance clinics take only preadolescents. Hospital programs are seldom aimed at the special needs of adolescents. Adolescents are in need of mental health services at every level from prevention and early treatment to service for the severely psychotic youth. Such drastic need cannot be met unless we recognize it as a problem of national importance and turn our enormous resources and know-how to its solution.

The Task Force therefore recommends that emergency and counseling services for adolescents be given a high priority in order to stem the rising rate of emotionally disturbed and antisocial youth. Such services must be provided in courts, detention centers, and correctional institutions as well as in hospitals and community clinics. Such services must be available on a drop-in basis and preferably open 24 hours a day.

"Halfway homes" should be established within communities to serve adolescents after institutionalization and as a preventive measure before institutionalization becomes necessary.

Where applicable, the Task Force recommends that programs for the emotionally disturbed adolescent be patterned after the Re-ED model.

Research is needed to construct a more coherent theory of adolescent psychology including a better understanding of differences between early and late adolescence for males and females. The rising rate of psychoneuroses among female adolescents is a particular issue.

Research is needed on the efficacy of various treatment modalities to the adolescent population, including the relationship to psychiatric diagnostic category and the specific population served, for example, the disadvantaged adolescent.

Research is needed on the relationship between class membership and the etiology of certain neuropsychiatric disorders and mental retardation; the reported differential correlations between sex, class, and/ or ethnic membership and delinquency and psychopathology; and the higher incidence of juvenile delinquency and/or psychopathology reported among some socially disorganized areas and among some lower-class populations.

Placement of the adolescent away from home should occur only when the home cannot meet the developmental needs of the adolescent, and should be viewed as a total process which includes a complex of facilities. Advisory boards should be established in each county under governmental auspices. Such boards should include representatives of private and public welfare, mental health organizations, and other required professionals. Placement agencies should report at least annually to these boards, which should function as a referral service and stimulate the development of adequate facilities.

Treatment of the adolescent in placement must be based on a multidisciplinary approach, including an overseer (e.g., a social worker or other appropriate person) who assesses the treatment independent of the setting in which the child lives.

Screening procedures should be employed to delineate those delinquents who are emotionally disturbed and in need of mental health supports. Placement, including a period of control and training, should be viewed as a *process* and include a variety of facilities.

Unified national standards for placement should be developed. Geographical residence of parents should not determine the kind of treatment received by the youngster.

Every adolescent has the right to the kind of treatment he requires, irrespective of his parents' income. A fair distribution of cost should be made among federal, state, and local governments and parents, based on their respective capacities to pay.

The government should fund qualified placement and treatment facilities of private agencies, universities, hospitals, and other voluntary organizations.

To meet the manpower crisis, general subsidies and proper legislation should be directed toward: the organization of and/or support of special training for the professionally trained staff, the child care worker, and foster parent; the uplifting of salaries and working conditions of child care personnel; and draft-deferred status for such workers.

Research should be part of all programs dealing with disturbed adolescents. Research and experimentation may be done in conjunction with universities; however, all efforts must be coordinated on a regional and national basis. (For discussion of the above recommendations see pp. 290–332.)

Some groups of adolescents and youth have particular needs because of their membership in a specific population segment. The Task Force turned its attention to some, though by no means all, of these special services required by our youth. The special needs of college students have led to the introduction of college psychiatry. The Task Force viewed the college experience not as a series of isolated, discrete relationships with peers, teachers, or counselors, but rather as that expansion and integration of the student's intellectual, ethical, and emotional capabilities which can best take place during the college years. Besides the treatment of psychological disorders, the Task Force felt that psychological services have a powerful role to play in facilitating student development within the college experience. The academic and emotional life of the college student must be viewed as interrelated, and American colleges must recognize the impact of the college experience upon both the student's mind and his personality.

The Task Force therefore recommends that all college students have the opportunity to obtain adequate mental health service, the *extent* of which has been clearly defined in advance of admission to the school. Every college must maintain a system of advisers and counselors who have daily contact with students, are sensitive to student responses, and are appointed to vital faculty and administrative bodies.

The college counseling service must have a clearly defined relationship to the rest of the college (particularly in regard to campus activities) and must provide adequate treatment for psychologically disturbed students, must facilitate student development within the college experience and play a major role in the creation of a college climate which will help in preventing serious emotional disturbance.

A clear separation should be made between police, teaching, and counseling functions. It is crucial to provide clear definitions for the specific functions of each role and to avoid the fusion of counseling and treatment with grading or policing function in the same staff person with regard to any one student.

All student communications to the counseling service must be guaranteed confidential. Records concerning the student's academic and nonacademic participation and behavior should be made available only to the student himself or to others with the student's consent.

There should be federal-state-community support as well as greater investment by the colleges in mental health activities. This would include training programs in college mental health for qualified workers from a variety of fields.

Schools should expand research on student development and the effect of the school upon the psychological development of its students, investigation of the routes and pathways currently used by distressed students in seeking help, and a frank evaluation of the adequacy of existing facilities. Federal support for research in these areas should be coordinated. (For discussion of the above recommendations see pp. 307–321.)

Suicide has assumed a relative importance as a leading cause of death among the young. It is the second leading cause of death among the college population and ranks consistently high among other young age groups. On a worldwide basis suicide among young persons has been on the upswing since the early fifties. It is now well established that the suicidal person gives many clues regarding his intentions. The first step in preventing suicide is the recognition of these warning signs.

The Task Force therefore recommends that federal, state, and local community governments establish a public information program on suicide. All who come into constant contact with the young—parents, teachers, family doctors, ministers, counselors, and others—should be aware of suicidal symptoms and where to go for help.

Centers for the prevention of suicide of children and adolescents should be established within a variety of accessible community and college settings. Such services should include not only crisis intervention, but after-care for the potential suicide and his family, particularly young siblings.

Research is needed on the etiology of youth suicide, particularly among the college population, where the rate is higher than among their noncollege same-age peers. Research is also needed on the differences by geographical areas or population segments on the death certification of young suicides. (See pp. 321–323.)

There is a growing tendency among the American people generally to use pharmacological agents as a device for altering the dimensions of consciousness. Aspirin, with its dulling of pain, is the most common example of this trend. The widespread use of tranquilizers, sleeping pills, and such stimulants as Benzedrine is rather more dramatic and telling, though probably less significant, than the annual outlays for nicotine, alcohol, and caffeine. The Task Force urges that the crucial problem of drug usage by young people be considered within the context of a society that is increasingly turning to pharmacological agents for the alteration of consciousness. The adolescent finds a troubling hypocrisy in the condemnation of marijuana expressed by his elders as they sip their third cocktail. Laws now on the books and taken often as a basis for prosecution are badly out of phase with knowledge about the drugs in question. Modernization of the relevant statutes and a more accurate and vigorous campaign of public education about marijuana, the hallucinogens, and narcotics seem very much in order. Hypocrisy, panic, and a kind of anti-intellectual brutality in both the existing laws and many patterns of their enforcement strike us as relevant factors in the discussion of increasing drug usage.

The Task Force therefore recommends that relevant drug statutes be modernized and discriminations made among marijuana, the major hallucinogens, and narcotics. Responsibility for control of marijuana and the major hallucinogens should be placed under the control of the Food and Drug Administration. Federal and state legislation should place heavy penalties on distribution and sale of marijuana but no penalties on possession for use beyond confiscation. There should be continuing review of policies concerning drug abuse as new scientific findings emerge.

The public should be accurately informed about the differences in drugs, their side effects and consequences. Such an educational program should be an integral part of programs in college, high school, junior high school, and primary school. Communities should initiate educative programs specifically aimed at parents and law enforcement officials.

Nonpunitive rehabilitative services for chronic drug users must be made available for all segments of the population. (See pp. 323–326.)

The relationship between mental illness and poverty is a very old concern. What is new is the positive emphasis. Whereas the concern once centered on the containment of charity cases, today it is directed toward the right of all people to optimal mental health. The debilitating frustrations and recurrent crises, the barren environment and unhealthy living conditions to which the poor are continually subjected, militate against mental health. Many aspects of the life style of the poor enable them to survive immediate problems, but are self-destructive in that they tend to perpetuate poverty. Perhaps the greatest tragedy confronting poor youth is that American society offers few opportunities for them to utilize the raw strengths that poverty fosters. Unless such opportunities are made available, millions of young Americans will live out their lives in poverty and become the parents of an even larger generation of deprived children. Measures to help the disadvantaged must allow for the diversity among the many subgroups of the poor.

The Task Force therefore recommends that research on the dynamics of cultural disadvantage and mental health should be directed toward: (1) the relationship between the incidence of mental health and the various types of disadvantage; (2) the effects of various programs for the disadvantaged adolescent on mental health; (3) defining what constitutes disrupted mental health among disadvantaged adolescents; (4) continuance of study to determine the more effective therapeutic methods for this group; (5) an analysis of the strengths of the poor adolescent which contribute to mental health.

Mental health services—of both a preventive and a treatment nature —should be available to all children in the poverty community so that the poor need not choose between preventive mental health and other essentials of life. Staff members should be willing to go into the homes of the poor, where necessary. Procedures (e.g., intake, scheduling of appointments, etc.) should indicate an understanding of the life style of disadvantaged communities; e.g., intake procedures should be as simple as possible, the scheduling of appointments should be flexible, and patients should feel free to come in when they perceive a crisis in their lives.

Adolescents of the poverty community should be involved in mental health programs by playing leadership roles in both planning and operation. Professionals should promote this involvement, e.g., by functioning as consultants to the poor in planning.

The mental health program should be an integrated part of the total community plan with coordination between the various institutions which cooperate to identify needs and establish priorities. New ways of implementing coordination among the services and of involving the poor in this integrating process should be explored. Mental health practitioners and representatives of various agencies should serve as resources to indigenous community leaders, seeking solutions to the negative social factors which bear on the mental health of the disadvantaged. (See pp. 326–332.)

It is a basic recommendation of the Task Force that all programs aimed at serving the adolescent population should include the use of adolescents and youth within the planning, implementation, and evaluation of the project. Adolescents should also be used in the implementation of programs aimed at younger children. Youth should serve as volunteers, paid workers, or as part of a national service project.

The adolescent has multiple and complicated problems to solve. Thus, the role of his particular environment is to provide multiple forms of assistance to him. The antisocial or disturbed adolescent manifests his disturbances by responses and behavior that are exaggerations of typical adolescent patterns. His behavior is evidence that he is overwhelmed either by the task of bringing order out of his emotional chaos or by the chaotic relationship between his internal confusion and his evaluation and response to the external world. He needs assistance in achieving his multiple tasks, assistance in any way he will accept it, if he is to reach an optimum self-fulfillment in the adult world he is about to share in creating. This Task Force has defined adolescence not so much a biological or a physiological determinant as a psychological and social opportunity. This definition assumes that adolescence is not a fixed number of years, or a biological or cognitive measurement, but rather a possibility for an experience of psychological growth which may occur after puberty. If emotional, ethical, and intellectual development is to continue through and beyond adolescence, then continual familial, educational, and societal confirmation and support of adolescent growth must be present.

With almost half of the population twenty-five years of age and younger, it seems clear that we must permit youth to exercise increasing influence on the social decisions that affect us all, or increasingly and understandably they will become more alienated, less contributive, and more a source of disruptive dissidence in public affairs. The central impact of this modern life upon adolescents and youth is uncertainty. Because of the new conditions of the world, yesterday's experience cannot be the sole guide for today's behavior; and today's learning may not effectively anticipate tomorrow's challenge. For young people, then, the basic issue is how to live zestfully, humanely, and individualistically in a world that is increasingly crowded, fluctuating, depersonalized, and ambiguous. To cope with the developmental tasks that are made more difficult by the uncertainties of contemporary society, the adolescent of whatever race, color, or creed must receive personalized support. No single institution—whether family, school, or treatment facility—has the tools to provide the essential help; we all must contribute from our own area of competence.

Appendix A

WORKING PAPERS OF TASK FORCE III

Charry, June, Ph.D., "Adolescence, Education and Preventive Mental Health," December 1967, 35 pp.
———, "What Do We Want from Education?" May 1967, 10 pp.
Groves, Eugene W., "Testimony in Favor of the 18 Year Old Vote," January 1968, 6 pp.
Keniston, Kenneth, Ph.D., "Dissent and Deviance in American College Students," September 1967, 72 pp.
———, "The Tasks of Adolescence," December 1967, 24 pp.
Kvaraceus, William C., Ph.D., "The Adolescent in School," November 1967, 7 pp.
———, "The Disadvantaged Learner: Some Implications for Teachers and Teaching," June 1967, 41 pp.
———, "Guiding the Adolescent in School," n.d., 6 pp.
Maldonado, Joe P., A.C.S.W., "The Mental Health of Disadvantaged Adolescents and Young Adults," November 1967, 47 pp.
Mayer, Morris F., Ph.D., "The Adolescent in Placement," n.d., 39 pp.
Pennington, R., M.A., "Mental Health Services as Related to the Lower-Class Adolescent."
Shoben, Edward Joseph, Jr., Ph.D., "To Temper the Sword of Intellect," n.d., 25 pp.
Sowder, Barbara, M.A., "The Question of Effective Treatment for Adolescents," December 1967, 58 pp.
Zinberg, Norman, M.D., "Draft on the Negro Adolescent," December 1967, 41 pp.
———, "The Mirage of Mental Health," December 1967, 16 pp.
———, and Keniston, Kenneth, Ph.D., "Mental Health Services in American Colleges," November 1967, 23 pp.

351

Appendix B

CONTRACTS FOR TASK FORCE III

Josselyn, Irene, M.D., "Adolescence," March, 1968, 178 pp.
Seiden, Richard H., Ph.D., "Review of Literature on Adolescent and College Student Suicides," November 1967, 135 pp.
Silverstein, Harry, "Some Themes Expressive of Alienated Youth," November 1967, 121 pp.

Appendix C: The Youth Power Act*

S. 1937—INTRODUCTION OF THE YOUTH POWER ACT

Mr. HATFIELD. Mr. President, in the belief that the talents and energies of young people should be more effectively devoted to voluntary service and learning opportunities to the benefit of the whole Nation, I offer for introduction today a bill to establish a National Youth Service Foundation and a National Youth Service Council. It is designated the "Youth Power Act of 1969." Senator MATHIAS, Senator PERCY, and Senator SAXBE join in the cosponsorship of this legislation.

Within the last half century, the potential role that youth might play in our society has grown tremendously. We have changed from a rural to an urban society. Better medicine and health have added to vigor and ability of young people to act upon their concerns. Available leisure time has been increased. The ideal of universal education has come closer to realization. The world of work has become more complex and more challenging. Young persons are raising fundamental questions about our society and are taking new and different views of the problems of life today. They seek to become the movers of our society rather than to be among the manipulated.

Yet, the potential role for youth in our society has not been nearly realized. Chances for creative work, learning and service to mankind have not kept pace with the increasing abilities and desires of our young citizens for such opportunities. Many millions of our under-27 citizens live in poverty while other millions of our youth sense that they are irrelevant to the myriad public and private institutions regulating their lives.

Since the establishment 8 years ago of the Peace Corps, the Federal Government has had an increasing commitment to lessen the gap between the potential service and learning roles and the actual service and learning roles of youth in our society. Following the Peace Corps came Volunteers in Service to

* The Congressional Record, 91st Congress, Sess. 1 (Senate), 115, 64 (Apr. 22, 1969), 3987–3990.

America—VISTA—the Teacher Corps, the Job Corps, and National Youth Corps. The attention given to youth problems at the national level has increased the awareness of the need to deal with these problems in the communities in all parts of our land.

It should be emphasized that private voluntary organizations have also been active in providing experiences of both service and learning for our youth.

The purpose of the bill which I am introducing today is to supplement and increase, not to replace, the service and learning opportunities currently available to our young people. The goal is to provide enough opportunities so that no young person is denied a chance to serve and to learn.

The extent of the broad effort required is well described in the following statement of Donald J. Eberly in the "Directory of Service Organizations," National Service Secretariat, Washington, D.C., 1968:

"We must ask our young people to engage themselves fully with the war on poverty, on disease, on illiteracy, on pollution. We must make it possible for every American youth who wants to serve his fellow man to do so. Black or white, rich or poor, from north or south, east or west, from slum or suburb, village or farm, from the school, the college or university, our young people are needed.

They are needed in our schools as tutors for young children. They are needed in our hospitals and clinics to assist doctors and nurses.

They are needed in our courts to work with youth who have started off on the wrong foot. They are needed as friends by old folks living alone, by the mentally retarded and the mentally ill. They are needed in our forests and open lands, to protect and conserve them. They are needed to respond to natural disasters, at home and overseas. They are needed to build new towns where there will be no discrimination, no illiteracy, no pollution, but opportunities for all to move with confidence into the 21st century.

Already the organizations exist to make this program possible. We shall ask the nation's schools, hospitals, churches, labor unions, businesses and industries, civic organizations, governmental departments at the local, state, regional and federal levels to provide opportunities for young people to serve.

We shall ask private citizens, foundations, profit-making organizations and, as necessary, Congress, for funds to provide the yearly subsistence that will be needed to feed, house, transport and give a living allowance to each young person in service.

We shall ask our colleges and universities, labor unions and industries to organize training and information programs so that each young person will be able to find the challenge he wants and will be able to meet that challenge."

As stated in the act's declaration of purpose, young people at all educational levels from high school dropouts through graduate students can and will take advantage of increased service and learning opportunities. A huge number of domestic tasks remain unmet which simultaneously provides a unique opportunity for young people to serve and learn. Future manpower requirements for increased skills in the fields of education, health, conservation, welfare, job training, and governmental affairs are increasingly difficult to fulfill, and can be alleviated by a coordinated effort to increase service and learning opportunities for young people. The experience young people acquire in service and learning projects will serve to increase manpower skills and to strengthen their understanding of the world in which they live. It is the purpose of the act to strengthen, supplement, and coordinate programs and activities contributing to these policy objectives.

NATIONAL YOUTH SERVICE FOUNDATION

The bill establishes a National Youth Service Foundation to be operated by a 21-member Board of Trustees, 15 of its members to be appointed by the President, by and with the advice and consent of the Senate, and the following to be ex officio members: Director of the Peace Corps; Director of the Teacher Corps; Assistant Director of the Office of Economic Opportunity for Volunteers in Service to America; Director of the Neighborhood Youth Corps; Director of the Job Corps; and the Director of the National Youth Service Foundation.

The Director and Deputy Director of the Foundation are to be appointed by the President, by and with the advice and consent of the Senate.

The National Youth Service Foundation is authorized to make grants to or contract with public and private nonprofit agencies for recruitment and training of 17 to 27 year olds, for periods up to 2 years for, and to conduct, youth service and learning programs as defined in the act; agree to furnish 17 to 27 year olds to public and private nonprofit agencies to carry out any youth service and learning program or any other program approved by the Foundation: recruit and train 17 to 27 year olds for, and to conduct, youth service and learning programs; provide technical assistance to any public and private nonprofit agency receiving assistance under the act; and develop and carry out a program to encourage greater participation by State and local agencies and by private agencies and organizations in programs offering greater opportunities for youth participation in projects for community betterment.

No payment may be made under the act in excess of 80 percent of the cost of the program. Not more than 12½ percent of the funds provided for grants and contracts shall be made available within any one State.

The Foundation shall submit to the President and to Congress an annual report of its operations and its recommendations.

The bill provides for an Advisory Council to the Board. The President would appoint the 24 members of the Council—at least eight of whom will be under 27 years of age—to advise the Board on board policy matters.

NATIONAL YOUTH SERVICE COUNCIL

The second major provision of the bill establishes a National Youth Service Council in the executive office of the President, who would be Chairman of the Council. In addition to the President, the Council would be composed of the Secretary of the Interior, the Secretary of Agriculture, the Secretary of Labor, the Secretary of Health, Education, and Welfare, the Secretary of Housing and Urban Development, the Chairman of the Civil Service Commission, the Commissioner of Education, the Director of the Peace Corps, the Director of the Teacher Corps, the Director of the Office of Economic Opportunity, the Assistant Director of the Office of Economic Opportunity for Volunteers in Service to America, and the Director of the National Youth Service Foundation.

The functions of the Council will be to advise and assist the President as to youth service and learning programs conducted or assisted by the Federal Government; to assure effective program planning for summer and other related youth programs of the Federal Government; coordinate youth programs and activities of all agencies of the Federal Government; encourage the adoption by appropriate agencies of the Federal Government of common procedures and simplified application forms for recruitment and transfer into youth service and learning programs conducted or assisted by any agency of the Federal Government, particularly with respect to the Job Corps, the Neighborhood Youth Corps, the Volunteers in Service to America, the Teacher Corps, the Peace Corps, and the National Youth Service Foundation; encourage each agency of the Federal Government administering a youth service and learning program to coordinate at the local level recruiting and informational activities; encourage development of cooperative programs among agencies of the Federal Government administering or conducting youth service and learning programs so as to more effectively meet the unmet community needs and services; encourage State and local agencies and private agencies and organizations to provide service and learning opportunities for youths; resolve differences between agencies of the Federal Government with respect to youth service and learning programs; and report to Congress at least once each year on the activities of the Council.

The Council may employ a staff to be headed by an executive director.

The bill provides that the functions of the President's Council on Youth Opportunity and the Citizens Advisory Board on Youth Opportunity established pursuant to Executive order, are transferred to the National Youth Service Council.

YOUTH SERVICE AND LEARNING PROGRAM

References are made throughout the bill to youth service and learning programs. Such a program is one primarily designed to improve educational opportunities of persons, improve health and welfare of persons, contribute to the development, conservation, or management of natural resources or recreational areas, strengthen library services, and improve community services.

AUTHORIZATIONS OF APPROPRIATIONS

There is authorized to be appropriated for the National Youth Service Council an amount not to exceed $2 million for any fiscal year. This is somewhat more than the $1.75 million recommended for the operation of the President's Council on Youth Opportunity for fiscal year 1970. As noted above, the functions of the President's Council on Youth Opportunity would be transferred, under the bill to the National Youth Service Council.

Authorizations for the National Youth Service Foundation are divided into: First, those for grant and contract awards; and, second, those for the activities carried on directly by the Foundation. In the first category, authorizations are provided of $75 million for the first fiscal year; $300 million for the second fiscal year; and $600 million for the third fiscal year. The second category provides for authorizations of $75 million for the first fiscal year; $200 million for the second fiscal year; and $300 million for the third fiscal year.

POSITIVE OBJECTIVE

I wish to stress the positive objective of the bill. We are passing through a time when the temptation is great to adopt measures designed to repress the energies of young people in the cities and on the campuses. But we have to recognize that energy per se is neither moral nor immoral. It is amoral. It can be used to shape a sword or a plowshare. By providing constructive ways for all young people to use their energies and talents, they will have a chance for a better life and a chance to relate to and serve their society—as well as to help peacefully improve it where necessary.

Mr. President, I ask unanimous consent that the bill which I have introduced be printed at this point in the RECORD.

The PRESIDENT pro tempore. The bill will be received and appropriately referred; and, without objection, the bill will be printed in the RECORD.

The bill (S. 1937) to supplement and strengthen voluntary youth service and learning opportunities supported or offered by the Federal Government by establishing a National Youth Service Council and a National Youth Service Foundation, and for other purposes, introduced by Mr. HATFIELD (for himself and others Senators), was received, read twice by its title, and referred to the Committee on Labor and Public Welfare.

S. 1937

Be it enacted by the Senate and House of Representatives of the United States of America in Congress assembled,

TITLE I—GENERAL PROVISIONS

SHORT TITLE

SECTION 101. This Act may be cited as the "Youth Power Act of 1969."

DECLARATION OF PURPOSE

SEC. 102. (a) The Congress hereby declares that it is the policy of the United States that the talents and energies of young people should be more effectively devoted to voluntary service and learning opportunities to the benefit of the whole nation.

(b) The Congress declares that young people at all educational levels from high school dropouts through graduate students can and will take advantage of increased service and learning opportunities; that a huge number of domestic tasks remain unmet which simultaneously provides a unique opportunity for young people to serve and learn; that future manpower requirements for increased skills in the fields of education, health, conservation, welfare, job training, and governmental affairs are increasingly difficult to fulfill, and can be alleviated by a coordinated effort to increase service and learning opportunities for young people; and that the experience young people acquire in service and learning projects will serve to increase manpower skills and to strengthen their understanding of the world in which they live.

(c) It is the purpose of this Act, therefore, to strengthen, supplement, and coordinate programs and activities contributing to the policy contained in this section.

DEFINITIONS

SEC. 103. As used in this Act—

(1) "Youth service and learning program" means a program primarily designed to—

(A) improve the educational opportunities of persons in the area to be served by any such program, including projects for counseling, custodial services, library assistance, tutorial work, teaching assistance, and maintenance of educational equipment;

(B) improve the health and welfare of the persons in the area to be served by any such program, including projects for clinical or clerical assistance in nonprofit private or public hospitals or public health centers or other related facilities; health surveys, increasing sanitation services, improving air and water pollution control services, and increasing services to the handicapped;

(C) contribute to the development, conservation, or management of natural resources or recreational areas in the area to be served by any such program, including projects for historical site restoration, camp site building and maintenance, trail construction and maintenance, protecting and maintaining forests, animal care and game services, grounds keeping and landscaping, soil surveys and water shed improvements;

(D) strengthen library services in the area to be served by any such program, including projects for increased staffing of bookmobiles, reading and recording services for the blind and young children, cataloguing, shelving and repairing books, and preparing exhibits; or

(E) improve community services available to persons in the area to be served by any such program, including projects for increased day camp and child care services, assistance for museum professional personnel, playground maintenance and operation, and assisting probationers and the disadvantaged, particularly helping unemployed youths locate services available to improve their skills and employability—

and is conducted or is to be conducted substantially for participation by persons who have attained 17 years of age but not 27 years of age. For the purpose of this paragraph "youth service and learning program" includes any program designed to increase the skills and employability of youths.

(2) "Private nonprofit agency" means any agency owned or operated by one or more corporations, organizations or associations no part of the net earnings of which inures, or may lawfully inure, to the benefit of any private shareholder or individual.

(3) "State" means each of the several States and the District of Columbia.

TITLE II—COORDINATION OF YOUTH SERVICE
AND LEARNING OPPORTUNITIES

ESTABLISHMENT OF THE NATIONAL YOUTH SERVICE COUNCIL

SEC. 201. (a) There is hereby established in the executive office of the President the National Youth Service Council (hereinafter referred to as the "Council") which shall be composed of—

(1) the President, who shall be Chairman of the Council;

(2) the Secretary of the Interior;

(3) the Secretary of Agriculture;

(4) the Secretary of Labor;

(5) the Secretary of Health, Education, and Welfare;

(6) the Secretary of Housing and Urban Development;

(7) the Chairman of the Civil Service Commission;

(8) the Commissioner of Education;

(9) the Director of the Peace Corps;

(10) the Director of the Teacher Corps;

(11) the Director of the Office of Economic Opportunity;

(12) the Assistant Director of the Office of Economic Opportunity for Volunteers in Service to America; and

(13) the Director of the National Youth Service Foundation.

(b) Each member of the Council from a department or agency of the Federal Government may designate another officer of his department or agency to serve on the Council as his alternate in his unavoidable absence.

(c) The President shall from time to time designate one of the members of the Council to preside over meetings of the Council during the absence, disability, or unavailability of the Chairman.

(d) Whenever any matter is considered by the Council relating to the interests of a Federal agency not represented on the Council, the Chairman shall invite the head of any such agency to participate in the business of the Council. The authority contained in this subsection may be exercised by the Chairman in any case in which the agency concerned is in a Federal department the head of which is a member of the Council.

FUNCTIONS

SEC. 202. It shall be the function of the Council to—

(1) advise and assist the President as he may request with respect to youth service and learning programs conducted or assisted by any agency of the Federal Government;

(2) assure effective program planning for summer and other related youth programs of the Federal Government;

(3) provide effective procedures for the coordination of youth programs and activities of all agencies of the Federal Government;

(4) develop and encourage, to the extent practicable, the adoption by appropriate agencies of the Federal Government of common procedures and simplified application forms for recruitment and transfer into any youth service and learning program conducted or assisted by any agency of the Federal Gov-

ernment, particularly with respect to the Job Corps, the Neighborhood Youth Corps, the Volunteers in Service to America, the Teacher Corps, the Peace Corps, and the National Youth Service Foundation;

(5) develop adequate procedures and encourage each agency of the Federal Government administering a youth service and learning program to coordinate at the local level recruiting and informational activities so that the young people in any such locality may be aware of the full range of service and learning opportunities available;

(6) to encourage the development of cooperative programs among agencies of the Federal Government administering or conducting youth service and learning programs with particular emphasis on cooperative programs designed to more effectively meet the unmet community needs and services;

(7) encourage State and local agencies and private nonprofit and other private agencies and organizations to participate fully in efforts to provide service and learning opportunities for youths;

(8) resolve differences arising among agencies of the Federal Government with respect to youth service and learning programs; and

(9) report to the Congress at least once in each fiscal year on the activities of the Council during the preceding fiscal year.

ADMINISTRATIVE PROVISIONS

Sec. 203. (a) The Council may employ a staff to be headed by an executive director and a deputy director. The executive director, subject to the direction of the Chairman, is authorized to—

(1) appoint and fix the compensation of such staff personnel, including not more than five persons who may be appointed without regard to the provisions of title 5, United States Code, governing appointments in the competitive service, and who may be compensated, without regard to the provisions of chapter 51 and subchapter III of chapter 53 of such title relating to classification and General Schedule pay rates, at rates not in excess of the maximum rate for GS–18 of the General Schedule under section 5332 of such title, as he deems necessary; and

(2) procure temporary and intermittent services to the same extent as is authorized by section 3109 of title 5, United States Code, but at rates not to exceed $100 a day for individuals.

(b) The Council shall, to the fullest extent possible, use the services, facilities, and information, including statistical information, of other Governmental agencies as well as private research agencies. Each department, agency, and instrumentality of the executive branch of the Government, including any independent agency, is authorized and directed to furnish to the Council, upon request made by the Chairman, such information as the Council deems necessary to carry out its functions under this title.

(c) The Council is authorized to establish an advisory committee and may consult with such representatives of State and local governments and other groups, organizations, and individuals as the Council deems advisable.

COMPENSATION OF THE EXECUTIVE DIRECTOR

SEC. 204. (a) Section 5315 of title 5, United States Code, is amended by adding at the end thereof the following new paragraph:

"(92) Executive Director—National Youth Service Council."

(b) Section 5316 of title 5, United States Code, is amended by adding at the end thereof the following new paragraph:

"(123) Deputy Director—National Youth Service Council."

TRANSFER OF FUNCTIONS OF PRESIDENT'S COUNCIL ON YOUTH OPPORTUNITY

SEC. 205. (a) The functions of the President's Council on Youth Opportunity and the Citizens Advisory Board on Youth Opportunity established pursuant to Executive Order 11330, approved March 6, 1967, are transferred to the Council.

(b) All personnel, assets, liabilities, property, and records as are determined by the Director of the Bureau of the Budget to be employed, held, or used primarily in connection with any function transferred by subsection (a) are transferred to the Council.

AUTHORIZATION OF APPROPRIATIONS

SEC. 206. There are authorized to be appropriated such sums as may be necessary, not to exceed $2,000,000 for any fiscal year, to carry out the provisions of this title.

TITLE III—NATIONAL YOUTH SERVICE FOUNDATION

ESTABLISHMENT OF FOUNDATION

SEC. 301. (a) In order to carry out the purposes of this Act, there is hereby established an agency to be known as the National Youth Service Foundation (hereinafter referred to as the "Foundation").

(b) The Foundation shall be subject to a Board of Trustees (hereinafter referred to as the "Board"). The Board shall be composed of 15 members who shall be appointed by the President, by and with the advice and consent of the Senate, of whom 4 members shall be appointed from among officials of agencies of the Federal Government, administering any youth service and learning program, and 11 members shall be appointed from among individuals from private life who are widely recognized by virtue of their experience or ability as specially qualified to serve on the Board. The Director of the Peace Corps, the Director of the Teacher Corps, the Assistant Director of the Office of Economic Opportunity for Volunteers in Service to America, the Director of the Neighborhood Youth Corps, the Director of the Job Corps, and the Director of the Foundation shall serve as ex officio members of the Board. In making appointments from private life, the President is requested to give consideration to the appointment of individuals who—

(1) will be representative of youth in the United States, and

(2) will provide collectively the appropriate regional balance on the Board.

(c) The term of office of each appointive trustee of the Foundation shall be six years; except that—

(1) the members first taking office shall serve as designated by the President,

five for terms of two years, five for terms of four years, and five for terms of six years, and

(2) any member appointed to fill a vacancy shall serve for the remainder of the term for which his predecessor was appointed.

(d) Members of the Board who are not regular full-time employees of the United States shall, while serving on business of the Foundation, be entitled to receive compensation at rates fixed by the President, but not exceeding $100 per diem, including travel time; and while so serving away from their homes or regular places of business, they may be allowed travel expenses, including per diem in lieu of subsistence, as authorized by section 5703 of title 5, United States Code, for persons in Government service employed intermittently.

(e) The President shall call the first meeting of the trustees of the Foundation, at which the first order of business shall be the election of a Chairman and a Vice Chairman, who shall serve until one year after the date of enactment of this title. Thereafter each Chairman and Vice Chairman shall be elected for a term of two years in duration. The Vice Chairman shall perform the duties of the Chairman in his absence. In case a vacancy occurs in the chairmanship or vice chairmanship, the Foundation shall elect an individual from among the trustees to fill such vacancy.

(f) A majority of the trustees of the Foundation shall constitute a quorum.

DIRECTOR AND DEPUTY DIRECTOR

SEC. 302. (a) There shall be a Director and a Deputy Director of the Foundation who shall be appointed by the President, by and with the advice and consent of the Senate. In making such appointments the President is requested to give due consideration to any recommendations submitted to him by the Board. The Director shall be the chief executive officer of the Foundation. The Director shall receive compensation at the rate provided for level IV of the Federal Executive Salary Schedule, and the Deputy Director shall receive compensation at the rate provided for level V of such Schedule. Each shall serve for a term of four years unless previously removed by the President. The Deputy Director shall perform such functions as the Director, with the approval of the Foundation, may prescribe, and be acting Director during the absence or disability of the Director or in the event of a vacancy in the office of the Director.

(b) The Director shall carry out the programs of the Foundation subject to its supervision and direction, and shall carry out such other functions as the Foundation may delegate to him consistent with the provisions of this title.

AUTHORITY OF THE FOUNDATION

SEC. 303. (a) The Foundation is authorized to—

(1) make grants, enter into contracts or other arrangements in any State with public and private nonprofit agencies, including junior colleges and other institutions of higher education, under which such agencies will recruit, select, train and enroll persons who have attained the age of 17 years of age but not 27 years of age, for periods up to two years in a youth service and learning program assisted under this title;

(2) make grants, enter into contracts or other arrangements in any State

with public and private nonprofit agencies to conduct youth service and learning programs;

(3) enter into arrangements in any State to furnish persons who have attained 17 years of age but not 27 years of age to public and private nonprofit agencies to carry out any youth service and learning program or any other program approved by the Foundation to be conducted by such agency or organization.

(4) to recruit, select, train and enroll persons who have attained 17 years of age but not 27 years of age for youth service and learning programs;

(5) conduct youth service and learning programs;

(6) provide technical assistance to any public and private nonprofit agency receiving assistance under this title;

(7) develop and carry out a program to encourage greater participation by State and local agencies and by private agencies and organizations in programs offering greater opportunities for youth participation in projects for the betterment of the community.

(b) No payment may be made under paragraphs (1), (2), (3), (6), and (7) of this section, except upon application therefor which is submitted to the Foundation in accordance with regulations and procedures established by the Board.

LIMITATIONS ON PAYMENTS

SEC. 304. (a) No payment may be made pursuant to this title in excess of 80 per centum of the cost of the program, project, activity, or award for which the application is made. Non-Federal contributions may be in cash or in kind, fairly evaluated, including, but not limited to, plant, equipment, or services. For the purposes of this subsection, financial assistance under any provision of Federal law other than this Act shall be considered financing from a non-Federal source.

(b) Not more than 12½ per centum of the funds provided in this title for grants or contracts pursuant to paragraphs (1), (2), and (3) of section 303(a) shall be made available within any one State.

(c) No compensation or stipend paid to any individual pursuant to this title may exceed $5,000 in any fiscal year. This limitation shall not apply to medical or travel expenses and other special expenses as determined by the Foundation.

(d) Assistance pursuant to this title shall not cover the cost of any land acquisition, construction, building acquisitions, or acquisition of major equipment.

(e) Nothing contained in this title shall be construed to authorize the making of any payment under this title for religious worship or instruction.

ADMINISTRATIVE PROVISIONS

SEC. 305. (a) In addition to any authority vested in it by other provisions of this title, the Foundation, in carrying out its functions, is authorized to—

(1) prescribe such regulations as it deems necessary governing the manner in which its functions shall be carried out;

(2) receive money and other property donated, bequeathed, or devised, without condition or restriction other than that it be used for the purposes of the Foundation; and to use, sell, or otherwise dispose of such property for the purpose of carrying out its functions;

(3) in the discretion of the Foundation, receive (and use, sell, or otherwise dispose of, in accordance with paragraph (2)) money and other property donated, bequeathed, or devised to the Foundation with a condition or restriction, including a condition that the Foundation use other funds of the Foundation for the purposes of the gift;

(4) appoint and fix the compensation of such personnel as may be necessary to carry out the provisions of this title;

(5) obtain the services of experts and consultants in accordance with the provisions of section 3109 of title 5, United States Code, at rates for individuals not to exceed $100 per diem;

(6) accept and utilize the services of voluntary and noncompensated personnel and reimburse them for travel expenses, including per diem, as authorized by section 5703 of title 5, United States Code;

(7) enter into contracts, grants or other arrangements, or modifications thereof to carry out the provisions of this title, and such contracts or modifications thereof may, with the concurrence of two-thirds of the members of the Board, be entered into without performance or other bonds, and without regard to section 3709 of the Revised Statutes, as amended (41 U.S.C. 5) or any other provision of law relating to competitive bidding;

(8) make advances, progress, and other payments which the Board deems necessary under this title without regard to the provisions of section 3648 of the Revised Statutes, as amended (31 U.S.C. 529);

(9) rent office space in the District of Columbia; and

(10) perform such other functions as are necessary to carry out the provisions of this title.

(b) The Foundation shall submit to the President and to the Congress an annual report of its operations under this title, which shall include a detailed statement of all private and public funds received and expended by it, and such recommendations as the Foundation deems appropriate.

ADVISORY COUNCIL OF YOUTH SERVICE AND LEARNING PROGRAMS

SEC. 306. (a) There is established an Advisory Council on Youth Service and Learning Programs (hereinafter referred to as the Advisory Council) composed of 24 members appointed by the President from among individuals who are widely recognized by reason of experience, education, or scholarship as specially qualified to serve on such Advisory Council. In making such appointments the President shall give due consideration to any recommendations submitted by the Board. At least 8 members appointed to the Advisory Council shall not have attained the age of 27 years on the date of appointment.

(b) The Advisory Council shall advise the Board on broad policy matters relating to the administration of this title. The Advisory Council shall select its own chairman and vice chairman.

(c) Each member of the Advisory Council who is appointed from private life shall receive $100 per diem (including travel time) for each day during which he is engaged in the actual performance of his duties as a member of the Council. A member of the Council who is an officer or employee of the Federal Government shall serve without additional compensation. All members of the Council shall be reimbursed for travel, subsistence, and other necessary expenses incurred by them in the performance of such duties.

AUTHORIZATION OF APPROPRIATIONS

SEC. 307. (a) For the purpose of making payments pursuant to paragraphs (1), (2), and (3) of section 303 (a) of this title there is authorized to be appropriated $75,000,000 for the fiscal year ending June 30, 1970, $300,000,000 for the fiscal year ending June 30, 1971, and $600,000,000 for the fiscal year ending June 30, 1972.

(b) For the purpose of carrying out other provisions of this title there are authorized to be appropriated $75,000,000 for the fiscal year ending June 30, 1970, $200,000,000 for the fiscal year ending June 30, 1971, and $300,000,000 for the fiscal year ending June 30, 1972.

References

Boulding, K. *The Meaning of the Twentieth Century*. New York: Harper & Row, 1964.

Bower, E. M. "Achievement of Competency," in *Learning and Mental Health in the School*, prepared by the ASCD 1966 Yearbook Committee, W. B. Waetjen, and R. R. Luper (eds.). Washington, D.C.: Association for Supervision and Curriculum Development, NEA, 1966, pp. 23–49.

Breuer, J., and Freud, S. *Studies in Hysteria*. New York and Washington: Nervous and Mental Disease Pub. Co., 1936, 241 pp. Nervous and Mental Disease Monograph Series No. 61.

Briar, S. "Clinical Judgment in Foster Care," *Child Welfare*, 13, 4 (1963).

Chilman, C. S. *Growing Up Poor*. Washington, D.C.: U.S. Dept. of Health, Education, and Welfare, 1966.

Conant, J. B. *The Education of American Teachers*. New York: McGraw-Hill, 1963.

———. *The Comprehensive High School*. New York: McGraw-Hill, 1967.

Cozzens, J. *By Love Possessed*. New York: Harcourt, Brace and World, 1957.

Crocker, D. "The Study of a Problem of Aggression," *The Psychoanalytic Study of the Child*, 10. New York: International University Press, 1955.

"Directory of Service Organizations." National Service Secretariat, 5140 Sherrier Place, N.W., Washington, D.C., 1968.

Duhl, L. J. "Environmental Health: Politics, Planning and Money," *American Journal of Public Health*, 58, 2 (Feb. 1968), 233.

Eisenberg, L. "The Sins of the Fathers: Urban Decay and Social Pathology," *American Journal of Orthopsychiatry*, XXXII, 1 (Jan. 1962), 5–17.

Erikson, E. "Identity and the Life Cycle," *Psychological Issues*, I, 1 (1959), 1–171.

———. "Ontogeny of Ritualization in Man," *Philosophical Transactions of the Royal Society of London*, Series B, 251, 772 (1966), 337–349.

———. *Identity: Youth and Crisis*. New York: W. W. Norton & Co., 1968.

Flacks, R. "The Liberated Generation: An Exploration of the Roots of Student Protest," *Journal of Social Issues*, XXIII, 3 (1967), 57–58.

"Foster Family Care for Emotionally Disturbed Children." New York: Child Welfare League of America, 1962.

Freud, S. "Analysis, Terminable and Interminable," *International Journal of Psycho-Analysis*, 18, 4 (Oct. 1937), 373–405.

Gage, N. L. "Desirable Behaviors of Teachers," in *Teachers for the Disadvantaged*, M. Usdan and F. Bertolaet (eds.). Chicago: Follett Publishing Co., 1966, pp. 4–13.

Garrett, B. L. "Meeting the Crisis in Foster Family Care," *Children*, 13, 1 (Jan.–Feb. 1966), 2–8.

Glasscote, R., Sanders, D., Forstenzer, H. M., and Foley, A. R. *The Community Mental Health Center: An Analysis of Existing Models,* Washington, D.C. A publication of the Joint Information Service of the American Psychiatric Association and the National Association for Mental Health in association with the Department of Mental Health, American Medical Association, and the Division of Community Psychiatry, Columbia University, Sept. 1964.

Glidewell, J., and Swallow, C. *The Prevalence of Maladjustment in Elementary Schools*. Chicago: University of Chicago, 1968.

Graves, W. A. "Teachers' Reading and Recreational Interests," *NEA Journal* (Nov. 1966), 17–19.

Group for the Advancement of Psychiatry. Committee on Adolescence. *Normal Adolescence: Its Dynamics and Impact*. New York: Charles Scribner's Sons, 1968.

———. "Normal Adolescence: Its Dynamics and Impact." Formulated by the Committee on Adolescence, VI, Report No. 68. New York: Mental Health Materials Center, Inc., Feb. 1968, p. 785.

Gula, M. "Agency Operated Group Homes: A Specialized Resource for Serving Children and Youth." U.S. Dept. of Health, Education, and Welfare, Children's Bureau, 1964.

Hoffman, M. E. "Problems of Identity in Foster Children," *Child Welfare*, 42, (1963), 10–17.

Holden, A., and Jackson, L. (eds.). *Perspectives on Poverty*. Health and Welfare Council of the National Capital Area. Washington, D.C.: CROSS-TELL (Communicating Research on the Urban Poor), Dec. 1967, p. 9.

Holt, J. *How Children Fail*. New York: Pitman, 1964.

Inhelder, B., and Piaget, J. *The Growth of Logical Thinking from Childhood to Adolescence*. New York: Basic Books, Inc., 1958.

Keniston, K. "Youth, Change and Violence," *The American Scholar* (Spring 1968).

Kimball, S .T., and McClellan, J. E., Jr. *Education and the New America*. New York: Random House, 1966.

Kohler, M. C. "Selected Youth Participation Projects." Paper prepared by the National Commission on Resources for Youth, Inc., for Task Force VI of the Joint Commission on Mental Health of Children, Inc., June 13, 1968.

Kramer, M. "Epidemiology, Biostatistics and Mental Health Planning." Address delivered at the American Psychiatric Association Regional Research Conference, Baltimore, Maryland, Apr. 21, 1966.

Lipset, S., *The Public Interest*. Fall 1968.

Manpower Report of the President. January 1969.

Mumford, L. *The Transformations of Man*. New York: Collier Books, 1962.

Musgrove, F. *Youth in the Social Order*. Bloomington: Indiana University Press, 1964.

National NDEA Institute for Advanced Study in Teaching Disadvantaged Youth. *Teachers Education: The Young Teacher's View*. Preliminary Report: Regional Conferences for Student Teachers and Beginning Teachers of the Disadvantaged, J. J. Kenney, P. Bartholomew, and W. C. Kvaraceus (eds.). 1967 (mimeo.).

National Student Association (2115 S Street, N.W., Washington, D.C.). "Community Action Curriculum Compendium." N.d.

Oakeshott, M. Lecture given at the London School of Economics, 1963.

"OEO Budget Call." Aug. 1969 (unpublished).

Peck, H. B. "Child and Juvenile Delinquency," *Psychodynamics,* Monograph Series. Washington, D.C., 1959.

Rabinow, I. "Agency Operated Group Homes: Group Homes in Perspective." Child Welfare League of America, 1964.

Report of the Committee on Clinical Issues. Report prepared for the Joint Commission on Mental Health of Children, Inc. May 1969.

Report of the National Advisory Commission on Selective Service. "In Pursuit of Equity: Who Serves When Not All Serve?" Washington, D.C.: U.S. Government Printing Office, Feb. 1967.

Rodman, H. "The Lower-Class Value Stretch," *Social Forces*, 42, 2 (Dec. 1963), 205–215.

Rosen, B. M., Bahn, R., Shellow, R., and Bower, E. M. "Adolescent Patients Served in Outpatient Psychiatric Clinics," *American Journal of Public Health,* 55 (1965), 1563–1577.

Rosen, B. M., Kramer, M., Redick, R. W., and Willner, S. G. "Utilization of Psychiatric Facilities by Children: Current Status, Trends, Implications." National Institute of Mental Health, Mental Health Statistics, Series B, No. 1, 1968.

Rubenfeld, S. *Family of Outcasts: A New Theory of Delinquency*. New York: Free Press, 1965.

Rustin, B. "The Anatomy of Frustration." Address delivered for the Anti-Defamation League of B'nai B'rith, New York, New York, May 6, 1968.

Silverstein, H., Rosenberg, B., and Weingarten, K. "Some Themes Expressive of Alienated Youth." Draft report to the Joint Commission on Mental Health of Children, Inc., Nov. 1967.

Smith, M. B. "Morality and Student Protest." Psi Chi invited address, American Psychological Association, San Francisco, Calif., Aug. 31, 1968.

Soddy, K., and Ahrenfeldt, R. H. (eds.). *Mental Health in the Service of the Community*. Vol. III of a report of an international and interprofessional study group convened by the World Federation for Mental Health. Tavistock Publications, J. B. Lippincott Co., 1967.

Sonis, M. "Patterns of Child Psychiatry," *Journal of the Academy of Child Psychiatry*, 3 (1964), 9–23.

"Student Protests: A Phenomenon for Behavioral Sciences Research." Statement of a group of Fellows at the Center for Advanced Study in the Behavioral Sciences, Stanford, Calif., *Science,* 161, 3836 (July 5, 1968), 20–23.

Tanner, J. M. *Growth at Adolescence.* London: Blackwell Scientific Publications, Ltd., 1962, p. 153.

U.S. Department of Health, Education, and Welfare. Public Health Service Publication No. 413, 1955. *Evaluation in Mental Health.* A Review of the Problem of Evaluating Mental Health Activities. Report of the Subcommittee on Evaluation of Mental Health Activities, Community Services Committee, National Advisory Mental Health Council.

————. *Vital Statistics of the United States*, II, Part A, Table 1-8. Public Health Service, National Center for Health Statistics, 1966.

Waelder, R. *Basic Theory of Psychoanalysis.* New York: International University Press, 1960.

White, R., Jr., and Fishman, R. "Proposal for a Survey of the Youth Patrol Movement." Submitted to Task Force III of the Joint Commission on Mental Health of Children, 1967.

IV

EDUCATION AND MENTAL HEALTH

REPORT OF THE COMMITTEE ON EDUCATION AND MENTAL HEALTH

Prepared by Abraham J. Tannenbaum, Ph.D.

The previous reports have provided a view of the developmental stages of human growth from conception through the age of twenty-four. As the reader will have noted, each of the Task Forces regarded the role of education as vital to the growth and mental health of children and youth. This view of education is in keeping with the importance given to this social institution by the Commission as a whole. The Commission, in fact, considered education so crucial to the mental health of children that a special study group was formed comprised of experts in the field of education. The report which follows is the result of the analyses of this Committee. Following the Report of the Committee on Education, this volume concludes with the Report of the Committee on Religion and Mental Health.

—EDITOR

MEMBERS OF THE COMMITTEE ON EDUCATION AND MENTAL HEALTH

MARTIN DEUTSCH, PH.D.
Department of Education
New York University
New York, New York

JAMES J. GALLAGHER, PH.D.
Bureau of Education for the
Handicapped
U.S. Office of Education
Washington, D.C.

NORRIS G. HARING, PH.D.
College of Education
University of Washington
Seattle, Washington

COMMISSIONER HAROLD HOWE
U.S. Office of Education
Washington, D.C.

PHILIP W. JACKSON, PH.D.
School of Education
University of Chicago
Chicago, Illinois

JAMES JARRETT, PH.D.
School of Education
University of California
Berkeley, California

MORTIMER KREUTER, PH.D.
Center for Urban Education
New York, New York

NADINE LAMBERT, PH.D.
Department of Education
University of California
Berkeley, California

MELVIN ROMAN, PH.D.
Mental Health Services
Lincoln Hospital
Bronx, New York

THOMAS A. SHELLHAMMER, PH.D.
California State Department
of Education
Sacramento, California

ABRAHAM J. TANNENBAUM, PH.D.
Teachers College
Columbia University
New York, New York

RALPH W. TYLER, PH.D.
Science Research Association
Chicago, Illinois

FRED WILHELMS, PH.D.
National Association of Secondary
School Principals
National Education Association
Washington, D.C.

LIAISON CONSULTANTS TO EDUCATION COMMITTEE

MILLIE ALMY, PH.D.—TASK FORCE I
Professor of Psychology and Education
Teachers College
New York, New York

MARY ENGEL, PH.D.—TASK FORCE II
Department of Psychology
City College of New York
New York, New York

BARBARA BIBER, PH.D.—TASK FORCE II
Research Division
Bank Street College of Education
New York, New York

WILLIAM C. KVARACEUS, PH.D.—
TASK FORCE III
Lincoln Filene Center for Citizenship
and Public Affairs
Medford, Massachusetts

JOHN H. NIEMEYER—TASK FORCE VI
Bank Street College of Education
New York, New York

LIAISON REPRESENTATIVE FROM GOVERNMENT AGENCY

ELI M. BOWER, ED.D.
Liaison Officer
National Institute of Mental Health
Chevy Chase, Maryland

Introduction

This report represents the results of four two-day meetings of educators and psychologists who were invited by the Joint Commission on Mental Health of Children to discuss some salient problems relevant to the positive promotion of mental health in the schools. The group's assignment was to formulate ways in which federal legislation could assist the school world in contributing optimally to the personal and social development of its pupils while realizing its substantive instructional aims. No detailed agenda was planned for the meetings, but there was general agreement that issues pertaining to education and mental health should be probed in all social milieus, with special emphasis on the depressed areas of the country which continue to suffer intensely from the scourge of educational failure and social pathology despite well-intentioned corrective measures that are currently being administered. There was general agreement that the problem of mediocre and irrelevant education in today's classrooms is not just localized in slum ghettos; conditions in these neighborhood schools only dramatize the universal inadequacies of our school systems in vitalizing education for *all* of today's children and youth. The recommended innovations for the disadvantaged groups, therefore, have their counterpart implications for the advantaged as well. These ideas are meant to be practical and programmatic in every instance, and the Committee considers them promising enough to warrant federal support for field testing on a large scale. Some are based on encouraging outcomes of laboratory and field research; others represent what has been learned from past intervention programs that have failed; still others grow out of the educated judgments of social and behavioral scientists who are deeply concerned about the unresolved problems of mental health in the schools.

Throughout its deliberations, the Committee operated with the understanding that the lawmakers and professional educators to whom this report is addressed are well oriented to the issues at hand. A conscious effort was therefore made to omit many self-evident, oft-repeated truisms that are familiar to such a reading audience, except when it was thought necessary to revive waning public attention to these ideas or when they lent dimension to the unique contributions of the group. Otherwise, the report would have been considerably more comprehensive than it is, with much of it bordering on the platitudinous. The intention here is not to demean by omission the familiar commentary on education and mental health but rather to capture the Committee's *distinctive* interpretation of the problem and its recommendations for dealing with it.

The Committee also took into account the fact that educational researchers and theoreticians have one advantage over the practitioner—they are not held to public accountability for their thinking about school matters. They can equivocate, defer judgment, or even remain silent without feeling compelled to contribute something of value to the practitioner's repertoire of day-to-day practices. They can also enjoy the luxury of lamenting conditions in the schools without having any professional stake in their improvement. From a sideline position it is safe to proclaim the need for a "new educational model" to replace the old, provided one is free of the responsibility of defining the new model and making it work. The Committee therefore made its recommendations with the practitioner's action commitments in mind. It took into account the constant pressures on him to make operational decisions in every phase of education; yet it recognized also the realities of life in school and society which delimit his options among policy alternatives.

The issues are presented in the form of critical realities in school and society that adversely affect education and mental health among the nation's children, and the recommendations are offered as practical measures for bringing about purposeful, sometimes radical, change in the schools in the interests of mental health. There is finally a discussion of legislative directions which attempts to provide guidelines for improving mental health in the schools through governmental intervention.

Fundamental Assertions About Education
and Mental Health

The first step toward helping the practitioner address the problems of mental health in the schools as he sees them is to suggest some basic premises from which he can proceed toward an analysis of his situation. He has to assume, a priori, that there is a relationship between educational and mental health goals and ways of achieving them. Otherwise, the non-academic aspects of child development would be of little more than academic interest to him. He might concede that they affect the child's progress at school, but he would feel neither obligated nor equipped to minister to them directly. He would probably consider health factors—mental *and* physical—as figuring prominently in the design of a teaching-learning *climate* rather than its *content* or *method*.

The Committee took a contrary position and assumed that education and mental health share some vital points of common relevance. Several of these points had to be explicated as a means of establishing a common ground for probing more deeply into existing problems and possible solutions. There was general consensus on the mutually reinforcing aspects of education and mental health; on the school's capabilities and limitations in fostering mental health; and on the disparities among American sub-cultures regarding the nature and extent of their dependency on the school to influence the development of their children. After reaching agreement on a series of basic premises, the Committee could then go beyond simply arguing that the educator can and should be strategically involved in the psychosocial development of children. It could specify in concrete terms *how* he should play his role. Such an understanding is necessary before it is possible to determine where and why he falls short of expectations and what changes are needed in the world of education to maximize his effectiveness as a professional.

1. *Sound educational principles contribute to the positive promotion of mental health.*

The major objective of the school is to transact ideas, skills, and competencies with children, not to serve as a mental institution. Yet, the success with which the school achieves its educational objectives is often a barometer of its success in the prevention of mental illness and in the nurture of healthy personal development. A sound education is not simply a non-interfering adjunct to effective personal guidance for schoolchildren; it is integral to the direct intervention measures aimed at facilitating desirable human maturation. From ages five to seventeen, practically all children spend from 25 to 40 percent of their waking hours in an educational environment. In most cases they spend more time in school than they do with their families. It follows, therefore, that the nature of the child's experience at school can be of great importance in determining the kind of adult he is going to be. It shades his attitudes toward himself and the world about him; it mediates his cultivation of basic skills and understandings; it leads him to the institutionalized means of meeting cultural expectations; and it structures a significant setting for interpersonal relations with age peers and adult authority figures.

Education also fosters the kinds of personal competence that enable the individual to interact effectively with his environment. It focuses, directs, and further stimulates his tendencies toward exploratory behavior which is seen by some psychologists as a basic, independent human process rather than a means of restoring functional equilibrium (White, 1959). Part of this process is the satisfaction of the need to explore and find novelty in the environment, to master it for the reason best expressed by mountain climbers struggling to "conquer" Mount Everest: "because it's there." Escalona (1967) aptly characterized the importance of individual competence in the healthy integration of the personality when she wrote:

The experience of learning and the perception of the self as one who *can* learn, generates a sense of the self as an active being, and a sense of the self as the carrier of power and of competence. It also makes available a source of pleasure and of satisfaction that is not directly dependent upon the quality of inter-personal relationships. Last, not least, each instance of successful learning makes the world more intelligible. Words, concepts, metaphors, and physical phenomena that are bewildering, out of context, and hence alien, become components of a comprehensible and orderly environment in consequence of successful learning (p. 2).

To the extent, then, that cognition and affect are conceptually inseparable (see Sanford, 1967), education is deeply involved in the mental health status of the child. His learning experience at school can have an ego-strengthening effect by bringing him into closer touch with the reality of the outer world and helping him regulate his own drives to imprint himself on that world. It can also sensitize him to the nuances of person-to-person relationships by orienting him to the transactional games people play and the variegated roles they assume. An enriching educational experience therefore enables him to study his environment so he can understand something about its orderliness and thereby derive self-confidence in predicting and judging events and in making personal decisions about where he fits in the scheme of things. By learning how to sensitize himself to complex external realities, he develops a repertoire of learning strategies that can be of enormous help to him when they are focused inwardly. They provide the means for him to build hypotheses and generalizations about his own motives, values, capabilities, tastes, and behaviors. They also facilitate self-probing as a requisite for resolving old conflicts and viewing his life style in a changing perspective. If he fails to sustain his healthy development and requires therapeutic intervention, he will then enter still another learning experience. For the psychotherapist's tactics in modifying deviant behavior parallel the educator's utilization of learning principles to guide and reinforce healthy personal development. In fact, Bandura (1961) demonstrated that methods of psychotherapy are frequently derived from an understanding of learning and motivation. Some of the learning mechanisms he discovered being employed in treating human deviance include counterconditioning, extinction, discrimination learning, reward, punishment, and social imitation.

Clearly, then, the rational mechanisms that are the stock in trade of school teaching and learning are the very ones used in understanding and controlling human life styles. By studying the world about him, the child moves closer toward a sense of independence and self-differentiation; by learning how to learn and utilizing that knowledge for greater self-understanding and social sensitivity, he moves closer toward clarifying his personal identity. Regardless of whether he is analyzing his outer or inner world, he is forced to make judgments regarding ideational consistencies, causality, relationships, and consequences. In both instances school is supposed to help him conceptualize at a sophisticated level and to utilize verbal abstractions necessary for communicating vital insights.

Part of the educative process is the attempt to release and regulate the imagination for creative productivity. Under proper tutelage, the child expands his universe not only by mastering it but also by bringing newness to it. Books introduce him to a fantasy world that he can manipulate and restructure freely. The encouragement to express original ideas or even conventional ones through fresh media and modes of communication is one way of loosening inhibitions and giving expression to primary impulses in a controlled, constructive way. A healthy fantasy and brain-storming life broadens cognitive horizons and provides the child with more degrees of freedom for responding to reality-based stimuli. He can strengthen his adaptiveness to external challenges by utilizing his imagination to prepare an array of alternative responses to them. This kind of personal flexibility in selecting from among alternative behavioral modes is regarded by some as a critical component of good mental health (Kubie, 1957; Bower *et al.,* 1958).

Education is concerned not only with life styles and coping mechanisms, but with behavior codes as well. This does not mean that schools are responsible for positing a set of human values to which children are compelled to adhere. In an age of moral and ethical relativism there are no persons or institutions capable of exercising that kind of authoritarian control. But the educator shares the responsibility of the humanist and the moral philosopher in passing *on* our cultural tradition, and that of the behavioral and social scientists in *passing* on our cultural tradition. As Smith (1961) points out, "drawing on the fund of human history and culture, with its stock of transmitted discriminations, they [the humanist and moral philosopher] can sensitize us to differentiations and potentialities of human experience which, unaided, we can never attain individually. Our value choices are enriched and modified by this exposure." On the other hand, the responsibility of "displaying the causal network in which value choice is embedded, is one for which the humane or behavioral scientist is uniquely qualified" (p. 302). In great measure, these roles are combined in the teacher of ideas and differentiate him from the dispenser of practical skills and habits.

Education's concern for values amounts to a quest for some kind of good life, however controversial the specifics of that objective may be, which cannot be overlooked in the pursuit of mental health. For it is impossible to characterize mental health without making value judgments concerning man's ultimate place in his universe. Certainly, schools are not in business to promote dogma, even if it were heavily weighted with ethical culture in the humanist tradition; such responsibility clearly belongs to the church and the family. However, the alternative to sectarianism in education need not be pure detachment from issues involving personal and social values. In fact, "pure detachment," if that is possible, is also a form of sectarianism and therefore inimical to healthy educational processes. The school can serve the child best by avoiding the extremes of either playing no part in helping him shape his belief system or of consciously indoctrinating him with a belief system. Effective education provides him with an abundance of ideas that enable him to fashion his own understanding not only of the objective world around him but also of the vital private world of right and wrong, interpersonal responsibility, social ideals, and political judgment.

2. *Sound mental health principles contribute to the promotion of
quality education.*

Just as education is of critical importance in attaining mental health
goals, the reverse is also true. Research in mental health provides valuable
insights into the facilitating and inhibiting factors of school success and
lends credence to the idea that a healthy environment for personal development is also a preferred setting for educational effectiveness (Ringness,
1968). This means that educators can profit from a variety of techniques
used by clinicians to overcome or reduce the personal and social inhibitors
of productive thinking. Moreover, since healthy emotional development is
in itself a legitimate curriculum goal, the teacher must accept the responsibility of helping his student become resilient enough to withstand the stresses
of his total life's experience. The interrelatedness of mental health and
learning success is so strong that one would expect to find an unusually
high incidence of learning failure among the emotionally disturbed. Indeed,
there is a considerable amount of empirical evidence to show that this is
so. Huff's (1964) survey of studies on the learning patterns of persons
with particular types of psychopathology clearly shows that their cognitive
functioning generally does not measure up to expectation. There is also
some evidence to show that even milder symptoms of deviant behavior
are associated with academic underachievement (See Raph and Tannenbaum, 1961). Although these emotional stresses are often stubbornly
rooted in the family milieu, the school can create a therapeutic environment through systematic application of mental health principles in the
educational program. Table 6 gives a small sample of these principles
and their implications.

Table 6.—MENTAL HEALTH PRINCIPLES IN THE EDUCATIONAL PROGRAM

MENTAL HEALTH PRINCIPLES	EDUCATIONAL IMPLICATIONS
1. The person who senses his own in-dividuality, who feels that he counts, who believes that his existence makes a dif-ference and that he exercises some con-trol over his own destiny, will be more likely to become a happy and productive member of society.	1. The child needs to have an instruc-tional program that bends to his individu-ality. Curriculum content and method can be based on a sensitive diagnosis of the status of his functioning, the modifi-ability of his functioning, and the realities of societal demands upon him. In the case of deviant children—the handi-capped and the talented—qualitatively different sets of experiences may be needed to realize this principle.
2. The child's social, emotional, and cog-nitive growth depends heavily on the kind	2. Although the family represents the key social unit of our society, the full

Table 6 (*continued*)

MENTAL HEALTH PRINCIPLES	EDUCATIONAL IMPLICATIONS
of home environment created by his parents or guardians during his infancy and early childhood.	development of the child takes precedence over maintaining the intactness of a family unit whose actions or inactions clearly suppress such development. Early intervention of health and education agencies are called for when the family is unable or unwilling to provide proper nurture for its offspring. All attempts to help the child should involve the family and strengthen the family unit as much as possible. On occasion, however, the child may be the only "reachable" person, so he should be given the chance to develop even if the helping services have to bypass the family in accomplishing their task.
3. Openness to a broad range of experiences and ideas, and the ability to see differing points of view, are vital to the healthy socialization of the individual.	3. Instructional materials representing one static prism through which to view the world can only distort by oversimplification. Students should not only receive many different points of view, but should also be taught the skills of making judgments among them. Children need practice in the search for self-knowledge and developing awareness of the role personal bias can play in tampering with reality. Self-knowledge and the ways of compensating for a unidimensional perspective on the world are explicit instructional goals for educational democracy.
4. The process of healthy attitudinal and behavioral maturation is facilitated through the child's emulation of significant models among peers and adults.	4. The teacher should be aware that his leadership role in the classroom automatically makes him a potential model for student behavior. Moreover, he should design the educational environment so that the pupil group contains desirable role models to enhance the personal development of its members.
5. Early childhood experiences designed to maximize healthy human development can have a permanent salutary effect on that development.	5. Since intervention efforts at modifying the rate and directionality of human growth have thus far been most successful in the child's early years, it is necessary to refine these measures to maximize their impact. Warmth and affection with reasonable demands for performance

Table 6 (*continued*)

MENTAL HEALTH PRINCIPLES	EDUCATIONAL IMPLICATIONS
	should be major components of early childhood education. Additionally, the schools cannot afford delaying the diagnosis and treatment of specific learning problems which may become increasingly resistant to treatment as the child grows older.
6. Self-actualization, as characterized by Maslow (1954), involves a number of competencies, including the ability to perceive and accept reality and to recognize one's own shortcomings and those of others; the ability and urge to improve oneself and eliminate discrepancies between what is and what ought to be; the ability to preserve one's own spontaneity and creative inclinations; the ability to focus attention on problems outside oneself, along with having a sense of mission in life which makes enormous demands on inner resources; the ability to cultivate in oneself a certain spirit of detachment, dignity, and independence from the environment; the ability to find satisfaction within oneself rather than relying on others to provide it; the ability to experience a sense of ecstasy, bordering on the mystical, inspired by the realities and promises of one's life experiences; the ability to identify with human beings in a compassionate way, and a desire to help the human race; and the ability to resist temptations to conform out of a sense of ritual rather than rational judgment.	6. One of the essential concerns of education is to help individuals become self-actualizing citizens in a democracy. A meaningful curriculum lays great stress on independent thinking, creative productivity, the formulation of a set of personal values, and the cultivation of interpersonal responsibility. The memorization of facts for their own sake has no place in such a program; facts are merely resource data for a profounder understanding of self and society. Nor is programming for creativity merely a signal to release basic instincts for expression; it involves also a highly sophisticated self-critical, self-regularizing process which determines its ultimate quality. In essence, then, education concerns itself with cognition and affect, with individuality and socialization, and with mastery and creativity.
7. A sense of human worth is enhanced by occupational activity that is both self-satisfying and socially rewarding.	7. The curriculum should provide a broad range of coping mechanisms necessary for vocational adjustment. These include the basic communication skills the worker needs in a modern industrial society. Also involved are on-the-job habitual demands such as dependability in completing an assignment, ability to get along with co-workers, adherence to prearranged time schedules, responsibility in living up to verbal agreements, and

Table 6 (*continued*)

MENTAL HEALTH PRINCIPLES	EDUCATIONAL IMPLICATIONS
	flexibility in the face of changing working conditions. Finally, there should be provision within the educational system to train young people in the specific skills required of their chosen vocation, provided they have the necessary basic aptitudes.

3. *The school is not equipped to assume sole responsibility for promoting mental health, nor is it restricted solely to pursuing mental health goals.*

The profound relevance of education to mental health should be appreciated in all of its ramifications. However, it can contribute to general euphoria regarding the power and responsibility of the school in nurturing the psychosocial development of children and youth. Many people have the same kind of fundamentalist faith in public education that others have in the church vis-à-vis its capabilities for solving human problems. They are convinced that personal defects can be corrected if a proper dosage of schooling is administered with enough skill and patience. Thus, education is above criticism, despite the fact that educators are fair game for attack. Its alleged bounty so dazzles public imagination that hardly anybody ever bothers to find out what it *cannot* do even under the best of circumstances. Who would argue, for example, that achieving 100 percent school retention is *not* a desirable goal? Certainly not industry and the labor unions, since they want to keep unskilled young people in school—and out of the glutted job market—for as long as possible. Certainly not the school administrator whose school subsidies are computed on a per capita attendance formula. Therefore, by emphasizing the importance of education, the public champions a noncontroversial cause that is in the best interests of everybody concerned, but in so doing, it is in danger of relieving itself of the responsibility of taking a realistic view of the *multiple* factors affecting mental health and the need for planning complex, expensive programs of prevention and rehabilitation. This is not to suggest that education is something of an opiate and should be exposed as such. It is, in fact, as indispensable to personal fulfillment as basic nutrition is to physical subsistence. However, it cannot guarantee good mental health any more than basic nutrients can guarantee good physical health.

Popular belief in the school as possessor of a potential cure-all for social ailments tends to blur its functional limits and makes it vulnerable to criticism for failing to accomplish things it was never designed to accomplish. It should be kept in mind that the school is no substitute for the mental health agency even though their objectives overlap. Both institutions share the following common concerns:

1. Increase the child's depth and range of self-understanding.
2. Increase the child's depth and range of sensitivity to the world around him.
3. Deepen the child's potentiality for differentiated interaction with people.
4. Foster the child's internalization of authority while helping him maintain his individuality.

But apart from its direct involvement in fostering mental health, the school assumes prime responsibility for actualizing the child's potentialities as a consumer and producer of knowledge. Its academic goals can be summarized as follows:

1. Promote the child's intellectual power and cognitive mastery.
2. Help the child develop techniques and attitudes for learning by discovery.
3. Help synthesize the child's learning experience through opportunity for symbolic expression.

Since there is commonality rather than congruence in the aims of education and of other helping services, the same is true for the professional roles played by exponents of these services. Effective teaching is supposed to incorporate some strategies that are the stock in trade of the counselor and therapist and others that are basically unique. These skills can help the teacher develop methods of early detection and treatment of deviant behavior in schoolchildren. The teacher can then extend his insight into human development and the varieties of behavior—including an understanding and appreciation of the multiple causes of behavior—and thus feel encouraged to apply this knowledge in his relations with the schoolchild. With these improved insights, he can modify his methods of handling children's problems and thus contribute to a healthy teacher-pupil relationship. That is why the teacher is sometimes seen as a curious amalgam consisting of part clinician, part social worker, part surrogate parent, part regulations legislator and enforcer, part dispenser of factual information, and part midwife to ideas. He shares with other adults the responsibility of serving as the child's mature companion with deep concerns about his personal problems and about ways of helping him deal with them. He also functions as an instructor who requires a special relationship with the child in order to do his job successfully.

The teacher is in some measure an authority figure who often plays a leadership role in determining what is to be learned and what behavior codes promise to create the best possible teaching-learning atmosphere. His primary concern is with the cultivation of knowledge, so he must possess it, know how to transmit it, and know how to stimulate children to create their own. No other public service shares these formal instructional tasks. Cutting back on these responsibilities in the interest of having him administer more direct mental health services would constitute a disservice both to education and to mental health.

4. *The quality of formal instruction at school is potentially a more critical determinant of educational attainment for some pupil populations than for others.*

The widely circulated Coleman report (1966) seems to indicate that variations in pupil success at school relate more directly to differences in home environment than to differences in teacher quality. This imbalance of home versus school influence must be changed to enable children whose families provide relatively little by way of school readiness opportunities to achieve success through formal education at school.

What, specifically, are some of the vital home experiences that relate directly to scholastic success? In an attempt to find answers to this question, Wolf (1964) examined several kinds of interaction patterns between parents and children and found the following to be most critical: (1) parental press for achievement motivation; (2) parental press for language development; and (3) the parents' provisions for the child to engage in out-of-school learning experiences. These so-called "process variables" appeared to account for nearly half the variance in school performance. Needless to say, variations in teaching methods and administrative policies at school do not correlate with school achievement nearly to that extent. Consequently, in the early years of schooling, at least, the child from an advantaged environment can compensate for mediocre instruction through his informal experiences at home and in the community. His social milieu is powerfully oriented toward achievement, and he learns early in life that success at school is vital to professional opportunities, social status, economic advancement, and personal happiness. Although his parents are concerned that he be exposed to the best in teaching methods at school, they insist that he compensate for the teacher's defects with a self-directed drive toward accomplishment. They also provide him with a rich variety of instructional aids and experiences to make the goals they have set for him more attainable.

The effect of family-supplied encouragement and enrichment is not simply to make the home a supportive collaborator with the school in achieving educational goals. Rather than playing the subordinate role, the home fills a dominant one. More specifically, for the advantaged child, home experiences that are continuous with the efforts of the school contribute more to educational progress than does the formal curriculum and methodology provided by the school. It follows, therefore, that if the family perseveres in its efforts on behalf of the child, laxity or mediocrity on the part of the teacher will not make much difference. This may help explain why Terman (1925), in his classic studies of gifted elementary school children coming for the most part from educationally rich and supportive environments and attending school anywhere from two to six years, found no correlation between academic achievement and length of school attendance.

In the case of the socially disadvantaged child the school cannot rely on the assumption that much of the readiness spadework is done by the family and that the remaining task is to channelize existing incentives, interests, and modes of social behavior to well-defined areas of productivity. Instead, it has to compensate for the lack of preconditions of school success. A ghetto home may recognize the importance of education and value it no less than other homes do, but it often does not or cannot exert the necessary pressures and inducements for the child to succeed at it. Too often, the child does not have an adult model whose power, self-sufficiency, and apparent freedom from fear he can envy and emulate. He is left to his own devices early in life without benefit of succorant care and disciplinary supervision at home. Upon entering the neighborhood and joining a peer group, he is unarmed with anything resembling a set of behavior principles and aspirations that reflect a value system he can associate with his parents. The absence of any clearly defined parental role model to serve as an anchorage forces him to substitute the values of the peer group and to acquire a premature independence that is often marked with rebelliousness and defiance rather than self-discipline and goal-directedness. His inner resources are so minimal that he tends to adopt a fatalistic belief in the power of external forces to shape his future. This places a greater responsibility on the school to help him compensate for his low self-esteem and for the lack of reinforcement of educational goals at home.

Critical Realities Affecting
Education and Mental Health

The great public investment in education reflects the importance Americans attach to enlightenment and personal happiness. It is generally acknowledged that any social engineering design for promoting mental health that does not contain a strong educational component stands little chance of success. The child requires a sound, complete education not only for its intrinsic values but for practical advantages as well. If he elects to discontinue his education before completing high school, he will become increasingly conspicuous as one of the near-vanishing few in his age group who could not or would not graduate. He relies on the high school diploma for its credential value, even if his achievement is minimal, because the spirit of the times demands it. Beyond that, he needs to show some modicum of satisfactory academic accomplishment because the criteria for minimum essentials in education are rising. We are fast approaching a time when the child may be relegated to a life of economic dependency and status depression unless he can master even more scholastic skills than are necessary to earn the high school diploma.

Because so much depends on the work of the schools, they are always vulnerable to attack for not doing enough or for doing their job badly. The criticism is severest in communities where mental health problems are most serious, particularly in the slum areas across the nation. Children coming from the ghettos grow up in an environment that is virtually barren of educational artifacts and preoccupations. Although their parents frequently recognize the importance of education, they are often not in a position to make the necessary sacrifices of time and money for their children to succeed at it. Moreover, there is some evidence (Schreiber, 1964) to show that slum parents' confidence in the neighborhood public schools is dangerously low, and this may be both a cause and a consequence of the inflated dropout rates in depressed areas. Small wonder that im-

389

poverished communities are confronting their schools with a staggering mandate to show more effectiveness in preventing the gulf between the "haves" and "have nots," and between the "more equal" and "less equal," from broadening in an affluent, democratic society.

It is not entirely clear just why schools fail to measure up to expectations. Undoubtedly some of these expectations are unrealistic, so it is futile to hope that schools can ever realize them under any circumstances. There are also inhibiting conditions over which educators have no control. But part of the unrealized potentialities must likewise be ascribed to the ineptitudes of school systems and the professionals who staff them. There is much that the school can do to put its house in order. At the same time, there are problems laid at its doorstep that really belong in the domain of other community institutions even though they need the school's help in developing solutions. Before any meaningful attempt can be made to improve public education, it is necessary to clarify some disturbing realities in which the school's legitimate concerns are embedded. The following reality factors are seen by the Committee as having a vital bearing both on education and on mental health.

1. *Schools are under enormous conflicting external pressure to undergo change.*

No other public institution (with the possible exception of law enforcement agencies) compares with the school in its exposure to persistent, massive, vigorous, and often conflicting external influences to engage in radical self-overhaul. Educators simply cannot move fast enough to meet the public demands for change, especially in depressed areas. In some instances, these pressures reverse their directionality after the so-called system has begun to respond to the initial influence. For example, when the Supreme Court decided in 1954 that racial separatism and equality were incompatible, the nation's schools moved slowly but inexorably toward integrated education. But in more recent years, there has been a groundswell of sentiment, partly stimulated by militant black separatists in Negro communities, to play down the importance of integration in favor of improved teaching services and methodology regardless of the racial composition of the classroom. For them, discussions of the alleged salutary effects of integration on the psychosocial development of children (see, for example, Group for the Advancement of Psychiatry, 1957) are purely academic and irrelevant to the needs of ghetto life. Consequently, the school finds itself in an unenviable position of having to decide not only how to respond but also how to respond fast enough to accommodate the sense of urgency among the interested parties.

Continuous exposure to pressures for change affects every aspect of school life. It has enormous implications for the structure and organization of the school as well as for the stability and continuity of educational programs. The educator must have a special aptitude for self-change in adapting to different professional roles, working conditions, and curriculum modifications. It may be uncomfortable for him to be accountable to the local community which is judging him constantly, but that is a condition of his chosen work.

Since schools have to operate in turbulent cross currents of influence, they are always apt to move too slowly for some, too rapidly for others. There are many educators whose conservatism, complacency, or indifference tends to impede any kind of progress in the schools. These are usually the stolid professionals in key positions who give the school system its ponderous, plodding image to the forces of reform. There is also a growing number of people—though still a minority—who are attuned to external pressures and highly responsive to them. For these educators the problem is to distinguish between personal flexibility and spinelessness and between progress and faddism. It takes great wisdom to determine the point on the conservatism-radicalism continuum that holds out the most promise for education today.

One clear fact seems to be emerging: Educators cannot continue playing the role of passive respondents to change pressures. Instructional goals have to relate to the realities of changing community life. It is the responsibility of professionals working with children to plan in advance for anticipated social change so that they can have the kind of experience in role playing, information gathering, and developing the understanding necessary to ameliorate the anxieties and stresses that often accompany social change. Moreover, school staffs are vulnerable to attack if local residents see them as visitors from other communities assigned to do a job in a neighborhood with which they do not identify, only to return after their working hours to places where their real loyalties lie. Since the school is an institution that is beginning to figure prominently in social action movements, involvement on the part of educators can have an uplifting effect on the school's image and influence. It can become a social force in the community, prepared even to exercise leadership if necessary, rather than remaining an object of manipulation among groups in the local power structure.

2. *As public satisfaction with the schools' accomplishments declines, and attacks on the public schools increase, communities tend to chip away at the school systems' autonomy in exercising control over their policies and structure.*

The large urban ghettos across the country are at the forefront of the campaign for educational reform. They feel that schools have let them down by failing to fulfill their mandate, as evidenced by the excessive school failure and dropout rates in these communities. They are convinced that the professional staffs are not really committed to the pursuit of excellence and do not demonstrate the necessary excitement and inspiration to engage the interests of their pupils. They are particularly displeased with the power network of the school, which seems to them more interested in preserving the structure of the institution than improving its function.

Regardless of how much or how little truth there is in these charges, the fact is that the school has developed a negative image among subpopulations that rely most heavily on its services and are most seriously victimized by problems pertaining to education and mental health. A barrier of distrust has come between the educator and the slum community as meaningful dialogue between them has failed to materialize. While under-utilizing knowledge in their own field, schools have attempted to offer services they are ill equipped to provide, thus aggravating their image of ineffectiveness. This is not to say that they are insensitive to the existence of vast numbers of poorly performing pupils. Contrary to charges that educators often sweep their problems under the rug, the greater tendency is to face reality and to do something about it. However, "members of the lodge" seek help primarily from within their ranks and give the impression of being exceedingly defensive about the quality of that help and its effectiveness. Even when a problem seems to resist efforts toward solution, it does not necessarily soften the school's resistance to help from the outside. Responsible and respected professionals proposing innovative ways to alleviate conditions in the schools are often viewed suspiciously if they are not part of the system. Their offer of assistance is interpreted as a lack of confidence in the school's ability or willingness to perform as it should. Thus, the school's need to present a solid front against external tamperers takes precedence over the objective pursuit of excellence in education.

Staffing policies that tend to ingrain existing ideas rather than accommodate new ones also contribute to the school's insularity against curriculum change. One generation of administrative leaders decides on the qualifications of succeeding generations, the criterion being how well the successor can emulate his predecessor. The preservation of staff regularity at the leadership level ensures similar regularity at the subordinate levels. Beyond the moment of induction and period of probation there is virtually no merit system in the schools to stimulate self-improvement. True, in some schools salary increments are awarded for continued graduate study, but there is an underlying unsubstantiated assumption that in-service training makes a meaningful difference in the teacher's classroom performance.

Once the professional achieves tenure, it is difficult for him to resist the feeling of complacency, even if he maintains some contact with the growth of knowledge in his field. Unless he has enormous personal pride, he will coast along from day to day, never straining to function at optimum capacity and never distinguishing himself among his colleagues. His supervisors have no way of rewarding him for excellence or punishing him for mediocrity, except in extreme situations, provided they are inclined to do so. If there is external pressure or internally felt needs to improve the pupil's scholastic record, the system's usual response is to bring in supplementary personnel rather than to force improvements in staff performance. Thus, while school budgets have risen dramatically in this decade the incline has been much steeper for out-of-classroom supportive services—including remedial, counseling, clinical, and social work help—than for classroom instruction. It raises the suspicion that much of this back-up assistance is makeshift patchwork to compensate for incompetence in the teaching and administrative staffs.

The school's stubborn conservatism is seen by many communities as a sign of institutional senility. Public-minded citizens in depressed areas especially are becoming convinced that there is no hope for meaningful educational change from within the system. To them, the only alternative is for the community to control the system either by having each locality take over the schools in its area or by making city-wide boards of education more representative of the districts they serve. There is, however, an alternative to writing off the school system as organizationally and programmatically inept. It involves establishing an elaborate communication network between the school and the community to facilitate a back-and-forth flow of ideas aimed at bringing about educational self-removal at the grassroots level. If this kind of cross fertilization could be initiated in a spirit of mutual trust it would sweep away many of the school-community relations problems. The schools have the means to attract a wealth of educational hypotheses from the community provided they are ready to examine these ideas on their own merit without fear of meddling from outsiders. For its part, the community should recognize the school as a potentially powerful agent for social reform rather than an uncommitted, fossilized institution in its midst. It is the educator's responsibility to enter into meaningful dialogue with the community concerning the educational needs of its children. In that way it may ultimately reap benefits from the wisdom and good will of the local citizenry while stemming the decline of its power in determining school policy.

3. *Education's "state of the art" is invoked to rationalize nonintervention for those who are most in need of intervention.*

Nobody has as yet fully explicated the precise capabilities of the school in influencing child development. This lack of clarity tends to rigidify the biases of those who expect too much or too little of the schools. Educators often ignore the serious imbalance between what is already known about the educative process and the application of this knowledge in the classroom. They claim there is not enough research evidence about how children learn that would justify changes in instructional practice; they prefer to maintain this inertia and ignore the growing research evidence that suggests change. When they are pressured to open their minds to alternative ways of doing their job, they frequently argue that no qualitative modifications in their programs would constitute improvement. Instead, the answer lies in quantitative supplementation of conventional goods and services: *more* teachers, *higher* salaries, *smaller* classes, *greater* supplies of teaching aids, *earlier* school admission, and an *increase* in the noninstructional staff. What results is a wasteful underutilization of the most advanced ideas in the field and an overutilization of outdated, ineffectual mechanisms.

While it is arrogant to claim complete knowledge of the psychoeducational and psychosocial life of the child, it is falsely modest to argue that nothing is known about it. Such arguments can be used mischievously to preserve a status quo know-nothing policy in the school. It is a form of anti-intellectualism among educators, even though it is covered with a veneer of scientific probity. The fact of the matter is, there is a vast amount of theory and research on the growth processes of children (Baldwin, 1967), the dynamics of the teaching-learning act (Gage, 1963), and the structure of intellect (Guilford, 1967) which educators need as a basis for making programmatic decisions. Part of the problem has been the time lag between the acquisition and application of knowledge. The schools need considerable help in streamlining their mechanism for feeding into the system those ideas for improvement they acknowledge possessing. They also have to be shown how to blueprint educational change on the basis of new research evidence concerning the nature and nurture of children. Too often, the laboratory researcher and theoretician assume that it is easy to make the leap from knowing the child to knowing what to do for (or about) him. However, insight does not always guarantee wise action inferences, even when practitioners look for them and are willing to accept them.

But whereas many professional educators underestimate the wisdom and potential strength of education, many nonprofessionals attempt to overestimate it. The well-meaning lay public frequently looks to education for panaceas and incorporates its sentiments into pressures for educational reform, especially in slum areas. Some social commentators advocating the cause of minority groups contend that schools could close the achievement gap between the socially advantaged and the disadvantaged if they matched their professional knowledge about teaching and learning with operational know-how for getting the education job done. Failure is seen as a lack of will—tacit indifference, even bigotry—not a lack of ways.

Realistically, education's "state of the art" is not nearly as advanced as some of its most hopeful critics imagine it to be, just as it is not nearly as primitive as some of its leading practitioners think it is. There is nothing resembling a programmatic design guaranteed to solve the problem of massive educational retardation in urban ghettos, nor does there exist a foolproof system for infusing school curriculums outside the ghetto areas with the kind of inspiration and challenge that educational experiences are meant to instill. Moreover, given the present organization of the school— its institutional structure, professional staff, instructional schedule, and the age span of its pupil population—it does not stand a chance of accomplishing the task even with the greatest of will power. The fact is that schools are floundering not simply for want of effort but because their responsibilities are too formidable under the ground rules covering their operations.

The educator's unwillingness to recognize progress in his field is sometimes used as a rationalization for the school's failure to accomplish its purposes, and the layman's exaggerated faith in the school is occasionally used to rationalize the ineptitude of other community institutions and services that influence the child's progress in education and mental health. Thus, the prevention and solution of many problems is left strictly to the schools, even though the work of other agencies sometimes has an important bearing on the outcomes. It is well known, for example, that there is an uncommonly high incidence of premature birth in slum communities which, in turn, relates directly to subsequent academic retardation. Yet, the popular feeling is that whatever the cause of school failure, it can be solved by improved instruction. The onus is on the school to overcome the problem, while there is relatively little pressure on public health agencies to help prevent it. Somehow, the child is "lost in the shuffle" as educators absolve themselves and laymen absolve other key professionals from doing what they can to help the child realize his learning potentialities.

One way out of the dilemma is for the schools and other public-serving institutions to engage in a collaborative effort in educating the community as to what it can rightfully expect from these local agencies. This would require first that the agencies engage in constant discussions among themselves regarding their present and projected functions. If there are plans for overlapping or combining services, they should be understood well in advance by the professional staffs and communicated in the best way possible to local residents. In some communities it isn't enough to wait for clients to avail themselves of existing services—the agencies have to reach out, uninvited, and provide help for the home. Schools can play an important role in initiating and coordinating this kind of vital service to the community, and thereby exercise the kind of leadership that is so desperately needed.

4. *There is frequent confusion and indecision about the mental health roles of key noninstructional, nonadministrative personnel.*

It is often claimed that the school does not have enough professional manpower concerned solely with the problems of mental health. There is also no universal agreement regarding the services which the mental health worker is supposed to render and how his work harmonizes with the educational activity of the school. It would seem that a job analysis of the mental health worker in ghetto schools would reveal at least four distinctive roles. First is the advocacy role which calls upon him to represent the interests of the child and of the teacher. Second is the administrative role involving class organization, staff relations, student advisement, and general instructional leadership. The third is the therapeutic role, which relates to personal and interpersonal problems, making referrals to other helping agencies, and establishing a cooperative relationship with the home on behalf of the child. The fourth is the educative role, which pertains to the in-service training of teachers and the orientation of the community to the mental health work of the school. These four task components are sometimes merged in one person. He is an advocate for the child, mediating between the slum environment and the school. However, when he assumes an administrative role he can no longer serve as mediator because the two roles are not compatible. He therefore tends to respond to administrative responsibilities, thus weakening his advocacy services. Moreover, pressures of administration prevent him from doing justice to his therapeutic and educational responsibilities, with the result that he becomes identified as part of the administrative staff.

There is also considerable confusion with respect to the advocacy role of the school mental health worker. He must decide whether he will represent the administration or whether he will identify primarily with the community or with the children. The problem is compounded by the inordinately great numbers of pupils in ghetto schools who need the help of a mental health worker. The existing counselor-pupil ratio makes it impossible for the helping services to provide anything resembling personal counseling. The mental health worker may therefore have to assume the role of advocate for the child, interpreting to the administration the implications of policy decisions that affect the mental health of pupils. In doing so, he must guard against becoming so problem-centered within the school that he fails to familiarize himself with the environmental conditions in the outside world where the child lives. He cannot allow himself to be regarded by the community as a stranger to its concerns and consequently incapable of advocating the needs of its children. To the extent, then, that the dynamics of community life have a powerful impact on the psychosocial growth processes of young people, the school mental health worker has to understand these influences and participate directly in shaping them. He may even have to serve as the community's advocate in the school.

Not only do the child, the school, and the community require the advocacy services of mental health workers—the classroom teacher requires services too. Every teacher should have somebody with whom to talk and from whom to get help in classroom management, in understanding the dynamics of pupil behavior, in learning how to deal effectively with parents, in preparing for home visits, and in utilizing resources that will contribute to effective teaching. The teacher's own intrapsychic condition has a profound influence on the social climate of the school and must be dealt with directly in any meaningful mental health program. Jersild's (1955) study of teachers' personal concerns revealed deep feelings of anxiety, loneliness, hostility, and a general need to clarify their own life's purposes. Many were desperately eager to discuss these concerns in depth as a means of becoming better integrated personalities and better able to help children face themselves. The school mental health worker can be most helpful in satisfying these needs.

Where, then, should the advocacy emphasis be? Should it be child-centered? Administration-centered? Community-centered? Teacher-centered? Or possibly a combination of these alternatives? Some kind of resolution is necessary for determining whether conventionally trained mental health workers can serve the schools adequately. Each school has to consider its own circumstances, including the staff and pupil composition, the neighborhood structure, and the program goals, before clarifying its own position in the matter.

5. *Teachers in ghetto schools frequently find the classroom an unmanageable administrative unit for purposes of instruction.*

There is no doubt that the problem of disruptive behavior in the classroom has discouraged large numbers of teachers from planning long professional careers in ghetto schools. It has been responsible in significant measure for the huge turnover rates in these schools and for the crippling morale problems among professionals who stay on for any length of time. The extent to which disruptiveness has spread in inner-city classrooms is not known, but some practitioners estimate that roughly 30 to 35 percent of the school population displays serious behavior disorders. From a mental health point of view, the problem has serious implications despite the fact that its origin may not be intrapsychic. In a noisy, chaotic atmosphere it is impossible for children to cultivate important interrelational sensitivities or the collaborative skills necessary for group productivity. The teacher is so preoccupied with his tense, disciplinary vigilance that children see him only in that role. He does not have the opportunity to present himself as a companion and critic, an instructor and counselor, and a stimulator of ideas and values.

Efforts at calming the learning environment in ghetto schools have not met with notable success. Experimenters have gone into these classrooms with a sincere desire to establish rapport by demonstrating to the pupils an abiding interest in their innermost concerns. They have worked with the children in small groups and, on occasion, on a one-to-one basis, in order to win their confidence and provide supportiveness in the most per-missive manner possible. One such well-publicized, well-endowed experi-ment in a New York City junior high school, considered one of the "worst" in the city (Bigart, 1967), illustrates the tragic outcomes of this kind of intervention. The object of the experiment was "to surround children with a team of adults who were sensitive to their needs and concerned with designing learning experiences to meet those particular needs." Unfortu-nately, these objectives were never met. The project director blamed the bureaucratic rigidity of the school system rather than student misconduct for the defeat of the experiment, while the school principal became disen-chanted with the air of permissiveness which he felt led to chaos. Thus, an initial outpouring of good intentions from all sides led nowhere. Missing were some systematic strategies for regulating classroom life for purposes of achieving educational objectives. The professionals from the university were no better able to make headway in modifying behavior or stimulating learning than were the school officials. After repeated failure, the spirit of despair began to tarnish initial enthusiasm and the project staff resorted to futile improvisation to quell the disruptive behavior.

Administrative solutions have not fared much better. In an effort to ameliorate the problem of disruptive behavior, boards of education have in some instances reduced class size and increased supportive services drastically at nearly three times the per-pupil cost. One such example is the More Effective Schools Program in New York City. An impartial assessment (Fox, 1967) reports that while the professional staffs were enthusiastic about these schools and their programs and optimistic about continued success, these positive feelings were not reflected in objective measures or in the reports of outside observers. "The data . . . show that children in classes in More Effective Schools were not behaving any dif-ferently than children in classes in the officially designated control schools or in classes in other special service schools" (Fox, 1967, p. 121).

From all indications, it would seem that no solution to the problem of disruptive behavior in ghetto schools is currently discernible. Perhaps there are no ways of establishing an environment for instruction in a class-room setting. The classroom as we know it may not be manageable enough to sustain ghetto children in learning activity. There is already some evi-dence to show that in some ghetto schools no more than 20 percent of the time is devoted to instruction while the rest is consumed by various kinds of managerial matters (Deutsch, 1960). The most widely proposed alter-native to socialized instruction in the classroom setting is individualized self-instruction in some kind of responsive environment or isolated carrel. If schools substitute individualized, for socialized, instruction, some critics will probably argue that such policy will emasculate the social learning aspects of the curriculum. However, despite the failure of many teachers to control children grouped in a classroom structure, isolating disruptive children for purposes of teaching them may not be necessary. Perhaps by varying his instructional strategies systematically according to a preordained model of methodological options and sensitizing himself to pupil responsiveness to these alternative stimuli, the teacher can locate the means of increasing pupil engagement in planned learning activity while reducing disruptiveness in the classroom. In order to accomplish this, he must learn to make use of a wide range of teaching tactics possible in a classroom situation. This means enriching his repertoire of teaching behaviors, monitoring them, and deriving some information about the instructional styles (as well as content) that tend to engage pupil attention. The assumption here is that each pupil responds best to a certain set of methodological stimuli, and the teacher can be taught how to find the best fit for each pupil. Therein lies the potential therapeutic value of this kind of prescriptive teaching.

Reducing frictions between teacher and pupil may require not only changes in classroom techniques—or even eliminating the classroom as the locus of instruction—but also a radical change in the way the school system relates to pupils. There is a great need to humanize education in order to make learning experiences relevant for the people who participate in it. Many kinds of constraints that exist within our schools hinder the humanization of school life. The grade system tends to fragment pupil populations, just as the grading system tends to lengthen the social distance between the grader and the graded. Pupils and their parents sense that school officials often regard administrative efficiency as more important than the "human factor." They are aware also of the bureaucratic pecking order, with its functionaries at every level of the status hierarchy busily working to preserve their own little domain and contributing their own share to the mountain of red tape that can stifle people attempting to influence change in the system. Rebelliousness among pupils sometimes appears to be the only way they can make themselves heard and show they are human in a dehumanized environment.

Unless the school takes a more critical look at its know-how in administering instruction and at its overall organizational image, the outlook for reducing friction between teachers and pupils can only worsen. The problem is already looming as a political football among laymen and professionals alike in depressed areas. Ghetto leaders are accusing schools of exaggerating the problem and using it to veil their prejudice against minority groups and as justification for their failure in teaching their children. Organized teacher groups are drawing attention to it while negotiating for improved working conditions. The infighting among school and community power structures may eventually determine who controls the schools, but it does not guarantee improved learning conditions for the children.

6. *Current instructional staffs and practices are often not attuned to engage the intellect, nurture personal sensitivities, or instill interpersonal responsibilities.*

The excessive problems in slum schools seem to demonstrate, in exacerbated form, what is generally wrong with educational methodology in schools everywhere. Even in so-called advantaged classrooms, there is evidence of silent dissent, apathy, and lack of commitment to the values preached by teachers, which is as symptomatic of pupil rebellion as disruptiveness in ghetto classrooms. Little is said about the constraints inherent in a graded school system or the abuses of success criteria that are evident in suburban as well as inner-city schools. The bitterest complaint among children in any school system is that classroom life is boring because teachers do not know how to do their jobs skillfully.

· Much of the pupil criticism is leveled against curriculum content that rarely stirs the imagination. Its sequential layout hardly takes into account the stages of early intellectual development and often underestimates the pupil's educability for problem solving. Facts are overstressed while processes are virtually ignored. Problem solving is viewed narrowly as an exercise in converging on the right answer, sometimes just guessing the answer that the teacher has in mind. Meanwhile, important dimensions of productive thinking remain largely unexplored. It is unusual for a teacher to educate children to become skilled problem finders, divergent thinkers, perceptive inquirers, and surveyors of the structure of academic fields. Children sense a void even if they do not know precisely what they are missing, and many drop out intellectually. Those who remain demonstrate their disenchantment by failing in coursework that they could otherwise master without difficulty, or they simply mark time while earning good grades in order to obtain the practical rewards our society grants for educational success.

Schools have also succeeded in creating a kind of antiseptic curriculum, relatively free of value preachments and administered by teachers who are trained to detach themselves from judging right from wrong and who therefore exert no character influence upon their pupils. The teacher seems to see himself only minimally involved in the personal and interpersonal life-patterning of his pupils. Thus, he is seen by them as something of a live teaching machine, cold and objective, and able to communicate only in content-related terms. They really never get to know him any better than he gets to know them in matters pertaining to personal affect. He reveals little about his personal taste, biases, worries, enthusiasms, fears, and satisfactions, and this creates a social distance between teacher and pupil which prevents mutual understanding, especially in a ghetto environment where the two represent such vastly different social backgrounds.

Teacher training institutions may be capable of adding new dimensions to the teacher's classroom image. To do so would involve new emphasis on helping him gain self-insight in relation to his professional roles. He would have to be educated to assume the responsibility of building the child's sense of competency in such a way as to support and integrate positive personality developmental processes. It means sensitizing the teacher not only to the pupil's thought patterns but also to the feeling tones of these thoughts during the learning act. Self-examination takes on new importance in modifying new instructional strategies, and curriculum change takes into account the mental health implications as well as the impact on cognitive growth. In short, instruction becomes comprehensive and multifaceted in the sense that larger segments of the personality configuration of pupils and teachers interact to vitalize life in the classroom.

But is it realistically possible for teacher training institutions to supply the profession with enough people who possess the qualities of a classroom virtuoso? Surely, the training programs need vast improvement, but it is unlikely that they can graduate large numbers of teachers to perform much beyond the mediocrity level. For quality teacher performance contains a touch of charisma, and those who possess it are the kinds of performing artists who cannot be mass-produced easily. If there were as many concert stages in search of recitalists as there are classrooms in search of teachers, the listening public would have to compromise its musical standards in the same way that the general population may have to resign itself to less-than-inspired education for the young. The fact is that given the realities of compulsory universal education and the present structure of the schools, it is impossible to adjust the demand for teacher-artists to the available supply.

The only way out is to change the present structure and maximize the utilization of existing resources in slightly modified roles. Professional responsibility would be restricted to conform to the teacher's special aptitudes and training. Organizationally, he might function as part of a group in a team teaching arrangement and would divide responsibilities with other colleagues according to the teaching strength of every team member. Thus, for example, the teacher with special skills for curriculum building might be spared some of the administrative chores in order to preoccupy himself with the work he does best. This organizational design is flexible enough to allow for a good deal of independent as well as cooperative planning among team members. It also eliminates the rigidity of the self-contained classroom structure and enables the children to identify with one of several possible role models on the team rather than just a single teacher who is in charge of his class day after day. The differentiation of responsibility also makes it possible for greater numbers of male teachers to join staffs and capitalize on their special talents. Children can be reorganized in groups ranging in size from 3 to 4 to 30 or 40 depending on the nature of activity and the physical accommodations of the school building.

The following kinds of specific personnel are needed to carry out the effective functioning of a team:

Educational Strategist: This is the knowledge organizer and inventive educational planner. He makes the curriculum decisions about children with assistance, rather than direction, from curriculum bulletins and other kinds of external resources. He is a master teacher with advanced training and superior teaching competence, and he serves the team as its leader in planning instruction and dealing with practical classroom problems as they arise.

Educational Technicians: These represent the more typical members of the teaching profession, having completed conventional training programs and demonstrated adequacy in their classroom performance. They either are not experienced enough or have not demonstrated superior performance, so they have to work closely with the educational strategist to implement the latter's instructional plans. While they serve in a subordinate position on the teaching team, they participate in designing curriculum and are given every opportunity to prove their readiness to become educational strategists.

Instructional Aides: These are nonprofessionals recruited from the immediate community to assist the classroom teacher in performing specific teaching tasks. They are not trained to improvise instructional method, but instead have to be given virtually "cookbook"-type instructions on how to tutor individuals and work with small groups in and out of the classroom. By demonstrating skill on the job, they can eventually become regular educational technicians and even strategists.

Teacher Aides: These are likewise recruited from the indigenous lay population to take care of various noninstructional chores such as clerical work and playground supervision. They can also move into the instructional phases of the program if they show the necessary aptitudes and interest.

Proposals for Promoting Mental Health in the Schools

Recommending cures for an ailing educational system may be as easy as diagnosing what ails it, but to justify the choice of treatment is another matter. In suggesting innovations, there is always the trap of making a fetish of novelty or of simply pontificating that people and their institutions ought to become better than they are. The recommendations set forth here attempt to avoid these pitfalls despite the fact that they are stated in general terms and are in need of careful blueprinting before they can become workable plans. Some of the suggested ideas have already been advanced by educators concerned about conditions in the schools, but they are worth repeating partly because they are directly relevant to the problem of mental health and partly because they have not yet gotten into the bloodstream of American education. Their chief virtue is that they *seem* promising although there is not enough scientific evidence to balance off polemical rationalization with equal measures of empiricism.

1. *Remove the restraints of current time, place, and staff specifications from public education.*

One need not be cynical to assert (with apologies to George Bernard Shaw) that education is becoming much too big and important these days to be confined to our schools. Society keeps demanding an ever better-educated citizenry in order to maintain its present course of growth, and the schools are buckling under these mounting pressures. The storehouse of human knowledge is expanding so phenomenally that schools are able to transmit a quickly shrinking proportion of that treasure to its pupils. We are approaching the day when a college graduate will have to continue on to graduate school in order to complete his basic education (if, indeed, "complete education" and "basic education" have any meaning at all any-more). At one time, not so long ago, an American dream was that every man, woman, and child in this country possess at least the basic literacy skills. Today, literacy skills are no more adequate as minimum essentials than is the once sought-after fifty-cents-an-hour minimum wage. The barely literate are rapidly becoming obsolete in our modern industrial society, but unfortunately, functional illiteracy is not becoming extinct.

Hardest hit by society's runaway educational demands and the school's growing failure to meet them are the so-called underprivileged groups con-centrated in the nation's blighted areas. Never before has their scholastic achievement been so inadequate to society's expectations, despite the fact that they have never reached as high a level of scholastic achievement as they do today.

One oft-repeated solution to the educational problems of the under-privileged is to improve the schools. There is, of course, always room for such improvement. But if we are going to judge the schools by their skill in educating the slum child to function adequately in the modern world, the odds against their earning much praise for demonstrating such skill in the foreseeable future are prohibitive. The magnitude of the problem is so great and its rate of aggravation so rapid that the schools as we know them now may *never* find the solution. For how much room do they have to maneuver if they are forced to administer education *only* through their present professional-type staff, to children *only* between the ages of six to sixteen, *only* within the present five- or six-hour school day, and *only* at the familiar school building? Formal education cannot, therefore, afford to be restricted to the formal classroom; it must also break out of the school as an institution and reach into the lives of the underprivileged in their homes, their places of work, their houses of worship, and their centers of social activity. The following specific recommendations are made to alleviate current restrictions on the school program:

Design a homebound educational program for pre-six-year-olds. One way to provide more latitude for schools to work effectively is to enlarge the slice of the child's life in which educational treatment is administered. The job of instilling in disadvantaged children the various coping mech-anisms with which to face up to the demands of an increasingly complex industrialized society is an enormous one. It involves far more than just teaching the child some communication skills in the elementary grades and encouraging him to stay on the education conveyor belt at least through adolescence. It must, instead, exert a powerful influence on the way he cultivates his cognitive aptitudes, his motivational structure, his value sys-tem, his self-image, and his *Weltanschauung*. This kind of intensive nurture may not be possible to accomplish without involving the home at some critical stages of childhood growth. The entire constellation of parent-child relationships from the moment of birth until the onset of schooling seems to have a persistent effect on the child's personal history. Skeels' (1966) follow-up studies of infants reared under different conditions in foundling homes revealed that poor mothering practices can inhibit healthy mental development even beyond the childhood stages despite the corrective influences of a normal environment beginning in post-infancy. To the extent, then, that early deprivation in the slum family is accountable for later failure at school, the damage is already done by the time the child is absorbed into a conventional preschool program.

The responsibility of education, then, is to breathe new meaning into early intervention by reaching the child in his own habitat long before he begins coming to the school building for formal group learning. It means heading off the deleterious effects of minimal succorant care in infancy, providing an environment of optimum cognitive stimulation at the earliest stages in life, and contributing to the young child's experiential background in preparation for learning. By departing from its policies concerning the age for the child's education, the school may succeed in intervening early enough to make a difference, especially if some of its work affects the learning climate in the home where the most influential behavior patterning seems to take place.

Spread education from the school building into the community for school-age and post-school-age youth. Intensifying the services for disadvantaged children beyond the school building requires that the school "infiltrate" into the various helping agencies in the community and introduce educational components into their existing programs. There is evidence (Roman, 1957) to show that in community mental health programs a combination of formal instruction and psychotherapy has a more positive effect on delinquent behavior than does either of the two approaches separately. This finding supports the assertion that proper education is an effective mechanism for achieving nonacademic goals, provided that it interacts with measures designed to help achieve these goals independently. Instruction outside the school building may indeed be necessary to help some children measure up to the rapidly rising minimum standards of basic education before they can benefit from the various social engineering programs designed to help them live productive lives. This means that carefully planned educational experiences will have to be available to ghetto residents of all ages. The programs will be designed and initiated by the school, but they will reach the population through such channels as community social agencies, neighborhood services, church programs, job training institutes, pediatric services, and mental health centers.

Adolescents in the ghetto are especially in need of educational experiences that are not part of the regular school program. Many of them are dropouts with bitter recollections of classroom life, and are reluctant to return to the school building for any kind of program, regardless of who sponsors it. For them, as well as for those still in the educational mainstream, the community can provide educational services that are administered away from the school. As demonstrated by the Berg Foundation Program, local businessmen, professionals, politicians, intellectuals, and artists have much to offer these young people if the trained educators assist them with the necessary materials and instructions for teaching. The school system can serve as that kind of resource in the community. In this capacity, it can also build educational programs into local business and industry to enable young apprentices and employees to make up for their inadequate schooling. As the schools find ways to make their programs less institution-bound, and communicate something of value to ghetto children regardless of time or place, they will come closer to a position of centrality in community life.

Stratify instructional staffs to include assisting adults and adolescents. Since compensatory education programs for the underprivileged usually represent an investment in "more of the same" goods and services found in programs for the privileged, there are some knotty logistic problems of finding enough extra funds to pay the bill, locating and recruiting enough trained manpower to fill the extra professional positions, and devising an appropriate "delivery system" so that the instructional treatments reach the multitudes who need them. Surely there is a limit to the potential supply of professional personnel for ghetto schools, and that limit will be reached when the cost of augmenting existing staffs to handle a radically reduced case load becomes prohibitive, or when teacher training institutions are unable to graduate enough qualified trainees to fill the added positions. One way out of the bind is to stratify teaching staffs to include not only the licensed professionals but also large numbers of untrained adolescents and adults living in depressed areas who have enough aptitude to learn some simple teaching skills and are willing to make up in sheer persistence, dedication, and frequency of contact for what they lack in professional sophistication.

School administrators are indeed turning to untrained personnel for help in getting the educational job done, and reports of mushrooming programs involving nonprofessionals are already being circulated in many parts of the country. These programs vary from one community to the next, as do the backgrounds, ages, and roles of the nonprofessionals serving in them. The impact of the laymen's contributions has not yet been assessed, but it is significant to know that there is little hesitation to involve them in instructional tasks. Schools that have enlisted their help are evidently convinced that the known methods of teaching young children are not so esoteric as to require full-scale professional training; adults and even adolescents with relatively little formal schooling can be taught some of the skills that may enable them to contribute something of value to the slum child's educational growth and perhaps even to their own. Involvement of aides is therefore not just a desperation move to fill teaching positions with any available warm bodies, but rather part of a plan to find a constructive role for the untrained in the educational enterprise. In this sense, education is following the lead of other professions, such as medicine and social work, that have long been making use of nonprofessionals.

2. Enrich professional training in teacher education programs.

Design a clear methodology for teaching. To be competent, the teacher needs a repertoire of teaching skills, not just a bag of tricks. This is one of many popular abstractions the teacher-in-training will encounter in his professional coursework. Just how "skills" differ from "tricks" is not fully clarified by his education professor, but he begins to sense some meaning when he confronts the difficult practical problems in working with children and is advised by his mentors to "let it be a challenge." At that point he sometimes wishes he had some tricks to fit the situation rather than the burden of applying some shadowy generalizations to meet a down-to-earth problem that can sometimes be threatening. Professional adaptability is a prime requisite for successful teaching, but if it isn't grounded in explicit methodology it is as useless as reasoning aptitude without supportive factual data.

Teacher training programs frequently indoctrinate trainees with a set of glittering educational objectives and then send them out to observe and imitate teachers who have long since lost sight of these objectives. Formal methodology courses that are supposed to enable the neophyte to achieve the noble aims he is told to achieve contain neither "tricks" nor "skills" to equip him for the task, and his preservice field experience enables him to learn some methods (good and bad) to attain a set of goals that his training institution places low on the priority list.

Bring teachers college faculties into closer touch with local schools. In many instances, teacher training institutions operate out of a set of unclear educational principles, without full understanding of the changing social realities of community life, and without a coherent instructional methodology to impart to their trainees. Faculty members responsible for preparing teachers to serve in the classrooms are themselves usually out of touch with classroom life. At the same time, there are master practitioners in the school system who are rarely given the opportunity to train others or to bring their skills onto the teachers college campuses. It is necessary, therefore, to initiate more collaborative action between the training institutions and the school system by releasing key faculty members from these colleges for purposes of keeping abreast of developments in the field and assisting the schools in their self-betterment efforts. In exchange, key school personnel could help the colleges improve their teacher training programs if they were invited to do so. This kind of mutual assistance is a beginning step toward a closer relationship than now exists between colleges and boards of education. The college faculties are interested, but essentially detached, observers of conditions in the schools. They often initiate experimental programs in the hope of locating improved ways for the schools to function; yet, they are not accountable to the community for their successes or failures. This luxury of uninvolvement is no longer tenable in an age when all available professional resources are needed to bolster public education in this country.

Establish an advanced study center for training educational statesmen for both the public schools and teacher education institutions. Some 100 Fellows should be brought into the center yearly for advanced training in the behavioral sciences, administrative leadership, dynamics of change, etc. Each Fellow should come from a leadership position in either the public schools or teacher education and agree to continue in such a position following training. Full salaries, plus all actual necessary expenses, should be paid the Fellows who are selected for such training.

Develop more training programs for educational leaders. Because change in teacher education must be accompanied by change in public schools, immediate attention should be given to training educational administrators, middle-level administrative-supervisory and specialist personnel, together with teachers and organized administrative groups. There are relatively few training programs for educational leaders currently offered in teacher training institutions, and those currently being offered rarely utilize the most advanced training methods to accomplish the task.

Develop more training programs for teacher trainers. A major problem of teacher education is that most training institutions do not prepare personnel to assume teacher education responsibilities at the advanced professional level. There is need to give immediate attention to the critical need for training college faculty members who, in turn, will be responsible for training classroom teachers.

Train teachers to collaborate with other helping services for deviant children. Teachers colleges should stop training teachers to rely on a large army of specialists to solve their critical classroom problems. Because of this orientation, teachers tend to remove children too quickly from the mainstream of education and place them under the care of other helping services. Teachers have to be taught to share responsibilities with non-instructional personnel in order to maintain the continuity of the child's educational experience.

3. *Enrich cultural-academic studies in teacher education programs.*

Before teachers-in-training can learn to be inspirational teachers, they must themselves be inspired. Inspiration comes from exposure to moving intellectual experiences that become the subject of the teaching-learning act. However, teacher education programs have failed to provide such experiences for trainees. They have exhorted trainees to make the world of ideas an exciting one for their pupils but have neglected to do the same for their own students. There is a desperate need to cut back on so-called Mickey Mouse courses and to redesign the programs of teacher training institutions in such a way as to reflect more vividly the objectives they preach for elementary and secondary schools. Thus, for example, if the elementary or high school teacher is expected to help pupils achieve better understanding of the self and of the world around them, it is the responsibility of the teacher training institution to do the same for him while instructing him on how to do it for others.

Barbara Biber (1967) has posited a set of educational goals and ways of attaining them that are as applicable for teacher training programs as they are for elementary and secondary curriculums. These include sensitivity, discovery, mastery, and synthesis.

Sensitivity. The school is obligated to broaden the child's sensory-perceptual responsiveness to the world about him by increasing the range of stimuli with which he can interact at various intellectual levels and through various modalities. The elaboration of external reality is brought about through exposure to creative variations in color, form, sound, and texture, and to the verbal world of facts, ideas, fantasies, and hypotheses. This can be as exciting an experience for the teacher-in-training as it is for the child he will someday teach. He can become an important role model for children to keep their "sensory antenna" extended for all kinds of signals as a means of gaining knowledge and aesthetic stimulation. This, in turn, will set the stage for developing information-processing strategies necessary for higher-level intellectual functioning.

Discovery. The inductive method for cultivating insights is in itself a vital experience which reinforces the desire for more knowledge. Suchman (1964) has made prominent use of inquiry training as a classroom technique of disciplining curiosity and turning problem solving into gamelike activity in which the "player" can improve his style by repeated practice. Problem finding and creative exploration among seemingly disordered stimuli also facilitate learning through the discovery method. This kind of experience is as uncommon to the elementary classroom as it is to the college lecture hall. In both settings, the students are far less skillful in utilizing these processes than they are in operating by deduction. An important aspect of the intellectual experience is shut to them, and these productive thinking processes remain underdeveloped. It is, of course, difficult to cultivate skills in the discovery method if the classroom teacher himself is provided with little experience in it during his professional training.

Mastery. In order to gain intellectual sophistication, it is necessary to master a vast storehouse of facts and ideas and to utilize them for creating new understandings. There is no shortcut to mastery. Information must be assembled before it can be processed; theories must be examined and understood before they can be tested; and fact must be separated from conjecture before inferences can be drawn. Training the mind is an endless process which can be highly productive if the learned principles are applied to follow and produce an upward spiral of interrelated ideas. Unfortunately, teachers themselves rarely embark on this kind of journey, and the institutions in which they receive their training seem to be relatively barren of intellectualism. One important step toward restoring the teaching profession to a more coveted spot on the prestige hierarchy of American occupations is to make teacher training more relevant to the stirring world of ideas and its trainees more deeply appreciative of them.

Synthesis. In recent years, there has been a great amount of work on the need and methodology for fostering creativity in the child's educational experience. It has been said that children should be taught to toy with ideas, to provide problem-solving alternatives, to visualize unforeseen consequences, to transform commonplace objects into new structures and ways of using them, and to be inventive in the arts and sciences. However, the emphasis in the school curriculum is primarily on "convergent thinking," to find the single solution to a problem, rather than on "divergent thinking," or the multiplicity and originality of solutions. In their own professional preparation, teachers learn that there is a single way to teach reading, a single way to teach mathematics, a single way to teach economics, and a single way to control the class, despite the protestations of their professors that there are many vantage points from which they can approach these tasks. There is relatively little opportunity for teachers to brainstorm ideas or to learn how to become facile with the existing methodological options available to them when they engage in instruction. Just being told to be flexible in the classroom is not enough for the trainee if he isn't given guided practice in improving his flexibility.

4. *Improve the diagnostic techniques, instructional content, and teaching methods in the school curriculum.*

Use diagnostic devices that reveal how far the child's mind can be stretched. Conventional assessment devices are generally designed to determine the status of the child's functioning rather than his capacity. These psychometric measures neglect what researchers consider to be the latent capabilities of children, especially those whose scores are depressed by impoverished social circumstances. The usual method for probing behind the veneer of manifest functioning and obtaining an uncontaminated measure of so-called true capabilities is to design culture-free and culture-fair tests that are supposed to measure what Cattell (1963) calls "fluid" (as against "crystallized") intelligence. However, these tests continue to discriminate among sociocultural groups in the same way that the allegedly biased tests do.

One of the most promising recent developments in test construction and tactics designed to tap the full capabilities of the child is the work of Reuben Feuerstein of Israel, whose Learning Potential Assessment Device (Feuerstein, 1968) attempts to reveal not only the status of the child's intellectual functioning but also the extent of its modifiability, the amount of teaching necessary to bring about improved performance, and the transferability of newly acquired understandings to other areas of productivity. Specifically, the test measures the capacity of the child to accommodate a set of principles, learning sets, skills and attitudes, and to apply these acquisitions to a variety of tasks progressively removed in complexity from the initial one on which the acquisition was induced. Measured, too, is the amount of investment required to raise the child from his initial performance status to the optimum modified level. Modifiability is measured in a variety of intellective processes, and careful note is taken of the transfer of training effect within and across classes of problems. In addition to providing the child with an understanding of the properties of problems he is required to solve, the examiner attempts to improve his work habits pertaining to perceptual analysis, the need for accuracy, proper exploratory behaviors, logical evidence, and consistency in the situations he confronts. This improvement is brought about by changing the nature of the relationship between examiner and examinee from neutrality and lack of involvement to a relationship that provides the child with orientation to the tasks at hand and enables him to express his feelings about them. The purpose is to change the child's attitude toward test taking and to build his self-confidence.

Provide the child with systematic instruction designed to cultivate his basic cognitive processes. Once the child's modifiability index has been obtained, the Feuerstein program provides "Instrumental Enrichment," consisting of a series of steps aimed at developing specific perceptual and cognitive functions which may be considered prerequisites for the individual's ability to engage in school-related problem solving. It directs its attack on the specific, diagnostically determined developing (or under-developing) intellective processes through the use of specifically designed exercises. Emphasis in these exercises is on learning how to learn, and they are administered by an adult trained to frame, select, focus, and feed back information on these patterns in order to create appropriate learning sets. By focusing on the learning sets, it is possible to restrict the field of external stimuli and enable intentional learning to take place.

A number of enrichment devices and materials have already been developed, and they may be described functionally as follows (see Feuerstein and Hamburger, 1965):

    I. The induction of "comparative" behavior patterns in areas such as:
        A. Sensorimotor
           a. visual
           b. auditory
           c. haptic
           d. olfactory
        B. Representational
           a. comparison of events
           b. comparison of emotions
   II. The development of active and systematic exploratory patterns
        A. Concrete materials and objects
           a. three-dimensional
           b. pictorial
           c. verbal-auditory and lexic material
           d. problem-solving instruments where trial and error is controlled and systematized
        B. Interiorized exploration
           a. anticipatory, planned behavior
           b. representation of movement
  III. The projection of perceptual-visual relationships
        A. Closure techniques
        B. Segregation
        C. Visual transport
  IV. Development of perceptual consistencies throughout varying conditions of exposure, such as conservation of form, direction and quantity
    V. Evaluation of quantities (measurement)
  VI. Spatial-perceptual orientation: concepts of right, left, up-down, in-out
 VII. Temporal orientation
VIII. Accuracy and precision
  IX. Cultivating the need for logical evidence
    X. Language enrichment

Design curriculum content that challenges and arouses students to search for profound ideas. It has often been said that many pupils find the conventional school curriculum barren of excitement, beauty, and meaningfulness. As Henry (1963) points out, "The function of education has never been to free the mind and the spirit of man, but to bind them; and to the end that the mind and spirit of his children should never escape *homo sapiens* has employed praise, ridicule, admonition, accusation, mutilation, and even torture to chain them to the culture pattern. Throughout most of his historic course *homo sapiens* has wanted from his children acquiescence, not originality" (p. 286). It is therefore to be expected that schools emphasize drill and fact acquisition rather than the understanding and creation of ideas.

Research during the past decade on intellective processes that have heretofore remained virtually ignored in the classroom (see, for example, Guilford, 1967; Torrance, 1965) provide educators with unprecedented opportunities to enrich the child's experience at school by adding new dimensions to curriculum content. Psychologists are arguing that the imbalance between problem-solving and problem-finding activities at school should be rectified. Children have to be trained to ask probing questions in the search for concepts. The questions should be pertinent and take into account a range of reasonable contingencies so that conceptual foresight will be developed. The broad domain of divergent thinking encompasses such processes as associational and ideational fluency, object synthesis, originality, and flexibility, all of which are still relatively untouched in the modern curriculum. Yet, classroom practitioners think primarily in terms of content areas rather than productive talents, including abilities in the academic and creative realms, communication skills, and skills in formulating plans and making decisions.

Most of all, education has to make a conscious effort to inspire love for knowledge for its own sake, not because knowledge is necessary for prestige or even survival. There is great emotion attached to great ideas, and it takes an inspiring teacher to preserve their vitality. There are too many able students who feel that the schools have dehumanized them by labeling them "human resources" being processed in the same way that "natural resources" are processed. They feel "discovered," "refined," and "channelized" for the betterment of society without enjoying the privilege of intellectual freedom and self-determination. They do not want to be manipulated at school; they want to learn how to consume and produce ideas and to discover themselves in the process.

Design instructional strategies to be prescriptive to individual capacities and learning styles. Measuring skill deficits is a far more precise task than determining the teaching strategies and perceptual modalities that are most appropriate for each child. This must be done before it is possible to implement individualized, diagnostic, prescriptive teaching. One attempt at filling in the gap is the development of a *Taxonomy of Instructional Treatments* (Tannenbaum and Cohen, 1967) which gives the classroom teacher specific guidelines for diagnosing learning needs and styles and for analyzing instructional methods and materials. It forces the teacher to become more aware of the great array of teaching behaviors that can be employed in the classroom and how many of them she has yet to add to her methodological arsenal. It allows the teacher to determine which basic skill and related subskills the child must master; at what difficulty level the content can be learned; the communications input that galvanizes maximum receptivity; the communications output that conducts maximum responsiveness; the instructional media most likely to accommodate behavioral needs; the instructional mode or strategy that engages attention and fixes interest in the learning task; and the instructional method of grouping to provide the most supportive, distraction-free environment for learning.

The taxonomy systematizes the teacher's stylistic repertoire by classifying the behavioral options open to her during the instructional act. To make these styles operative, it is necessary to create and assemble instructional materials that will plug appropriate content into every specified teaching style. Once the teacher has determined precisely what skill deficits handicap the child, she elects the preferred instructional content and teaching behavior from an array outlined in the taxonomy. She is then guided to the teaching aids that fit her requirement by the taxonomy code system which forms the indexing scheme for the materials. The task of the curriculum specialist is to keep the library of instructional aids stocked in such a manner as to fulfill the content and teacher behavior specifications suggested by the taxonomy. Thus, a diagnosis of individual learning needs is directly applicable to an educational catalog that provides sources of methods and materials to match the diagnosis. The result is diagnostic teaching and a broad diversification of approaches to instruction.

5. *Build up the teacher's competencies as a modifier of social behavior.*

Although behavior modification is enormously difficult for the teacher to accomplish in the classroom, it is not an excuse for shirking the attempt. Many children come to school with behavioral codes that are not only offensive but self-destructive as well. Any amount of rationalization concerning subcultural pluralism will not explain away the seriousness of the problem. What makes matters even more complicated is the fact that different personal attributes are adaptive in different social settings, so the need is to tease out the commonalities and focus on them.

One of the most neglected areas of the curriculum that has to do with behavior modification is character education. Kohlberg (1966) has formulated six hierarchical stages in the development of moral judgments among children and adolescents. It ranges from confusing the valuation of human life with that of physical objects to a belief in the sacredness of human life as representing a universal human value of respect for the individual. Kohlberg suggests that stimulating the development of moral judgment is not accomplished through exhortation in the conventional moral virtues. Instead, the teacher has to inspire the child's own predilection for reaching closure on moral issues. If the child is uninvolved because the teacher's lessons have all the answers, he will lose interest and make no moral commitment himself.

Introduce character education and training in human relations on a wider scale in the schools. Much of the work in character education has concentrated on the improvement of interpersonal sensitivities among people living and working together. An example of such a program is the one developed by Berlin and Wyckoff (1963). The stated goals are to deepen one's ability to be more aware of his own feelings and the feelings of others; to enhance one's appreciation of his own potentialities; to increase flexibility in both the emotional and the cognitive aspects of behavior; and to develop the ability to apply these new behavior patterns to live situations. In the first three (of a total of ten) sessions, it is pointed out that each participant is responsible in some measure for what the other will get out of this experience, and the main emphasis of the content of these sessions is on things that the individual can do that will help his partner get the most from the program. Attention is immediately focused on feelings as contrasted to facts, opinions, and problems, and on ways in which one may respond to another person's feelings. Participants learn that it is possible to respond to another person's expressed emotions in ways that will not make him feel foolish, ashamed, or inferior, but that such responses are neither common nor easy to learn. They are also shown that it is possible to allow another to have his feelings even when he does not argue with the other person's opinions and that in such cases hiding his disagreement is not necessary and often not desirable. Finally, it is pointed out that people can become more aware of how others feel by being alert to the sentiments that lie behind the questions and statements of other persons. Each of these points is developed in detail through multiple illustrations, practice at making the necessary discriminations, and various exercises ranging from examination of their own conversations to enacting short dramas in role-playing exercises.

The next three sessions are concerned with the relationship between the expression of feelings and self-awareness and self-understanding. It is emphasized that open expression of feelings is not always appropriate, but that advances in self-understanding occur most readily in situations in which true feelings are not kept hidden.

Beginning with the seventh session, the program presents a series of concepts which are designed to stimulate the participants to look at themselves and their relationships with others from a new viewpoint. In each case they are prompted to stop and examine themselves and others in the light of the particular concepts involved. Definitions of self-concept and self-ideal are introduced, and a distinction is made between the motivations for self-preservation and self-actualization. It is also pointed out that there are things people do which serve the purpose of shifting conversation away from themselves. These are identified as being "protective reactions." Examples include talking about something far away, "lecturing," and clinging unnecessarily to concepts in the program itself. These activities lead up to the final session, during which examination is made of the learning process through which individual change takes place. A distinction is made between intellectually understanding and "internalizing" a concept. This is seen as a gradual process which will continue after the program is finished.

Somewhat similar work with elementary and high school children has been conducted by Ralph Ojemann for some thirty years. His working hypothesis has been that if a teacher learns to understand the causes of behavior, his attitude toward the children will change and he will deal with children's behavior more satisfactorily. Objective testing of this hypothesis was conducted (Ojemann and Wilkinson, 1939), and the results sustained it. This investigation created interest in the capabilities of children to learn something about the dynamic approaches to behavior and to apply them in their relations with parents, teachers, and other adults. Several concepts were introduced into the curriculum, including the dynamics of multiple causation, the anatomy of motivation, and the relativistic nature of values. The instructional materials have been prepared in units to supplement sections of standard texts. These materials reorient the textbook content in terms of motivation and causation so that the understanding of behavior is made simpler. Thus, for example, the study of community structure in the seventh grade is supplemented by an analysis of community problems in terms of the dynamics of human behavior. In the preschool and primary grades, simple plays have been devised in which children can dramatize different ways of dealing with behavior which they meet in their child's world. Much of the work has focused on helping children become better aware of the principles of social causality (Ojemann, 1959), and the elaborate program material and evaluative measures deserve much wider testing in schools in which character education is not emphasized.

Add time and emphasis to social education in the high school. Once teachers develop a systematic, sequential methodology for dealing with personality variables it may result in some dramatic changes in the school curriculum, especially for older children. Preadolescents and adolescents can make good use of the steadily improving teaching aids to study the academic subjects independently, thus allowing for more time to concentrate on the nonintellective aspects of the curriculum. In high school it would mean cutting back sharply on the number of hours devoted to teacher-led lessons in selected subject matter, with self-instruction assignments that are not bound to classroom scheduling making up the difference. The rest of the day could then be spent in intensive counseling sessions, guided service to the community through local agencies, sex education, training in group dynamics, discussions of youth's quest for identity and personal aspirations, and an orientation to the realities of the growth process in adolescence.

6. *Train and deputize indigenous nonprofessionals to become a task force of educators in their communities.*

A recent study (Tannenbaum, 1968) of a program involving the training of nonprofessionals to instruct socially disadvantaged parents in methods of tutoring their young children in beginning reading demonstrated that this kind of intervention can be an effective weapon against educational retardation among young slum children. If repeated assessments confirm the initial positive results, the practicality and flexibility of the model should stimulate replication efforts. The program's cost is relatively low by school budget standards. A single well-trained, well-paid teacher can multiply his efforts with the help of the nonprofessional aides by providing indirect services to many times the number of pupils he ordinarily reaches, at a supplementary cost determined by hourly rates paid unskilled workers. This necessitates a role change for the professional. Instead of spending his time teaching children, he devotes it to training the aides and supervising their work in the field. If the expense were computed in terms of tutorial time provided for the children, the cost per hour would be relatively minimal.

Perhaps the most promising feature of a well-planned educational program utilizing nonprofessionals is its adaptability in attacking hitherto inaccessible roots of problems plaguing ghetto schools. With the help of nonprofessionals, the educator can gain access to the home long before the child is of school age and breathe new meaning into early intervention. His aim would be to head off the deleterious effects of minimal succorant care in infancy, provide an environment of optimal cognitive stimulation at the earliest stages of life, and build the young child's experiential background in preparation for learning.

The availability of nonprofessionals makes it possible to plan on a broad scale a number of ambitious programs that hardly exist today, even on a small scale. For example, there would be some practical purpose to analyzing the medical and psychological literature on the specific deprivations that seem to retard normal growth and extrapolating some guidelines for designing clear-cut, sequential parent-child activities in the home. Such a curriculum would also include making practical use of information regarding the scope of experiences afforded children in homes where the environment for school readiness is challenging and supportive. The aides could be trained to utilize some of this information in helping mothers enrich their child-rearing practices and thus prepare them for school learning. This might be a first step toward testing the hypothesis that early intervention programs stand the best chance of success if they (1) intervene as early as the child's infancy and (2) attempt to modify the home environment during the child's preschool years.

Another promising aspect of a program that trains and deputizes indigenous nonprofessionals to serve their own communities is its contribution to the social structure of the inner city. Usually, efforts aimed at rehabilitating ghetto life are administered by people who are not themselves identified with the target community. The teacher in the slum school lives outside the ghetto area, as does the antipoverty social worker or the physician in the local free dispensary. Most of those who were born in the ghettos and have "made it" socially, economically, or professionally have long since moved out to more advantaged surroundings, thus leaving behind a critical shortage of talent and buying power. Under these circumstances, a self-help movement is virtually impossible. The familiar gambit for filling the ghetto's skill and money void is to infuse it with huge job training programs; but the training is generally restricted to blue-collar skills which guarantee little status mobility even if such jobs should succeed in surviving the inroads of automation. Preparing adults to assist professionals in attacking the problems of their own ghettos may contribute something of permanent value to community life. Talents cultivated among the nonprofessional aides will remain in the community as an *internal* force for reducing its dependency relationship with the outside world.

The aides' behavioral orientation toward the target groups is often different from that of the "outside" professional serving the same population. Informal observations of the work of nonprofessionals indicate that they are less patient with uncooperative clients, less tolerant of their hardships in participating rehabilitative programs, and quicker to recommend dropping difficult clients than their professional counterparts often are. Some talk forcibly and unpretentiously to parents about their children's progress and occasionally have to be restrained by the supervisors from acting impatiently when problems arise. Yet, it is quite possible that the client from the slum is exceptionally receptive to the indigenous aide's ministrations despite the blunt familiarity that occasionally exists between them. Similarity in social background and community identification may effect a reduction of social distance between aide and client that professionals from the outside cannot accomplish, even with the greatest measure of good will.

The feeling of pride and self-fulfillment among nonprofessionals engaged in educating others is one of the most important by-products of such a program. The aides know they are doing a meaningful job, one that may someday carry with it special prestige in the community. In addition to offering direct tutorial help at home and at school they can be trained to assist the professional educator in bringing slum parents into closer contact with the school. Their job would be to galvanize parents to participate more actively in school activities that bear directly on their children's progress. Experience with educational programs involving working with slum families indicates that clients seek their help in many matters pertaining to the social, economic, medical, and physical conditions of the home. The aides therefore need some training in methods of handling the multitude of depressing confidences shared with them in their visits to the family. However, care should be taken not to divert the aides from concentrating on their primary assignments. It is important to keep in mind that an aide cannot be a generalist in the helping services. He must be trained to do a specific job and to avoid dissipating his energies by attempting to do singlehandedly what can be accomplished only through massive, collaborative services administered by large cadres of professionals and nonprofessionals.

7. *Establish Parent and Child Centers to service communities in every state in the Union.*

The Committee strongly endorses the cooperative work of several governmental agencies in designing Parent and Child Centers (Office of Economic Opportunity, 1967) to offer day care, medical services, mental health consultation, and educational programs for disadvantaged families. Although the structure and organization of these agencies should vary in accordance with the needs of the populations they serve, it is recommended that they accommodate children from the earliest years of life to a maximum age of eight or nine, and that no child leave the Center program until he shows evidence of succeeding in school. For those who are handicapped in their mental development, there is need for special compensatory provisions from a staff trained to deal with various forms of exceptionality. The entire Center program should be geared not only to intervention but also to ongoing self-evaluation and longitudinal research activity.

Some of the programmatic developments that are essential to the Parent and Child Center could be described as follows:

Provide assistance to underprivileged families. Parental participation is mandatory if the Center program can hope to succeed. The children enrolled in the Center are potentially quite different from the families that enroll them. They have the capacity to become intellectually more advanced, socially more mobile, and personally more self-confident about controlling their future. The mere fact that the Center can be a "hothouse" for nurturing their children's talents and ambitions may create serious anxieties in many of the client families. In contrast to the homes from which they come, the Center would encourage children to ask probing questions about their environment; it would try to fill their hours with serious, organized, productive activity; and it would attempt to build up their conceptually oriented modes of expression while reducing their reliance on motoric tendencies. It is therefore necessary to alleviate as much as possible whatever conflicts may develop between life styles and expectations of the home and those of the Center. The concern here is not only for the mental health of the families but also for the need to help parents understand and support the Center program. To achieve this, it is necessary for Center administrators, child care workers, teachers, and researchers to establish meaningful and positive relationships with the children's parents. A long-term relationship with the child care workers should be a basic feature of the program. A team working with each family should remain intact in order to minimize the confusion and frustration brought on by changes in helping personnel and the resulting breakdown of communications within the team. The Center should be open evenings and on weekends as a facility which parents can use regularly for themselves, for recreation, continued schooling, and social brokerage. In addition, a public health nurse and social worker are needed to keep in touch with the family to help solve or ameliorate the problems they face in maintaining a healthy social climate in the home.

Provide intensive medical and dental care for children. An integral part of the program is the comprehensive health care rendered to each child by a staff of pediatricians, dentists, and nurses available at all times. Infirmary facilities should accommodate children well enough to be moved from their homes but needing more intensive, more specialized care than can be provided by the family. A good deal of research and experimentation is needed to determine the best design for the public health facility at the center. It is apparent that initial contacts with the families of most of the children need to be made during the mother's pregnancy, and careful records should be kept of prenatal as well as postnatal health data. Although clinical facilities are currently available to families in depressed areas, these facilities are routinely used primarily for emergency care. Little effort is made to develop a program that makes use of the latest knowledge in preventive medicine, and there is rarely a continuing, close relationship between the clinic staff and the clients. It is hoped, therefore, that the medical and dental care offered by the Center will make up for these deficiencies in public health services for the socially disadvantaged.

Provide elaborate school readiness services to children. The Center staff representing the various helping services should exercise independent control over the total Center program, but the local schools ought to have a hand in planning educational intervention, just as the local medical center is needed to assist in planning health services. A strong educational program would help fill gaps in the child's readiness experiences and also reinforce the work of the schools. These services cannot have their full impact if they are circumscribed within the Center; they have to be carried into the home even if it means stimulating the family's willingness to accept them. Substantively, they ought to consist of more than just improvised play and companionship. Since there is enough research evidence to show that young children, even during infancy, are clearly affected by the ways in which they interact with their immediate environment (Horowitz, 1968), it is fruitful to experiment with educational intervention from the earliest days of the child's life. What would hopefully emerge from such research is a curriculum that makes the total environment a facilitator of educational growth. Specifically, the curriculum would emphasize the following programmatic ideas:

a. *Improved mothering practices.* These involve instructions to mothers and would-be mothers on the preferred ways of handling infants, fondling them, providing their nutritional needs, and protecting them from disease and infection. The object is to enhance the mother's awareness of the child's need for succorant care during the earliest period of his life. The slum home is frequently so overcrowded and poorly furnished that the parent cannot give enough attention to the infant under distraction-free circumstances. She therefore needs considerable help in planning time and space allowances for the infant, as well as many specific techniques of child care. These include learning some of the basic hygienic principles and how to apply them in dingy, unhygienic surroundings.

b. *Early cognitive stimulation.* This includes the elaborate exercises such as those developed by Uzgiris and Hunt (1966) and by Gordon (1967) in their work with infants and toddlers. Stimulus activities include simple games involving sensorimotor adaptiveness, reaction to sound, language comprehension, and various forms of symbolic discrimination. Instructions to parents are designed with "cookbook" simplicity and can be administered with the help of trained nonprofessionals. Parents see the purposes of the activities clearly and enjoy watching their children's responses to the games. The effects of early cognitive stimulation on later intellectual development remain yet to be assessed, but large-scale experimentation along these lines deserves encouragement and support.

c. *Experiential enrichment.* This involves exposure of preschool children to meaningful places and persons around them in order to help build their language skills, their power of conceptualization, and their range of interests. The slum child's home and neighborhood offer a great wealth of differentiated stimuli that can improve school readiness. The child can learn a great deal from labeling and classifying appurtenances in his home; he can begin to appreciate exciting features of his social world by getting to know what community workers do for him and his neighbors; he can become oriented to language symbolism by distinguishing the shapes, colors, and sizes of written signs he sees in his surroundings; and he can begin to appreciate the codes of social behavior he will eventually adopt by understanding the ground rules governing relationships among people he sees every day. In order to bring meaning to these experiences, the child needs mentors who can help him organize them and extrapolate generalizations that are both challenging and useful.

d. *Expanded school readiness experiences.* These are built around an elaborate program of diagnosing cognitive and behavioral deficits among children who require greater readiness for language experiences in the first grade. According to Lesser and Lazarus (1967) the treatment aspect of such a program consists of three phases: (1) learning how to learn, which involves the teacher's giving specific training in impulse control and the development of attention to visual and auditory directions; (2) beginning steps toward formal learning which approximates the readiness experiences of the regular first grade, but with materials that are far more structured and elaborate; and (3) formal learning with the help of more conventional methods and materials as the child shows less need for special kinds of intervention.

e. *School orientation for parents.* This involves introducing parents to the power structure of the school, the organization of classes, the content of the curriculum, the teacher's instructional methods, the school's expectations, and the parents' role in influencing school policy. The school world is a maze to parents from disadvantaged neighborhoods, and they lack the know-how to make its staff serve their children's needs. They are not clear on what they can rightfully expect of the various officials responsible for the school curriculum, nor are they likely to receive and accept much opportunity to find out. Once they learn how the school functions and where they stand in relation to its program, they may be in a better position to reinforce the professional's efforts in behalf of their children and make education instrumental in serving their aspirations.

f. *Strengthened press for achievement in the home.* This involves systematic efforts to help parents set standards of excellence that are compatible with the child's intellectual capabilities. Parents should be instructed on what they can rightfully expect of the child in his performance at school and helped in formulating some realistic aspirations on the basis of that information. The home needs to provide the child with meaningful rewards for intellectual accomplishment as well as the necessary enrichment experiences that make such rewards more reachable. In these ways, the disadvantaged home will be able to create an environment for learning that is fully competitive with that of the more affluent home.

8. *Enhance the vocational readiness of all school-age youth.*

Schools have long acknowledged the critical importance of preparing the adolescent for the job world in order to build his self-image as a productive member of society. The communication and socialization skills that are taught at school are important to the worker on his job, regardless of whether it is on the farm, in the factory, or in the office. Those students who continue on to college and aspire to white-collar work are especially trained at school to qualify for the kinds of employment they will seek. However, those who lack the academic aptitudes and interests necessary for higher education or for the high school diploma often find themselves poorly prepared in any marketable occupational skills. These marginal students are caught between a school program that rarely provides adequate vocational education and a world of work that hardly offers much training. The only hope for these students is to bring together the resources of the school, the business community, and the public and private service agencies and work out a comprehensive program that will adjust a variety of job preparation resources to the capacities and aspirations of each adolescent. Salient features of such a program would be as follows:

Provide vocational preparation at school. In view of the sharp criticism of vocational high schools as dumping grounds for failing and unwanted students—and where the dropout rate is more than 60 percent higher than in academic high schools—it is suggested that exploratory work courses be offered to all students in all high schools (see Kohler, 1962; Public Education Association Committee on Education, Guidance, and Work, 1963). These experiences would hopefully help the adolescent make wiser career choices by the time he graduates. Training in specific vocational skills would be deferred until after school completion, allowing more undergraduate time to be spent in much-needed basic academic skills. This amounts to an elimination of the dual academic and vocational school system, with the most desirable features of both preserved in a comprehensive-type institution.

Expand work-study provisions in the schools. Opportunities to earn and learn simultaneously may convince many students that it pays to stay in school from both financial and educational standpoints. Such programs should be planned in three stages. First, pupils of junior high school age work completely under teacher supervision either in special workshops at school or in selected places in the community. During this time they would be taught such basic work habits as punctuality, courtesy, and responsibility. A second stage is part-time work with employers in private and public enterprises under close supervision, with some training at school. Finally, the student enters full-time employment while continuing to receive limited guidance from the school-based counselors.

Expand out-of-school opportunities for vocational preparation. There are young people who simply cannot or will not function at school but need certain basic skills to enter the job market. The school is out of the picture insofar as special assistance is concerned, and it remains for public and private community agencies to take a huge share of the responsibility.

Among the various services that can be offered in community-based programs are physical and psychological testing, counseling on work habits and job opportunities, referral to special training centers, and job placement. Many occupational tryouts should be set up by local governments in their own offices and work centers to get youth started on socially useful projects. Arrangements should also be made for training adolescents both in apprenticeship positions in private industry and in specially organized production and service centers run on a profit-seeking basis by the trainees under experienced supervision. These work-training programs should be supplemented with tutoring in basic language and number skills because so many of the young people placed in such programs would need them desperately.

Support training and retraining programs in private industry. A growing number of businessmen are beginning to realize that they cannot look passively at the economic problem of unskilled, impoverished youth and allow the schools and social agencies to carry full responsibility. These young people are potential customers who can become chronic relief cases and heavy tax burdens upon society unless prospective employers provide some assistance. There are, of course, several calculated risks involved. Singling out poorly educated adolescents for special opportunities in industry may eventually induce would-be school graduates to discontinue school. Furthermore, if the marginal students prove to be serious employment risks, these well-meaning efforts by private businessmen may backfire to the embarrassment of all concerned. Nevertheless, it is important that the private sector become one of several training grounds for youth preparing to enter the job world and that the schools serve as an available resource to help design the academic and social learning aspects of these programs.

Savitsky (1965) has suggested several practical guidelines for classroom teachers to follow in order to facilitate vocational preparedness among children and youth. They are as follows:

Personalize instruction. Bring the student into focus by making learning content relevant to his own experiences and aspirations. What is of practical interest to a child from a disadvantaged background may be quite different from what appeals to children who live in favored environments.

Orient the child to job experiences and the world of work. The disadvantaged pupil is job conscious and seeking a short-range goal that holds some promise of economic stability. Anything that helps prepare him for the world of work is meaningful to him. This basic interest may be used as a medium for improving instruction in the basic skills as well as preparing him to be a successful job seeker.

Use current events to stimulate the acquisition of meaningful ideas. All pupils need to benefit from general education, not just the skills that are of practical, immediate value. Teachers can capitalize on the disadvantaged pupils' concern with the here-and-now world by introducing present-day problems as a springboard toward formulating more generalized concepts.

Adapt or arrange test materials to fit reading levels, interests, and needs. Most of the existing textbooks do not take into consideration the special backgrounds, vocabulary, and interests of disadvantaged children. These pupils need content that is more relevant to their everyday lives and with which they can readily identify. It may be simpler to elicit responsiveness by developing textbook content at their interest levels without overburdening them with complex language structure.

Cross subject area lines to develop course content. Fragmentation of instruction at the junior high school level and beyond may, in effect, depersonalize learning for the socially disadvantaged, and thereby discourage them from making progress. If teachers could operate as teams, pooling information and relating course content, the students might come to realize that their learning interests are not being neglected.

Concentrate on oral communication skills. Verbal interaction is one of the key elements of socialized behavior. Teachers often discourage the development of oral communication skills among disadvantaged children when they sense the difficulties these pupils have in utilizing them. The teacher gives up prematurely, and the child is afflicted with a permanent handicap.

Work for standards. Disadvantaged pupils are capable of learning and should be required and encouraged to accept standards of accomplishment. This is necessary to build the child's self-esteem in the school world. However, these responsibilities should be the kind that are attainable by the student; otherwise, failure may be compounded and he may even be discouraged from coming to grips with those learning tasks that he is capable of negotiating.

Organize short but achievable units. These shorter units facilitate mastery by gradation and posit achievable goals for pupils whose attention spans are short and whose work habits are poorly organized.

Build in elements of success. Positive reinforcement of correct learning responses can be a powerful encouragement for continued concentration and learning success. The disadvantaged child rarely experiences success in and out of school and is therefore often unable to assess his true capabilities. Providing him with meaningful success experiences can help counteract the debilitating effects of repeated frustration.

Provide for exploration and discovery, including learning how to think. Help these students develop their own strategies for problem solving which they can utilize independently and with skill. Once the child has developed a method of attack, with the help of a talented teacher, he will reach out into worlds of ambiguity and know how to achieve clarity by himself.

9. *Incorporate into the curriculum a carefully designed program to combat racism and to promote the liberalist tradition.*

The existence of racism in American society antedates the establishment of an independent republic on these shores. As the *Report of the National Advisory Commission on Civil Disorders* (1968) forcefully demonstrates, there are two Americas, unequal in power, prestige, education, and economic status. The problem is not simply that of inequities in our opportunity structure or a lack of complete openness in what is supposed to be an open society. The fundamental malady is the castelike conditions in a nation that professes human equality while clinging to a belief that the white majority is racially superior to the black minority. These attitudes pervade every sector of our social structure, including the schools, where educators and students go about their work under an assumption of black inferiority in learning potential, which becomes a self-fulfilling prophecy.

Despite the legislation passed in recent years to support a great variety of programs designed to facilitate interracial harmony, the cleavage between whites and blacks has rarely been wider. A recent Harris survey (1968) revealed that nearly three-quarters of both whites and blacks say they would make personal sacrifices to improve Negro living conditions, but no more than 39 percent were willing to pay higher taxes to rebuild the ghettos. Nine out of ten whites think black people live in miserable conditions, but fewer than half favor open housing legislation. Despite the fact that nearly 80 percent of whites believe the inequality for Negroes in the United States hurts the country's image abroad, as many as 69 percent of the whites also think that Negroes are asking for more than they are ready to absorb. Shortly before Dr. Martin Luther King's death, whites and Negroes showed alarming signs of polarizing into two armed camps. Some 55 percent of all whites and 32 percent of the Negroes had guns in their homes in March 1968. When asked if they would use their guns against other people in case of a riot, 51 percent of all gun owners said they would, a sharp rise from a comparable 29 percent the previous August. Yet, in spite of the growing signs of racial separatism and hostility, the majority of whites simply do not feel that white racism is a major root cause of black disorders, while a majority of Negroes feel that it is.

Among the most unfortunate by-products of racism have been extremist reactions that threaten the liberal tradition in this country. A growing number of people who are sickened by the American caste system, but who accept the basic characteristics of the existing political and economic structure and believe that the government should be an active instrument for improving the lives of its citizens, have been lured into supporting movements that seek to break down the democratic processes for achieving desirable social change. Under a camouflage of avowed racial egalitarianism, the sponsors of these radical movements violate the liberal tradition that accommodates open forum, persuasion, negotiation, consensus, and conciliation when they promote civil disobedience with impunity or violence in order to advance their Cause. Noble as their sentiments surely are, it is self-righteously hypocritical for them to preach social justice while slurring and overriding the rights of others who disagree with their methods of attaining it, especially in instances when the others constitute a majority. In the long run, they can nullify the gains they seek by destroying the social order they want to improve.

In an era of racism and counterracism, violence and counterviolence, and reactionary antidemocracy countered by radical antidemocracy, educators cannot sit back and assume an attitude of noninvolvement. The school is responsible for preserving the liberal tradition through active, programmatic intervention in the classroom and in the community. It is difficult for school-age children and youth to appreciate the obedience of law as anything other than a practical, expedient way of preventing social chaos if they are not exposed to the moral and ethical bases of law. Yet, constitutional law is hardly given much attention in social studies programs at the precollege levels. Children need to know the political principles that dictate public policy and how threats to these principles constitute threats to liberalism. They also have to understand how the mass media can be powerful forces to promote or distort justice. The *Report of the National Advisory Commission on Civil Disorders* (1968) dramatically illustrates the inciting effects of radio news commentary on civil disorders:

> News presented on local "rock" stations seldom constitutes much more than terse headline items which may startle or frighten but seldom inform. Radio disc jockeys and those who preside over the popular "talk" shows keep a steady patter of information going over the air. When a city is beset by civil strife, this patter can both inform transistor-radio-carrying young people where the action is, and terrify their elders and much of the white community. "Burn, baby, burn," the slogan of the Watts Riot was inadvertently originated by a radio disc jockey (p. 376).

Part of the information-filtering process has to do with the appreciation of semantic shadings of verbal messages that are received. Children need to understand how to recognize propagandistic coloration in an age when public issues are often debated in a no-holds-barred atmosphere. Even some of the arguments supporting perfectly desirable causes are antirational, but they are persuasive because children are not sensitized to evaluate content that is presented in dazzling form. As a result, many uninformed points of view have a contagion effect and build into a massive anti-intellectual movement that threatens the very foundations of centers of inquiry, which schools are supposed to be. Teachers owe children an opportunity to build reading and listening skills that reduce their vulnerability to deception by words. There are instructional materials now in existence that can be adopted or adapted for this purpose.

10. *Establish the position of child development specialist to provide supportive services in the schools.*

Educators generally concede that the mental health services currently available in the schools are not sufficient to accommodate the many children who need them. This is not simply a manpower problem but also one of making qualitative changes in the way the services are designed and administered. A new type of professional is required—a child development specialist—who is capable of bridging the gap between the community and the school, bringing together the child and the curriculum, consulting on learning and behavior of children with school personnel, communicating and translating the concepts of the traditional mental health professions and services to the teacher, working with the teacher in enabling him to work with the students as a group, and working with parents on a variety of child-rearing problems.

One of the most important skills of the child development specialist is that of facilitating the educational development of all children by helping to improve the conditions of learning in the schools. He should therefore be well trained to understand the factors affecting academic achievement, interpersonal skills, and emotional stability. He should also learn observational techniques, how to use knowledge of feedback in order to effect tension reduction, how to intervene in a system as opposed to tinkering with it, and how to effect change as a result of introducing himself into the system. Thus, he plays the role of making the system more flexible while helping the child develop competence in handling the demands of the system.

The child development specialist should be able to deal with a range of difficulties presented by the teacher, the child, and the school. He should be in the same school every day and sensitive to the school as a complex social structure. As a consultant to the teacher, he needs to be oriented to the realities of the classroom and to the way the teacher interprets these realities. Most of all, he should understand theory and research on child development and its application to the educative process.

The extent of training required of the child development specialist depends on the kinds of competence required by the role he is to play in the school. In some instances, a bachelor's degree may be appropriate, and in others, doctoral training may be necessary. Generally, however, he needs a two- or three-year program beyond the baccalaureate which then extends into in-service training. A typical training program is designed primarily but not exclusively to enable teachers and nonteachers with backgrounds in the behavioral sciences to fill the newly designed role. They would attend regular seminars dealing with the problems of understanding the school and the community. From there, the trainees would move on to a clarification of the child development specialist's job responsibilities in relation to the organization of the school system. Finally, they would engage in formal academic coursework organized around the interrelatedness of knowledge about human functioning. Having completed the program, the trainee would combine some of the characteristics of the school social worker, the school psychologist, and the guidance counselor, without necessarily replacing them in the staff organization.

11. *Organize a series of residential remedial schools for educationally and behaviorally disordered children.*

Perhaps the most advanced model for such a program is represented by Re-ED, which is defined as a "project for the re-education of emotionally disturbed children" (Hobbs, 1967, p. 340).

Two residential schools currently offer this program and are staffed for the most part by teacher-counselors carefully selected from among candidates who have experience in working with children and have completed a special nine-month training program. A staff social worker develops community resources in the interest of the child and his family, and his Re-ED teacher maintains close communication with the child's regular school. Supporting the professional staff is a group of consultants from education, social work, psychiatry, and psychology.

The program is based on several principles, including the assumption that laws of learning can explain the acquisition of deviant behavior patterns and play a key role in therapy. The child is seen as having learned to construe the world in a manner that will lead to his rejection from that world and as having acquired ways of interacting with his environment that may be immediately rewarding but ultimately defeating. What the child needs, then, is a reeducation that will lead to more effective functioning. Thus, treatment veers away from techniques that derive from "dynamic" psychology. Such psychoanalytic concepts as transference, regression, interpretation, and insight do not play an important part in the program. Instead, it emphasizes the following processes:

The development of trust. The disturbed child often finds it difficult to learn from adults because he assumes they are deceptive and unpredictable. In his relationship with them, he generally anticipates the kinds of behavior that are calculated to hurt him. Reeducation, therefore, emphasizes the development of trust and understanding between child and adult, so that the child could benefit from that relationship in ways he considers vital to his own growth and happiness. The manner in which the teacher-counselor relates to the child is basic to the entire program, since any formal teacher intervention techniques are useless unless they are administered in a climate of trust.

The gaining of confidence. In an achievement-minded society, the ability to perform well in socially approved activities is essential for one's self-respect and for gaining respect from others. It is unrealistic to hope that the child can cultivate a complete personal identity or gain social status without being capable of some kind of productive work. Accepting him for what he is involves also accepting him for what he can do. It is therefore not surprising to find that children with learning handicaps in the Re-ED program tend to improve in behavior and attitude when they make gains in basic communication skills. The cause-and-effect relationship between learning competence and general adjustment is not clear, but experience in the program seems to indicate that there are interaction effects. Each facilitates the other to an extent that is often not appreciated by therapists working with deviant children.

The control of symptoms. Although psychotherapists minimize the importance of symptoms in favor of underlying causes, the Re-ED program orients its staff to take more serious cognizance of symptoms and the need to change them. Some manifest behaviors alienate the child from other children or from adults and can be the source of great disturbance. He can benefit greatly from identifying the habits that stand in the way of normal development and making the attempt to eliminate or change them for his own ultimate benefit.

Learning middle-class values. Whereas the well-adjusted child can afford to adopt certain unconventional values and behaviors in a predominantly middle-class milieu, the deviant child cannot risk the added social strain. It is therefore necessary to create an environment which will help him conform to middle-class standards of good manners, cleanliness, good language, achievement orientation, and interest in books. It is not always easy to accomplish this while maintaining the child's individuality and need for personal identity. However, the image he presents to the world about him is too critical a factor of his rehabilitation to be overlooked.

Gaining cognitive control over today and tomorrow. Although the Re-ED program has not placed primary emphasis on insight therapy, it does regard communication skills as vital to the symbolic representation of experience and the mechanism for self-initiated behavior control. It enables the children to meet together and, under the guidance of the teacher-counselor, discuss the events of the day, evaluate them, and make plans for the immediate future. Talking things over means taking one step closer to the control of events and the strengthening of self-regulatory systems.

The development of community ties. Most children in the program come from families that are hostile to the community power system and are not recognized enough to influence it. The child learns that local agencies exist either to patronize or to hurt him rather than to provide assistance. Part of his education, then, is to learn how these institutions can be instrumental in enriching his life in many essential ways. He is therefore introduced into the work of the local settlement houses, museums, playgrounds, churches, libraries, and recreational facilities. He learns how these services are organized, who runs them, and how local residents can have a voice in formulating their policies.

Physical experience as a basis for greater awareness of self. The idea of building confidence in the physical self and appreciating its power and skill is an important component of the Re-ED program. The contribution of physical skill to psychological fitness has hardly been investigated, but there is a good bit of conjecture that the relationship is real and strong. The program therefore places a good deal of emphasis on sports, clay modeling, building, and even some acrobatics.

The knowing of joy. The treatment of deviant behavior should emphasize not only the avoidance of pain or discomfort, but also skill in developing joy in the child's experience. Planning pleasure-giving experiences is an important part of the program, and it requires sensitivity on the part of the teacher-counselor regarding the ways the individual child reacts to such stimuli. What may seem pleasure-giving to the adult is not necessarily regarded as such by the child, nor does the adult always appreciate how seemingly inconsequential experiences can be memorably pleasurable to children. Those who have experienced the pain and occasional horror of ego-damaging events in life should be given the opportunity to build a personal history of joyful occasions to help build strength and add purpose to life.

Some Concluding Legislative Considerations

The most obvious problem in considering federal legislation to upgrade education and mental health in the schools is that of exercising leverage to influence educational policies that are under local control. One way of accomplishing this is to evaluate the programs that are federally funded and locally administered and call attention to the degree of their success. The Title I program of the Elementary and Secondary Education Act makes it possible for the United States Office of Education to conduct that kind of monitoring and dissemination of research outcomes. Another point of direct leverage derives from the National Defense Education Act of 1958, which enabled the federal government to become deeply involved with teacher education. However, that piece of legislation was concerned primarily with the teacher's mastery of subject matter rather than with teaching strategies and the structure of the school. The newly approved Education Professions Development Act encompasses many more aspects of teacher training and includes in its target group various kinds of personnel on school staffs.

Thus, the federal government is making headway toward influencing the course of American education without violating the principle of local control. With this power comes the responsibility of asserting leadership through the encouragement and assessment of promising innovation. The following legislative considerations may suggest further ways to exercise that power:

Present compulsory education laws established in the states may soon become obsolete and require major revision at the urging of federal authorities. The requirement that all children attend school from about age six to sixteen was established by an industrialized democracy that could not tolerate an illiterate citizenry. But societal conditions have changed, bringing on new necessities for survival. The goal of basic literacy for all has virtually been reached, but the level of communication skills necessary for social and economic survival is much higher than it ever was, and significant segments of the population cannot measure up even after spending the usual ten- or twelve-year period of their lives at school.

Currently, the greatest hope for averting school failure is being vested in early intervention programs. The conceptual designs of these readiness programs have begun to vary widely and will vary even more as additional federal research monies become available. Justification for the massive preschool efforts derives from the hypothesis that human potentialities are most amenable to modification during the years preceding school entrance (Bloom, 1964). Experimentation is still in its early stages, so there is not enough evidence to confirm this hypothesis. However, it is possible that at least some of the preventive measures being tested in preschool programs will reduce the skill deficits and the rates of progressive retardation among the socially disadvantaged. The evidence may even show that unless ghetto children can receive certain kinds of help at a specified early age a large majority of them may be seriously handicapped at school.

Significant outcomes of research on preschool education can suggest the need for reexamination of public policy on compulsory schooling. Huge outlays of federal funds are making this experimentation possible. It would be unfortunate if the returns for such an investment were distributed only among those who asked for it. As long as education prior to age five or six is voluntary, not all of the children who need it desperately will reap its benefits. If empirical data prove the necessity of lowering the age of schooling in order to give large numbers of children a chance to succeed in their studies, then there is no more reason to reject the possibility of making preschool education compulsory, even from the moment of birth, than there is to make inoculation against fatal childhood diseases a matter of choice. This does not mean that children have to be wrested from their homes and educated in schoolrooms, thus leading to possible estrangement from parents. On the contrary, a successful early intervention program at home and at a neighborhood Parent and Child Center could help the parents cultivate a more meaningful and productive relationship with their children than would otherwise be possible.

The upper age limit for compulsory schooling is also less meaningful today than it once was. Those who leave school at age sixteen or seventeen are usually marginal students, unfit for entrance into the labor market except at the lowest skill levels and unable to function as enlightened citizens in a democracy. Even high school completion has become less and less a mark of achievement as more and more students are allowed to graduate each year. As a matter of fact, a kind of "Gresham's Law" is beginning to operate, with easy-to-obtain diplomas driving down the credential value of those that are more dearly earned.

What, then, do the present compulsory statutes mean for those who do little more than mark time at school until they can withdraw legally? With this population it may be necessary to take a more flexible approach to age limits and a less flexible approach to achievement expectations. Some could probably benefit more if they were excused from classroom attendance and placed in paid positions which would require that they learn some meaningful job skills as well as the basic academic subjects. Others may have to be subsidized beyond age sixteen in a compulsory program that would take them through junior college.[1] Changing conditions in American life make it imperative to determine what is in the best interest of children and youth at school and to adjust legislation in such a way as to enhance their chances for educational success.

Increased support for research activity should lead to the establishment of national laboratories devoted to the production of educational standards. It is useless to talk about innovation without emphasizing the indispensability of research activity. Educational research is often so loose and fractionated that practitioners in the classroom are bewildered by it all. One of the missing links in the research-to-policy chain is something akin to a medical research center concerned mainly with improving treatment. Present-day educational research and demonstration institutes operate differently from these centers in the sense that they are not concerned with counterposing differential approaches to solving massive problems. Instead, they develop a single experimental strategy and test it against conventional controls. Educational research has reached the point where it is prepared to deal systematically with programmatic *alternatives* without investing preferential hope or confidence in any one. This would be a long step toward reducing halo effects and self-fulfilling prophecies.

A research center concerned with the establishment of standards would carve out for itself a clearly visible problem area in education. Two of the most significant problem areas today are (1) preschool and (2) beginning reading instruction for socially disadvantaged children. A laboratory preschool in a slum neighborhood would serve as a self-administered testing ground for various methodological emphases. Its purpose would be to obtain insights into the strengths and weaknesses of newly developed treatments and thereby provide guidance to inner-city schools in their plans for adopting early intervention programs. These programs would be evaluated on a comparative basis, provided they represent different theoretical rationales for reversing school readiness. For example, curriculums heavily loaded with sensorimotor training might be compared with those that offer intensive language orientation. The intention is to evaluate the *conceptual bases* of the

---

1. Editor's note: In its final report, the Commission recommends that high-quality preschool education be universally available as a public utility and that free public education be extended at least two years beyond high school. See *Crisis in Child Mental Health: Challenge for the 1970's* (New York: Harper & Row, 1970).

different treatments rather than any specific treatment per se. The laboratory school for primary grade children should also be established to evaluate beginning reading programs that vary in symbol systems, degrees of pre-structure, and the extent of synthetic versus analytic methods. The mere existence of such research centers might stimulate would-be program designers to compare experimental cures for educational ailments much in the same way that medical research centers attract new ideas for battling disease. These are the kinds of institutes that the federal government would call upon to develop and demonstrate the best known standards of educational effectiveness.

Although there is growing support for research and demonstration in public schools, there is great need to align educational practices with research evidence. The road from research to policy implementation is often a long and difficult one. The federal government has been supporting pilot studies designed to reassess ongoing school practices. In too many instances, however, studies effect little or no change in the schools even if the outcomes are inordinately promising. The time has come when the federal government can look beyond the limitations of short-term research activity and encourage simplifying the procedures and shortening the time currently needed for applying research findings in the classroom.

In most instances, educational research originates at a university or a community agency rather than within a school system. The success of these efforts depends, therefore, not only on their merit but also on the dynamics of interinstitutional relationships involving the agency that initiates the project and the school that allows it to be initiated. Not all schools are receptive to recommended innovations originating outside the system, even if they are based on experimentation conducted in the schools with their permission. To many school administrators, the outside researcher is using the children as "guinea pigs" to facilitate work that is not directly relevant to classroom practices. Some may resent it and others may tolerate it, but few are ready to make commitments subject to outcomes.

Even when research originates within the school system, it is rarely a force for bringing about quick, meaningful change. Educational leaders are not usually oriented to utilize empirical evidence for supporting programmatic innovation, except when the evidence also conforms to prior convictions about needed reform. The famous fifty-year lag between the birth of an idea and its implementation betrays not only a creaky administrative machinery in the schools but also a lack of sensitivity to the value of research as a tool for improving decision making rather than supporting previous biases. Unless there is a respectful understanding of empirical findings among educational leaders, it is unlikely that research activity can ever be worth the investment for its support. Research on educational needs and outcomes should therefore be accomplished in school settings jointly

Table 7.—Phases of Knowledge and Action and Types of Organizational Support Needed for Educational Change

DEVELOPMENTAL PHASE	PURPOSE	SUPPORTING ORGANIZATIONS
Research	The discovery of new knowledge about handicapped children or about those intellectual and personality processes that can be applied to these children.	These are usually research centers and institutions, often found in universities, which can provide organizational support for long-range attacks on difficult research problems.
Development	Knowledge, to be educationally useful, must be organized or packaged into sequences of activities or curriculums that fit the needs of particular groups of children.	Sometimes done through research and development centers which concentrate on sequencing of existing knowledge—basic setting is still the university.
Demonstration	There must be an effective conjunction of organized knowledge and child. This conjunction must be demonstrated in a school setting to be believable.	A combination of university or government and school operation required. Usually, the elementary or secondary school is the physical setting while additional resources are supplied by the other agency.
Implementation	Local school systems with local needs usually wish to try out, on a pilot basis, the effective demonstrations they have observed elsewhere to establish their viability in a local setting.	Additional funds for retraining personnel and for establishing a new program locally are needed. Some type of university, state, or federal support often needed as the catalyst to bring about this additional stage.
Adoption	To establish the new program as part of the educational operation. Without acceptance of new program at the policy level, demonstration and implementation stages can atrophy.	Organized attempts need to be made to involve policy decision makers (i.e., school board members, superintendents, etc.) in the preceding developmental phases. Items like cost effectiveness need to be developed to help policy makers decide.

with personnel of public schools and of competent research institutions. Support for experimentation should be incorporated into support for a total plan of policy review which includes the establishment of an administrative process for implementing research implications. Thus, the federal government could exercise important leverage for hastening educational progress without abridging local autonomy. Table 7 suggests the relevant developmental phases, their purposes, and their supporting organizations.

References

Baldwin, A. L. *Theories of Child Development.* New York: John Wiley & Sons, 1967.

Bandura, A. "Psychotherapy as a Learning Process," *Psychological Bulletin,* 58 (Mar. 1961), 143–159.

Berlin, J. I., and Wyckoff, L. B. *The Teaching of Improved Interpersonal Relations Through Programmed Instruction for Two People Working Together.* Paper presented at the American Psychological Association Convention, 1963.

Biber, Barbara. "A Learning-Teaching Paradigm Integrating Intellectual and Affective Processes," in *Behavioral Science Frontiers in Education,* ed. by Eli M. Bower and William G. Hollister. New York: John Wiley & Sons, 1967, pp. 111–155.

Bigart, H. "N.Y.U. Clinic Stalled in Trying to Improve School," *New York Times,* Nov. 26, 1967.

Bloom, B. *Stability and Change in Human Characteristics.* New York: John Wiley & Sons, 1964.

Bower, E. M. *et al. A Process for Early Identification of Emotionally Disturbed Children.* Bulletin No. 6. Sacramento: California State Department of Education, Aug. 1958.

Cattell, R. B. "Theory of Fluid and Crystallized Intelligence," *Journal of Educational Psychology,* 54 (Feb. 1963), 1–22.

Coleman, J. *et al. Equality of Educational Opportunity.* Washington D.C.: U.S. Government Printing Office, 1966.

Deutsch, M. *Minority Groups and Class Status as Related to Social and Personality Factors in Scholastic Achievements.* Monographs of the Society for Applied Anthropology, 1960.

Escalona, Sybil K. "Mental Health, the Educational Process and the Schools," *American Journal of Orthopsychiatry,* 37 (Jan. 1967), 1–4.

Feuerstein, R. *The Learning Potential Assessment Device: A New Method for*

438

Assessing Modifiability of the Cognitive Functioning of Socio-Culturally Disadvantaged Adolescents. Jerusalem: The Youth Aliya Department of the Jewish Agency, 1968 (mimeo).

Feuerstein, R., and Hamburger, M. *A Proposal to Study the Process of Redevelopment in Several Groups of Deprived Early Adolescents in Both Residential and Non-Residential Settings.* Jerusalem, Israel: The Youth Aliya Department of the Jewish Agency, Nov. 1965.

Fox, D. J. *Expansion of the More Effective School Programs.* New York: The Center for Urban Education, Sept. 1967.

Gage, N. L. (ed.). *Handbook of Research on Teaching.* Chicago: Rand McNally, 1963.

Gordon, I. J. *Intellectual Stimulation for Infants and Toddlers: A Brief Scientific Introduction.* Gainesville, Fla.: Institute for Development of Human Resources, University of Florida, Aug. 1967 (mimeo).

Group for the Advancement of Psychiatry. *Psychiatric Aspects of School Desegregation.* New York: The Group, 1957.

Guilford, J. P. *The Nature of Human Intelligence.* New York: McGraw-Hill, 1967.

Harris, L. "The Racial Gap," *New York Post,* Apr. 18, 1968.

Henry, J. *Culture Against Man.* New York: Vintage Books, 1963.

Hobbs, N. "The Reeducation of Emotionally Disturbed Children," in *Behavioral Science Frontiers in Education,* ed. by Eli M. Bower and William G. Hollister. New York: John Wiley & Sons, 1967, pp. 335–354.

Horowitz, Frances Degen. "Infant Learning and Development: Retrospect and Prospect," *Merrill-Palmer Quarterly,* 14 (Jan. 1968), 101–120.

Huff, F. W. "Learning and Psychopathology," *Psychological Bulletin,* 61 (June 1964), 459–468.

Jersild, A. T. *When Teachers Face Themselves.* New York: Teachers College Bureau of Publications, Teachers College, Columbia University, 1955.

Kohlberg, L. "Moral Education in the Schools: A Developmental View," *School Review,* 74 (Spring 1966), 1–29.

Kohler, Mary Conway. *Youth in the World of Work.* New York: The Taconic Foundation, Oct. 1962.

Kubie, L. S. "Social Forces and the Neurotic Process," in *Explorations in Social Psychiatry,* ed. by Alexander Leighton *et al.* New York: Basic Books, 1957, pp. 77–104.

Lesser, I. J., and Lazarus, Phoebe W. *A Multi-District Evaluation of a Two-Year Extended Readiness Class Program.* New York: The Education Council, Levittown Public Schools, 1967.

Maslow, A. H. *Motivation and Personality.* New York: Harper & Brothers, 1954.

Office of Economic Opportunity. *Parent and Child Centers.* Washington, D.C.: The Office, 1967.

Ojemann, R. H. *Developing a Program for Education in Human Behavior.* Iowa City: Preventive Psychiatry Program, State University of Iowa, 1959.

Ojemann, R. H., and Wilkinson, F. R. "The Effect on Pupil Growth of an Increase in Teacher's Understanding of Pupil Behavior," *Journal of Experimental Education,* 8 (1939), 143–147.

Public Education Association Committee on Education, Guidance, and Work. *Reorganizing Secondary Education in New York City*. New York: The Association, 1963.

Raph, Jane Beasley, and Tannenbaum, A. J. *Review of Research on Under-achievement*. New York: Horace Mann-Lincoln Institute of School Experimentation, Teachers College, Columbia University, 1961 (mimeo).

Report of the National Advisory Commission on Civil Disorders. New York: E. P. Dutton, 1968.

Ringness, T. A. *Mental Health in the Schools*. New York: Random House, 1968.

Roman, M. *Reaching Delinquents Through Reading*. Springfield, Ill.: Charles C. Thomas, 1957.

Sanford, N. "The Development of Cognitive-Affective Processes Through Education," in *Behavioral Science Frontiers in Education*, ed. by Eli M. Bower and William G. Hollister. New York: John Wiley & Sons, 1967, pp. 73–87.

Savitsky, C. "Reaching the Disadvantaged," in *Mental Health and Achievement: Increasing Potential and Reducing School Dropout*, ed. by E. Paul Torrance and Robert D. Strom. New York: John Wiley & Sons, 1965, pp. 305–311.

Schreiber, D. *Holding Power: Large City School Systems*. Washington, D.C.: National Education Association, 1964.

Skeels, H. M. *Adult Status of Children with Contrasting Early Life Experiences*. Monographs of the Society for Research in Child Development, 1966.

Smith, M. B. "Mental Health Reconsidered: A Special Case of the Problem of Values in Psychology," *American Psychologist,* 16 (June 1961), 299–306.

Suchman, J. R. "The Child and the Inquiry Process," in *Intellectual Development: Another Look*, ed. by A. Harry Passow and Robert R. Leeper. Washington, D.C.: Association for Supervision and Curriculum Development, 1964, pp. 59–77.

Tannenbaum, A. J. "An Evaluation of STAR: A Non-Professional Tutoring Program." *Teachers College Record*, 69 (Feb. 1968), 433–448.

Tannenbaum, A. J., and Cohen, S. A. *Taxonomy of Instructional Treatments*. New York: Research and Demonstration Center on the Education of the Handicapped, Teachers College, Columbia University, 1967 (mimeo).

Terman, L. M. *Genetic Studies of Genius*: Vol. 1, *Mental and Physical Traits of a Thousand Gifted Children*. Stanford, Calif.: Stanford University Press, 1925.

Torrance, E. P. *Rewarding Creative Behavior*. Englewood Cliffs, N.J.: Prentice-Hall, 1965.

Uzgiris, I. C., and Hunt, J. McV. *An Instrument for Assessing Psychological Development*. Urbana, Ill.: University of Illinois, Feb. 1966 (mimeo).

White, R. W. "Motivation Reconsidered: The Concept of Competence," *Psychological Review*, 66 (1959), 297–333.

Wolf, R. M. "The Identification and Measurement of Environmental Process Variables." Unpublished doctoral dissertation, University of Chicago, 1964.

V

RELIGION AND MENTAL HEALTH

REPORT OF THE COMMITTEE ON RELIGION AND MENTAL HEALTH

Edited by Rabbi I. Fred Hollander
and the Reverend Leo N. Kisrow

MEMBERS OF THE COMMITTEE ON RELIGION AND MENTAL HEALTH

Religion in Child Mental Health Development

THE PLACE OF RELIGION IN THE TRANSMISSION OF VALUES

The joint Commission on the Mental Health of Children addresses itself to the potentials in our society which promote the mental health of children. Resources of many kinds, tapped and untapped, are available. The values inherent in religion constitute one of these resources. For example, families in trouble frequently turn first to the clergy and to religion for advice, solace, and support. Therefore, it is appropriate for the Joint Commission on the Mental Health of Children to consider the role that religion plays in the mental health of children.

In order to properly evaluate the place of religion, it is necessary to emphasize the significance of its value systems with respect to mental health situations. It is recognized today that a positive set of values by which a person may live is not alone a subject of concern to philosophers and theologians; it also is very much a sickness and health issue for the individual. In the past three decades, modern psychology and psychiatry have demonstrated that people who are unable to cultivate values which deepen their sense of security, belonging, and self-acceptance often find themselves overwhelmed by the psychologically incapacitating effects of sickness or the many other forms of stress with which they are confronted.

While many aspects of society project values—social, economic, cultural—which the individual can utilize to achieve positive emotional stature, those values derived from religious sources have something distinctive and timeless to offer which supplement the values society provides. Such distinctives as the affirmation of the infinite worth of the individual, the capacity to face the ultimate questions of life with equanimity, and the acceptance of man's reason for being are an indication of the kind of uniquenesses religion offers.

444

Thus, at a time in history when violence and murder have become part of our daily lives, when racism and poverty are dividing our nation into divisive factions, and when the younger generation is becoming increasingly alienated from its parents, we must speak in humility about the role of religion in the transmission of positive values. Religion, traditionally, has emphasized the value of human dignity and individual worth. The continuing desperate need for the incorporation of more positive values in society is ample demonstration that the role of organized religion in the transmission of values is still unfulfilled.

In a society that has become increasingly materialistic, where a man's worth is often judged by the quantity of his possessions, and where our youth are frequently troubled by conflicts between their own idealistic values and the materialism that is honored by society, religion can provide support for these idealistic aims of the younger generation.

Further, in a society which is becoming more and more "group"-oriented, the church and synagogue have a special role in asserting both the value of each individual human life and the role of personal responsibility within that life. Thus religion, in the framework of its distinctive value systems, can play a significant role in modifying the negative aspects of an increasingly group-oriented culture.

TASK OF IMPLEMENTATION

It is the Committee's observation that the optimal utilization of religious values in relation to the mental health of children is contingent upon the following factors:

1. Clergy who have acquired the education and experience necessary to prepare them to participate responsibly in the area of child mental health development.

2. A social milieu conducive to the utilization of clergy and other religious resources in the area of child mental health development.

3. Mental health workers who have the skill and the desire to co-operate and work with the clergy toward the effective utilization of religious resources in child mental health development.

THE CLERGY

The clergyman's involvement in the area of child mental health development may assume forms like these:

1. To act as a resource person to facilities concerned with child mental health development. The clergyman needs to make himself available to social agencies, hospitals, institutions, and community health centers. He, more than any other person, has the unique responsibility

and opportunity to channel the resources of religion into facilities concerned with the mental health development of children.

2. In addition to serving as a resource person to mental health facilities, the clergyman must also participate more actively in the mental health problems of the children within his own congregation and in the community. The clergyman must understand that his religious role in mental health is not limited to adults seeking help. He must be equally available where the mental health of children is concerned and particularly at the point of preventive intervention which may help to keep problems from developing. This includes dealing with problems such as when marriage partners face crises which impinge upon the welfare of the children in the family unit. It also includes problems of parents who have to accept limitations in their children owing to mental illness or deficiency. He needs also to cooperate with clinicians in the management and treatment of disturbed children and their families within the community.

3. Finally, the clergyman's mental health role demands of him to serve as a *community leader* in promoting the cause of child mental health development. Because of the important contribution that religion can make to this area, the clergy must become a significant nucleus within community activities. The clergy and religious groups may provide local leadership in stimulating the community to provide facilities and personnel, and to establish mental health services and mental health centers, day-care facilities for working mothers, and centers for teen-agers where young people can meet, exchange ideas, and become involved in constructive activities. The clergy are in a unique position to be particularly sensitive to community needs in these areas and can play a major role in identifying social and community factors which militate against good mental health of children, as well as those which promote it.

PERCEPT AND PRECEPT

One of the basic tenets of child development is that children learn more by percept than by precept. For instance, it has been demonstrated that children who share life experiences with those of different ethnic, religious, and economic backgrounds tend to be less prejudiced than those who grow up in racial and economic isolation. It is therefore evident that the child's direct experience modifies his behavior as much as, or more than, the words that he hears at home, in school, in church or synagogue. Thus, if positive values are to be transmitted to children, the children must witness the practice of these values by their parents, clergyman, teachers, and other responsible adults about them. Religious institutions may fulfill their commitment to families and to mental health by demonstrating their convictions in support of integrated, denominationally related or supported facilities, services, schools, and hospitals, as well as by initiating and supporting communication and interaction for the common good of *all* racial, national, and economic groups.

THE CLERGYMAN'S EDUCATION FOR HIS MENTAL HEALTH ROLE

Training in the area of mental health is an indispensable ingredient in the preparation of the clergyman to exercise his threefold mental health role. The clergyman cannot do justice to this role simply on the basis of his general education in the seminary and his commitment to the cause of human welfare. Without specific training in mental health, the clergyman's capacity to communicate religious values, as a means of mental health assistance, is seriously diminished.

It must be emphasized, however, that a mental health education whose sole principal aim is to provide the clergyman with a professional understanding of the subject is not adequate to prepare him for his mental health role. The training that he requires is more than a comprehensive understanding of the mental health sciences. Its form and content must be specifically geared to provide him with the *capacity to understand the nature of religion's role in mental health and the knowledge to effectively utilize his role toward this end.* This demands a focused type of education aimed at clarifying to the clergyman the basic nature of his involvement.

A general outline of content that merits consideration in a mental health education program for clergy might include the following:

1. *A Basis for the Clergyman's Mental Health Role*

The clergyman's ability to be a person of helpfulness in this area is ultimately derived from the fact that he is a representative of the God who cares for and watches over all people. It is this factor that is essentially responsible for his acceptance as a helping person by individuals in need. No other individual engaged in the area of mental health has a relationship with people in need which is derived from such a unique source. The clergyman, by the very nature of his role, has a unique capacity to broaden the meaning and value of such social institutions as marriage, home, and family, so that they may become instrumentalities of greater mental health value to the people involved.

2. *Uniqueness of Religiously Derived Values*

The religious values that the clergyman may channel to mental health possess distinctive elements:

a. Religious values are endowed, by virtue of their very origin, with a sense of the permanent which enables them to impart to their adherents the psychological satisfaction of investing oneself into value systems which are not simply a product of transient cultural determinism.

b. Religious values possess a basic validity for their adherents which gives them a timelessness which culturally determined values do not necessarily have.

c. Religious, moral, and ethical values address themselves to fundamental questions of existence within a different framework than do culturally derived values. For instance, religion attempts to formulate answers to questions of life and death, pain and suffering, as well as to the ultimate goals and purposes for human existence and striving.

3. Religious Values as a Motivating Force

Religious resources in the form of ideas, concepts, and values function as motivating and stabilizing forces in some of the following ways:

a. *Clarifying the concept of the nature of man.* Religion has a dual concept with respect to the question of what man is. It views him as a biological organism—a living entity united with inferior one-celled organisms through the bond of mortal existence. Religion, however, also encourages man to recognize that, even though he is an organism, he nonetheless has been endowed with the potential capacity of almost unlimited creativity. It is this concept which can serve to encourage and motivate man to use his faculties to the fullest. The further concept of the infinite worth of the individual and the intimations of timeless existence which are inherent in his very being add still deeper dimensions to man's reason for being.

b. *Developing a firm social fabric.* Religion serves as a motivating force by providing man with a basis for developing a firm social fabric to enable him to live in harmony with his fellowman. Moral and ethical value systems, especially those of the religions of Western civilization, have proven themselves to be of great value in helping persons evolve a pattern of social existence which enables them to live more adequately with themselves, their families, and their neighbors. The Ten Commandments and the Golden Rule are outstanding examples of some basic ideals and standards that have helped determine the shape and destiny of Western civilization. The clergy can help make these moral and ethical systems effective instrumentalities of mental health in the establishment of sound relationships between man and his fellowman. These systems have served repeatedly as preventatives to social chaos throughout history.

It is important, however, to recognize that moral and ethical systems are important to people not simply because of the logic and reasonableness of such systems. A great deal of their importance is derived from the belief and conviction that these systems stem from an Eternal Source and are not simply products of social necessity. It is this special factor that enhances the ability of the clergy to utilize effectively the moral and ethical systems to help persons.

c. *Coping with the incapacitating effects of stress.* Religion serves as a motivating and stabilizing force by providing man with the strength to more adequately cope with the incapacitating effects of stress. Modern medicine presently views the term "total man" as expressing a philosophy that sickness affects not only an individual's physical body but also his personality and behavior as a whole. Sickness has this effect, since it strips man of an important basis for his day-to-day security, his health, and his ability to exercise his physical and mental capacities to the fullest. Religion helps a person to cope with these negative forces in some of the following ways:

By encouraging man with the affirmation that there is a God who cares for and watches over the destinies of all human beings regardless of physical condition.

By providing man with a unique concept of the ultimate basis for human worth. Religion encourages man to believe that his sense of innate worth ultimately is not determined by youth, beauty, intellect, or physical vigor. Religion teaches man that he is a unique individual because he has been so designed by his Maker.

By providing man with the means of attaining a sense of security and belonging. One can posit two forms of security which persons endeavor to achieve. There is the normal sense of security without which a person loses his ability to function in normal daily activities and, in some extreme cases, ceases to function in the outside world. There is a need for a deeper kind of security. This is a sense of security which enables man to continue his day-to-day functioning although it may be at less than his optimum level. To the religiously minded modern man, the religious value systems which reflect the conviction that the world is divinely guided offer him the basis for attainment of both of these forms of security.

d. *Dealing with the crisis of mortal existence.* Religion serves as a motivating force by providing man with a viable approach to the crisis of mortal existence. Religion's concept of mortal existence is such that it provides the religiously committed person with a philosophical ground for an optimistic approach toward life while helping him accept the fact that death, or the cessation of mortal existence, is a natural and normal part of his destiny.

CLINICAL AND FIELD WORK TRAINING
AND EXPERIENCE FOR THE CLERGYMAN

The clergyman's capacity to utilize religious resources effectively and appropriately in mental health situations is contingent upon his acquiring the training necessary to carry out this function. Mental health training in a classroom atmosphere only, no matter how relevant, is not by itself adequate to prepare the clergyman. To utilize religious resources as a medium of assistance in the areas of prevention, care, and management, the clergyman requires field and clinical experience also. It is this experience, combined with his mental health education on an academic level, that places him in a position of being of help.

It should be pointed out, however, that just as the clergyman's mental health education on an academic level must be focused toward helping him in the discharge of his special role, likewise the field and clinical experience must be of a comparable focused nature.

To be suitable for the clergyman, the mental health knowledge and experience to which he is exposed in a mental health facility should reflect the following basic principles:

1. Psychological stress produces medically significant changes in the human organism. *Forces* other than physical or chemical ones can produce medically important changes in the human organism. This implies that emotions may produce conditions of illness in the human being in much the same way as does an infectious process. Emotions also contribute to conditions of health within the human organism. This observation of the psychological significance of emotions in sickness and health can help the clergyman more fully to appreciate the importance of his pastoral role in helping persons cope with their fears, guilts, and insecurities.

2. Such methods of rendering assistance as the communication of values are medically valid ways to help the individual cope with stress situations which threaten to immobilize him. *Methods* of intervention into the human organism, other than physical or chemical ones, can produce conditions of sickness or health in the individual. This implies that verbal and nonverbal means of intervention can be forces for sickness or health. If they are of a positive nature they may be helpful in the development of stable personality; if negative, they may be a factor in the precipitation of emotional disturbances.

This observation of the psychological significance of verbal and nonverbal methods of intervention in a clinical setting helps the student to see that, through his methods of communication, he can render assistance that may produce changes in personality and behavior which are medically significant, in addition to their being of spiritual and religious value.

3. A system of identifiable causal relationships exists in regard to the two observations above. This means that the mental health aspects of religious resources and their place in the management of mental health problems can presently be assessed and evaluated. It means that it is possible for the student to apply the scientific methods of evaluation to measure the results of his helping resources.

MENTAL HEALTH FACILITIES

A second condition—the first condition being a better-trained clergy—to be met is the creation within society of a milieu which is conducive to the utilization of the clergyman and of religious resources in child mental health development.

For a milieu to be thus conducive it must demonstrate a positive attitude toward the value of religion as an integral facet in the process of child mental health development. This means that the mental health team will be freed to make it possible for the clergyman to appropriately utilize his religious resources in this area. It means also that the approach to child mental health development in terms of care, management, and treatment will incorporate the clergyman's contribution as a natural and ongoing part of the care and treatment process of the helping facility.

Finally, a mental health facility for clergy training and involvement must be of the type that it can serve as a place where the clergyman can *regularly* practice his role. This means that the clergyman's function in child mental health development ought not be confined only to those who come to seek his help in the privacy of his study. The bulk of child care and development, of necessity, must be carried forth in agencies and facilities developed for that purpose. Therefore, by integrating the clergyman's functions with those of the mental health worker, the facility makes possible the optimal use of both in the area of child mental health development.

THE MENTAL HEALTH WORKER

The third condition to be met to make adequate use of religious resources in child mental health development relates to the participation of the mental health worker. This assumes a number of forms. The most critical factor is that there be a positive attitude toward the value of religious resources in child mental health development; and a concomitant positive attitude toward the role of the clergyman in utilizing these religious resources in child mental health development.

This demands the development of a more professional relationship between the clergyman and the mental health worker if the contribution of the clergyman to child mental health development is to have more than tangential value. A meaningful collaborative relationship needs to have the following characteristics:

1. The acceptance of the clergyman by the hospital or agency staff as a bona fide resource person.
2. A willingness on the part of the hospital or agency staff to be of

direct assistance to the clergyman by making available the agency facilities for training as well as for the discharge of his function.

Assistance rendered by the agency staff to the clergy training process ought to include the following:

1. Delineation and selection by the mental health worker of those cases in which the clergyman's resources are of demonstrable value with respect to the management of the problem.

2. Apprising the client and his family unit of:

   a. The availability of the services of the clergyman.

   b. The relevance of the clergyman's services with respect to the management of mental health problems.

   c. The importance of the resources offered through the clergyman with respect to the successful resolution or management of the problem for which the client is seeking agency assistance.

   d. Determination of the time when the clergyman's intervention with his special resources would be of maximum value toward the management of the client's problems.

SUMMARY

It is the observation of the Committee on Religion and Mental Health that there is not now available an adequate mental health education program for clergy which optimally reflects the subject matter described in this paper. Nor is there a sufficiently conducive milieu which will encourage clergy participation and utilization in child mental health development. Attempts, however, are being made to develop and design this type of focused mental health education program and to establish such a milieu. The results of such programs will be to markedly enhance the clergyman's potential capacity to utilize religious values in this very critical area of child mental health development.

It is the consensus of the Committee that, inasmuch as the purpose of the Joint Commission on the Mental Health of Children is to seek out potentials in our society which will promote child mental health development, and since religious values have been shown to intrinsically offer a potential source of support, it can therefore be assumed that religion has a valid role to play in this area.

The implementation of religion's role in child mental health is contingent upon:

1. Enlistment of clergy who have received the type of focused mental health education and clinical and field training and experience which will equip them to exercise responsibly their role in child mental health development.

2. Creation of a social milieu in which religious resources may find their appropriate place in child mental health development.

3. Establishing a more professional relationship between clergy and mental health workers and agencies through which they may work together to provide more adequate services to the child in mental health development.

Index

73 74 75 10 9 8 7 6 5 4 3 2 1